KNOTS UNTIED

Being plain statements on disputed points in
Religion from the standpoint of an
Evangelical Churchman

by

J. C. Ryle

Printed on acid free ANSI archival quality paper.
ISBN: 978-1-78139-877-7.
© 2017 Benediction Classics, Oxford.

CONTENTS

I

EVANGELICAL RELIGION

IT may be laid down as a rule, with tolerable confidence, that the absence of accurate definitions is the very life of religious controversy. If men would only define with precision the theological terms which they use, many disputes would die. Scores of excited disputants would discover that they do not really differ, and that their disputes have arisen from their own neglect of the great duty of explaining the meaning of words.

In opening the subject of this paper, I desire to remember carefully this important rule. Without further preface, I shall begin by explaining what I mean when I speak of "Evangelical Religion."

By "Evangelical Religion," I do not mean Christianity as compared with Heathenism, or Protestantism as compared with Romanism, or Trinitarianism as compared with Socinianism or Deism. I do not propose to argue with the Sceptic or the Modernist, with the Papist or the Jew. What I do want to consider is the religion which is peculiar to that party in the Church of England which is commonly called "Evangelical." To that point I shall confine myself, and to that alone.

I will not waste time by proving the existence of such a party as "the Evangelical party." It is a fact as patent as the sun in heaven. When it began first to be called by this name, and why it was so called, are points into which it is not worth while now to inquire. It is a simple fact that it exists. Whether we like it or not, whether it be right or wrong, the well-known tripartite division is correct and may be assumed as true. There are three great schools of thought in the Church of England,—High Church, Broad Church, and Evangelical;—and the man who cannot see them is in a very curious state of mind.* Now what are the distinctive peculiarities of the religion of the Evangelical school? That it has some leading tenets or principles is unmistakable and undeniable. What are those principles which distinguish it from other schools? This in plain words is my subject,— Has Evangelical Religion any distinctive principles? I answer, it has.— Are they worth contending for? I answer, they are.

I approach the subject with a deep sense of its difficulty. It cannot be

.* Beneath this tripartite division there are, no doubt, many sub-divisions, and subordinate shades of difference. There is certainly a very distinct line of demarcation between the old High Church party and the modern Ritualistic section of the Church of England.

1

handled without touching points of extreme nicety, and treading on very delicate ground. It necessitates comparison between section and section of our Church; and all comparisons are odious. It lays a writer open to the charge of being "party-spirited, narrow-minded, combative, pugnacious," and what not. But there are times when comparisons are a positive duty. It is an apostolic command to "try things that differ." (Phil. i. 10.) The existence of diversities in the Church of England is a fact that cannot be ignored. To pretend that *we* do not see them is absurd. Everybody else can see them, talk about them, and criticise them. To attempt to deny their existence is mere squeamishness and affectation. Whether we like it or not, there they are, and the world around us knows it.

But while I have a deep sense of the difficulty of the subject, I have a deeper sense of its importance. The clouds are gathering round the Church of England; her very existence is in peril. Conflicting opinions bid fair to rend her in twain. A strife has arisen within her pale in the last thirty or forty years, not about the trappings and vestments of religion, but about the very foundations of the Gospel. It remains to be seen whether our beloved Church will survive the struggle. Surely it is high time for Evangelical clergymen and laymen to review calmly their position, and to consider seriously what it is they have got to maintain and defend. Let us walk round our lines. Let us mark well our bulwarks. Let us distinctly understand the principles which are characteristic of our body. It must do us good; it can do us no harm.

In defining what Evangelical Religion is, I admit at the outset that I have no written creed, no formal declaration of principles, to refer to. The reader will do me the justice to believe that I feel that want very keenly. I can only bring forward the results of such reading, study, and observation, as are within the reach of all ordinary men. But for many years I have examined carefully the published works of most of the Fathers of the Evangelical school, and especially of the men of the last century, and I have formed decided opinions about their peculiar principles. I may be wrong in my estimate of their merits; but I can honestly say that I have not arrived at my conclusions without prayer, thought, and pains.*

There are three questions which I wish to bring under the notice of the readers of this paper.

    I. What Evangelical Religion is.
    II. What it is not.
    III. What makes much religion not Evangelical.

* Of course my readers will understand that, throughout this paper, I am only expressing my own individual opinion. I do not for a moment pretend to be a mouthpiece of the Evangelical party, or to speak for anybody but myself. Indeed I am not sure that all who are called Evangelical will agree with all that this paper contains. I am only describing what I, personally, believe to be the leading sentiments of most Evangelical Churchmen, and my description must be taken for what it is worth.

Each of these questions I shall attempt to touch very briefly.

I. To the question *"what Evangelical Religion is?"* the simplest answer I can give is to point out what appear to be its leading features. These I consider to be five in number.

(*a*) The first leading feature in Evangelical Religion is the *absolute supremacy it assigns to Holy Scripture*, as the only rule of faith and practice, the only test of truth, the only judge of controversy.

Its theory is that man is required to believe nothing, as necessary to salvation, which is not read in God's Word written, or can be proved thereby. It totally denies that there is any other guide for man's soul, co-equal or co-ordinate with the Bible. It refuses to listen to such arguments as "the Church says so,"—"the Fathers say so,"—"primitive antiquity says so,"—"Catholic tradition says so,"—"the Councils say so,"—"the ancient liturgies say so,"—"the Prayer-book says so,"—"the universal conscience of mankind says so,"—"the verifying light within says so,"—unless it can be shown that what is said is in harmony with Scripture.

The supreme authority of the Bible, in one word, is one of the corner-stones of our system. Show us anything plainly written in that Book, and, however trying to flesh and blood, we will receive it, believe it, and submit to it. Show us anything, as religion, which is contrary to that Book, and, however specious, plausible, beautiful, and apparently desirable, we will not have it at any price. It may come before us endorsed by Fathers, schoolmen, and catholic writers;—it may be commended by reason, philosophy, science, the inner light, the verifying faculty, the universal conscience of mankind. It signifies nothing. Give us rather a few plain texts. If the thing is not in the Bible, deducible from the Bible, or in manifest harmony with the Bible, we will have none of it. Like the forbidden fruit, we dare not touch it, lest we die. Our faith can find no resting-place except in the Bible, or in Bible arguments. Here is rock: all else is sand.

(*b*) The second leading feature in Evangelical Religion is *the depth and prominence it assigns to the doctrine of human sinfulness and corruption*.

Its theory is that in consequence of Adam's fall, all men are as far as possible gone from original righteousness, and are of their own natures inclined to evil. They are not only in a miserable, pitiable, and bankrupt condition, but in a state of guilt, imminent danger, and condemnation before God. They are not only at enmity with their Maker, and have no title to heaven, but they have no will to serve their Maker, no love to their Maker, and no meetness for heaven.

We hold that a mighty spiritual disease like this requires a mighty spiritual medicine for its cure. We dread giving the slightest countenance to any religious system of dealing with man's soul, which even *seems* to encourage the notion that his deadly wound can be easily healed. We dread fostering man's favourite notion that a little church-going and sacrament-receiving,—a little patching, and mending, and whitewashing, and gilding, and polishing, and varnishing, and painting the outside,—is all that his case requires. Hence we protest with all our heart against formalism, sacramentalism, and every species of mere external or vicarious Christianity. We maintain that all such religion is founded on an inadequate view of man's spiritual need. It requires far more than this to save, or satisfy, or sanctify, a soul. It requires nothing less than the blood of God the Son applied to the conscience, and the grace of God the Holy Ghost entirely renewing the heart. Man is radically diseased, and man needs a radical cure. I believe that ignorance of the extent of the fall, and of the whole doctrine of original sin, is one grand reason why many can neither understand, appreciate, nor receive Evangelical Religion. Next to the Bible, as its foundation, it is based on a clear view of original sin.

(c) The third leading feature of Evangelical Religion is the *paramount importance it attaches to the work and office of our Lord Jesus Christ*, and to the nature of the salvation which He has wrought out for man.

Its theory is that the eternal Son of God, Jesus Christ, has by His life, death, and resurrection, as our Representative and Substitute, obtained a complete salvation for sinners, and a redemption from the guilt, power, and consequences of sin, and that all who believe on Him are, even while they live, completely forgiven and justified from all things,—are reckoned completely righteous before God,—are interested in Christ and all His benefits.

We hold that nothing whatever is needed between the soul of man the sinner and Christ the Saviour, but simple, childlike faith, and that all means, helps, ministers, and ordinances are useful just so far as they help this faith, but no further;—but that rested in and relied on as ends and not as means, they become downright poison to the soul.

We hold that an experimental knowledge of Christ crucified and interceding, is the very essence of Christianity, and that in teaching men the Christian religion we can never dwell too much on Christ Himself, and can never speak too strongly of the fulness, freeness, presentness, and simplicity of the salvation there is in Him for every one that believes.

Not least, we hold most firmly that the true doctrine about Christ is precisely that which the natural heart most dislikes. The religion which man craves after is one of sight and sense, and not of faith. An external religion, of which the essence is "doing something,"—and not an inward and spiritual one, of which the essence is "believing," this is the religion that man naturally loves. Hence we maintain that people ought to be continually warned not to make a Christ of the Church, or of the ministry, or of the forms of worship, or of baptism, or of the Lord's Supper. We say that life eternal is to know Christ, believe in Christ, abide in Christ, have daily heart communion with Christ, by simple personal faith,—and that everything in religion is useful so far as it helps forward that life of faith, but no further.

(*d*) The fourth leading feature in Evangelical Religion is the *high place which it assigns to the inward work of the Holy Spirit in the heart of man.*

Its theory is that the root and foundation of all vital Christianity in any one, is a work of grace in the heart, and that until there is real experimental business within a man, his religion is a mere husk, and shell, and name, and form, and can neither comfort nor save. We maintain'that the things which need most to be pressed on men's attention are those mighty works of the Holy Spirit, inward repentance, inward faith, inward hope, inward hatred of sin, and inward love to God's law. And we say that to tell men to take comfort in their baptism or Church-membership, when these all-important graces are unknown, is not merely a mistake, but positive cruelty.

We hold that, as an inward work of the Holy Ghost is a necessary thing to a man's salvation, so also it is a thing that must be inwardly *felt*. We admit that feelings are often deceptive, and that a man may feel much, or weep much, or rejoice much, and yet remain dead in trespasses and sins. But we maintain firmly that there can be no real conversion to God, no new creation in Christ, no new birth of the Spirit, where there is nothing felt and experienced within. We hold that the witness of the Spirit, however much it may be abused, is a real, true thing. We deem it a solemn duty to be no less jealous about the work of the Holy Ghost, in its place and degree, than we are about the work of Christ. And we insist that where there is nothing *felt* within the heart of a man, there is nothing really possessed.

(*e*) The fifth and last leading feature in Evangelical Religion is *the importance which it attaches to the outward and visible work of the Holy Ghost in the life of man.*

Its theory is that the true grace of God is a thing that will always make itself manifest in the conduct, behaviour, tastes, ways, choices, and habits of him who has it. It is not a *dormant* thing, that can be within a man and not show itself without. The heavenly seed is "not corruptible, but incorruptible." It is a seed which is distinctly said to "remain" in every one that is born of God. (1 Peter i. 23; 1 John iii. 9.) Where the Spirit is, He will always make His presence known.

We hold that it is wrong to tell men that they are "children of God, and members of Christ, and heirs of the kingdom of heaven," unless they really overcome the world, the flesh, and the devil. We maintain that to tell a man he is "born of God," or regenerated, while he is living in carelessness or sin, is a dangerous delusion, and calculated to do infinite mischief to his soul. We affirm confidently that "fruit" is the only certain evidence of a man's spiritual condition; that if we would know whose he is and whom he serves, we must look first at his life. Where there is the grace of the Spirit there will be always more or less fruit of the Spirit. Grace that cannot be seen is no grace at all, and nothing better than Antinomianism. Note, in short, we believe that where there is nothing *seen*, there is nothing possessed.

Such are the leading features of Evangelical Religion. Such are the main principles which characterize the teaching of the Evangelical school in the Church of England. To my eyes they seem to stand out in the theological horizon like Tabor and Hermon among the mountains, and to tower upward like cathedral spires in our English plains. It will readily be perceived that I have only sketched them in outline. I have purposely avoided much that might have been said in the way of amplification and demonstration. I have omitted many things which might have been handled as parts and portions of our system, not because they are not important, but because they are comparatively of secondary importance. But enough has probably been said to serve my present purpose. I have pointed out what I conscientiously believe are the five distinctive doctrinal marks by which the members of the Evangelical body may be discerned. Rightly or wrongly, I have laid them down plainly. I venture to think that my statement will hold water and stand the fire.

I do not for a moment deny, be it remembered, that many Churchmen who are outside the Evangelical body, are sound in the main about the five points I have named, if you take them one by one. Propound them separately, as points to be believed, and they would admit them every one. But they do not give them the prominence, position, rank, degree, priority, dignity, and precedence which we do. And this I hold to be a most important difference between us and them. It is the *position* which we assign to these points, which is one of the grand characteristics of Evangelical theology. We say boldly that they are first, foremost, chief, and principal things in Christianity, and that want of attention to their position mars and spoils the teaching of many well-meaning Churchmen.

To show all the foundations on which Evangelical Religion is based, would be clearly impossible in a paper like this. We appeal boldly to the Holy Scriptures, and challenge any one to examine our system by the light of the New Testament.—We appeal boldly to the Thirty-nine Articles of our own Church, and assert unhesitatingly that they are on our side.—We appeal boldly to the writings of our leading Divines, from the Reformation down to the time of Archbishop Laud, and invite any man to compare our teaching with theirs.—We repudiate with scorn the vulgar charge of novelty, and tell the man who makes it that he only exposes his own ignorance. We ask him to turn again to his New Testament, to study afresh the Thirty-nine Articles, to take down and read once more the English theology of the pre-Caroline age. We court the fullest, strictest investigation into our case, and shall abide the result without fear. Of ourselves and our imperfections we may well be ashamed; but of what is called

"Evangelical Religion" we have no cause to be ashamed at all. Let men say what they please. Nothing is easier than to call names, affix odious epithets, and frighten ignorant people, by raising the cry of "Calvinism" or "Puritanism" against the Evangelical school. "The curse causeless shall not come." (Prov. xxvi. 2.) I believe firmly that impartial inquiry will always show that Evangelical Religion is the religion of Scripture and of the Church of England.

II. I turn now to the negative side of my subject. Having shown what Evangelical Religion is, it becomes my duty next to show *what it is not*.

I am almost ashamed to take up time by saying anything on this point. But slanders and false reports about Evangelical Religion are so sadly numerous, and shameless misrepresentations of its nature are so widely current, that I can hardly pass over this branch of my subject. We are not perfect, we know to our sorrow. We have many faults and defects, we humbly confess. But to many charges brought against us we plead "Not guilty." We say they are not true.

(1) I begin then by saying that Evangelical Religion *does not despise learning*, research, or the wisdom of days gone by. It is not true to say that we do. In thorough appreciation of anything that throws light on God's Word, we give place to none. Let any one look over the lists of those who in days gone by have been eminent for theological scholarship in this country, and I am bold to say he will find some of the most eminent are Evangelical men. Ridley, Jewell, Usher, Lightfoot, Davenant, Hall, Whittaker, Willett, Reynolds, Leighton, Owen, Baxter, Manton, are names that for profound learning stand second to none. To what school do they belong, I should like to know, if not to the Evangelical? What school, I ask confidently, has done more for the exposition and interpreta- tion of Scripture than the Evangelical school? What school has given to the world more Commentaries? Poole's *Synopsis* and Owen on *Hebrews* are alone sufficient to show that Evangelical men do read and can think. Even in the Egyptian darkness of last century, there were few English divines who showed more real learning than Hervey, Romaine, and Toplady.

Turn even to our own day, and I say, unhesitatingly, that we have no cause to be ashamed. To name divines of our own generation is somewhat invidious. Yet I do not shrink from saying that the three great books of Dean Goode on *Scripture*, *Baptism*, and the *Lord's Supper*, remain to the present day unanswered by the opponents of the Evangelical school. Coarse sneers about ignorance and shallowness may be safely disregarded, while books like these are unrefuted.

But while we do not despise learning, we steadily refuse to place any uninspired writings on a level with revelation. We refuse to call any man "father" or "master," however learned or intellectual he may be. We will follow no guide but Scripture. We own no master over conscience in religious matters, except the Bible. We leave it to others to talk of "primitive antiquity" and "Catholic truth." To us there is but one test of truth: "What is written in the Scripture? What saith the Lord?"

(2) I go on to say that Evangelical Religion *does not undervalue the Church*, or think lightly of its privileges. It is not true to say that we do. In sincere and loyal attachment to the Church of England we give place to none. We value its form of government, its Confession of Faith, its mode of worship, as much as any within its pale. We have stuck by it through evil report and good report, while many who once talked more loudly about their Churchmanship have seceded and gone over to Rome. We stick by it still, and will resist all attempts to Romanize it to the very death! We know its value, and would hand it down unimpaired to our children's children.

But we steadily refuse to exalt the Church above Christ, or to teach our people that membership of the Church is identical with membership of Christ. We refuse to assign it an authority for which we find no warrant either in Scripture or the Articles. We protest against the modern practice of first personifying the Church, then deifying it, and finally idolizing it. We hold that Church councils, Church synods, and Church convocations, may err, and that "things ordained by them as necessary to salvation have neither strength nor authority, unless it may be declared that they be taken out of Holy Scripture." We can find no proof in the Bible that the Lord Jesus Christ ever meant a body of erring mortals, whether ordained nor not ordained, to be treated as infallible. We consequently hold that a vast quantity of language in this day about "the Church" and the "voice of the Church" is mere unmeaning verbiage. It is "the talk of the lips, which tendeth only to penury." (Prov. xiv. 23.)

(3) I go on to say that Evangelical Religion *does not under value the Christian ministry*. It is not true to say that we do. We regard it as an honourable office instituted by Christ Himself, and of general necessity for carrying on the work of the Gospel. We look on ministers as preachers of God's Word, God's ambassadors, God's messengers, God's servants, God's shepherds, God's stewards, God's overseers, and labourers in God's vineyard.

But we steadily refuse to admit that Christian ministers are in any sense sacrificing priests, mediators between God and man, lords of men's consciences, or private confessors. We refuse it, not only because we cannot see it in the Bible, but also because we have read the lessons of Church history. We find that Sacerdotalism, or priestcraft, has frequently been the curse of Christianity, and the ruin of true religion. And we say boldly that the exaltation of the ministerial office to an unscriptural place and extravagant dignity in the Church of England in the present day, is likely to alienate the affections of the laity, to ruin the Church, and to be the source of every kind of error and superstition.

(4) I go on to say that Evangelical Religion *does not undervalue the Sacraments of Baptism and the Lord's Supper*. It is not true to say that we do. We honour them as holy ordinances appointed by Christ Himself, and as blessed means of grace, which in all who use them rightly, worthily, and with faith, "have a wholesome effect or operation."

But we steadily refuse to admit that Christ's Sacraments convey grace *ex opere operato*, and that in every case where they are administered, good must of necessity be done. We refuse to admit that they are the grand media between Christ and the soul,—above faith, above preaching, and above prayer. We protest against the idea that in baptism the use of water, in the name of the Trinity, is invariably and necessarily accompanied by regeneration. We protest against the practice of encouraging any one to come to the Lord's Table unless he repents truly of sin, has a lively faith in Christ, and is in charity with all men. We protest against the theory that the Lord's Supper is a sacrifice, as a theory alike contrary to the Bible, Articles, and Prayer-book. And above all, we protest against the notion of any corporal presence of Christ's flesh and blood in the Lord's Supper, under the forms of bread and wine, as an "idolatry to be abhorred of all faithful Christians."

(5) I go on to say that Evangelical Religion *does not undervalue the English Prayer-book*. It is not true to say that we do. We honour that excellent book as a matchless form of public worship, and one most admirably adapted to the wants of human nature. We use it with pleasure in our public ministrations, and should grieve to see the day when its use is forbidden.

But we do not presume to say there can be no acceptable worship of God without the Prayer-book. It does not possess the same authority as the Bible. We steadily refuse to give to the Prayer-book the honour which is only due to the Holy Scriptures, or to regard it as forming, together with the Bible, the rule of faith for the Church of England. We deny that it contains one single truth of religion, besides, over and above what is contained in God's Word. And we hold that to say the Bible and Prayer-book together are "the Church's Creed," is foolish and absurd.

(6) I go on to say that Evangelical Religion *does not undervalue Episcopacy*. It is not true to say that we do. We give to our Bishops as much honour and respect as any section of the Church of England does, and in reality a great deal more. We thoroughly believe that Episcopal government, rightly administered, is the best form of Church government that can be had in this evil world.

But we steadily refuse to believe that Bishops are infallible, or that their words are to be believed when they are not in harmony with the Scriptures, —or that Episcopacy is the first test of a Church being a true Church,—

or that Presbyterian orders are not valid orders, or that non-Episcopal Christians are to be handed over to the uncovenanted mercies of God. We hold as firmly as any that "from the beginning there have been bishops, priests, and deacons." But we refuse to join in the bigoted cry, "No bishop, no Church."

I repeat that in due respect to the Episcopal office we yield to none. But we never will admit that the acts and doings and deliverances of any Bishops, however numerous, and by whatever name they are called, whether a Pan-Anglican Synod or not, are to be received as infallible, and not to be submitted to free criticism. We cannot forget that erring Bishops ruined the Church of England in the days of Charles the First,—almost ruined it again in 1662, when they cast out the Puritans,—and nearly ruined it once more in the last century, when they shut out the Methodists. No! we have read history, and we have not forgotten that while we have had a Cranmer and a Parker, we have also had a Sheldon and a Laud; and that while we have had stars in our ecclesiastical firmament like Hooper, Ridley, and Jewell, we have also had men who were a disgrace to their office, like the semi-papists, Cheyney and Montague, and the subtle politician, Atterbury.

(7) I go on to say that Evangelical Religion *does not object to handsome churches*, good ecclesiastical architecture, a well-ordered ceremonial, and a well-conducted service. It is not true to say that we do. We like handsome, well-arranged places of worship, when we can get them. We abhor slovenliness and disorder in God's service, as much as any. We would have all things done "decently and in order." (1 Cor. xiv. 40.)

But we steadily maintain that simplicity should be the grand characteristic of Christian worship. We hold that human nature is so easily led astray, and so thoroughly inclined to idolatry, that ornament in Christian worship should be used with a very sparing hand. We firmly believe that the tendency of excessive ornament, and a theatrical ceremonial, is to defeat the primary end for which worship was established, to draw away men's minds from Christ, and to make them walk by sight and not by faith. We hold above all that the inward and spiritual character of the congregation is of far more importance than the architecture and adornments of the church. We dare not forget the great principle of Scripture, that "man looketh on the outward appearance, but the Lord looketh on the heart." (1 Sam. xvi. 7.)

(8) I go on to say that Evangelical religion *does not undervalue unity*. It is not true to say that we do. We love harmony and peace as much as any Christians in the world. We long for that day when there shall be no more controversy, strife, and division; when Ephraim shall no longer vex Judah, nor Judah Ephraim.

But we firmly maintain that there can be no real unity without oneness in the faith. We protest against the idea of unity based on a common

Episcopacy, and not on a common belief of Christ's Gospel. As for the theories of those who make advances to Rome, and hold out the hand to the Church of Bonner and Gardiner, while they turn their backs on the Church of Knox and Rutherford, Chalmers and M'Cheyne, we repudiate them with indignation as unworthy of English Churchmen. We abhor the very idea of reunion with Rome, unless Rome first purges herself from her many false doctrines and superstitions.

(9) Last, but not least, I say that Evangelical Religion *does not undervalue Christian holiness and self-denial.* It is not true to say that we do. We desire as much as any to promote habitual spirituality of heart and life in Christians. We give place to none in exalting humility, charity, meekness, gentleness, temperance, purity, self-denial, good works, and separation from the world. With all our defects, we are second to no section of Christ's Church in attaching the utmost importance to private prayer, private Bible-reading, and private communion with God.

But we steadily deny that true holiness consists in calling everything "holy" in religion, and thrusting forward the word "holy" with sickening frequency at every turn. We will not allow that it is really promoted by an ostentatious observance of Lent, by keeping Ecclesiastical fasts and saints' days, by frequent communion, by joining Houses of mercy, by doing penance, by going to confession, by wearing peculiar dresses, by decorating our persons with enormous crosses, by frequent gestures, and postures expressive of humility, in public worship, by walking in procession and the like. We believe, on the contrary, that such holiness (so-called) too often begins from the outside, and is a complete delusion. It has a "show of wisdom," and may satisfy silly young women and brainless young men, who like to compound for races and balls one part of their week, by asceticism and will-worship at another. But we utterly deny that it is the holiness recommended by St. Paul and St. Peter, St. James and St. John.*

* I am aware that this paragraph is likely to be misinterpreted, and may give offence. A captious reader may say that I consider keeping Lent and saints' days and fasts is wrong. I beg to remind him that I say nothing of the kind. I only say that these things do not constitute Christian holiness. I will go even further I will say that the history of the last three hundred years in England does not incline me to think that these things, however well meant, are conducive to real holiness.

I am quite sure that the substance of this paragraph is imperatively demanded by the times. Things have come to this pass in England that thousands of Churchmen are making the whole of religion to consist in externals. Against such a religion, as long as I live, I desire to protest. It may suit an Italian bandit, who oscillates between Lent and Carnival, between fasting and robbing. It ought never to satisfy a Bible-reading Christian. It is the religion that the natural heart likes, but it is not the religion of God.

When I speak of an "ostentatious" observance of Lent, I do it with a reason. There are hundreds of people who "scruple" at weddings and dinner parties in Lent, but rush to balls, theatres, and races as soon as Lent is over! If this is Christian holiness, we may throw our Bibles to the winds.

I leave my list of negatives here. I have not time to dwell on them further. The sum of the whole matter is this:—we give all lawful honour to learning, the Church, the ministry, the Sacrament, Episcopacy, the Prayer-book, Church ornament, unity, and holiness; but we firmly decline to give them more honour than we find given to them in God's Word.

We dare not take up any other position, because of the plain teaching of the Scriptures. We read there how the ark itself was utterly useless to Israel when trusted in as a saviour, and exalted into the place of God.— We read there how God Himself has said, that the sacrifices and feasts which He Himself had appointed, were "abominations" and a "weariness" to Him, when rested on as ends and not as means.—We read there how the very temple itself, with all its divinely ordained services, was denounced as a "den of thieves," by Christ Himself. (1 Sam. iv. 1–11; Isa. 1. 11–15; Luke xix. 46.)

And what do we learn from all this? We learn that we must be very careful how we give primary honour to things invented by man, or even to things which, though ordained by God, are secondary things in religion. We learn, above all, that those who accuse us of undervaluing the things I have mentioned, because we refuse to make them idols, are only exposing their own ignorance of Scripture. They know not what they say, nor whereof they affirm. We may listen to their slanderous charges and misrepresentations with calm indifference. Let them show us that we do not estimate learning, the Church, the Ministry, the Sacraments, the Prayer-book, Episcopacy, unity, and holiness, with the estimate of Scripture, and we will confess that we have erred. But till they can do that, we shall firmly maintain that we are right and they are wrong.

III. It only remains for me to say a few words on the last question I propose to consider:—"*What is it that makes much religion appear to us not Evangelical?*"

This is no doubt a delicate point, but a very serious and important one. I repeat here what I have remarked before. We do not say that men who are not professedly Evangelical ignore and disbelieve the leading doctrines of the Evangelical creed. We say nothing of the kind. But we do say confidently, that there are many ways in which the faith of Christ may be marred and spoiled, without being positively denied. And here we venture to think is the very reason that so much religion called Christian, is not truly Evangelical. The Gospel in fact is a most curiously and delicately compounded medicine, and a medicine that is very easily spoiled.

You may spoil the Gospel by *substitution*. You have only to withdraw from the eyes of the sinner the grand object which the Bible proposes to faith,—Jesus Christ; and to substitute another object in His place,—the Church, the Ministry, the Confessional, Baptism, or the Lord's Supper,— and the mischief is done. Substitute anything for Christ, and the Gospel is totally spoiled! Do this, either directly or indirectly, and your religion ceases to be Evangelical.

You may spoil the Gospel by *addition*. You have only to add to Christ, the grand object of faith, some other objects as equally worthy of honour, and the mischief is done. Add anything to Christ, and the Gospel ceases to be a pure Gospel! Do this, either directly or indirectly, and your religion ceases to be Evangelical.

You may spoil the Gospel by *interposition*. You have only to push something between Christ and the eye of the soul, to draw away the sinner's attention from the Saviour, and the mischief is done. Interpose anything between man and Christ, and man will neglect Christ for the thing interposed! Do this, either directly or indirectly, and your religion ceases to be Evangelical.

You may spoil the Gospel by *disproportion*. You have only to attach an exaggerated importance to the secondary things of Christianity, and a diminished importance to the first things, and the mischief is done. Once alter the proportion of the parts of truth, and truth soon becomes downright error! Do this, either directly or indirectly, and your religion ceases to be Evangelical.

Lastly, but not least, you may completely spoil the Gospel by *confused and contradictory directions*. Complicated and obscure statements about faith, baptism, Church privileges, and the benefits of the Lord's Supper, all jumbled together, and thrown down without order before hearers, make the Gospel no Gospel at all! Confused and disorderly statements of Christianity are almost as bad as no statement at all! Religion of this sort is not Evangelical.

I know not whether I succeed in making my meaning clear. I am very anxious to do so. Myriads of our fellow-countrymen are utterly unable to see any difference between one thing and another in religion, and are hence continually led astray. Thousands can see no distinct difference between sermons and sermons, and preachers and preachers, and have only a vague idea that "sometimes all is not right." I will endeavour, therefore, to illustrate my subject by two familiar illustrations.

A doctor's prescription of a medicine often contains five or six different ingredients. There is so much of one drug and so much of another; a little of this, and a good deal of that. Now what man of common sense can fail to see that the whole value of the prescription depends on a faithful and honest use of it? Take away one ingredient, and substitute another; leave out one ingredient altogether; add a little to the quantity of one drug; take away a little from the quantity of another. Do this, I say, to the prescription, my good friend, and it is a thousand chances to one that you spoil it altogether. The thing that was meant for your health, you have converted into downright poison.

Apply this little simple parable to the Gospel. Regard it as a medicine sent down from heaven, for the curing of man's spiritual disease, by a Physician of infinite skill and power; a medicine of singular efficacy, which man with all his wisdom could never have devised. Tell me now, as one of common sense, does it not stand to reason that this medicine should be used without the slightest alteration, and precisely in the manner and proportion that the great Physician intended? Tell me whether you have the least right to expect good from it, if you have tampered with it in the smallest degree? You know what the answer to these questions must be: your conscience will give the reply. Spoil the proportions of your doctor's prescription, and you will spoil its usefulness, even though you may call it medicine. Spoil the proportions of Christ's Gospel, and you spoil its efficacy. You may call it religion if you like; but you must not call it Evangelical. The several doctrines may be there, but they are useless if you have not observed the *proportions*.

The brazen serpent supplies another valuable illustration of my meaning. The whole efficacy of that miraculous remedy, we must remember, depended on using it precisely in the way that God directed.—It was *the serpent* of brass, and nothing else, that brought health to him that looked at it. The man who thought it wise to look at the brazen altar, or at the pole on which the serpent hung, would have died of his wounds.—It was the serpent *looked at*, and only looked at, that cured the poor bitten Israelite. The man who fancied it would be better to touch the serpent, or to offer a sacrifice to it, would have got no benefit.—It was the serpent looked at by each sufferer *with his own eyes*, and not with the eyes of another, that healed. The man who bade another look for him, would have found a vicarious look useless.—Looking, looking, only looking, was the prescription.—The sufferer, and only the sufferer, must look for himself with his own eyes.—The serpent, the brazen serpent, and nothing but the serpent, was the object for the eye.

Let us apply that marvellous and most deeply typical history to the Gospel. We have no warrant for expecting the slightest benefit for our souls from Christ's salvation, unless we use it precisely in the way that Christ appointed. If we add anything to it, take anything away from it, try to improve the terms, depart in the slightest degree from the path which the Bible marks out for us, we have no right whatever to look for any good being done. God's plan of salvation cannot possibly be mended or improved. He who tries to amend or improve it, will find that he spoils it altogether.

In one word I wind up this last part of my subject by saying, that a religion to be really "Evangelical" and really good, must be the Gospel, the whole Gospel, and nothing but the Gospel, as Christ prescribed it and expounded it to the Apostles;—the truth, the whole truth, and nothing but the truth;—the terms, the whole terms, and nothing but the terms,—in all their fulness, all their freeness, all their simplicity, all their presentness.

Here, I am sorry to say, a vast quantity of so-called religion in the present day appears to me to break down. It does not come up to the standard I have just given. Things are added to it, or things are taken away, or things are put in their wrong places, or things are set forth in their wrong proportions. And hence, painful as it is, I cannot avoid the conclusion that much of the religion of our own times does not deserve to be called Evangelical. I do not charge all clergymen who are not "Evangelical" with not being "Christians." I do not say that the religion they teach is not Christianity. I trust I am not so uncharitable as to say anything of this kind. But I do say that, for the reasons already assigned, they appear to me to teach that which is not Christ's whole truth. In a word, they do not give full weight, full measure, and the prescription of the Gospel accurately made up. The parts are there, but not the proportions.

I cannot bring my paper to a conclusion without offering some practical suggestions about the present duties of the Evangelical body. We have been considering what Evangelical religion is and is not. A few pages devoted to our immediate duties, in the present position of the Church, can hardly be thought misapplied.

The times no doubt are very critical, full of danger to our beloved Church, full of danger to the nation. Never has there been such an unblushing avowal of Popish opinions among Churchmen, and such shameless additions to the faith as defined in our Articles. The grand question is, whether our Protestantism shall die or live? Now I believe much depends on the attitude and line of conduct taken up by the Evangelical body. If they know the times and do their duty, there is hope for the Church. If they are timid, supine, compromising, vacillating, and indolent, there is no hope at all.

(1) I suggest, for one thing, that we ought to exercise a special jealousy over *our own personal religion*. Let us take heed that it is thoroughly and entirely Evangelical. The times we live in are desperately unfavourable to a sharply-cut, decided, distinct, doctrinal Christianity. A fog of vague liberalism overspreads the ecclesiastical horizon. A settled determination to think everybody is right, and nobody is wrong, everything is true, and nothing is false, meets us at every turn. The world is possessed with a devil of false charity about religion. Men try to persuade us, like Gallio, that the alleged differences between creeds and schools of thought are only about "words and names," and that it is "all the same thing." In times like these, let us be on our guard, and take heed to our souls.—"Watch ye: stand fast in the faith. Quit you like men: be strong." (1 Cor. xvi. 13.) Let us steadfastly resolve to stand fast in the old paths, the good way of our Protestant Reformers. Narrow, old-fashioned, obsolete, as some may be pleased to call that way, they will never show us a better. The nearer we draw to the great realities of death, judgment, and eternity, the more

excellent will that way appear. When I go down the valley of the shadow of death, and my feet touch the cold waters, I want something better than vague, high-sounding words, or the painted playthings and gilded trifles of man-made ceremonials. Give me no stone altars and would-be confessors. Give me no surpliced priests or pretended sacrifice in my bedroom. Put no man or form between me and Christ. Give me a real staff for my hand such as David had, and real meat and drink for my soul such as aged Paul felt within him, and feeling cried, "I am not ashamed." (2 Tim. i. 12.) I must know distinctly whom I believe, what I believe, and why I believe and in what manner I believe. Nothing, nothing will answer these questions satisfactorily, but thorough, downright Evangelical Religion. Let us make sure that this religion is our own.

(2) I suggest, secondly, that ministers who call themselves Evangelical, ought to be specially *careful that they do not compromise their principles*, and damage their testimony, by vain attempts to conciliate the world.

This is a great danger in these days. It is a sunken rock, on which I fear many are striking, and doing themselves immense harm. The plausible pretext of making our services more attractive, and cutting the ground from under the feet of Ritualists, too often induces Evangelical ministers to do things which they had far better let alone. New church decorations, new church music, and a semi-histrionic mode of going through church worship, are things which I suggest that we must watch most narrowly, and keep at arm's length. They are points on which we must take heed that we do not let in the Pope and the devil.

Tampering with these things, we may be sure, does no real good. It may seem to please the world, and have a "show of wisdom," but it never converts the world, and makes the world believe. We had far better leave it alone. Some Evangelical clergymen, I suspect, have begun flirting and trifling with these things with the best intentions, and have ended by losing their own characters, disgusting their true believing hearers, making themselves miserable, and going out of the world under a cloud.

Oh, no! we cannot be too jealous in these days about the slightest departure from the "faith once delivered to the saints," and from the worship handed down to us by the Reformers. We cannot be too careful to add nothing to, and take nothing away from, the simplicity of the Gospel, and to do nothing in our worship, which seems to cast the slightest reflection on Evangelical principles.—"A little leaven leaveneth the whole lump."—"Take heed and beware of the leaven of the Pharisees and Sadducees." (Gal. v. 9; Matt. xvi. 6.)

Let us mark the testimony of Scripture on this subject. The Epistle to the Galatians is the inspired handbook for these times. Mark how in that Epistle St. Paul declares, "Though we, or an angel from heaven, preach any other Gospel unto you than that which we have preached unto you, let him be accursed."—Mark how he repeats it: "As we said before, so we say again, If any man preach any other Gospel than that ye have received, let him be accursed."—Mark how he tells us that "when he came to Antioch he withstood Peter to the face, because he was to be blamed."—Mark how he says to the Galatians, "Ye observe days, and months, and times, and years." And then comes the solemn and weighty remark which ought to ring in the ears of many: "I am afraid of you." (Gal. i. 9; ii. 11; iv. 10, 11.)

Let us carefully observe how little good they do who attempt to mix up Evangelical preaching and a Ritual ceremonial. Little, did I say?—they do no good at all! The world is never won by trimming, and compromising, by facing both ways, and trying to please all. The cross of Christ is never made more acceptable by sawing off its corners, or by polishing, varnishing, and adorning it. Processions, and banners, and flowers, and crosses, and excessive quantity of music, and elaborate services, and beautiful vestments, may please children and weak-minded people. But they never helped forward heart-conversion and heart-sanctification, and they never will. Scores of English clergymen, I strongly suspect, have found out too late that St. Paul's words are deeply true, when he says, "It is a good thing that the heart be established with grace; not with meats, which have not profited them that have been occupied therein." (Heb. xiii. 9.)

I grant freely that we have need of much patience in these times. No doubt it is very provoking to be twitted with the nakedness, poverty, and meagreness (so called) of Evangelical worship. It is very annoying to see our younger members slipping away to churches where there are processions, banners, flowers, incense, and a thoroughly histrionic and gorgeous ceremonial. It is vexing to hear them say, that "they feel so much better after these services." But none of these things must move us. "He that believeth shall not make haste." (Isaiah xxviii. 16.) The end will never justify illicit means. Let us never leave the high ground of principle under any false pressure, from whatever side it may come. Let us hold on our own way, and be jealously sensitive of any departure from simplicity. Popularity obtained by pandering to the senses or the sentiment of our hearers is not worth anything. Worshippers who are not content with the Bible, the cross of Christ, simple prayers and simple praise, are worshippers of little value. It is useless to try to please them, because their spiritual taste is diseased.

Let us remember, not least, the enormous injury which we may do to souls, if we once allow ourselves to depart in the least degree from the simplicity of the Gospel either in our doctrine or in our worship. Who can estimate the shipwrecks that might occur in a single night, and the lives that might be lost, if a light-house keeper dared to alter but a *little* the colour of his light?—Who can estimate the deaths that might take place in a town, if the chemist took on himself to depart but a *little* from the doctor's prescriptions?—Who can estimate the wholesale misery that might be caused in a war, by maps a *little* wrong and charts a little in-

correct?—Who can estimate these things?—Then perhaps you may have
some idea of the spiritual harm that ministers may do by departing in the
slightest degree from the Scriptural proportions of the Gospel, or by
trying to catch the world by dressing simple old Evangelical Religion in
new clothes.

(3) I suggest, finally, that *we must not allow Evangelical Religion to be
thrust out of the Church of England without a struggle.*

It is a religion which is worth a struggle; for it can point to works which
no other school in the Church of England has ever equalled. In this matter
we fear no comparison, if honestly and fairly made. We confess with
sorrow that we have done but little compared to what we ought to have
done; and yet we say boldly, that both abroad and at home no Churchmen
have done so much good to souls as those who are called Evangelical.
What Sierra Leone can the extreme Ritualists place before us as the result
of their system? What Tinnevelly bears testimony to the truth of their
school? What manufacturing towns have they rescued from semi-
heathenism? What mining districts have they Christianized? What teeming
populations of poor in our large cities can they point to, as evangelized by
their agencies? We boldly challenge a reply. Let them come forward and
name them. In the day when Evangelical Religion is cast out of the Church
of England, the usefulness of the Church will be ended and gone. Nothing
gives the Church of England such power and influence as genuine, well-
worked, well-administered Evangelical Religion.

But it is a religion that can only be preserved amongst us just now by a
great effort, and a mighty struggle. For our nation's sake, for our children's
sake, for the world's sake, for the honour and glory of our God, let us gird
up the loins of our minds, and resolve that the struggle shall be made.

It is a struggle, we can honestly call the world to witness, which is not
one of our seeking. The controversy is thrust upon us, whether we like it
or not. We are driven to a painful dilemma. We must either sit by in
silence, like sneaks and cowards, and let the Church of England be
unprotestantized and re-united with Rome;—or else we must basely desert
the dear old Church and let traitors work their will;—or else we must
look the danger manfully in the face, and *fight!*—Our fight, of course, is to
be carried on with the same Word that Cranmer, Latimer, and Ridley
fought with, and not with carnal weapons. But as they did, so must we do:
we must stand up and fight. Yes! even if a secession of our antagonists is
the consequence, we must not shrink from fighting. Let every man go to the
place that suits him best. Let Papists join the Pope, and Romanists retire to
Rome.* But if we want our Church to continue Protestant and Evangelical,

---

* I trust that no one will misunderstand me here. If any one supposes that
I want to narrow the pale of the Church of England, and to make it the Church
of one particular party, he is totally mistaken. I am quite aware that my Church
is eminently liberal, truly comprehensive, and tolerant of wide differences of

we must not be afraid to fight. There are times when there is a mine of deep meaning in our Lord's words,—"He that hath no sword, let him sell his garment, and buy one." (Luke xxii, 36.) To such times we have come.

Does any one ask me what is to be done? I answer that the path of duty, to my mind, is clear, plain, and unmistakable. Union and organization of all Protestant and Evangelical Churchmen,—untiring exposure of the Popish dealings of our antagonists, by the pulpit, the platform, and the press,—lawsuits whenever there is a reasonable hope of success,—appeals to Parliament for declarative statutes, and the reform of our Ecclesiastical courts,—bold, decided, prompt action, the moment any necessity requires,—these are the weapons of our warfare. They are weapons which, from one end of the country to the other, we ought to wield, boldly, untiringly, unflinchingly, be the sacrifice and cost what it may. But I say, "No surrender! No desertion! No compromise! No disgraceful peace!"

Let us then resolve to "contend earnestly for the faith." By preaching and by praying, by pulpit and by platform, by pen and by tongue, by printing and by speaking, let us labour to maintain Evangelical Religion within the Church of England, and to resist the enemies which we see around us.—We are not weak if we stand together and act together. The middle classes and the poor are yet sound at heart. They do not love Popery. God Himself has not forsaken us, and truth is on our side.— But, be the issue of the conflict what it may, let us nail our colours to the mast; and, if need be, go down with our colours flying. Let us only settle it deeply in our minds, that without Protestant and Evangelical principles, a Church is as useless as a well without water. In one word, when the Church of England becomes Popish once more, it will be a Church not worth preserving.

opinion. But I deny that the Church ever meant its members to be downright Papists.

The Church has always found room in its ranks for men of very different schools of thought. There has been room for Ridley, and room for Hooper,— room for Jewell, and room for Hooker,—room for Whitgift, and room for Tillotson,—room for Usher, and room for Jeremy Taylor,—room for Davenant, and room for Andrews,—room for Waterland, and room for Beveridge,—room for Chillingworth, and room for Bull,—room for Whitby, and room for Scott, —room for Toplady, and room for Fletcher. Where is the Churchman who would like any one of these men to have been shut out of the Church of England? If there is such an one, I do not agree with him.

But if any man wants me to believe that our Church ever meant to allow its clergy to teach the Romish doctrine of the Real Presence, the sacrifice of the Mass, and the practice of auricular confession, without let or hindrance, I tell him plainly that I cannot believe it. My common sense revolts against it. I would as soon believe that black is white, or that two and two make five.

Between the old High Churchman and the Ritualists I draw a broad line of distinction. With all his faults and mistakes, in my judgment, the old High Churchman is a true Churchman, and is thoroughly and heartily opposed to Popery. The Ritualists, on the other hand, scorn the very name of Protestant; and, if words mean anything, are so like Roman Catholics, that a plain man can see no difference between their tenets and those of Rome.

II

ONLY ONE WAY OF SALVATION

Is there more than one road to heaven? Is there more than one way in which the soul of man can be saved? This is the question which I propose to consider in this paper, and I shall begin the consideration by quoting a text of Scripture: "Neither is there salvation in any other: for there is none other name under heaven given among men, whereby we must be saved." (Acts iv. 12.)

These words are striking in themselves; but they are much more striking if we observe when and by whom they were spoken.

They were spoken by a poor and friendless Christian, in the midst of a persecuting Jewish Council. It was a grand confession of Christ.

They were spoken by the lips of the Apostle Peter. This is the man who a few weeks before forsook Jesus and fled: this is the very man who three times over denied his Lord. There is another spirit in him now! He stands up boldly before priests and Sadducees, and tells them the truth to their face: "This is the stone that was set at naught of you builders, which is become the head of the corner. Neither is there salvation in any other: for there is none other name under heaven given among men, whereby we must be saved."

Now, I need hardly tell a well-informed reader that this text is one of the principal foundations on which the Eighteenth Article of the Church of England is built.

That article runs as follows: "They also are to be had accursed that presume to say that every man shall be saved by the law or sect he professeth, so that he be diligent to frame his life according to that law and the light of nature. For Holy Scripture doth set out unto us only the name of Jesus Christ whereby men must be saved."

There are few stronger assertions than this throughout the whole Thirty-nine Articles. It is the only anathema pronounced by our Church from one end of her great Confession of faith to the other. The Council of Trent in her decrees anathematizes continually. The Church of England uses an anathema or curse once, and once only; and that she does it on good grounds I propose to show, by an examination of the Apostle Peter's words.

In considering this solemn subject, there are three things I wish to do.

I. First, I wish to explain the doctrine here laid down by the Apostle.

II. Secondly, I wish to supply some reasons why this doctrine must be true.

III. Thirdly, I wish to show some consequences which naturally flow from the doctrine.

I. *First, let me explain the doctrine laid down by St. Peter.*

Let us make sure that we rightly understand what the Apostle means. He says of Christ, "Neither is there salvation in any other." Now, what does this mean? On our clearly seeing this very much depends.

He means that no one can be saved from sin,—its guilt, its power, and its consequences,—excepting by Jesus Christ.

He means that no one can have peace with God the Father,—obtain pardon in this world, and escape wrath to come in the next,—excepting through the atonement and mediation of Jesus Christ.

In Christ alone God's rich provision of salvation for sinners is treasured up: by Christ alone God's abundant mercies come down from heaven to earth. Christ's blood alone can cleanse us; Christ's righteousness alone can clothe us; Christ's merit alone can give us a title to heaven. Jews and Gentiles, learned and unlearned, kings and poor men,—all alike must either be saved by the Lord Jesus, or lost for ever.

And the Apostle adds emphatically, "There is none other name under heaven given among men, whereby we must be saved." There is no other person commissioned, sealed, and appointed by God the Father to be the Saviour of sinners excepting Christ. The keys of Life and Death are committed to His hand, and all who would be saved must go to Him.

There was but one place of safety in the day when the flood came upon the earth: that place was Noah's ark. All other places and devices,—mountains, towers, trees, rafts, boats,—all were alike useless. So also there is but one hiding-place for the sinner who would escape the storm of God's anger; he must venture his soul on Christ.

There was but one man to whom the Egyptians could go in the time of famine, when they wanted food. They must go to Joseph: it was a waste of time to go to any one else. So also there is but One to whom hungering souls must go, if they would not perish for ever: they must go to Christ.

There was but one word that could save the lives of the Ephraimites in the day when the Gileadites contended with them, and took the fords of Jordan (Judges xi.): they must say "Shibboleth," or die. Just so there is but one name that will avail us when we stand at the gate of heaven: we must name the name of Jesus as our only hope, or be cast away everlastingly.

Such is the doctrine of the text. "No salvation but by Jesus Christ;—in Him plenty of salvation,—salvation to the uttermost, salvation for the very chief of sinners;—out of Him no salvation at all." It is in perfect harmony with our Lord's own words in St. John's Gospel,—"I am the way, the truth, and the life: no man cometh unto the Father, but by Me." (John xiv. 6.) It is the same thing that Paul tells the Corinthians,—"Other foundation can no man lay than that is laid, which is Jesus Christ." (1 Cor. iii. 11.) And it is the same that St. John tells us in his first Epistle,— "God hath given to us eternal life, and this life is in His Son. He that hath the Son hath life, and he that hath not the Son of God hath not life." (1 John v. 12.) All these texts come to one and the same point,—no salvation but by Jesus Christ.

Let us make sure that we understand this before we pass on. Men are apt to think, "This is all old news;—these are ancient things: who knoweth not such truths as these? Of course we believe there is no salvation but by Christ." But I ask my readers to mark well what I say. Make sure that you understand this doctrine, or else by and by you will stumble, and be offended at the statements I have yet to make in this paper.

We are to venture the whole salvation of our souls on Christ, and on Christ only. We are to cast loose completely and entirely from all other hopes and trusts. We are not to rest partly on Christ,—partly on doing all we can,—partly on keeping our church,—partly on receiving the sacrament. In the matter of our justification Christ is to be *all*. This is the doctrine of the text.

Heaven is before us, and Christ the only door into it; hell beneath us, and Christ alone able to deliver from it; the devil behind us, and Christ the only refuge from his wrath and accusations; the law against us, and Christ alone able to redeem us; sin weighing us down, and Christ alone able to put it away. This is the doctrine of the text.

Now do we see it? I hope we do. But I fear many think so who may find, before laying down this paper, that they do not.

II. *Let me, in the second place, supply some reasons why the doctrine of the text must be true.*

I might cut short this part of the subject by one simple argument: "God says so." "One plain text," said an old divine, " is as good as a thousand reasons."

But I will not do this. I wish to meet the objections that are ready to rise in many hearts against this doctrine, by pointing out the strong foundations on which it stands.

(1) Let me then say, for one thing, the doctrine of the text must be true, *because man is what man is.*

Now, what is man? There is one broad, sweeping answer, which takes in the whole human race: man is a sinful being. All children of Adam born into the world, whatever be their name or nation, are corrupt, wicked, and defiled in the sight of God. Their thoughts, words, ways, and actions are all, more or less, defective and imperfect.

Is there no country on the face of the globe where sin does not reign? Is there no happy valley, no secluded island, where innocence is to be found? Is there no tribe on earth, where, far away from civilization, and commerce, and money, and gunpowder, and luxury, and books, morality and purity flourish? No! there is none. Look over all the voyages and travels you can lay your hand on, from Columbus down to Cook, and from Cook to Livingstone, and you will see the truth of what I am asserting. The most solitary islands of the Pacific Ocean,—islands cut off from all the rest of the world,—islands where people were alike ignorant of Rome and Paris, London and Jerusalem,—these islands, when first discovered, have been found full of impurity, cruelty, and idolatry. The footprints of the devil have been traced on every shore. The veracity of the third chapter of Genesis has everywhere been established. Whatever else savages have been found ignorant of, they have never been found ignorant of sin.

But are there no men and women in the world who are free from this corruption of nature? Have there not been high-minded and exalted beings who have every now and then lived faultless lives? Have there not been some, if it be only a few, who have done all that God requires, and thus proved that sinless perfection is a possibility? No! there have been none. Look over all the biographies and lives of the holiest Christians; mark how the brightest and best of Christ's people have always had the deepest sense of their own defectiveness and corruption. They groan, they mourn, they sigh, they weep over their own shortcomings: it is one of the common grounds on which they meet. Patriarchs and Apostles, Fathers and Reformers, Episcopalians and Presbyterians, Luther and Calvin, Knox and Bradford, Rutherford and Bishop Hall, Wesley and Whitefield, Martyn and M'Cheyne,—all are alike agreed in feeling their own sinfulness. The more light they have, the more humble and self-abased they seem to be; the more holy they are, the more they seem to feel their own unworthiness.

Now what does all this seem to prove? To my eyes it seems to prove that human nature is so tainted and corrupt that, left to himself, no man could be saved. Man's case appears to be a hopeless one without a Saviour,—and that a mighty Saviour too. There must be a Mediator, an Atonement, an Advocate, to make such poor sinful beings acceptable with God; and I find this nowhere, excepting in Jesus Christ. Heaven for man without an almighty Redeemer, peace with God for man without a divine Intercessor, eternal life for man without an eternal Saviour,—in one word, salvation without Christ,—all alike, in the face of the plain facts about human nature, appear utter impossibilities.

I lay these things before thinking men, and I ask them to consider them. I know it is one of the hardest things in the world to realize the sinfulness of sin. *To say* we are all sinners is one thing; to have an idea what sin must be in the sight of God is quite another. Sin is too much part of ourselves to allow us to see it as it is: we do not feel our own moral deformity. We are like those animals in creation which are vile and loathsome to our senses, but are not so to themselves, nor yet to one another: their loathsomeness is their nature, and they do not perceive it. Just in the same way our corruption is part and parcel of ourselves, and at our best we have but a feeble comprehension of its intensity.

But this we may be sure of,—if we could see our own lives with the eyes of the angels who never fell, we should never doubt this point for a moment. In a word, no one can really know what man is, and not see that the doctrine of our text must be true. We are shut up to the Apostle Peter's conclusion. There can be no salvation except by Christ.

(2) Let me say another thing. The doctrine of our text must be true, *because God is what God is*.

Now what is God? That is a deep question indeed. We know something of His attributes: He has not left Himself without witness in creation; He has mercifully revealed to us many things about Himself in His Word. We know that God is a Spirit,—eternal, invisible, almighty,—the Maker of all things, the Preserver of all things,—holy, just, all-seeing, all-knowing, all-remembering,—infinite in mercy, in wisdom, in purity.

But, alas, after all, how low and grovelling are our highest ideas, when we come to put down on paper what we believe God to be! How many words and expressions we use whose full meaning we cannot fathom! How many things our tongues say of Him which our minds are utterly unable to conceive!

How small a part of Him do we see! How little of Him can we possibly know! How mean and paltry are any words of ours to convey any idea of Him who made this mighty world out of nothing, and with Whom one day is as a thousand years, and a thousand years as one day! How weak and inadequate are our poor feeble intellects to form any conception of Him Who is perfect in all His works,—perfect in the greatest as well as perfect in the smallest,—perfect in appointing the days and hours, and minutes and seconds in which Jupiter, with all his satellites, shall travel round the sun,—perfect in forming the smallest insect that creeps over a few feet of our little globe! How little can our busy helplessness comprehend a Being who is ever ordering all things, in heaven and earth, by universal providence: ordering the rise and fall of nations and dynasties, like Nineveh and Carthage; ordering the exact length to which men like Alexander and Napoleon shall extend their conquests; ordering the least step in the life of the humblest believer among His people: all at the same time, all unceasingly, all perfectly,—all for His own glory.

The blind man is no judge of the paintings of Rubens or Titian; the deaf man is insensible to the beauty of Handel's music; the Greenlander can have but a faint notion of the climate of the tropics; the South Sea islander can form but a remote conception of a locomotive engine, however well you may describe it. There is no faculty in their minds which can take in these things; they have no set of thoughts which can comprehend them; they have no mental fingers to grasp them. And just in the same way, the best and brightest ideas that man can form of God, compared to the reality which we shall one day see, are weak and faint indeed.

But one thing, I think, is very clear: and that is this. The more any man considers calmly what God really is, the more he must feel the immeasurable distance between God and himself; the more he meditates, the more he must see that there is a great gulf between him and God. His conscience, I think, will tell him, if he will let it speak, that God is perfect, and he imperfect; that God is very high, and he very low; that God is glorious majesty, and he a poor worm; and that if ever he is to stand before Him in judgment with comfort, he must have some mighty Helper, or he will not be saved.

And what is all this but the very doctrine of the text with which I began this paper? What is all this but coming round to the conclusion I am urging upon my readers? With such an one as God to give account to, we must have a mighty Saviour. To give us peace with such a glorious being as God, we must have an almighty Mediator, a Friend and Advocate on our side,—an Advocate who can answer every charge that can be laid against us, and plead our cause with God on equal terms. We want this, and nothing less than this. Vague notions of mercy will never give true peace. And such a Saviour, such a Friend, such an Advocate is nowhere to be found excepting in the person of Jesus Christ.

I lay this reason also before thinking men. I know well that people may have false notions of God as well as everything else, and shut their eyes against truth. But I say boldly and confidently, No man can have really high and honourable views of what God is, and escape the conclusion that the doctrine of our text must be true. We are shut up to the truth of St. Peter's declaration. There can be no possible salvation but by Jesus Christ.

(3) Let me say, in the third place, this doctrine must be true *because the Bible is what the Bible is.* If we do not believe the doctrine, we must give up the Bible as the only rule of faith.

All through the Bible, from Genesis down to Revelation, there is only one simple account of the way in which man must be saved. It is always the same: only for the sake of our Lord Jesus Christ,—through faith; not for our own works and deservings.

We see it dimly revealed at first: it looms through the mist of a few promises; but there it is.

We have it more plainly afterwards: it is taught by the pictures and emblems of the law of Moses, the schoolmaster dispensation.

We have it still more clearly by and by: the Prophets saw in vision many particulars about the Redeemer yet to come.

We have it fully at last, in the sunshine of New Testament history: Christ incarnate,—Christ crucified,—Christ rising again,—Christ preached to the world.

But one golden chain runs through the whole volume: no salvation excepting by Jesus Christ. The bruising of the serpent's head foretold in the day of the fall; the clothing of our first parents with skins; the sacrifices of Noah, Abraham, Isaac, and Jacob; the passover, and all the particulars of the Jewish law,—the high priest, the altar, the daily offering of the lamb, the holy of holies entered only by blood, the scape-goat, the cities of refuge;—all are so many witnesses to the truth set forth in the text. All preach with one voice, salvation only by Jesus Christ.

In fact, this truth appears to be the grand object of the Bible, and all the different parts and portions of the book are meant to pour light upon it. I can gather from it no ideas of pardon and peace with God excepting in connection with this truth. If I could read of one soul in it who was saved without faith in a Saviour, I might perhaps not speak so confidently. But when I see that faith in Christ,—whether a coming Christ or a crucified Christ,—was the prominent feature in the religion of all who went to heaven;—when I see Abel owning Christ in his "better sacrifice" at one end of the Bible, and the saints in glory in John's vision rejoicing in Christ at the other end of the Bible;—when I see a man like Cornelius, who was devout, and feared God, and gave alms and prayed, not told that he had done all, and would of course be saved, but ordered to send for Peter, and hear of Christ;—when I see all these things, I say, I feel bound to believe that the doctrine of the text is the doctrine of the whole Bible. The Word of God, fairly examined and interpreted, shuts me up to the truth laid down by St. Peter. No salvation, no way to heaven, excepting by Jesus Christ.

Such are the reasons which seem to me to confirm the truth which forms the subject of this paper. What man is,—what God is,—what the Bible is,—all appear to me to lead on to the same great conclusion: no possible salvation without Christ. I leave them here, and pass on.

III. And now, in the third and last place, *let me show some consequences which flow naturally out of the doctrine declared by St. Peter.*

There are few parts of the subject which seem to me more important than this. The truth I have been trying to set before my readers bears so strongly on the condition of a great proportion of mankind, that I consider it would be mere affectation on my part not to say something about it. If Christ is the only way of salvation, what are we to feel about many people in the world? This is the point I am now going to take up.

I believe that many persons would go with me so far as I have gone, and would go no further. They will allow my premises: they will have nothing to say to my conclusions. They think it uncharitable to say anything which appears to condemn others. For my part I cannot understand such charity.

It seems to me the kind of charity which would see a neighbour drinking slow poison, but never interfere to stop him;—which would allow emigrants to embark in a leaky, ill-found vessel, and not interfere to prevent them;—which would see a blind man walking near a precipice, and think it wrong to cry out, and tell him there was danger.

The greatest charity is to tell the greatest quantity of truth. It is no charity to hide the legitimate consequences of such a saying of St. Peter as we are now considering, or to shut our eyes against them. And I solemnly call on every one who really believes there is no salvation in any but Christ,—and none other name given under heaven whereby we must be saved,—I solemnly call on that person to give me his attention, while I set before him some of the tremendous consequences which the doctrine we are considering involves.

I am not going to speak of the heathen who have never heard the Gospel. Their final state is a great depth, which the mightiest minds have been unable to fathom: I am not ashamed of leaving it alone. One thing only I will say. If any of the heathen, who die heathen, are saved, I believe they will owe their salvation, however little they may know it on this side of the grave, to the work and atonement of Christ. Just as infants and idiots among ourselves will find at the last day they owed all to Christ, though they never knew Him, so I believe it will be with the heathen, if any of them are saved, whether many or few. This at any rate I am sure of—there is no such thing as creature merit. My own private opinion is that the highest Archangel (though, of course, in a very different way and degree from us) will be found in some way to owe his standing to Christ; and that things in heaven, as well as things on earth, will be found ultimately all indebted to the name of Jesus. But I leave the case of the heathen to others, and will speak of matters nearer home.

(a) One mighty consequence then which seems to be learned from the text which forms the keynote of this paper, *is the utter uselessness of any religion without Christ.*

There are many to be found in Christendom at this day who have a religion of this kind. They would not like to be called Deists, but Deists they are. That there is a God, that there is what they are pleased to call Providence, that God is merciful, that there will be a state after death,—this is about the sum and substance of their creed; and as to the distinguishing tenets of Christianity, they do not seem to recognize them at all. Now I denounce such a system as a baseless fabric,—its seeming foundation man's fancy,—its hopes an utter delusion. The god of such people is an idol of their own invention, and not the glorious God of the Scriptures,—a miserably imperfect being, even on their own showing,—without holiness, without justice, without any attribute but that of vague, indiscriminate mercy. Such a religion may possibly do as a toy to live with: it is far too unreal to die with. It utterly fails to meet the wants of man's conscience:

it offers no remedy; it affords no rest for the soles of our feet; it cannot comfort, for it cannot save. Let us beware of it, if we love life. *Let us beware of a religion without Christ.*

(*b*) Another consequence to be learned from the text is, *the folly of any religion in which Christ has not the first place.*

I need not remind my readers how many hold a system of this kind. The Socinian tells us that Christ was a mere man; that His blood had no more efficacy than that of another; that His death on the cross was not a real atonement and propitiation of man's sins; and that, after all, doing is the way to heaven, and not believing. I solemnly declare that I believe such a system is ruinous to men's souls. It seems to me to strike at the root of the whole plan of salvation which God has revealed in the Bible, and practically to nullify the greater part of the Scriptures. It overthrows the priesthood of the Lord Jesus, and strips Him of His office. It converts the whole system of the law of Moses, touching sacrifices and ordinances, into a meaningless form. It seems to say that the sacrifice of Cain was just as good as the sacrifice of Abel. It turns man adrift on a sea of uncertainty, by plucking from under him the finished work of a divine Mediator. Let us beware of it, no less than of Deism, if we love life. Let us beware of the least attempt to depreciate and undervalue Christ's person, offices, or work. The name whereby alone we can be saved, is a name above every name, and the slightest contempt poured upon it is an insult to the King of kings. The salvation of our souls has been laid by God the Father on Christ, and no other. If He were not very God of very God, He never could accomplish it, and there could be no salvation at all.

(*c*) Another consequence to be learned from our text, is the *great error committed by those who add anything to Christ, as necessary to salvation.*

It is an easy thing to profess belief in the Trinity, and reverence for our Lord Jesus Christ, and yet to make some addition to Christ as the ground of hope, and so to overthrow the doctrine of the text as really and completely as by denying it altogether.

The Church of Rome does this systematically. She adds things to Christianity over and above the requirements of the Gospel, of her own invention. She speaks as if Christ's finished work was not a sufficient foundation for a sinner's soul, and as if it were not enough to say, "Believe on the Lord Jesus Christ, and thou shalt be saved." She sends men to priests and confessors, to penances and absolution, to masses and extreme unction, to fasting and bodily mortification, to the Virgin Mary and the saints,—as if these things could add to the safety there is in Christ Jesus. And in doing this she sins against the doctrine of God's Word with a high hand. Let us beware of any Romish hankering after additions to the simple way of the Gospel, from whatever quarter it may come.

But I fear the Church of Rome does not stand alone in this matter.

I fear there are thousands of professing Protestants who are often erring in the same direction, although, of course, in a very different degree. They get into a way of adding, perhaps insensibly, other things to the name of Christ, or attaching an importance to them which they never ought to receive. The ultra Churchman in England, who thinks God's covenanted mercies are tied to Episcopacy,—the ultra Presbyterian in Scotland, who cannot reconcile prelacy with an intelligent knowledge of the Gospel,—the ultra Free-kirk man by his side, who seems to think lay patronage and vital Christianity almost incompatible,—the ultra Dissenter, who traces every evil in the Church to its connection with the State, and can talk of nothing but the voluntary system,—the ultra Baptist, who shuts out from the Lord's table every one who has not received his peculiar views of adult baptism,—the ultra Plymouth Brother, who believes all knowledge to reside with his own body, and condemns every one outside as a poor weak babe;—all these, I say, however unwittingly, exhibit a most uncomfortable tendency to add to the doctrine of our text. All seem to me to be practically declaring that salvation is not to be found simply and solely in Christ. All seem to me to be practically adding another name to the name of Jesus, whereby men must be saved,—even the name of their own party and sect. All seem to me to be practically replying to the question, "What shall I do to be saved?" not merely, "Believe on the Lord Jesus Christ," but also "Come and join us."

Now I call upon every true Christian to beware of such ultraism, in whatever form he may be inclined to it. In saying this I would not be misunderstood. I like every one to be decided in his views of ecclesiastical matters, and to be fully persuaded of their correctness. All I ask is, that men will not put these things in the place of Christ, or place them anywhere near Him, or speak of them as if they thought them needful to salvation. However dear to us our own peculiar views may be, let us beware of thrusting them in between the sinner and the Saviour. In the things of God's Word, be it remembered, addition, as well as subtraction, is a great sin.

(d) The last consequence which seems to me to be learned from our text is, *the utter absurdity of supposing that we ought to be satisfied with a man's state of soul, if he is only earnest and sincere.*

This is a very common heresy indeed, and one against which we all need to be on our guard. There are thousands who say in the present day, "We have nothing to do with the opinions of others. They may perhaps be mistaken, though it is possible they are right and we wrong: but, if they are sincere and earnest, we hope they will be saved even as we." And all this sounds liberal and charitable, and people like to fancy their own views are so! To such an extreme length has this erroneous idea run, that many are content to describe a Christian as "an earnest man," and seem to think this vague definition is quite sufficient!

Now I believe such notions are entirely contradictory to the Bible, whatever else they may be. I cannot find in Scripture that any one ever got to heaven merely by sincerity, or was accepted with God if he was only earnest in maintaining his own views. The priests of Baal were earnest and sincere when they cut themselves with knives and lancets till the blood gushed out; but that did not prevent Elijah from commanding them to be treated as wicked idolators.—Manasseh, King of Judah, was doubtless earnest and sincere when he burned his children in the fire to Moloch; but who does not know that he brought on himself great guilt by so doing?—The Apostle Paul, when a Pharisee, was earnest and sincere while he made havoc of the Church, but when his eyes were opened he mourned over this as a special wickedness. Let us beware of allowing for a moment that sincerity is everything, and that we have no right to speak ill of a man's spiritual state because of the opinions he holds, if he is only *earnest* in holding them. On such principles, the Druidical sacrifices, the car of Juggernaut, the Indian suttees, the systematic murders of the Thugs, the fires of Smithfield, might each and all be defended. It will not stand: it will not bear the test of Scripture. Once allow such notions to be true, and we may as well throw our Bibles aside altogether. Sincerity is not Christ, and therefore sincerity cannot put away sin.

I dare be sure these consequences sound very unpleasant to the minds of some who may read them. But I say, calmly and advisedly, that a religion without Christ, a religion that takes away from Christ, a religion that adds anything to Christ, a religion that puts sincerity in the place of Christ,—all are dangerous: all are to be avoided, because all are alike contrary to the doctrine of Scripture.

Some readers may not like this. I am sorry for it. They think me uncharitable, illiberal, narrow-minded, bigoted, and so forth. Be it so. But they will not tell me my doctrine is not that of the Word of God and of the Church of England, whose minister I am. That doctrine is, salvation in Christ to the very uttermost,—but out of Christ no salvation at all.

I feel it a duty to bear my solemn testimony against the spirit of the day we live in; to warn men against its infection. It is not Atheism I fear so much, in the present times, as Pantheism. It is not the system which says nothing is true, so much as the system which says everything is true. It is not the system which says there is no Saviour, so much as the system which says there are many saviours, and many ways to peace!—It is the system which is so liberal, that it dares not say anything is false. It is the system which is so charitable, that it will allow everything to be true. It is the system which seems ready to honour others as well as our Lord Jesus Christ, to class them all together, and to think well of all. Confucius and Zoroaster, Socrates and Mahomet, the Indian Brahmins and the

African devil-worshippers, Arius and Pelagius, Ignatius Loyola and Socinus,—all are to be treated respectfully: none are to be condemned. It is the system which bids us smile complacently on all creeds and systems of religion. The Bible and the Koran, the old wives' fables of Rabbinical writers and the rubbish of Patristic traditions, the revelations of Emmanuel Swedenborg and the book of Mormon of Joseph Smith,—all, all are to be listened to: none are to be denounced as lies. It is the system which is so scrupulous about the feelings of others, that we are never to say they are wrong. It is the system which is so liberal that it calls a man a bigot if he dares to say, "I know my views are right." This is the system, this is the tone of feeling which I fear in this day, and this is the system which I desire emphatically to testify against and denounce.

What is it all but a bowing down before a great idol, speciously called liberality? What is it all but a sacrificing of truth upon the altar of a caricature of charity? What is it all but the worship of a shadow, a phantom, and an unreality? What can be more absurd than to profess ourselves content with "earnestness," when we do not know what we are earnest about? Let us take heed lest we are carried away by the delusion. Has the Lord God spoken to us in the Bible, or has He not? Has He shown us the way of salvation plainly and distinctly in that Bible, or has He not? Has He declared to us the dangerous state of all out of that way, or has He not? Let us gird up the loins of our minds, and look these questions fairly in the face, and give them an honest answer. Tell us that there is some other inspired book beside the Bible, and then we shall know what you mean. Tell us that the whole Bible is not inspired, and then we shall know where to meet you. But grant for a moment that the Bible, the whole Bible, and nothing but the Bible is God's truth, and then I know not in what way we can escape the doctrine of the text. From the liberality which says everybody is right, from the charity which forbids us to say anybody is wrong, from the peace which is bought at the expense of truth,—may the good Lord deliver us!

For my own part, I frankly confess, I find no resting-place between downright distinct Evangelical Christianity and downright infidelity, whatever others may find. I see no half-way house between them; or else I see houses that are roofless and cannot shelter my weary soul. I can see consistency in an infidel, however much I may pity him. I can see consistency in the full maintenance of Evangelical truth. But as to a middle course between the two,—I cannot see it; and I say so plainly. Let it be called illiberal and uncharitable. I can hear God's voice nowhere except in the Bible, and I can see no salvation for sinners in the Bible excepting through Jesus Christ. In Him I see abundance: out of Him I see none. And as for those who hold religions in which Christ is not all, whoever they may be, I have a most uncomfortable feeling about their safety. I do not for a moment say that none of them will be saved;

but I say that those who are saved will be saved by their disagreement with their own principles, and in spite of their own systems. The man who wrote the famous line,

"He can't be wrong whose life is in the right,"

was a great poet undoubtedly, but he was a wretched divine.

Let me conclude this paper with a few words by way of application.

(1) *First of all*, if there is no salvation excepting in Christ, let us make sure that we have an interest in that salvation ourselves. Let us not be content with hearing, and approving, and assenting to the truth, and going no further. Let us seek to have a personal interest in this salvation. Let us not rest till we know and feel that we have got actual possession of that peace with God which Jesus offers, and that Christ is ours, and we are Christ's. If there were two, or three, or more ways of getting to heaven, there would be no necessity for pressing this matter. But if there is *only one way*, who can wonder that I say, "Make sure that you are in it."

(2) *Secondly*, if there is no salvation excepting in Christ, let us try to do good to the souls of all who do not know Him as a Saviour. There are millions in this miserable condition,—millions in foreign lands, millions in our own country, millions who are not trusting in Christ. We ought to feel for them if we are true Christians; we ought to pray for them; we ought to work for them, while there is yet time. Do we really believe that Christ is the only way to heaven? Then let us live as if we believed it.

Let us look round the circle of our own relatives and friends, count them up one by one, and think how many of them are not yet in Christ. Let us try to do good to them in some way or other, and act as a man should act who believes his friends to be in danger. Let us not be content with their being kind and amiable, gentle and good-tempered, moral and courteous. Let us rather be miserable about them till they come to Christ, and trust in Him. I know all this may sound like enthusiasm and fanaticism. I wish there was more of it in the world. Anything, I am sure, is better than a quiet indifference about the souls of others, as if everybody was in the way to heaven. Nothing, to my mind, so proves our little faith, as our little feeling about the spiritual condition of those around us.

(3) *Thirdly*, if there is no salvation excepting in Christ, let us love all who love the Lord Jesus in sincerity, and exalt Him as their Saviour, whoever they may be. Let us not draw back and look shy on others, because they do not see eye to eye with ourselves in everything. Whether a man be a Free-kirk man or an Independent, a Wesleyan or a Baptist, let us love him if he loves Christ, and gives Christ His rightful place. We are all fast travelling toward a place where names and forms and

Church-government will be nothing, and Christ will be all. Let us get ready for that place betimes, by loving all who are in the way that leads to it.

This is the true charity, to believe all things and hope all things, so long as we see Bible doctrines maintained and Christ exalted. Christ must be the single standard by which all opinions must be measured. Let us honour all who honour Him: but let us never forget that the same Apostle Paul who wrote about charity, says also, "If any man love not the Lord Jesus Christ, let him be Anathema." If our charity and liberality are wider than that of the Bible, they are worth nothing at all. Indiscriminate love is no love at all, and indiscriminate approbation of all religious opinions, is only a new name for infidelity. Let us hold out the right hand to all who love the Lord Jesus, but let us beware how we go beyond this.

(4) *Lastly*, if there is no salvation excepting by Christ, we must not be surprised if ministers of the Gospel preach much about Him. They cannot tell us too much about the name which is above every name. We cannot hear of Him too often. We may hear too much about controversy in sermons,—we may hear too much of works and duties, of forms, of ceremonies, of sacraments and ordinances,—but there is one subject which we never hear too much of: we can never hear too much of Christ.

When ministers are wearied of preaching Him, they are false ministers: when people are wearied of hearing of Him, their souls are in an unhealthy state. When ministers have preached Him all their lives, the half of His excellence will remain untold. When hearers see Him face to face in the day of His appearing, they will find there was more in Him than their hearts ever conceived.

Let me conclude this paper with the words of an old writer, to which I desire humbly to subscribe. "I know no true religion but Christianity; no true Christianity but the doctrine of Christ; the doctrine of His divine person, of His divine office, of His divine righteousness, and of His divine Spirit, which all that are His receive. I know no true ministers of Christ but such as make it their business, in their calling, to commend Jesus Christ, in His saving fulness of grace and glory, to the faith and love of men; no true Christian but one united to Christ by faith and love, unto the glorifying of the name of Jesus Christ, in the beauty of Gospel holiness. Ministers and Christians of this spirit have been for many years my brethren and companions, and I hope shall ever be, whithersoever the hand of God shall lead me."

—(ROBERT TRAILL.)

III

PRIVATE JUDGMENT

"Prove all things; hold fast that which is good."—1 Thess. v. 21.

There were three great doctrines or principles which won the battle of the Protestant Reformation. These three were: (1) the sufficiency and supremacy of Holy Scripture, (2) the right of private judgment, and (3) justification by faith only, without the deeds of the law.

These three principles were the keys of the whole controversy between the Reformers and the Church of Rome. If we keep firm hold of them when we argue with a Roman Catholic, our position is unassailable: no weapon that the Church of Rome can forge against us will prosper. If we give up any one of them, our cause is lost. Like Samson, with his hair shorn, our strength is gone. Like the Spartans, betrayed at Thermopylæ, we are out-flanked and surrounded. We cannot maintain our ground. Resistance is useless. Sooner or later we shall have to lay down our arms, and surrender at discretion.

Let us carefully remember this. The Roman Catholic controversy is upon us once more. We must put on the old armour, if we would not have our faith overthrown. The sufficiency of Holy Scripture,—the right of private judgment,—justification by faith only,—these are the three great principles to which we must always cling. Let us grasp them firmly, and never let them go.

One of the three great principles to which I have referred appears to me to stand forth in the verse of Scripture which heads this paper. I mean the right of private judgment. I wish to say something about that principle.

The Holy Ghost, by the mouth of St. Paul, says to us, "Prove all things; hold fast that which is good." In these words we have two great truths.

I. The right, duty, and necessity of private judgment:
"Prove all things."

II. The duty and necessity of keeping firm hold upon truth:
"Hold fast that which is good."

In this paper I propose to dwell a little on both these points.

I. Let me speak first, of the *right, duty, and necessity of private judgment.*

34

When I say the *right* of private judgment, I mean that every individual Christian has a right to judge for himself by the Word of God, whether that which is put before him as religious truth is God's truth, or is not.

When I say the *duty* of private judgment, I mean that God requires every Christian man to use the right of which I have just spoken;—to compare man's words and man's writings with God's revelation, and to make sure that he is not deluded and taken in by false teaching.

And when I say the *necessity* of private judgment, I mean this,—that it is absolutely needful for every Christian who loves his soul and would not be deceived, to exercise the right, and discharge the duty to which I have referred; seeing that experience shows that the neglect of private judgment has always been the cause of immense evils in the Church of Christ.

Now the Apostle Paul urges all these three points upon our notice when he uses those remarkable words, "Prove all things." I ask particular attention to that expression. In every point of view it is most weighty and instructive.

Here, we must remember, the Apostle Paul is writing to the Thessalonians,—to a Church which he himself had founded. Here is an inspired Apostle writing to young inexperienced Christians,—writing to the whole professing Church in a certain city, containing laity as well as clergy,—writing, too, with especial reference to matters of doctrine and preaching, as we know by the verse preceding the text: "Despise not prophesyings." And yet mark what he says,—"Prove all things."

He does not say, "Whatsoever Apostles,—whatsoever evangelists, pastors, and teachers,—whatsoever your Bishops,—whatsoever your ministers tell you is truth, that you are to believe." No! he says, "Prove all things." He does not say, "Whatsoever the universal Church pronounces true, that you are to hold." No! he says, "Prove all things."

The principle laid down is this: "Prove all things by the Word of God;— all ministers, all teaching, all preaching, all doctrines, all sermons, all writings, all opinions, all practices,—prove all by the Word of God. Measure all by the measure of the Bible.—Compare all with the standard of the Bible.—Weigh all in the balances of the Bible.—Examine all by the light of the Bible.—Test all in the crucible of the Bible. That which can abide the fire of the Bible, receive, hold, believe, and obey. That which cannot abide the fire of the Bible, reject, refuse, repudiate, and cast away."

This is private judgment. This is the right we are to exercise if we love our souls. We are not to believe things in religion merely because they are said by Popes or Cardinals,—by Bishops or Priests,—by Presbyters or Deacons,—by Churches, Councils, or Synods,—by Fathers, Puritans, or Reformers. We are not to argue, "Such and such things must be true, because these men say so." We are not to do so. We are to prove all things by the Word of God.

Now I know such doctrine sounds startling in some men's ears. But I write it down advisedly, and believe it cannot be disproved. I should be sorry to encourage any man in ignorant presumption or ignorant contempt. I praise not the man who seldom reads his Bible, and yet sets himself up to pick holes in his minister's sermons. I praise not the man who knows nothing but a few texts in the New Testament, and yet undertakes to settle questions in divinity which have puzzled God's wisest children. But still I hold with Bishop Bilson (A.D. 1575), that "all hearers have both liberty to discern and a charge to beware of seducers; and woe to them that do it not." And I say with Bishop Davenant (A.D. 1627) "We are not to believe all who undertake to teach in the Church, but, must take care and weigh with serious examination, whether their doctrine be sound or not."*

Some men I know, refuse to believe this doctrine of private judgment; but I assert confidently that it is continually taught in the Word of God.

This is the principle laid down by the prophet Isaiah. (Isa. viii. 19.) His words were written, we should remember, at a time when God was more immediately King over His Church, and had more direct communication with it than He has now. They were written at a time when there were men upon earth who had express revelations from God. Yet what does Isaiah say?—"When they shall say unto you, Seek unto them that have familiar spirits, and unto wizards that peep, and that mutter: should not a people seek unto their God? for the living to the dead? To the law and to the testimony: if they speak not according to this word, it is because there is no light in them." If this be not private judgment, what is?

This, again, is the principle laid down by our Lord Jesus Christ in the Sermon on the Mount. The Head of the Church says there:—"Beware of false prophets which come to you in sheep's clothing, but inwardly they are ravening wolves. Ye shall know them by their fruit." (Matt. vii. 15.) How is it possible that men shall know these false prophets, except they exercise their private judgment as to what their fruits are?

This is the practice we find commended in the Bereans, in the Acts of the Apostles. They did not take the Apostle Paul's word for granted, when he came to preach to them. We are told, that they "searched the Scriptures daily, whether those things were so," and "*therefore*," it is

* The people of God are called to try the truth, to judge between good and ill, between light and darkness. God hath made them the promise of His Spirit, and hath left unto them His Word. They of Berea, when they heard the preaching of Paul, searched the Scriptures daily, whether those things were so as he taught them, and many of them believed. So do you: give heed to instruction, and yet receive not all things without proof and trial that they are not contrary to the wholesome doctrine of the Word of God."—*Bishop Jewell, author of the "Apology of the Church of England."* 1583.

said, "many of them believed." (Acts xvii. 11, 12.) What was this again but private judgment?

This is the spirit of the advice given in 1 Cor. x. 15,—"I speak as unto wise men; judge ye what I say:" and in Col. ii. 18,—"Beware lest any man spoil you through philosophy and vain deceit;" and in 1 John iv. 1,— "Beloved, believe not every spirit, but try the spirits, whether they are of God;" and in 2 John 10,—"If there come any unto you, and bring not this doctrine, receive him not into your house." If these passages do not recommend the use of private judgment, I do not know what words mean. To my mind they seem to say to every individual Christian, "Prove all things."

Whatever men may say against private judgment, we may be sure it cannot be neglected without immense danger to the soul. We may not like it; but we never know what we may come to if we refuse to use it. No man can say into what depths of false doctrine we may be drawn if we will not do what God requires of us, and "prove all things."

Suppose that, in fear of private judgment, we resolve to believe whatever *the Church* believes. Where is our security against error? The Church is not infallible. There was a time when almost the whole of Christendom embraced the Arian heresy, and did not acknowledge the Lord Jesus Christ to be equal with the Father in all things. There was a time, before the Reformation, when the darkness over the face of Europe was a darkness that might be felt.—The General *Councils* of the Church are not infallible. When the whole Church is gathered together in a General Council, what says our Twenty-first Article? "They may err, and sometimes have erred, even in things pertaining unto God. Wherefore things ordained by them as necessary to salvation, have neither strength nor authority, unless it may be declared that they be taken out of Holy Scripture."—The particular *branches of the Church* are not infallible. Any one of them may err. Many of them have fallen foully, or have been swept away. Where is the Church of Ephesus at this day? Where is the Church of Sardis at the present time? Where is Augustine's Church of Hippo in Africa? Where is Cyprian's Church of Carthage? They are all gone! Not a vestige of any of them is left! Shall we then be content to err merely because the Church errs? Will our company be any excuse for our error? Will our erring in company with the Church remove our responsibility for our own souls? Surely it is a thousand times better for a man to stand alone and be saved, than to err in company with the Church, and be lost? It is better to "prove all things" and go to heaven, than to say, "I dare not think for myself," and go to hell.

But suppose that, to cut matters short, we resolve to believe whatever *our minister* believes. Once more I ask,—Where is our security against error? Ministers are not infallible, any more than Churches. All of them have not the Spirit of God. The very best of them are only men. Call them

Bishops, Priests, Deacons, or whatever names you please, they are all earthen vessels. I speak not merely of Popes, who have promulgated awful superstitions, and led abominable lives. I would rather point to the very best of Protestants, and say, "Beware of looking upon them as infallible,—beware of thinking of any man (whoever that man may be) that he cannot err." Luther held consubstantiation;—that was a mighty error. Calvin, the Geneva Reformer, advised the burning of Servetus; —that was a mighty error. Cranmer and Ridley urged the putting of Hooper into prison because of some trifling dispute about vestments;— that was a mighty error. Whitgift persecuted the Puritans;—that was a mighty error. Wesley and Toplady in the last century quarrelled fiercely about Calvinism;—that was a mighty error. All these things are warnings, if we will only take them. All say, "Cease ye from man." All show us that if a man's religion hangs on ministers, whoever they may be, and not on the Word of God, it hangs on a broken reed. Let us never make ministers Popes. Let us follow them so far as they follow Christ, but not a hair's breadth further. Let us believe whatever they can show us out of the Bible, but not a single word more. If we neglect the duty of private judgment, we may find, to our cost, the truth of what Whitby says: "The best of overseers do sometimes make oversights." We may live to experience the truth of what the Lord said about the Pharisees: "If the blind lead the blind, both shall fall into the ditch." (Matt. xv. 14.) We may be very sure no man is safe against error, unless he acts on St. Paul's injunction,—unless he "proves all things" by the Word of God.

I have said that it is impossible to overrate the *evils* that may arise from neglecting to exercise private judgment. I will go further, and say that it is impossible to overrate the *blessings* which private judgment has conferred both on the world and on the Church.

I ask my readers, then, to remember that the greatest discoveries in science and in philosophy, beyond all controversy, have arisen from the use of private judgment. To this we owe the discovery of Galileo, that the earth went round the sun, and not the sun round the earth.—To this we owe Columbus' discovery of the continent of America.—To this we owe Harvey's discovery of the circulation of the blood.—To this we owe Jenner's discovery of vaccination.—To this we owe the printing press, the steam engine, the powerloom, the electric telegraph, railways, and gas. For all these discoveries we are indebted to men who dared to "think for themselves." They were not content with the beaten path of those who had gone before. They were not satisfied with taking for granted that what their fathers believed must be true. They made experiments for themselves. They brought old-established theories to the proof, and found that they were worthless. They proclaimed new systems, and invited men to examine them, and test their truth. They bore storms of obloquy and ridicule unmoved. They heard the clamour of prejudiced lovers of old traditions without flinching. And they prospered and succeeded in what they did. We see it now. And we who live in the nineteenth century are reaping the fruit of their use of private judgment.

And as it has been in science, so also it has been in the history of the Christian religion. The martyrs who stood alone in their day, and shed that blood which has been the seed of Christ's Gospel throughout the world,—the Reformers, who, one after another, rose up in their might to enter the lists with the Church of Rome,—all did what they did, suffered what they suffered, proclaimed what they proclaimed, simply because they exercised their private judgment about what was Christ's truth. —Private judgment made the Waldensians, the Albigensians, and the Lollards, count not their lives dear to them, rather than believe the doctrines of the Church of Rome.—Private judgment made Wickliffe search the Bible in our own land, denounce the Romish friars, and all their impostures, translate the Scriptures into the vulgar tongue, and become "the morning star" of the Reformation.—Private judgment made Luther examine Tetzel's abominable system of indulgences by the light of the Word.—Private judgment led him on, step by step, from one thing to another, guided by the same light, till at length the gulf between him and Rome was a gulf that could not be passed, and the Pope's power in Germany was completely broken.—Private judgment made our own English Reformers examine for themselves, and inquire for themselves, as to the true nature of that corrupt system under which they had been born and brought up.—Private judgment made them cast off the abominations of Popery, and circulate the Bible among the laity.—Private judgment made them draw from the Bible our Articles, compile our Prayerbook, and constitute the Church of England as it is. They broke the fetters of tradition, and dared to think for themselves. They refused to take for granted Rome's pretensions and assertions. They examined them all by the Bible, and because they would not abide the examination, they broke with Rome altogether. All the blessings of Protestantism in England, all that we are enjoying at this very day, we owe to the right exercise of private judgment. Surely if we do not honour private judgment, we are thankless and ungrateful indeed!

Let us not be moved by the common argument, that the right of private judgment is liable to be abused,—that private judgment has done great harm, and should be avoided as a dangerous thing. Never was there a more miserable argument! Never was there one which, when thrashed, proves so full of chaff!

Private judgment has been abused! I would like the objector to tell me what good gift of God has not been abused? What high principle can be named that has not been employed for the very worst of purposes? Strength may become tyranny, when it is employed by the stronger to coerce the weaker; yet strength is a blessing when properly employed.

Liberty may become licentiousness, when every man does that which is right in his own eyes, without regarding the rights and feelings of others; yet liberty, rightly used, is a mighty blessing. Because many things may be used improperly, are we therefore to give them up altogether? Because opium is used improperly by some, is it not to be used as a medicine on any occasion at all? Because money may be used improperly, is all money to be cast into the sea? You cannot have good in this world without evil. You cannot have private judgment without some abusing it, and turning it to bad account.

But private judgment, people say, *has done more harm than good!* What harm has private judgment done, I would like to know, in matters of religion, compared to the harm that has been done by the neglect of it? Some are fond of telling us that among Protestants who allow private judgment, there are divisions, and that in the Church of Rome, where private judgment is forbidden, there are no divisions. I might easily show such objectors that Romish unity is far more seeming than real. Bishop Hall, in his book called *The Peace of Rome*, numbers up no less than three hundred differences of opinion existing in the Romish Church. I might easily show that the divisions of Protestants are exceedingly exaggerated, and that most of them are upon points of minor importance. I might show that, with all the "varieties of Protestantism," as men call them, there is still a vast amount of fundamental unity and substantial agreement among Protestants. No man can read the *Harmony of Protestant Confessions* without seeing that.

But grant for a moment that private judgment has led to divisions, and brought about varieties. I say that these divisions and varieties are but a drop of water when compared with the torrent of abominations that have arisen from the Church of Rome's practice of disallowing private judgment altogether. Place the evils in two scales,—the evils that have arisen from private judgment, and those that have arisen from no man being allowed to think for himself. Weigh the evils one against another, and I have no doubt as to which will be the greatest. Give me Protestant divisions, certainly, rather than Popish unity, with the fruit that it brings forth. Give me Protestant variations, whatever a man like Bossuet may say about them, rather than Romish ignorance, Romish superstition, Romish darkness, and Romish idolatry. Give me the Protestant diversities of England and Scotland, with all their disadvantages, rather than the dead level, both intellectual and spiritual, of the Italian peninsula. Let the two systems be tried by their fruits,—the system that says, "Prove all things," and the system that says, "Dare to have no opinion of your own;"—let them be tried by their fruits in the hearts, in the intellects, in the lives, in all the ways of men, and I have no doubt as to the result.

In any case let us not be moved by the specious argument, that it is *humility* to disallow private judgment, and to have no opinion of our own, that it is the part of a true Christian not to think for himself!

I tell men boldly that such humility is a false humility, a humility that does not deserve that blessed name. Call it rather laziness, idleness, and sloth. It makes a man strip himself of all his responsibility, and throw the whole burden of his soul into the hands of the minister and the Church. It gives a man a mere vicarious religion, a religion by which he places his conscience and all his spiritual concerns under the care of others. He need not trouble himself! He need no longer think for himself! He has embarked in a safe ship, and placed his soul under a safe pilot, and will get to heaven! Oh, let us beware of supposing that this deserves the name of humility! It is refusing to exercise the gift that God has given us. It is refusing to employ the sword of the Spirit which God has forged for the use of our hand. Blessed be God, our forefathers did not act upon such principles! Had they done so, we should never have had the Reformation. Had they done so, we might have been bowing down to the image of the Virgin Mary at this moment, or praying to the spirits of departed saints, or having a service performed in Latin. From such humility may the good Lord ever deliver us!

As long as we live, let us resolve that we will read for ourselves, think for ourselves, judge of the Bible for ourselves, in the great matters of our souls. Let us dare to have an opinion of our own. Let us never be ashamed of saying, "I think that this is right, because I find it in the Bible;" and "I think that this is wrong, because I do not find it in the Bible." "Let us prove all things," and prove them by the Word of God.

As long as we live, let us beware of the blindfold system, which many commend in the present day,—the system of following a leader, and having no opinion of our own,—the system which practically says, "Only keep your Church, only receive the Sacraments, only believe what the ordained ministers who are set over you tell you, and then all shall be well." I warn men that this will not do. If we are content with this kind of religion, we are perilling our immortal souls. Let the Bible, and not any Church upon earth, or any minister upon earth, be our rule of faith. "Prove all things" by the Word of God.

Above all, as long as we live, let us habitually look forward to the great day of judgment. Let us think of the solemn account which every one of us will have to give in that day before the judgment-seat of Christ. We shall not be judged by Churches. We shall not be judged by whole congregations. We shall be judged individually, each by himself. What shall it profit us in that day to say, "Lord, Lord, I believed everything the Church told me. I received and believed everything ordained ministers set before me. I thought that whatever the Church and the ministers said must be right"? What shall it profit us to say this, if we have held some deadly error? Surely, the voice of Him that sits upon the throne will reply, "You had the Scriptures. You had a book, plain and easy to him that will read it and search it in a child-like spirit. Why did you not use the Word of God when it was given to you? You had a reasonable soul given you to understand that Bible. Why did you not 'Prove all things,' and thus keep clear of error?" If we refuse to exercise our private judgment, let us think of that awful day, and beware.

II. And now let me speak of the *duty and necessity of keeping firm hold upon God's truth.*

The words of the Apostle on this subject are pithy and forcible. "Hold fast," he says, "that which is good." It is as if he said to us, "When you have found the truth for yourself, and when you are satisfied that it is Christ's truth,—that truth which the Scriptures set forth,—then get a firm hold upon it, grasp it, keep it in your heart, never let it go."

St. Paul speaks as one who knew what the hearts of all Christians are. He knew that our grasp of the Gospel, at our best, is very cold,—that our love soon waxes feeble,—that our faith soon wavers,—that our zeal soon flags,—that familiarity with Christ's truth often brings with it a species of contempt,—that, like Israel, we are apt to be discouraged by the length of our journey,—and, like Peter, ready to sleep one moment and fight the next,—but, like Peter, not ready to "watch and pray." All this St. Paul remembered, and, like a faithful watchman, he cries, by the Holy Ghost, "Hold fast that which is good."

He speaks as if he foresaw by the Spirit that the good tidings of the Gospel would soon be corrupted, spoiled, and plucked away from the Church at Thessalonica. He speaks as one who foresaw that Satan and all his agents would labour hard to cast down Christ's truth. He writes as though he would forewarn men of this danger, and he cries, "Hold fast that which is good."

The advice is always needed,—needed as long as the world stands. There is a tendency to decay in the very best of human institutions. The best visible Church of Christ is not free from a liability to degenerate. It is made up of fallible men. There is always in it a tendency to leave its first love. We see the leaven of evil creeping into many a Church, even in the Apostle's time. There were evils in the Corinthian Church, evils in the Ephesian Church, evils in the Galatian Church. All these things are meant to be beacons in these latter times. All show the great necessity laid upon the Church to remember the Apostle's words: "Hold fast that which is good."

Many Churches of Christ since then have fallen away for the want of remembering this principle. Their ministers and members forgot that Satan is always labouring to bring in false doctrine. They forgot that he can transform himself into an angel of light,—that he can make darkness appear light, and light darkness, truth appear falsehood, and falsehood truth. If he cannot destroy Christianity, he ever tries to spoil it. If he cannot prevent the form of godliness, he endeavours to rob Churches of the power. No Church is ever safe that forgets these things, and does not bear in mind the Apostle's injunction: "Hold fast that which is good."

If ever there was a time in the world when Churches were put upon their trial, whether they would hold fast the truth or not, that time is the present time, and those Churches are the Protestant Churches of our own land. Popery, that old enemy of our nation, is coming in upon us in this day like a flood. We are assaulted by open enemies without, and betrayed continually by false friends within. The number of Roman Catholic churches, and chapels, and schools, and conventual and monastic establishments, is continually increasing around us. Already the clergy of the Church of Rome are using great swelling words about things to come, and boasting that, sooner or later, England shall once more be brought back to the orbit from whence she fell, and take her place in the Catholic system. Surely now or never, we ought all of us to awake, and "Hold fast that which is good."

Perhaps we supposed, some of us, in our blindness, that the power of the Church of Rome was ended. We dreamed, in our folly, that the Reformation had ended the Popish controversy, and that if Romanism did survive, Romanism was altogether changed. If we did think so, we have lived to learn that we made a most grievous mistake. Rome never changes. It is her boast that she is always the same. The snake is not killed. He was scotched at the time of the Reformation, but was not destroyed. The Romish Antichrist is not dead. He was cast down for a little season, like the fabled giant buried under Ætna, but his deadly wound is healed, the grave is opening once more, and Antichrist is coming forth. The unclean spirit of Popery is not laid in his own place. Rather he seems to say, "My house in England is now swept and garnished for me; let me return to the place from whence I came forth."

And the question is now, whether we are going to abide quietly, sit still, and fold our hands, and do nothing to resist the assault. Are we really men of understanding of the times? Do we know the day of our visitation? Surely this is a crisis in the history of our Churches and of our land. It is a time which will soon prove whether we know the value of our privileges, or whether, like Amalek, "the first of the nations," our "latter end shall be that we perish for ever." It is a time which will soon prove whether we intend to allow our candlestick to be removed, or to repent, and do our first works, lest any man should take our crown. If we love the open Bible,—if we love the preaching of the Gospel,—if we love the privilege of reading that Bible, no man letting or hindering us, and the opportunity of hearing that Gospel, no man forbidding us,— if we love civil liberty,—if we love religious liberty,—if these things are

precious to our souls, we must make up our minds to "hold fast," lest
by and by we lose all.

If we mean to "hold fast," every parish, every congregation, every
Christian man, and every Christian woman, must do their part in contending for the truth. Each one of us should work, and pray, and labour as
if the preservation of the pure Gospel depended upon himself or herself,
and upon no one else at all. The Bishops must not leave the matter to
the priests, nor the priests leave the matter to the Bishops. The clergy
must not leave the matter to the laity, nor the laity to the clergy. The
Parliament must not leave the matter to the country, nor the country to
the Parliament. The rich must not leave the matter to the poor, nor the
poor to the rich. We must all work. Every living soul has a sphere of
influence. Let him see to it that he fills it. Every living soul can throw
some weight into the scale of the Gospel. Let him see to it that he casts
it in. Let every one know his own individual responsibility in this matter;
and all, by God's help, will be well.

If we would "hold fast" that which is good, we must never tolerate
or countenance any doctrine which is not the pure doctrine of Christ's
Gospel. There is a hatred which is downright charity,—that is, the hatred
of erroneous doctrine. There is an intolerance which is downright praise-
worthy,—that is, the intolerance of false teaching in the pulpit. Who
would ever think of tolerating a little poison given to him day by day?
If men come among us who do not preach "all the counsel of God,"
who do not preach of Christ, and sin, and holiness, of ruin, and redemption,
and regeneration, and do not preach of these things in a Scriptural way,
we ought to cease to hear them. We ought to act upon the injunction
given by the Holy Ghost in the Old Testament: "Cease, my son, to hear
the instruction which causes to err from the words of knowledge."
(Prov. xix. 27.) We ought to carry out the spirit shown by the Apostle
Paul, in Gal. i. 8: "Though we, or an angel from heaven, preach any other
doctrine unto you than that which we have preached, let him be accursed."
If we can bear to hear Christ's truth mangled or adulterated,—and can
see no harm in listening to that which is another Gospel,—and can sit
at ease while sham Christianity is poured into our ears,—and can go home
comfortably afterwards, and not burn with holy indignation,—if this be
the case, there is little chance of our ever doing much to resist Rome.
If we are content to hear Jesus Christ not put in His rightful place, we
are not men and women who are likely to do Christ much service, or fight
a good fight on His side. He that is not zealous against error, is not likely
to be zealous for truth.

If we would hold fast the truth, we must be ready to unite with all
who hold the truth, and love the Lord Jesus Christ in sincerity. We must
be ready to lay aside all minor questions as things of subordinate
importance. Establishment or no Establishment, Liturgy or no Liturgy,

surplice or no surplice, Bishops or Presbyters,—all these points of difference, however important they may be in their place and in their proportion,
—all ought to be regarded as subordinate questions. I ask no man to
give up his private opinions about them. I wish no man to do violence
to his conscience. All I say is, that these questions are wood, hay, and
stubble, when the very foundations of the faith are in danger. The
Philistines are upon us. Can we make common cause against them, or
can we not? This is the one point for our consideration. Surely it is not
right to say that we expect to spend eternity with men in heaven, and yet
cannot work for a few years with them in this world. It is nonsense to talk
of alliance and union, if there is to be no co-operation. The presence of
a common foe ought to sink minor differences. We must hold together,
if we mean to "hold fast that which is good."

Some men may say, "This is very troublesome." Some may say, "Why
not sit still and be quiet?" Some may say, "Oh, that horrid controversy!
What need is there for all this trouble? Why should we care so much
about these points of difference?" I ask, what good thing was ever got,
or ever kept, without trouble? Gold does not lie in English corn-fields,
but at the bottom of Californian rivers, and Australian quartz reefs.
Pearls do not grow on English hedges, but deep down in Indian seas.
Difficulties are never overcome without struggles. Mountains are seldom
climbed without fatigue. Oceans are not crossed without tossings on the
waves. Peace is seldom obtained without war. And Christ's truth is
seldom made a nation's property, and kept a nation's property, without
pains, without struggles, and without trouble.

Let the man who talks of "*trouble*" tell us where we should be at this
day, if our forefathers had not taken some trouble? Where would be the
Gospel in England, if martyrs had not given their bodies to be burned?
Who shall estimate our debt to Cranmer, Latimer, Hooper, Ridley, and
Taylor, and their brethren? They "held fast that which is good." They
would not give up one jot of Christ's truth. They counted not their lives
dear for the Gospel's sake. They laboured and travailed, and we have
entered into their labours. Shame upon us, if we will not take a little
trouble to keep with us what they so nobly won! Trouble or no trouble,—
pains or no pains,—controversy or no controversy,—one thing is very
sure, that nothing but Christ's Gospel will ever do good to our own
souls. Nothing else will maintain our Churches. Nothing else will ever
bring down God's blessing upon our land. If, therefore, we love our own
souls, or if we love our country's prosperity, or if we love to keep our
Churches standing, we must remember the Apostle's words, and "hold
fast" firmly the Gospel, and refuse to let it go.

I have set forth in plain language two things. *One* is the right, the duty,
and necessity of private judgment. *The other* is the duty and necessity

of keeping firm hold upon truth.—It only remains to apply these things to the individual consciences of my readers, by a few concluding words.

(1) For one thing, if it be our duty to "prove all things," let me beseech and exhort all English Churchmen to arm themselves with a thorough knowledge of the written Word of God. Let us read our Bibles regularly, and become familiar with their contents. Let us prove all religious teaching, when it is brought before us, by the Bible. A little knowledge of the Bible will not suffice. A man must know his Bible well, if he is to prove religion by it; and he must read it regularly, if he would know it well. There is no royal road to a knowledge of the Bible. There must be patient, daily, systematic reading of the Book, or the Book will not be known. As one said quaintly, but most truly, "Justification may be by faith, but a knowledge of the Bible comes only by works." The devil can quote Scripture. He could go to our Lord and quote a text when he wished to tempt Him. A man must be able to say, when he hears Scripture falsely quoted, perverted, and misapplied, "It is written again," lest he be deceived. Let a man neglect his Bible, and I see nothing to prevent his becoming a Roman Catholic, an Arian, a Socinian, a Jew, or a Turk, if a plausible advocate of any of these false systems shall happen to meet him.

(2) For another thing, if it be right to "prove all things," let us take special care to try every Roman Catholic doctrine, by whomsoever put forward, by the written Word of God. Let us believe nothing, however speciously advanced,—believe nothing, with whatever weight of authority brought forward,—believe nothing, though supported by all the Fathers, —believe nothing, except it can be proved to us out of the Scripture. The Bible alone is infallible. That alone is light. That alone is God's measure of truth and falsehood. "Let God be true, and every man a liar." The New Zealander's answer to the Romish priests when they first went among them, was an answer never to be forgotten. They heard these priests urge upon them the worship of the Virgin Mary. They heard them recommend prayer to the dead saints, the use of images, the mass and the confessional. They heard them speak of the authority of the Church of Rome, the supremacy of the Pope, the antiquity of the Romish Communion. They knew the Bible, and heard all this calmly, and gave one simple but memorable answer: "*It cannot be true, because it is not in the Book.*" All the learning in the world could never have supplied a better answer than that. Latimer, or Knox, or Owen, could never have made a more crushing reply. Let this be our rule when we are attacked by Romanists, or semi-Romanists; let us hold fast the sword of the Spirit; and say, in reply to all their arguments, "*It cannot be true, because it is not in the Book.*"

(3) Last of all, if it be right to "hold fast that which is good," let us make sure that we have each laid hold personally upon Christ's truth

for ourselves. It will not save us to know all controversies, and to be able to detect everything which is false. Head knowledge will never bring us to heaven. It will not save us to be able to argue and reason with Roman Catholics, or to detect the errors of Popes' Bulls, or Pastoral Letters. Let us see that we each lay hold upon Jesus Christ for ourselves, by our own personal faith. Let us see to it that we each flee for refuge, and lay hold upon the hope set before us in His glorious Gospel. Let us do this, and all shall be well with us, whatever else may go ill. Let us do this, and then all things are ours. The Church may fail. The State may go to ruin. The foundations of all establishments may be shaken. The enemies of truth may for a season prevail. But as for us, all shall be well. We shall have in this world peace, and in the world which is to come, life everlasting; for we shall have Christ, and having Him, we have all. This is real "good," lasting good, good in sickness, good in health, good in life, good in death, good in time, and good in eternity. All other things are but uncertain. They all wear out. They fade. They droop. They wither. They decay. The longer we have them the more worthless we find them, and the more satisfied we become, that everything here below is "vanity and vexation of spirit." But as for hope in Christ, that is *always* good. The longer we use it the better it seems. The more we wear it in our hearts the brighter it will look. It is good when we first have it. It is better far when we grow older. It is better still in the day of trial, and the hour of death. And it will prove best of all in the day of judgment.

IV

THE THIRTY-NINE ARTICLES

I MUST begin this paper with an apology. My subject may seem at first sight dry, dull, and uninteresting. But I ask my readers to believe that it is not so in reality. There are few points about which it is so important for English Churchmen to have clear and correct views, as about the nature, position, and authority of the Thirty-nine Articles.

Marriage settlements and wills are not very lively reading. Like all carefully-drawn legal documents, they are extremely unattractive to general readers. The language seems cramped and old-fashioned; the amount of verbiage and circumlocution in them appears positively astounding; yet none but a child or fool would ever dare to say that wills and marriage settlements are of no use. The happiness of whole families often turns upon the meaning of their contents. It is even so with the Thirty-nine Articles. Dry, and dull, and uninteresting as they may appear to some, they are in one sense the backbone of the Church of England. Surely some knowledge of them ought to be sought after by every sensible and intelligent member of our Communion.

Who is the "true Churchman"? That is a question which is shaking the Established Church of England to the very centre, and will shake it a good deal more, I suspect, before the end of the world comes. It is becoming a very large and serious question, and one which imperatively demands an answer.

It is not enough to say that everybody who goes to church is a "true Churchman." That reply, I think, will content nobody. There are scores of people occupying our pews and benches every Sunday, who know nothing whatever about religion. They could not tell you, if life depended on it, what they believe or don't believe, hold or don't hold, think or don't think, about any doctrine of Christianity. They are totally in the dark about the whole subject. Politics they know, and business they know, and science perhaps they know, and possibly they know something about the amusements of this world. But as to the composition of a "true Churchman's" creed, they can tell you nothing whatever. They "go to church" on Sundays; and that is all. Surely this will never do! Ignorance, complete ignorance, can never be the qualification of a true Churchman.

But perhaps it is enough to say that everybody who goes to church,

48

and is zealous and earnest in his religion, is a "true Churchman"? That is a very wide question, and opens up an entirely new line of thought. But I fear it will not land us in any satisfactory conclusion. "Earnestness" is the attribute of men of the most opposite and contradictory creeds. "Earnestness is the character of religionists who are as wide apart as black and white, light and darkness, bitter and sweet, hot and cold.—You see it outside the Church of England. The Mohametans who overran the rotten Churches of Africa and Western Asia, crying, "the Koran or the sword,"—the Jesuit, who saps and mines, and compasses sea and land to make one proselyte,—the Mormonite, who crosses half the globe to die in the Salt Lake City, and calls Joe Smith a prophet,—all these undeniably were and are earnest men.—You see it inside the Church of England at this very day. The Ritualist, the Rationalist, the Evangelical,—all are in earnest. Yet every one knows that their differences are grave, wide, deep, and irreconcilable. Surely this will never do. Earnestness alone is no proof that a man is a true Churchman. The devil is in earnest. Infidels are in earnest. Deists are in earnest. Socinians are in earnest. Papists are in earnest. Pharisees were in earnest. Sadducees were in earnest. Earnestness alone proves nothing more than this,—that a man has a good deal of steam and energy and "go" about him, and will not go to sleep. But it certainly does not prove that a man is a "true Churchman." What is the man earnest about? This is the question that ought to be asked, and deserves to be answered.

Once for all, I must protest against the modern notion, that it does not matter the least what religious opinions a man holds, so long as he is in "earnest" about them,—that one creed is just as good as another,—and that all "earnest" men will somehow or other at last find themselves in heaven. I cannot hold such an opinion, so long as I believe that the Bible is a revelation from God. I would extend to every one the widest liberty and toleration. I abhor the idea of persecuting any one for his opinions. I would "think and let think." But so long as I have breath in my body, I shall always contend that there is such a thing as revealed truth,—that men may find out what truth is if they will honestly seek for it,—and that mere earnestness and zeal, without Scriptural knowledge, will never give any one comfort in life, peace in death, or boldness in the day of judgment.

But how are we to find out who is the "true Churchman"? some one will ask me. Men complain with good reason that they feel puzzled, perplexed, embarrassed, bewildered, posed, and mystified by the question. Rationalists, Ritualists, and Evangelicals, all call themselves "Churchmen." Who is right?—The name "Churchman" is bandied about from side to side, like a shuttlecock, and men lay claim to it who on many points are diametrically opposed to one another. Now how are we to settle the question? What are we to believe? What are we to think?

How shall we distinguish the good coin from the bad? In one word, is there any test, any legal, authorized test of a true Churchman?

My answer to all these inquiries is short, plain, and most decided. I assert confidently that the Church of England has provided a test of true Churchmanship, and one that is recognized by the law of the land. This test is to be found in "the Thirty-nine Articles of Religion." I say, furthermore, that the Thirty-nine Articles of Religion form a test which any plain man can easily understand, if he will only give his mind to a study of them. An honest examination of these Articles will show any one at this day who is the best, the truest, the most genuine style of Churchman. To exhibit the authority, nature, and characteristics of the Thirty-nine Articles, is the simple object for which I send forth the paper which is now in the reader's hands.

I. Now, first of all, *what are the Thirty-nine Articles?* This is a question which many will be ready to ask, and one to which it is absolutely necessary to return an answer. It is a melancholy fact, explain it as we may, that for the last 200 years the Articles have fallen into great and undeserved neglect. Thousands and myriads of Churchmen, I am fully persuaded, have never read them, never even looked at them, and of course know nothing whatever of their contents. I make no apology therefore for beginning with that which every Churchman ought to know. I will briefly state what the Thirty-nine Articles are.

The Thirty-nine Articles are a brief and condensed statement, under thirty-nine heads or propositions, of what the Church of England regards as the chief doctrines which her chief members ought to hold and believe. They were, most of them, gathered by our Reformers out of Holy Scripture. They were carefully packed up and summarized in the most accurate and precise language, of which every word was delicately weighed, and had a special meaning. Some of the Articles are positive, and declare directly what the Church of England regards as Bible truth and worthy of belief. Some of them are negative, and declare what the Church of England considers erroneous and unworthy of credence. Some few of them are simple statements of the Church's judgment on points which were somewhat controverted, even among Protestants, 300 years ago, and on which Churchmen might need an expression of opinion. Such is the document commonly called the Thirty-nine Articles; and all who wish to read it will find it at the end of every properly printed Prayer-book. At all events, any Prayer-book which does not contain the Articles is a most imperfect, mutilated, and barely honest copy of the Liturgy.

When and by whom were these Articles first drawn up? They were first composed by our Reformers in the days of that admirable young King, Edward the Sixth. Who had the chief hand in the work, history does not reveal; but there is every reason to believe that Cranmer and

Ridley our two most learned martyrs, had more to do with it than any. When first sent forth, they were forty-two in number. Afterwards, when Queen Elizabeth came to the throne, they were reduced by Archbishop Parker and his helpers, of whom Bishop Jewell was probably the chief, to their present number, with a few unimportant alterations. They were finally confirmed and ratified by Crown, Convocation, and Parliament, in the year 1571, and from 1571 down to this day not a single word in them has been altered.

The object for which the Articles were drawn up is clearly stated in the title of them, which any one will find in a proper Prayer-book. They are called "Articles agreed upon by the Archbishops and Bishops of both provinces, and the whole clergy, in the Convocation holden at London in the year 1562, for avoiding of diversities of opinion, and for the establishment of consent touching true religion." About the real, plain, honest meaning of this title, I think there ought to be no doubt. It proves that the Thirty-nine Articles are intended to be "the Church of England's Confession of faith." Every well-organized Church throughout Christendom has its Confession of faith: that is, it has a carefully composed statement of the main things in religion which it considers its members ought to believe. Every reading man knows this. The Augsburg Confession, the Creed of Pope Pius IV., the Decrees of the Council of Trent, the Westminster Confession, are documents with which every student of ecclesiastical history is familiar. Common sense shows the necessity and convenience of such Confessions. In a fallen world like this the terms of membership in any ecclesiastical corporation must be written down in black and white, or else the whole body is liable to fall into disorder and confusion. Every member of a Church ought to be able to render a reason of his membership, and to say what are the great principles of his Church. To do this his Church supplies him with a short creed, manual, or Confession, to which at any time he may refer inquirers. This was the object of the Thirty-nine Articles of the Church of England. They were intended to be "the Churchman's Confession of his faith."

The substance of the Thirty-nine Articles is a point on which I shall say but little at present, because I propose to dwell on it by and by. Let it suffice to say that they contain most admirable, terse, clear statements of Scriptural truth, according to the judgment of our Reformers, on almost every point in the Christian religion. The titles overleaf speak for themselves.

Some of these points are handled in a more firm, strong, and decided manner than others, and the curiously different tone of the Articles, according to their subject-matter, is a matter on which I shall have more to say by and by. But taking them for all in all, as a Church's statement of things to be believed, I think that no Church on earth has a better "Confession of faith" than the Church of England. I have no wish to find fault with other Churches. God forbid! We have faults and defects enough to keep us humble within the Anglican Communion. But after carefully examining other Confessions of faith, I find none which seem comparable to our own. Some Confessions are too long. Some go into particulars too much. Some define what had better be left undefined, and shut up sharply what had better be left a little open. For a combination of fulness, boldness, clearness, brevity, moderation, and wisdom, I find no Confession which comes near the Thirty-nine Articles of the Church of England.*

A Table of the Articles

1. Of Faith in the Holy Trinity.	22. Of Purgatory.
2. Of Christ the Son of God.	23. Of Ministering in the Congregation.
3. Of His going down into Hell.	
4. Of His resurrection.	24. Of Speaking in the Congregation.
5. Of the Holy Ghost.	
6. Of the Sufficiency of the Scripture.	25. Of the Sacraments.
	26. Of the Unworthiness of Ministers.
7. Of the Old Testament.	
8. Of the Three Creeds.	27. Of Baptism.
9. Of Original or Birth-sin.	28. Of the Lord's Supper.
10. Of Free-will.	29. Of the Wicked which eat not the Body of Christ.
11. Of Justification.	
12. Of Good Works.	30. Of both kinds.
13. Of Works before Justification.	31. Of Christ's one Oblation.
14. Of Works of Supererogation.	32. Of the Marriage of Priests.
15. Of Christ alone without Sin.	33. Of Excommunicate Persons.
16. Of Sin after Baptism.	34. Of the Traditions of the Church.
17. Of Predestination and Election.	35. Of Homilies.
18. Of obtaining Salvation by Christ.	36. Of Consecrating of Ministers.
19. Of the Church.	37. Of Civil Magistrates.
20. Of the Authority of the Church.	38. Of Christian Men's Goods.
21. Of the Authority of General Councils.	39. Of a Christian Man's Oath.

So much for what we mean when we talk of the Thirty-nine Articles. For dwelling so much on the point, I shall make little apology. The intrinsic importance of it, and the singular ignorance of most Churchmen about it, are my best excuse. The times we live in make it imperatively necessary to look up and ventilate these old questions. The perilous position of the Church of England requires all her sons to spread light and information. He that would know what a true Churchman is, must be content to begin by finding out what is meant by "the Thirty-nine Articles."

II.   I must now take up a question which is of great and serious importance. To prevent mistakes I shall state it as clearly and logically

---

*The famous historian Bingham, in his curious book on the French Protestant Church, quotes a remarkable testimony to the Articles from the French divine Le Moyne, a man of great note in his day:—"No Confession can be contrived more wisely than the English is, and the Articles of Faith were never collected with a more just and reasonable discretion."—*Bingham's Works*, Oxf. Edit., vol. x., p. 95.

as I can. "*What is the precise rank, authority, and position of the Thirty-nine Articles?* Are they, or are they not, the chief, foremost, primary and principal test of true Churchmanship?"

My reasons for going into this point are as follows. Some clergymen and laymen in the present day are fond of saying that the Prayer-book, and not the Articles, is the real measure and gauge of a Churchman. "The Prayer-book! the Prayer-book!" is the incessant cry of these people. "We want no other standard of doctrine but the Prayer-book."—Is it a controverted point about the Church? What says the Prayer-book?—Is it a doctrine that is disputed? What says the Prayer-book?—Is it the effect of baptism, or the nature of the Lord's Supper, that is under discussion? What says the Prayer-book?—To the Articles these gentlemen seem to have a peculiar dislike, an hydrophobic aversion. They seldom refer to them, unless perhaps to sneer at them as the "forty stripes save one." They never quote them, never bring them forward if they can possibly help it. What intelligent observer of religious questions among Churchmen does not know perfectly well the class of men whom I have in view? They are to be found all over England. We meet them in newspapers and books. We hear them in pulpits and on platforms. They are ever thrusting on the public their favourite "Diana of the Ephesians,"—their darling notion that the Prayer-book, and not the Articles, is the test of a Churchman.

Now, with all respect to these worthy people, I venture to say that their favourite notion is as real an idol as the Ephesian "Diana" was of old. I shall try to show the reader that in exalting the Prayer-book above the Articles, they have taken up a position that cannot possibly be maintained. I shall try to show, by evidence that cannot be gainsayed, that the true state of the case is exactly the reverse of what they are so fond of proclaiming. I am not going to say anything against the Prayer-book. It is a matchless book of devotion. But I am going to say, and to prove, that the Articles, and not the Prayer-book, are the first, foremost, and principal test of a true Churchman.

I shall dismiss briefly four points that I might dwell upon at length, if it were worth while.

(*a*) I pass over the obvious suspiciousness of any Churchman ignoring the Articles, giving them the cold shoulder, and talking only about the Prayer-book, when he is speaking of the tests of a Churchman's religion. That many do so it is quite needless to say. Yet the fifth Canon, of 1604, contains the following words: "Whosoever shall hereafter affirm that any of the Thirty-nine Articles agreed upon by the Archbishops and Bishops of both provinces, in the Convocation holden at London in the year of our Lord God 1562, for avoiding diversities of opinion, and establishing of consent touching true religion, are in any part superstitious, or erroneous, or such as he may not with a good conscience subscribe unto, let him be excommunicated *ipso facto*, and not restored but only by the Archbishops, after his repentance and public revocation of such his wicked errors." Plain language that! Certain Churchmen who are fond of pelting Evangelical Churchmen with Canons would do well to remember that Canon.

(b) I pass over the implied insinuation that there is any contradiction between the Articles and the Prayer-book. Many talk and write as if there was. It is a notion unworthy of any one of common sense. The man who supposes that divines of such grace and learning as the Elizabethan Reformers would ever with the same hands draw up Articles and a Prayer-book containing two different doctrines, must be in a strange state of mind? Reason itself points out that the Prayer-book and Articles were meant to teach the same doctrines, and that no interpretation which makes them jar and contradict one another can be correct. Lord Chatham's famous dictum, that the Church of England has a Popish Liturgy, an Arminian clergy, and a Calvinistic set of Articles, was doubtless very smart, but it was not true.

(c) I pass over the unreasonableness of setting up a book of devotion, like the Liturgy, as a better test of Churchmanship than a Confession of faith like the Articles. Prayers, in the very nature of things, are compositions which are not so precisely framed and worded as cold, dry, dogmatic statements of doctrine. They are what the rhetorical speech of the advocate is, compared to the cautiously-balanced decision of the judge. "In the Prayer-book," says Dean Goode, "we have a collection of national formularies of devotion, written at a time when a large proportion of the people were inclined to Romanism, and at the same time compelled to attend the services of the national Churches,—and consequently carefully drawn up, so as to give as little offence as possible to Romish prejudices. Is such a book calculated to serve the purposes of a standard of faith?"—"In the Articles," he adds, on the other hand, "we have a precise Confession of faith on all the great points of Christian doctrine, drawn up in dogmatic propositions, as a test of doctrinal soundness for the clergy." The Liturgy is an excellent book. But to say that in the nature of things it can serve the purpose of a standard of faith so well as the Articles, is absurd.

(d) I pass over the glaring foolishness of the common remark, that those who are fond of maintaining the primary authority of the Articles cast discredit upon the Creeds. The authors of this notable charge must surely have forgotten that one whole Article—the eighth—is devoted to the three Creeds! So far from the admirers of the Articles dishonouring and disparaging the Creeds, they are specially bound to honour, reverence, and defend them. Such vague argumentation goes far to show that many who speak slightly of the Articles do not even know what the Articles contain! They "speak evil of things which they know not." (Jude 10.)

But I pass over all these points. I desire to go straight to the mark, and to give direct proofs of the position that I take up. What I deliberately assert is, that the Thirty-nine Articles were always intended to be, and are at this day, the first, foremost, chief, and principal test of a Churchman, and that in this point of view there is nothing else that stands on a level with them. In proof of this assertion I shall now bring forward a few witnesses.

(1) My first witness shall be a very simple one. I mean the title of the Articles, which is prefixed to them in every complete and unmutilated Prayer-book. They are called, "Articles agreed upon for the avoiding of Diversities of Opinion, and for the stablishing of Consent touching true Religion." This title was first given to them by Thomas Cranmer, Archbishop of Canterbury, in the reign of Edward VI., 1552; and afterwards given a second time by Matthew Parker, Archbishop of Canterbury, in Queen Elizabeth's reign, in 1562. I want no plainer language than the words of this title. The man who tries to get away from it and evade it is like a viper biting a file.*

* Archbishop Parker's Correspondence, published in the Parker Society's series, supplies remarkable evidence of the importance attached to the Thirty-nine Articles by the Elizabethan Reformers. This evidence will be found in a letter addressed to the Queen, by the Archbishop and thirteen other Bishops, in which they pray her to facilitate the passing of a Bill through Parliament for the confirmation of the Articles. The reason why the Queen interposed any delay does not appear to have been any dislike to the Articles, but her characteristic Tudor jealousy of any thing being done in Church or State which did not originate from herself. In short, she affected to consider the initiation of a Bill affecting religion by the Commons, was an infringement of her ecclesiastical supremacy!

The reasons against delay which the Archbishop and Bishops pressed on the Queen's attention deserve special notice. They say:—"First, the matter itself tendeth to the glory of God, the advancement of true religion, and the salvation of Christian souls, and therefore ought principally, chiefly, and before all other things to be sought.

"Secondly, in the book which is now desired to be confirmed are contained the principal Articles of Christian religion most agreeable to God's Word, publicly, since the beginning of your Majesty's reign, professed, and by your Highness' authority set forth and maintained.

"Thirdly, divers and sundry errors, and namely, such as have been in the realm wickedly and obstinately by the adversaries of the Gospel defended, are by the same Articles condemned.

"Fourthly, the approbation of these Articles by your Majesty shall be a very good mean to establish and confirm all your Majesty's subjects in one consent and unity of true doctrine, to the great quiet and safety of your Majesty and this free realm; whereas now, for want of plain certainty of Articles of doctrine by law to be declared, great distraction and dissension of minds is at this present among your subjects."—*Parker Correspondence, Parker Society*, p. 293.

Notwithstanding this letter, the prayer of the Bishop appears not to have been granted until the year 1571. It is only one among many illustrations of the immense difficulties which the Elizabethan Reformers had to contend with, in consequence of the abitrary and self-willed character of their Sovereign. I venture the opinion that few English Monarchs have been so much over-praised and misunderstood as Elizabeth. I suspect the English Reformation would have been a far more perfect and complete work if the Queen had allowed the Reformers to do all that they wanted to do.

(2) My second witness shall be the statute law of the realm. I refer to two Acts of Parliament. One is called the 13th of Elizabeth, cap. 12, and entitled "An Act for *Ministers of the Church to be of sound religion.*" The other Act is called the 28th and 29th Victoria, cap. 122, and is entitled "An Act to Amend the Law as to the declarations and subscriptions to be made, and Oaths to be taken by the Clergy," and was passed in the year 1865.

The Act of Elizabeth, in the second section declares, that "if any person ecclesiastical, or which shall have any ecclesiastical living, shall advisedly maintain or affirm any doctrine directly contrary or repugnant to any of the said Thirty-nine Articles; and being convicted before the Bishop of the Diocese, or the Ordinary, or before the Queen's Commissioner in causes ecclesiastical, shall persist therein, or not revoke his error, or after such revocation affirm such untrue doctrine, such maintaining, or affirming, or persisting shall be just cause to deprive such person of his ecclesiastical functions; and it shall be lawful for the Bishop of the Diocese, or Ordinary, or such Commissioner, to deprive such person."

Comment on the evidence of this witness is needless. There is no way of honestly evading the edge and point of this yet unrepealed Act of Parliament. In a decision of all the judges, in the twenty-third year of Elizabeth, it was declared that the Act of 13th Elizabeth was made for avoiding a diversity of opinion, and that the "prevention of such diversity was the scope of the statute." (*Coke's Institut.* 1865.) The provisions of this Act of Elizabeth are in full force at this very day, and form the basis of any proceedings against a clergyman in matters of religion.

The Act of the 28th and 29th of Victoria is even more remarkable than the 13th of Elizabeth. The seventh section requires every person instituted to any living, on the first Lord's Day in which he officiates in his church, "publicly and openly in the presence of his congregation, to read the whole Thirty-nine Articles of Religion, and immediately after reading to make the declaration of assent to them."

Up to the year 1865, we must remember, a clergyman was required to read over the whole Morning and Evening Service as well as the Articles, and then declare his assent and consent to the use of the Book of Common Prayer. This was dispensed with by the Act of Victoria. But *the requirement to read the Thirty-nine Articles was carefully retained!* The result is, that every beneficed clergyman in the Church of England has not only declared his assent to the Thirty-nine Articles, but has done it in the most public way, after reading them over before his congregation.

(3) My third witness shall be the Royal Declaration prefixed to the Articles in 1628, by King Charles I. It is a document which will be found at length in every complete and unmutilated Prayer-book. It contains the following passage: "We hold it most agreeable to this our Kingly

office, and our own religious zeal, to conserve and maintain the Church committed to our charge, in unity of true religion, and in the bond of peace; and not to suffer unnecessary disputations, altercations, or questions to be raised, which may nourish faction both in the Church and Commonwealth. We have therefore, upon mature deliberation, and with the advice of so many of our Bishops as might conveniently be called together, thought fit to make this declaration following:—

"That the Articles of the Church of England (which have been allowed and authorized heretofore, and which our clergy generally have subscribed unto) do contain the true doctrine of the Church of England agreeable to God's Word: which we do therefore ratify and confirm, requiring all our loving subjects to continue in the uniform profession thereof, and prohibiting the least difference from the said Articles." Admirable words these! Well would it have been if the unhappy Monarch who put forth this declaration, had afterwards adhered more decidedly to the doctrine of the Articles, and not ruined himself and the Church by patronizing and supporting such men as Archbishop Laud.

(4) My fourth witness shall be a remarkable letter or circular issued by the Crown in 1721, entitled "Directions to our Archbishops and Bishops for the preservation of unity in the Church and the purity of the Christian faith, particularly in the doctrine of the Holy Trinity." The charge given to the Bishops in these directions is as follows: "You shall, without delay, signify to the clergy of your several dioceses this our Royal command, which we require you to see duly published and decreed: *viz.*, that no preacher whatsoever in his sermons or lectures do presume to deliver any other doctrines concerning the great and fundamental truths of our most holy religion, and particularly concerning the blessed Trinity, than what are contained in the Holy Scriptures, and are agreeable to the three Creeds and the Thirty-nine Articles of religion." The circular proceeds to direct the Bishops to put in force the famous statute of Elizabeth already quoted. But not one word do we find about the Prayer-book, from beginning to end. Of course these "directions" have no binding force now, but as evidence of what men thought the test of Church religion in 1721, they are remarkable.

(5) My fifth witness shall be Thomas Rogers, chaplain to Archbishop Bancroft, who published in 1607, the first Exposition of the Articles which ever appeared. This book, we must remember, was written within forty years of the time when the Articles were finally ratified. It was a work of great authority at the time, and was dedicated to the Archbishop. In the preface to this work Rogers says:—

"The purpose of our Church is best known by the doctrine which she does profess: the doctrine by the Thirty-nine Articles established by Act of Parliament; the Articles by the words whereby they are expressed: and other doctrine than in the said Articles is contained, our Church neither hath nor holdeth, and other sense they cannot yield than their words do import."

Strong language that from an Archbishop's chaplain! I heartily wish we had a few more chaplains like him.

(6) My sixth and last evidence, for brevity's sake, I will give you all at once, in the words of five well-known Bishops of the Church, who have long passed away. They were men very unlike one another, and belonged to very different schools of thought. But their testimonies to the value and rightful position of the Articles are so curiously harmonious, that it is interesting to have them brought together.

(*a*) Let us hear then what great and good Bishop Hall says, in his work on "*The Old Religion:*" "The Church of England, in whose motherhood we have all come to pride ourselves, hath in much wisdom and piety delivered her judgment concerning all necessary points of religion, in so complete a body of divinity as all hearts may rest in. These we read, these we write under, as professing not their truth only, but their sufficiency also. The voice of God our Father, in His Scriptures, and, out of them, the voice of the Church our mother, in her Articles, is that which must both guide and settle our resolutions. Whatsoever is beside these, is either private, or unnecessary, or uncertain."—*Hall's Works.* Oxford Edition. Vol. ix., p. 308.

(*b*) Let us hear next what Bishop Stillingfleet says in his *Unreasonableness of Separation:* "This we all say, that the doctrine of the Church of England is contained in the Thirty-nine Articles; and whatever the opinions of private persons may be, this is the standard by which the sense of our Church is to be taken."—London, 4to edition, p. 95. 1631.

(*c*) Let us hear next what Bishop Burnet says: "The Thirty-nine Articles are the sum of our doctrines, and the confession of our faith.—*Burnet on Articles*, pref., p. 1. Oxford Edition. 1831.

(*d*) Let us hear next what Bishop Beveridge says, in the preface to his great work on the Articles: "The Bishops and clergy of both provinces of this nation, in a Council held at London, 1562, agreed upon certain Articles of Religion, to the number of thirty-nine, which to this day remain the constant and settled doctrine of our Church; which, by an Act of Parliament of the 13th of Queen Elizabeth, 1571, all that are entrusted with any ecclesiastical preferments, are bound to subscribe to."—*Beveridge on Articles*, vol. i., p. 9. Oxford Edition. 1840.

(*e*) Let us hear, lastly, what Bishop Tomline says: "The Thirty-nine Articles are the criterion of the faith of the members of the Church of England."—*Elements of Theol.*, vol. ii., p. 34. 1799.

Such are the testimonies which I offer to the attention of my readers, in proof of my assertion that the Articles, much more than the Prayer-book, are the true test of Churchmanship. The title prefixed to the Articles by Cranmer and Parker;—the famous statutes of the 13th Elizabeth and

28th and 29th Victoria;—the Royal Declaration of Charles I., in 1628;—the Royal Circular to the Bishops in 1721;—the express opinion of Rogers, Archbishop Bancroft's private chaplain;—the deliberately expressed judgment of five such men as Hall, Stillingfleet, Burnet, Beveridge, and Tomline,—all these witnesses, taken together, supply a mass of evidence which to my eyes seem perfectly unanswerable. In the face of such evidence I dare not, as an honest man, refuse the conclusion, that the truest Churchman is the man who most truly agrees with the Thirty-nine Articles.

It would be easy to multiply witnesses, and to overload the subject with evidence. But in these matters enough is as good as a feast. Enough, probably, has been said to satisfy any candid and impartial mind that the ground I have taken up about the Articles has not been taken up in vain. He that desires to go more deeply into the subject would do well to consult Dean Goode's writings about it, in a controversy which he held with the late Bishop of Exeter. In that remarkable controversy, I am bold to say, the Dean proved himself more than a match for the Bishop. (Goode's *Defence of Thirty-nine Articles, and Vindication of Defence*. Hatchard. 1848.)

One remark I must make, in self-defence, before leaving this branch of my subject. I particularly request that no reader will misunderstand the grounds I have been taking up. Let no one suppose that I think lightly of the Prayer-book, because I do not regard it as the Church of England's standard and test of truth. Nothing could be more erroneous than such an idea. In loyal love to the Prayer-book, and deep admiration of its contents, I give place to no man. Taken for all in all, as an uninspired work, it is an incomparable book of devotion for the use of a Christian congregation. This is a position I would defend anywhere and everywhere. But the Church of England's Book of Common Prayer was never intended to be the Church's standard of doctrine in the same way that the Articles were. This was not meant to be its office; this was not the purpose for which it was compiled. It is a manual of public devotion: it is not a Confession of faith. Let us love it, honour it, prize it, reverence it, admire it, use it. But let us not exalt it to the place which the Thirty-nine Articles alone can fill, and which common sense, statute law, and the express opinions of eminent divines unanimously agree in assigning to them. The Articles, far more than the Prayer-book, are the Church's standard of sound doctrine, and the real test of true Churchmanship.*

* If any reader supposes that there is anything peculiar or extravagant in the position I take up about the authority of the Articles, as compared to the Prayer-book, I ask him to remember that Lord Hatherley, in his judgment in the famous "Voysey" case, takes up precisely the same ground. These are his words, as reported in the *Guardian:* "We have not, in this our decision, referred

III. One more point now remains to be considered, which is of so
much importance that I dare not pass it by unnoticed. What the Articles
are we have seen. What their position and authority is in the Church of
England we have also seen. Ought we not now to see what are the *great
leading characteristics of the Articles?* I think we ought, unless we mean
to leave our subject unfinished. There are certain grand features in them,
without descending into particulars, which stand out prominently, like
mountains in a landscape. What those features are we ought to know.
I shall therefore proceed to point them out to the reader, and try to
impress them on his attention. If those who are induced to read them with
attention, in consequence of this paper, are not struck with the singular
distinctness and prominence of these leading features in the Articles, I
shall be greatly mistaken. To my eyes they stand out in bold, clear, and
sharply-cut relief. I ask the reader to give me his attention for a very few
minutes, and I will show him what I mean.

(1) Let us mark, then, for one thing, as we read the Articles, the strong
and decided language which they use in speaking of *things which are
essential to salvation.*

Concerning the nature of God and the Holy Trinity,—concerning the
sufficiency and authority of Scripture,—concerning the sinfulness and
helplessness of natural man,—concerning justification by faith alone,—
concerning the place and value of good works,—concerning salvation
only by the name of Christ; concerning all these grand foundations of
the Christian religion, it is hard to conceive language more decided,
clear, distinct, ringing, and trumpet-toned than that of the Thirty-nine
Articles. There is no doubtfulness, or hesitancy, or faltering, or timidity,
or uncertainty, or compromise about their statements. There is no attempt
to gratify undecided theologians by saying, "It is probably so,"—or,
"Perhaps it may be so,"—or, "There are some grounds for thinking so,"—
and all that sort of language which is so pleasing to what are called "broad"
Christians. Nothing of the kind! On all the points I have named the
Articles speak out boldly, roundly, frankly, and honestly, in a most
unmistakable tone. "This is the Church of England's judgment, "they seem
to say; and "these are the views which every Churchman ought to hold."

I ask special attention to this point. We live in days when many loudly
declare that it is not right to be positive about anything in religion. The
clergyman who dares to say of any theological question, "This is true,

to any of the formularies of the Church, other than the Articles of Religion.
We have been mindful of the authorities which have held that *pious expressions
of devotion are not to be taken as binding declarations of doctrine.*"

In commenting on this judgment, the *Solicitor's Journal,* which certainly is
not the organ of any theological party, uses the following remarkable language:
"The Judicial Committee have adhered to the principles of previous decisions
in their recent judgment. The Articles of Religion, *and these alone,* are to be
considered as the code of doctrine of the Church of England.

and that is false,—this is right, and that is wrong,"—is pretty sure to be denounced as a narrow-minded, illiberal, uncharitable man. Nothing delights many Churchmen so much as to proclaim that they "belong to no party,"—that they are "moderate men,"—that they "hold no extreme views." Well! I only ask these Churchmen to settle matters with the Thirty-nine Articles. I want no clergyman to go a bit beyond the authoritative statements of his own Church; but I do want every clergyman not to fall below them. And I shall always maintain, publicly or privately, that to call any one an "extreme" man, or a "party" man, because his doctrinal views are in harmony with the bold, decided statements of the Articles, is neither just, nor fair, nor reasonable, nor consistent with common sense. Give me the clergyman who, after reading the Articles to his congregation, and solemnly promising to abide by them, acts up to his promise, and speaks out boldly, decidedly, and unhesitatingly, like a man, about all the leading doctrines of Christianity. As for the clergyman who, after declaring his assent to the Articles, flinches from their doctrinal distinctness, and preaches hesitatingly, as if he hardly knew what he believed, I am sorry for him. He may be a charitable, a liberal, a learned man, but he is not in the right place in the pulpit of the Church of England.

(2) Let us mark, in the next place, as we read the Articles, their *studied moderation about things non-essential to salvation*, and things about which good Christian men may differ.

About sin after baptism,—about predestination and election,—about the definition of the Church,—about the ministry,—about the ceremonies and rights of every particular or national Church,—about all these points it is most striking to observe the calm, gentle, tender, conciliatory tone which runs throughout the Articles; a tone the more remarkable when contrasted with the firm and decided language on essential points, to which I have just been referring.

It is clear as daylight to my mind, that the authors of the Articles intended to admit the possibility of difference on the points which I have just been enumerating. They saw the possibility of men differing about predestination and election, as Fletcher and Toplady did. How cautious are their statements, and how carefully guarded and fenced!—They believed that there might be Churches differently organized to our own, that there might be many good Christian ministers who were not Episcopalians, and many useful rites and ceremonies of worship unlike those of the Church of England. They take care to say nothing which could possibly give offence.—They scrupulously avoid condemning and denouncing other Churches and other Christians. In short, their maxim seems to have been, "*in necessariis unitas, in non-necessariis libertas, in omnibus caritas.*"

I greatly admire this moderation in non-essentials. I heartily wish that the spirit of it had been more acted upon in days gone by, by the rulers of the Church of England. To the blind intolerance and fanaticism of days gone by, to the insane and senseless wish to cram Episcopacy and Liturgy down the throats of every man by force, and excommunicate him if he would not swallow them,—to this we owe an immense proportion of our English Dissent. And the root of all this has been departure from the spirit of the Thirty-nine Articles.

I frankly own that I belong to a school in the Church of England, which is incorrectly and unfairly called "low." And why are we called so? Simply because we will not condemn every Church which is not governed by Bishops; simply because we will not denounce every one as greatly in error who worships without a surplice and a Prayer-book! But I venture to tell our accusers that their charges fall very lightly on us. When they can prove that our standard is not the standard of the Thirty-nine Articles,—when they can show that we take lower ground than our own Church takes in her authorized Confession of faith,—then we will allow there is something in what they say against us. But till they can do that, and they have not done it yet, I tell them that we shall remain unmoved. We may be called "low" Churchmen, but we are "true."

(3) Let us mark, in the next place, as we read the Articles, their *wise, discreet, and well-balanced statements about the Sacraments.* They declare plainly the divine authority of Baptism and the Lord's Supper. They use high and reverent language about them both, as means of grace, "by the which God doth work invisibly in us, and doth not only quicken, but strengthen and confirm our faith in Him."

But after saying all this, it is most instructive to observe how carefully the Articles repudiate the Romish doctrine of grace being imparted by the Sacraments "*ex opere operato.*" "The Sacraments," says the Twenty-fifth Article, "were not ordained of Christ to be gazed upon, or to be carried about, but that we should duly use them. And in such only as worthily receive the same they have a wholesome effect or operation."

Now if there is any one thing that is laid to the charge of us Evangelical clergy, it is this,—that we deny sacramental grace. "Excellent, worthy, hard-working men," we are sometimes called; "but unhappily they do not hold right Church views about the Sacraments."—Men who talk in this manner are talking rashly, and saying what they cannot prove. Evangelical clergymen yield to none in willingness to give rightful honour to Baptism and the Lord's Supper. All we say is, that grace is not tied to the Sacraments, and that a man may receive them, and be none the better for it. And what is all this but the doctrine of the Thirty-nine Articles?

(4) Let us mark, in the fourth place, as we read the Articles, the *thoroughly Protestant spirit* which runs throughout them, and the boldness of their language about Romish error.

What says the Nineteenth Article? "The Church of Rome hath erred, not only in living and manner of ceremonies, but also in matters of faith."

What says the Twenty-second Article? "The Romish doctrine concerning purgatory, pardons, worshipping and adoration, as well of images as of reliques, and also of invocation of saints, is a fond thing vainly invented, and grounded upon no warranty of Scripture, but rather repugnant to the Word of God."

What says the Twenty-fourth Article? It forbids the Romish custom of having public prayers and ministering the Sacraments in Latin.

What says the Twenty-fifth Article? It declares that the five Romish sacraments of confirmation, penance, orders, matrimony, and extreme unction, are not to be accounted sacraments of the Gospel.

What says the Twenty-eighth Article? It declares that "transubstantiation, or the change of the substance of bread and wine in the Lord's Supper, cannot be proved by Holy Writ, is repugnant to the plain words of Scripture, overthroweth the nature of a sacrament, and hath given occasion to many superstitions." It also declares that "the Sacrament of the Lord's Supper was not by Christ's ordinance reserved, carried about, lifted up, or worshipped."

What says the Thirtieth Article? "The cup of the Lord is not to be denied to the lay-people."

What saith the Thirty-first Article? "The sacrifices of masses, in which it was commonly said the priest did offer Christ for the quick and dead, to have remission of pain and guilt, were blasphemous fables and dangerous deceit."

What says the Thirty-second Article? "Bishops, priests, and deacons are not commanded by God's laws to vow the estate of single life, or to abstain from marriage."

What says the Thirty-seventh Article? "The Bishop of Rome hath no jurisdiction in this realm of England."

Now what shall we say to all this? Nine times over the Thirty-nine Articles condemn, in plain and unmistakable language, the leading doctrines of the Church of Rome, and declare in favour of what must be called Protestant views. And yet men dare to tell us that we Evangelical clergymen have no right to denounce Popery,—that it is very wrong and very uncharitable to be so hot in favour of Protestantism,—that Romanism is a pretty good sort of thing,—and that by making such a piece of work about Popery, and Protestantism, and Ritualism, and semi-Popery, we are only troubling the country and doing more harm than good. Well! I am content to point to the Thirty-nine Articles. There is my apology! There is my defence! I will take up no other ground at present. I will not say, as I might do, that Popery is an unscriptural system, which every free nation ought to dread, and every Bible-reading Christian of any nation ought to oppose. I simply point to the Thirty-nine Articles.

I ask any one to explain how any English clergyman can be acting consistently, if he does not oppose, denounce, expose, and resist Popery in every shape, either within the Church or without. Other Christians may do as they please, and countenance Popery if they like. But so long as the Articles stand unrepealed and unaltered, it is the bounden duty of every clergyman of the Church of England to oppose Popery.

(5) Let us mark, in the last place, as we read the Articles, the unvarying *reverence with which they always speak of Holy Scripture.* The inspiration of the Bible, no doubt, is never distinctly asserted. It is evidently taken for granted as a first principle, which need not be proved. But if constant references to Scripture, and constant appeals to the authority of Scripture, as God's Word, are allowed to prove anything, in no document does the Bible receive more honour than in the Articles.

The Sixth Article declares that "Holy Scripture contains all things necessary to salvation, and that whatsoever is not read therein, nor may be proved thereby, is not to be required of any man, that it should be believed as an article of faith, or be thought requisite and necessary to salvation."

The Eighth Article says that "the three Creeds ought thoroughly to be believed and received, for they may be proved by most certain warranty of Holy Scripture."

The Twentieth Article says, "It is not lawful for the Church to ordain anything that is contrary to God's Word written, neither may it so expound one place of Scripture that it be repugnant to another."

The Twenty-first Article says that "things ordained by General Councils as necessary to salvation, have neither strength nor authority, unless it be declared that they be taken from Holy Scripture."

The Twenty-second Article condemns certain Romish functions, "because they are grounded on no warranty of Scripture, but are rather repugnant to the Word of God."

The Twenty-eighth Article condemns Transubstantiation, "because it cannot be proved by Holy Writ, but is repugnant to the plain words of Scripture."

The Thirty-fourth Article says that "traditions and ceremonies of the Church may be changed, so long as nothing is ordained against God's Word."

Now I see in all this abundant proof that the Bible is the rule of faith in the Church of England, and that no doctrine is "Church doctrine" which cannot be reconciled with God's Word. I see a complete answer to those who tell us that we make an idol of the Bible, and that we ought to go to the voice of the Church and to the Prayer-book for direction. I see that any sense placed on any part of the Prayer-book which is not reconcilable with Scripture, must be a mistake, and ought not to be received. I see, above all, that all who pour contempt on the Bible, as an uninspired, imperfect, defective Book, which ought not to be believed, if it contradicts "modern thought," are taking up ground which is at variance with the Church's own Confession of faith. They may be clever, liberal, scientific, and confident; but they are contradicting the Articles, and they are not sound Churchmen.

Such are the leading features, in my judgment, of the Thirty-nine Articles. I commend them to the attention of my readers, and ask that they may be carefully weighed. No doubt men may say that the Articles admit of more than one interpretation, and that my interpretation is not the correct one. My reply to all this is short and simple. I ask in what sense the Reformers who drew up the Articles meant them to be interpreted? Let men answer that. It is an acknowledged axiom in interpreting all public documents, such as treaties, covenants, wills, articles of faith, and religious formularies, that in any case of doubt or dispute the true sense is the sense of those who drew them up and imposed them. Waterland and Sanderson have abundantly shown that. Upon this principle I take my stand. I only want the Thirty-nine Articles to be interpreted in the sense in which the Reformers first imposed them, and I believe it impossible to avoid the conclusion you arrive at. That conclusion is, that the Thirty-nine Articles are in general tone, temper, spirit, intention, and meaning, eminently Protestant and eminently Evangelical.

And now I draw my subject to a conclusion. I have shown the reader, to the best of my ability, what the Articles are,—what is the position and authority which they hold in the Church of England,—and what are the leading features of their contents. It only remains for me to point out a few practical conclusions, which I venture to think are peculiarly suited to the times.

(1) In the first place, I ask every Churchman who reads this paper *to read the Thirty-nine Articles regularly at least once every year*, and to make himself thoroughly familiar with their contents.

It is not a reading age, I fear. Newspapers, and periodicals, and novels absorb the greater part of the time given to reading. I am sorry for it. If I could only reach the ear of all thinking lay Churchmen, I should like to say, "Do read your Articles." As for clergymen, if I had my own way I would require them to read the Articles publicly in church once every year.

Ignorance, I am compelled to say, is one of the grand dangers of members of the Church of England. The bulk of her people neither know, nor understand, nor seem to care about the inside of any of the great religious questions of the day. Presbyterians know their system. Baptists, Independents, and Methodists know theirs. Papists are all trained controversialists. Churchmen alone, as a body, are generally very ignorant of their own Church, and all its privileges, doctrines, and history. Not one in twenty could tell you why he is a Churchman.

Let us cast aside this reproach. Let all Churchmen awake and rub their eyes, and begin to read up their own Church and its doctrines. And if any man wants to know where to begin, I advise him to begin with the Thirty-nine Articles.

(2) In the second place, I ask all who read this paper *to teach the Thirty-nine Articles* to all young people who are yet of an age to be taught. It is a burning shame that the Articles are not made an essential part of the system of every school connected with the Church of England, whether for high or low, for rich or poor.

I do not say this without reason. It is a simple fact, that the beginning of any clear doctrinal views I have ever attained myself, was reading up the Articles at Eton, for the Newcastle Scholarship, and attending a lecture, at Christ Church, Oxford, on the Articles, by a college tutor. I shall always thank God for what I learned then. Before that time I really knew nothing systematically of Christianity. I knew not what came first or what last. I had a religion without order in my head. What I found good myself I commend to others. If you love young people's souls, and would ground them, and stablish them, and arm them against error betimes, take care that you teach them not only the Catechism, but also the Articles.

(3) In the third place, I advise all who read this paper *to test all Churchmanship by the test of the Articles.* Be not carried away by those who talk of "nice Church views," "Catholic ceremonies," "holy, earnest, parish priests," and the like. Try all that is preached and taught by one simple measure,—does it or does it not agree with the Articles? You have an undoubted right to do this, and no English clergyman has any right to object to your doing it. Say to him, if he does object, "You publicly read and subscribed to the Articles when you accepted your cure of souls. Do you or do you not abide by your subscription?"

This is the simple ground we take up in the various societies which, amidst much abuse, obloquy, and opposition, are labouring to maintain the Protestant character of the Church of England. They are not intolerant, whatever some may please to say. They do not want to narrow the limits of our Church. But we do say that any one who holds preferment in the Church of England ought to be bound by the laws of the Church of England, so long as those laws are unrepealed. Repeal the Act of Parliament called the 13th of Elizabeth, and cast out the Thirty-nine Articles, and we will cease to oppose Ritualism, and will concede that a Churchman may be anything, or everything, in opinion. But so long as things are as they are, we say we have a right to demand that respect should be paid to the Articles.

(4) Finally, let me advise every Churchman who values his soul *never*

to be ashamed of the great leading doctrines which are so nobly set forth in the Articles.

Never mind if people call you extreme, party-spirited, going too far, Puritanical, ultra-Methodist, and the like.—Ask them if they have ever read the first nineteen Articles of their own Church. Tell them, so long as you are a Churchman, you will never be ashamed of holding Church doctrine, and that you know what Church doctrine is, if they do not.

Remember, above all, that nothing but clear, distinct views of doctrine, such views as you will find in the Articles, will ever give you peace while you live, and comfort when you die.

"Earnestness" is a fine, vague, high-sounding term, and is very beautiful to look at and talk about, when we are well, and happy, and prosperous. But when the stern realities of life break in upon us, and we are in trouble,—when the valley of death looms in sight, and the cold river must be crossed,—in seasons like those, we want something better than mere "earnestness" to support our souls. Oh, no! it is cold comfort then, as our feet touch the chill waters, to be told, "Never mind! Be in earnest! Take comfort! Only be in earnest!"—It will never, never do! We want them to know if God is our God, if Christ is our Christ, if we have the Spirit within us, if our sins are pardoned, if our souls are justified, if our hearts are changed, if our faith is genuine and real. "Earnestness" will not be enough then. It will prove a mere fine-weather religion. Nothing, in short, will do in that solemn hour but clear, distinct doctrine, embraced by our inward man, and made our own. "Earnestness" then proves nothing but a dream. Doctrines such as those set forth in the Articles are the only doctrines which are life, and health, and strength, and peace. Let us never be ashamed of laying hold of them, maintaining them, and making them our own. Those doctrines are the religion of the Bible and of the Church of England!

V

BAPTISM

THERE is perhaps no subject in Christianity about which such difference of opinion exists as the sacrament of baptism. The very name recalls to one's mind an endless list of strifes, disputes, heart-burnings, controversies, and divisions.

It is a subject, moreover, on which even eminent Christians have long been greatly divided. Praying, Bible-reading, holy men, who can agree on all other points, find themselves hopelessly divided about baptism. The fall of man has affected the understanding as well as the will. Fallen indeed must human nature be, when millions who agree about sin, and Christ, and grace, are as the poles asunder about baptism.

I propose in the following pages to offer a few remarks on this disputed subject. I am not vain enough to suppose that I can throw any light on a controversy which so many great and good men have handled in vain. But I know that every additional witness is useful in a disputed case. I wish to strengthen the hands of those I agree with, and to show them that we have no reason to be ashamed of our opinions. I wish to suggest a few things for the consideration of those I do not agree with, and to show them that the Scriptural argument in this matter is not, as some suppose, all on one side.

There are four points which I propose to examine in considering the subject:—

    I.   What baptism is,—its *nature*.

    II. In what manner baptism should be administered,—its *mode*.

    III. Who ought to be baptized,—its *subjects*.

    IV. What place baptism ought to occupy in religion,—its *true position*.

If I can supply a satisfactory answer to these four questions, I feel that I shall have contributed something to the clearing of many minds.

    I. Let us consider first the *nature of baptism,—what is it?*

(1) Baptism is an ordinance appointed by our Lord Jesus Christ, for the continual admission of fresh members into His visible Church. In the army every new soldier is formally added to the muster-roll of his regiment. In a school every new scholar is formally entered on the books

of the school. And every Christian begins his Church-membership by being baptized.*

(2) Baptism is an ordinance of great simplicity. The outward part or sign is water, administered in the name of the Father, the Son, and the Holy Ghost, or in the name of Christ. The inward part, or thing signified, is that washing in the blood of Christ, and inward cleansing of the heart by the Holy Ghost, without which no one can be saved. The Twenty-seventh Article of the Church of England says rightly,—"Baptism is not only a sign of profession and mark of difference, whereby Christian men are discerned from others that be not christened, but it is also *a sign* of regeneration or new birth."

(3) Baptism is an ordinance on which we may confidently expect the highest blessings, when it is rightly used. It is unreasonable to suppose that the Lord Jesus, the Great Head of the Church, would solemnly appoint an ordinance which was to be as useless to the soul as a mere human enrolment or an act of civil registration. The sacrament we are considering is not a mere man-made appointment, but an institution appointed by the King of kings. When faith and prayer accompany baptism, and a diligent use of Scriptural means follows it, we are justified in looking for much spiritual blessing. Without faith and prayer baptism becomes a mere form.

(4) Baptism is an ordinance which is expressly named in the New Testament about eighty times. Almost the last words of our Lord Jesus Christ were a command to baptize: "Go ye, and teach all nations, baptizing them in the name of the Father, and of the Son, and of the Holy Ghost." (Matt. xxviii. 19.) We find Peter saying on the day of Pentecost,— "Repent, and be baptized every one of you;"—and asking in the house of Cornelius,—"Can any man forbid water, that these should not be baptized?" (Acts ii. 38; x. 47.) We find St. Paul was not only baptized himself, but baptized disciples wherever he went. To say, as some do, in the face of these texts, that baptism is an institution of no importance, is to pour contempt on the Bible. To say, as others do, that baptism is only a thing of the heart,† and not an outward ordinance at all, is to say that which seems flatly contradictory to the Bible.

---

* This is a point which ought to be carefully noticed. Here lies the one simple reason why the children of Baptists, or any other unbaptized persons, cannot have the Burial Service of the Prayer-book read over them, when they are buried. It is a service expressly intended for members of the professing Church. An unbaptized person is not such a member. There is, therefore, no Service that we can read. To suppose that we pronounce any opinion on a man's state of soul and consider him lost, because we read no Service over him, is simply absurd! We pronounce no opinion at all. He may be in paradise with the penitent thief for anything we know. His soul after death is not affected either by reading a Service or by not reading one. The plain reason is *we have nothing to read!*

† I am quite aware that the whole body of Christians called Friends, or Quakers, reject water-baptism, and allow of no baptism except the inward

(5) Baptism is an ordinance which, according to Scripture, a man may receive, and yet get no good from it. Can any one doubt that Judas Iscariot, Simon Magus, Ananias and Sapphira, Demas, Hymenæus, Philetus, and Nicolas, were all baptized people? Yet what benefit did they receive from baptism? Clearly, for anything that we can see, none at all! Their hearts were "not right in the sight of God." (Acts viii. 21.) They remained "dead in trespasses and sins," and were "dead while they lived." (Ephes. ii. 1; 1 Tim. v. 6.)

(6) Baptism is an ordinance which in Apostolic times went together with the first beginnings of a man's religion. In the very day that many of the early Christians repented and believed, in that very day they were baptized. Baptism was the expression of their new-born faith, and the starting-point in their Christianity. No wonder that in such cases it was regarded as the vehicle of all spiritual blessings. The Scriptural expressions, "buried with Christ in baptism"—"putting on Christ in baptism"— "baptism doth also save us"—would be full of deep meaning to such persons. (Rom. vi. 4; Col. ii. 12; Gal. iii. 27; 1 Pet. iii. 21.) They would exactly tally with their experience. But to apply such expressions indiscriminately to the baptism of infants in our own day is, in my judgment, unreasonable and unfair. It is an application of Scripture which, I believe, was never intended.

(7) Baptism is an ordinance which a man may never receive, and yet be a true Christian and be saved. The case of the penitent thief is sufficient to prove this. Here was a man who repented, believed, was converted and gave evidence of true grace, if any one ever did. We read of no one else to whom such marvellous words were addressed as the famous sentence, "To-day shalt thou be with Me in paradise." (Luke xxiii. 42.) And yet there is not the slightest proof that this man was ever baptized at all! Without baptism and the Lord's Supper he received the highest spiritual blessings while he lived, and was with Christ in paradise when he died! To assert, in the face of such a case, that baptism is *absolutely necessary* to salvation is something monstrous. To say that baptism is the *only* means of regeneration, and that all who die unbaptized are lost for ever, is to say that which cannot be proved by Scripture, and is revolting to common sense.

baptism of the heart. To their own Master they must stand or fall. I am not their Judge. The grace, faith, and holiness of many Quakers are beyond all question. They are simple matters of fact. Christians like Mrs. Fry and J. J. Gurney most evidently had received the Holy Ghost, and would reflect honour on any Church. Would God that many baptized Christians were like them! But the best people are fallible at their best. How people, so sensible and well read as many Quakers have been and are, can possibly refuse to see water-baptism in Scripture, as an ordinance obligatory on all professing Christians, is a problem which I cannot pretend to solve. It passes my understanding. I can only suppose that God allows the Quakers to be a perpetual testimony against Romish views of water-baptism, and a standing witness to the Churches that God can, in some cases, give grace without the use of any sacraments at all!

I leave this part of my subject here. I commend the seven propositions which I have laid down to the serious attention of all who wish to obtain clear views about baptism. In considering the two sacraments of the Christian religion, I hold it to be of primary importance to put away from us the vagueness and mysteriousness with which too many surround them. Above all, let us be careful that we believe neither more nor less about them than we can prove by plain texts of Scripture.

There is a baptism which is absolutely necessary to salvation, beyond all question. There is a baptism without which no one, whether old or young, has ever gone to heaven. But what baptism is this? It is not the baptism of *water*, but the inward baptism which the Holy Ghost gives to the *heart*. It is not a baptism which any man can offer, whether ordained or unordained. It is the baptism which it is the special privilege of the Lord Jesus Christ to give to all His mystical members. It is not a baptism which man's eye can see, but an invisible operation on the inward nature. "Baptism," says St. Peter, "saves us." But what baptism does he tell us he means? Not the washing of water, "not the putting away the filth of the flesh. (1 Peter iii. 21.) "By one spirit are we all baptized into one body." (1 Cor. xii. 13.) It is the peculiar prerogative of the Lord Jesus to give this inward and spiritual baptism. "He it is," said John the Baptist, "which baptizeth with the Holy Ghost." (John i. 33.)

Let us take heed that we know something of this saving baptism, the inward baptism of the Holy Ghost. Without this it signifies little what we think about the baptism of water. No man, whether High Churchman or Low Churchman, Baptist or Episcopalian, no man was ever yet saved without the baptism of the Holy Ghost. It is a weighty and true saying of the Regius Professor of Divinity at Cambridge, in the reign of Edward VI.,—"By the baptism of water we are received into the outward Church of God: by the baptism of the Spirit into the inward." (*Bucer*, on John i. 33.)

II. Let us now consider the *mode of Baptism. In what way ought it to be administered?*

This is a point on which a wide difference of opinion prevails. Some Christians maintain strongly that complete immersion in water is absolutely necessary and essential to make a valid baptism. They hold that no person is really baptized unless he is entirely "dipped," and covered over with water. Others, on the contrary, maintain with equal decision that immersion is not necessary at all, and that sprinkling, or pouring a small quantity of water on the person baptized, fulfils all the requirements of Christ.

My own opinion is distinct and decided, that Scripture leaves the point an open question. I can find nothing in the Bible to warrant the assertion that either dipping, or pouring, or sprinkling, is *essential* to

baptism. I believe it would be impossible to prove that either way of
baptizing is exclusively right, or that either is downright wrong. So long
as water is used in the name of the Trinity, the precise mode of administering the ordinance is left an open question.

This is the view adopted by the Church of England. The Baptismal
Service expressly sanctions "dipping" in the most plain terms.* To say,
as many Baptists do, that the Church of England is *opposed* to baptism
by immersion, is a melancholy proof of the ignorance in which many
Dissenters live. Thousands, I am afraid, find fault with the Prayer-book
without having ever examined its contents! If any one wishes to be
baptized by "dipping" in the Church of England, let him understand
that the parish clergyman is just as ready to dip him as the Baptist minister,
and that he may be baptized by "immersion" in church as well as in
chapel.

There is a large body of Christians, however, who are not satisfied
with this moderate view of the question. They will have it that baptism
by dipping or immersion is the *only* Scriptural baptism. They say that
all the persons whose baptism we read of in the Bible were "dipped."
They hold, in short, that where there is no immersion there is no baptism.

I fear it is almost waste of time to attempt to say anything on this
much-disputed question. So much has been written on both sides without
effect, during the last two hundred years, that I cannot hope to throw
any new light on the subject. The utmost that I shall try to do is to suggest
a few considerations to any whose minds are in doubt. I only ask them
to remember that I do not say that baptism by "dipping" is positively
wrong. All I say is, that it is not absolutely necessary, and is not absolutely
commanded in Scripture.

I ask, then, any doubting mind to consider whether it is in the least
probable that all the cases of baptism described in Scripture were cases
of complete immersion? The three thousand baptized in one day at the
feast of Pentecost (Acts ii. 41),—the jailor at Philippi suddenly baptized
at midnight in prison (Acts xvi. 33)—is it at all likely or probable that
they were all "dipped"? To my own mind, trying to take an impartial
view, it seems in the highest degree improbable. Let those believe it
who can.

I ask any one to consider, furthermore, whether it is at all probable
that a mode of baptism would have been enjoined as necessary, which
in some climates is impracticable? At the North and South Poles, for
example, the temperature, for many months, is many degrees below
freezing-point. In tropical countries, on the other hand, water is often
so extremely scarce that it is almost impossible to find enough for common

* The rubric of the Prayer-book Service for the Public Baptism of Infants
says,—"If the godfather and godmother shall certify to the priest that the child
may well endure it, he shall dip it in the water discreetly and warily."

drinking purposes. Now will any maintain that in such climates there can be no baptism without "immersion"? Will any one tell us that in such climates it is really necessary that every candidate for baptism should be completely "dipped"? Let those believe it who can.

I ask any one to consider, further, whether it is at all probable that a mode of baptism would have been enjoined which, in some conditions of health, is simply impossible. There are thousands of persons whose lungs and general constitution are in so delicate a state that total immersion in water, and especially in cold water, would damage their health. Now will any maintain that such persons ought to be debarred from baptism unless they are "dipped"? Let those believe it who can.

I ask any one to consider, further, whether it is probable that a mode of baptizing would be enjoined, which in many countries would practically exclude women from baptism. The sensitiveness and strictness of Eastern nations about the treatment of their wives and daughters are notorious facts. There are many parts of the world in which women are so completely separated and secluded from the other sex, that there is the greatest difficulty in even speaking to them about religion. To talk of such an ordinance as baptizing them by "immersion" would, in hundreds of cases, be perfectly absurd. The feelings of fathers, husbands, and brothers, however personally disposed to Christian teaching, would be revolted by the mention of it. And will any one maintain that such women are to be left unbaptized altogether because they cannot be "dipped"? Let those believe it who can.

I believe I might well leave the subject of the mode of baptism at this point. But there are two favourite arguments which the advocates of immersion are constantly bringing forward, about which I think it right to say something.

(a) One of these favourite arguments is based on the meaning of the Greek word in the New Testament, which we translate "to baptize." It is constantly asserted that this word can mean nothing else but dipping, or complete "immersion." The reply to this argument is short and simple. The assertion is utterly destitute of foundation. Those who are best acquainted with New Testament Greek are decidedly of opinion that to baptize means "to wash or cleanse with water," but whether by immersion or not must be entirely decided by the context. We read in St. Luke (xi. 38) that when our Lord dined with a certain Pharisee, "the Pharisee marvelled that He had not first washed before dinner." It may surprise some readers, perhaps, to hear that these words would have been rendered more literally, "that He had not first been *baptized* before dinner." —Yet it is evident to common sense that the Pharisee could not have expected our Lord to immerse or dip Himself over head in water before dining! It simply means that he expected Him to perform some ablution, or to pour water over His hands, before the meal. But if this is so, what becomes of the argument that to baptize *always* means complete "immersion"? It is cut from under the feet of the advocate of "dipping," and to reason further about it is mere waste of time.

(*b*) Another favourite argument in favour of baptism by immersion is drawn from the expression "buried with Christ in baptism," which St. Paul uses on two occasions. (Rom. vi. 4; Col. ii. 12.) It is asserted that going down into the water of baptism, and being completely "dipped" under it, is an exact figure of Christ's burial and coming up out of the grave, and represents our union with Christ and participation in all the benefits of His death and resurrection. But unfortunately for this argument there is no proof whatever that Christ's burial was a going down into a hole dug in the ground. On the contrary, it is far more probable that His grave was a cave cut out of the side of a rock, like that of Lazarus, and on a level with the surrounding ground. Such, at least, was the common mode of burying round Jerusalem. At this rate there is no resemblance whatever between going down into a bath, or baptistry, and the burial of our Lord. The actions are not like one another. That by profession of a lively faith in Christ at baptism a believer declares his union with Christ, both in His death and resurrection, is undoubtedly true. But to say that in "going down into the water" he is burying his body just as His Master's body was buried in the grave, is to say what cannot be proved.

In saying all this I should be very sorry to be mistaken. God forbid that I should wound the feelings of any brother who has conscientious scruples on this subject, and prefers baptism by dipping to baptism by sprinkling. I condemn him not. To his own Master he stands or falls. He that conscientiously prefers dipping may be dipped in the Church of England, and have all his children dipped if he pleases. What I contend for is *liberty*. I find no certain law laid down as to the mode in which baptism is to be administered, so long as water is used in the name of the Trinity. Let every man be persuaded in his own mind. He that sprinkles or simply pours water in baptism has no right to excommunicate him that dips;—and he that dips has no right to excommunicate him that sprinkles or pours water. Neither of them can possibly prove that the other is entirely wrong.

I leave this part of my subject here. Whatever some may think, I am content to regard the precise mode of baptizing as a thing indifferent, as a thing on which every one may use his liberty. I firmly believe that this liberty was intended of God. It is in keeping with many other things in the Christian dispensation. I find nothing precise laid down in the New Testament about ceremonies, or vestments, or liturgies, or church music, or the shape of churches, or the hours of service, or the quantity of bread and wine to be used at the Lord's Supper, or the position and attitude of communicants. On all these points I see a liberal discretion allowed to the Church of Christ. So long as things are "done to edifying," the principle of the New Testament is to allow a wide liberty.

I hold firmly, myself, that the validity and benefit of baptism do not depend on the *quantity of water* employed, but on the state of heart in which the sacrament is used. Those who insist on every grown-up person being plunged over head in a baptistry, and those who insist on splashing an immense handful of water in the face of every tender infant they receive into the Church at the font, are both alike, in my judgment, greatly mistaken. Both are attaching far more importance to the quantity of water used than I can find warranted in Scripture. It has been well said by a great divine,—"A little drop of water may serve to seal the fulness of divine grace in baptizing as well as a small piece of bread and the least tasting of wine in the Holy Supper." (Witsius, *Econ. Fed.* 1. 4, ch. xvi. 30.). To that opinion I entirely subscribe.

III. Let us next consider *the subjects of baptism. To whom ought baptism to be administered?*

It is impossible to handle this branch of the question without coming into direct collision with the opinions of others. But I hope it is possible to handle it in a kindly and temperate spirit. At any rate it is no use to avoid discussion for fear of offending Baptists. Disputed points in theology are never likely to be settled unless men on both sides will say out plainly what they think, and give their reasons for their opinions. To avoid the subject, because it is a controversial one, is neither honest nor wise. A clergyman has no right to complain that his parishioners become Baptists if he never instructs them about infant baptism.

I begin by laying it down as a point almost undisputed, that all grown-up converts at missionary stations among the heathen ought to be baptized. As soon as they embrace the Gospel and make a credible profession of repentance and faith in Christ, they ought at once to receive baptism. This is the doctrine and practice of Episcopal, Presbyterian, Wesleyan, and Independent missionaries, just as much as it is the doctrine of Baptists. Let there be no mistake on this point. To talk, as some Baptists do, of "believer's baptism," as if it was a kind of baptism peculiar to their own body, is simply nonsense! Believer's baptism is known and practised in every successful Protestant mission throughout the world.

But I now go a step further. I lay it down as a Christian truth that the children of all professing Christians have a right to baptism, if their parents require it, as well as their parents. Of course the children of professed unbelievers and heathen have no title to baptism, so long as they are under the charge of their parents. But the children of professing Christians are in an entirely different position. If their fathers and mothers offer them to be baptized, the Church ought to receive them in baptism, and has no right to refuse them.

It is precisely at this point that the grave division of opinion exists between the body of Christians called Baptists and the greater part of Christians throughout the world. The Baptist asserts that no one ought to be baptized who does not make a personal profession of repentance and faith, and that as children cannot do this they ought not to be baptized. I think that this assertion is not borne out by Scripture, and I shall proceed to give the reasons why I think so. I believe it can be shown that the children of professing Christians have a right to baptism, and that it is a complete mistake not to baptize them.

Let me remind the reader at the outset, that the question under consideration is not the Baptismal Service of the Church of England. Whether that service is right or wrong,—whether it is useful to have godfathers and godmothers,—are not the points in dispute. It is mere waste of time to say anything about them.* The question before us is simply whether infant baptism is right in *principle*. That it is right is held by Presbyterians, Independents, and Methodists, who use no Prayer-book, just as stoutly as it is by Churchmen. To the consideration of this one question I shall strictly confine myself. There is not the slightest necessary connection between the Liturgy and infant baptism. I heartily wish that some people would remember this. To insist on dragging in the Liturgy, and mixing it up with the abstract question of infant baptism, is not a sign of good logic, fairness, or common sense.

Let me clear the way, furthermore, by observing that I will not be drawn away from the real point at issue by the ludicrous descriptions which Baptists often give of the *abuse* of infant baptism. No doubt it is easy for popular writers and preachers among the Baptists, to draw a vivid picture of an ignorant, prayerless couple of peasants, bringing an unconscious infant to be sprinkled at the font by a careless sporting parson! It is easy to finish off the picture by saying, "What good can infant baptism do?" Such pictures are very amusing, perhaps, but they are no argument against the *principle* of infant baptism. The abuse of a thing is no proof that it ought to be disused and is wrong. Moreover, those who live in glass-houses had better not throw stones. Strange pictures might be drawn of what happens sometimes in chapels at adult baptisms! But I forbear. I want the reader to look not at pictures but at Scriptural principles.

Let me now supply a few simple reasons why I hold, in common with all Episcopalians, Presbyterians, Methodists, and Independents throughout the world, that infant baptism is a right thing, and that in denying baptism to children the Baptists are mistaken. The reasons are as follows.

(*a*) Children were *admitted into the Old Testament Church by a formal*

---

* Readers who wish to examine the true meaning of the Baptismal Service are requested to read the paper in this volume, called "Prayer-book Statements about Regeneration."

ordinance, from the time of Abraham downwards. That ordinance was circumcision. It was an ordinance which God Himself appointed, and the neglect of which was denounced as a great sin. It was an ordinance about which the highest language is used in the New Testament. St. Paul calls it "a seal of the righteousness of faith." (Rom. ii. 4.) Now, if children were considered to be capable of admission into the Church by an ordinance in the Old Testament, it is difficult to see why they cannot be admitted in the New. The general tendency of the Gospel is to increase men's spiritual privileges and not to diminish them. Nothing, I believe, would astonish a Jewish convert so much as to tell him his children could *not* be baptized! "If they are fit to receive circumcision," he would reply, "why are they not fit to receive baptism?" And my own firm conviction has long been that no Baptist could give him an answer. In fact I never heard of a converted Jew becoming a Baptist, and I never saw an argument against infant baptism that might not have been equally directed against infant circumcision. No man, I suppose, in his sober senses, would presume to say that infant circumcision was wrong.

(*b*) The baptism of children is *nowhere forbidden in the New Testament.* There is not a single text, from Matthew to Revelation, which either directly or indirectly hints that infants should *not* be baptized. Some, perhaps, may see little in this silence. To my mind it is a silence full of meaning and instruction. The first Christians, be it remembered, were many of them by birth Jews. They had been accustomed in the Jewish Church, before their conversion, to have their children admitted into church-membership by a solemn ordinance, as a matter of course. Without a distinct prohibition from our Lord Jesus Christ, they would naturally go on with the same system of proceeding, and bring their children to be baptized. But *we find no such prohibition!* That absence of a prohibition, to my mind, speaks volumes. It satisfies me that no change was intended by Christ about children. If He had intended a change He would have said something to teach it. But He says not a word! That very silence is, to my mind, a most powerful and convincing argument. As God commanded Old Testament children to be circumcised, so God intends New Testament children to be baptized.

(*c*) The *baptism of households* is specially mentioned in the New Testament. We read in the Acts that Lydia was baptized "and her household," and that the jailer of Philippi "was baptized: he and all his." (Acts xvi. 15, 33.) We read in the Epistle to the Corinthians that St. Paul baptized "the household of Stephanas." (1 Cor. i. 16.) Now what meaning would any one attach to these expressions, if he had no theory to maintain, and could view them dispassionately? Would he not explain the "household" to include young as well as old,—children as well as grown-up people? Who doubts when he reads the words of Joseph in Genesis,— "take food for the famine of your households" (Gen. xlii. 33);—or, "take

your father and your households and come unto me" (Gen. xlv. 18),
that children are included? Who can possibly deny that when God said
to Noah, "Come thou and all thy house into the ark," He meant Noah's
sons? Gen. vii. 1.) For my own part I cannot see how these questions
can be answered without establishing the principle of infant baptism.
Admitting most fully that it is not directly said that St. Paul baptized
little children, it seems to my mind the highest probability that the
"households" he baptized comprised children as well as grown-up
people.

(d) The *behaviour of our Lord Jesus Christ to little children*, as recorded
in the Gospels, is very peculiar and full of meaning. The well-known
passage in St. Mark is an instance of what I mean. "They brought young
children* to Him, that He should touch them: and His disciples rebuked
those that brought them. But when Jesus saw it, He was much displeased,
and said unto them, Suffer the little children to come unto Me, and
forbid them not: for of such is the kingdom of God. Verily I say unto
you, Whosoever shall not receive the kingdom of God as a little child,
he shall not enter therein. And He took them up in His arms, put His
hands upon them, and blessed them." (Mark x. 13–16.)

Now I do not pretend for a moment to say that this passage is a *direct*
proof of infant baptism. It is nothing of the kind. But I do say that it
supplies a curious answer to some of the arguments in common use among
those who object to infant baptism. That infants are *capable* of receiving
some benefit from our Lord, that the conduct of those who would have
kept them from Him was *wrong* in our Lord's eyes, that He was ready
and willing to bless them, even when they were *too young to understand*
what He said or did,—all these things stand out as clearly as if written
with a sunbeam! A direct argument in favour of infant baptism the
passage certainly is not. But a stronger indirect testimony it seems to me
impossible to conceive.

I might easily add to these arguments. I might strengthen the position
I have taken up by several considerations which seem to me to deserve
very serious attention.

I might show, from the writings of old Dr. Lightfoot, that the baptism
of little children was a practice with which the Jews were perfectly familiar.
When proselytes were received into the Jewish Church by baptism, before
our Lord Jesus Christ came, their infants were received, and baptized
with them, as a matter of course.

I might show that infant baptism was uniformly practised by all the
early Christians. Every Christian writer of any repute during the first
1500 years after Christ, with the single exception of perhaps Tertullian,

* In the parallel passage in St. Luke's Gospel the word "infants" is used,
and the Greek word so rendered can only be used of infants too young to speak
or be called intelligent.

speaks of infant baptism as a custom which the Church has always maintained.

I might show that the vast majority of eminent Christians from the period of the Protestant Reformation down to the present day, have maintained the rights of infants to be baptized. Luther, Calvin, Melanchthon, and all the Continental Reformers,—Cranmer, Ridley, Latimer, and all the English Reformers,—the great body of all the English Puritans,—the whole of the Episcopal, Presbyterian, Independent, and Methodist Churches of the present day,—are all of one mind on this point. They all hold infant baptism!

But I will not weary the reader by going over this ground. I will proceed to notice two arguments which are commonly used against infant baptism, and are thought by some to be unanswerable. Whether they really are so I will leave the reader to judge.

(1) The first favourite argument against infant baptism is the entire absence of any direct text or precept in its favour in the New Testament. "Show me a plain text," says many a Baptist, "commanding me to baptize little children. Without a plain text the thing ought not to be done."

I reply, for one thing, that the absence of any text about infant baptism is, to my mind, one of the strongest evidences in its favour. That infants were formally admitted into the Church by an outward ordinance, for centuries before Christ came, is a fact that cannot be denied. Now, if He had meant to change the practice, and exclude infants from baptism, I should expect to find some plain text about it. But I find none, and therefore I conclude that there was to be no alteration and no change. The very *absence* of any direct command, on which the Baptists lay such stress, is, in reality, one of the strongest arguments against them! No change and therefore no text!

But I reply, for another thing, that the absence of some plain text or command is not a sufficient argument against infant baptism. There are not a few things which can be proved and inferred from Scripture, though they are not plainly and directly taught. Let the Baptist show us a single plain text which directly warrants the admission of women to the Lord's Supper.—Let him show us one which directly teaches the keeping of the Sabbath on the first day of the week instead of the seventh.—Let him show us one which directly forbids gambling. Any well-instructed Baptist knows that it cannot be done. But surely, if this is the case, there is an end of this famous argument against infant baptism! It falls to the ground.

(2) The second favourite argument against infant baptism is the inability of infants to repent and believe. "What can be more monstrous," says many a Baptist, "than to administer an ordinance to an unconscious babe? It cannot possibly know anything of repentance and faith, and

therefore it ought not to be baptized. The Scripture says, 'He that believeth and is baptized shall be saved:' and, 'Repent, and be baptized.' " (Mark xvi. 16; Acts ii. 38.)

In reply to this argument, I ask to be shown a single text which says that *nobody* ought to be baptized until he repents and believes. I shall ask in vain. The texts just quoted prove conclusively that grown-up people who repent and believe when missionaries preach the Gospel to them, ought at once to be baptized. But they do not prove that their children ought not to be baptized together with them, even though they are too young to believe. I find St. Paul baptized "the household of Stephanas" (1 Cor. i. 16); but I do not find a word about their believing at the time of their baptism. The truth is that the often-quoted texts, "He that believeth and is baptized shall be saved,"—and "Repent ye, and be baptized," will never carry the weight that Baptists lay upon them. To assert that they forbid any one to be baptized *unless* he repents and believes, is to put a meaning on the words which they were never meant to bear. They leave the whole question of infants entirely out of sight. The text "nobody shall be baptized except he repents and believes," would no doubt have been a very conclusive one. But such a text cannot be found!

After all, will any one tell us that an intelligent profession of repentance and faith is absolutely necessary to salvation? Would even the most rigid Baptist say that because infants cannot believe, all infants must be damned? Yet our Lord said plainly, "He that believeth not shall be damned." (Mark xvi. 16.)—Will any man pretend to say that infants cannot receive grace and the Holy Ghost? John the Baptist, we know, was filled with the Holy Ghost from his mother's womb. (Luke i. 15.)— Will any one dare to tell us that infants cannot be elect,—cannot be in the covenant,—cannot be members of Christ,—cannot be children of God,—cannot have new hearts,—cannot be born again,—cannot go to heaven when they die?—These are solemn and serious questions. I cannot believe that any well-informed Baptist would give them any but one answer. Yet surely those who may be members of the glorious Church above, may be admitted to the Church below! Those who are washed with the blood of Christ, may surely be washed with the water of baptism! Those who can be capable of being baptized with the Holy Ghost, may surely be baptized with water! Let these things be calmly weighed. I have seen many arguments against infant baptism, which, traced to their logical conclusion, are arguments against infant salvation, and condemn all infants to eternal ruin!

I leave this part of my subject here. I am almost ashamed of having said so much about it. But the times in which we live are my plea and justification. I do not write so much to convince Baptists, as to establish and confirm Churchmen. I have often been surprised to see how ignorant some Churchmen are of the grounds on which infant baptism may be defended. If I have done anything to show Churchmen the strength of their own position, I feel that I shall not have written in vain.

IV. Let us now consider, in the last place, *what position baptism ought to hold in our religion.*

This is a point of great importance. In matters of opinion man is ever liable to go into extremes. In nothing does this tendency appear so strongly as in the matter of religion. In no part of religion is man in so much danger of erring, either on the right hand or the left, as about the sacraments. In order to arrive at a settled judgment about baptism, we must beware both of the error of defect, and of the error of excess.

We must beware, for one thing, of *despising baptism.* This is the error of defect. Many in the present day seem to regard it with perfect indifference. They pass it by, and give it no place or position in their religion. Because, in many cases, it seems to confer no benefit, they appear to jump to the conclusion that it can confer none. They care nothing if baptism is never named in the sermon. They dislike to have it publicly administered in the congregation. In short, they seem to regard the whole subject of baptism as a troublesome question, which they are determined to let alone. They are neither satisfied with it, nor without it.

Now, I only ask such persons to consider gravely, whether their attitude of mind is justified by Scripture. Let them remember our Lord's distinct and precise command to "baptize," when He left His disciples alone in the world. Let them remember the invariable practice of the Apostles, wherever they went preaching the Gospel. Let them mark the language used about baptism in several places in the Epistles. Now, is it likely,—is it probable,—is it agreeable to reason and common sense,— that baptism can be safely regarded as a dropped subject, and quietly laid on the shelf? Surely, I think these questions can only receive one answer.

It is simply unreasonable to suppose that the Great Head of the Church would burden His people in all ages with an empty, powerless, unprofitable institution. It is ridiculous to suppose His Apostles would speak as they do about baptism, if, in no case, and under no circumstances, could it be of any use or help to man's soul. Let these things be calmly weighed. Let us take heed, lest in fleeing from blind superstition, we are found equally blind in another way, and pour contempt on an appointment of Christ.

We must beware, for another thing, of *making an idol of baptism.* This is the error of excess. Many in the present day exalt baptism to a position which nothing in Scripture can possibly justify. If they hold infant baptism, they will tell you that the grace of the Holy Ghost invariably accompanies the administration of the ordinance,—that in every case, a seed of Divine life is implanted in the heart, to which all subsequent religious movement must be traced,—and that all baptized children are, as a matter of course, born again, and made partakers of the Holy Ghost!—If they do not hold infant baptism, they will tell you that to go down into the water with a profession of faith and repentance is the very turning-point in a man's religion,—that until we have gone down into the water we are nothing,—and that when we have gone down into the water, we have taken the first step toward heaven! It is notorious that many High Churchmen and Baptists hold these opinions, though not all. And I say that, although they may not mean it, they are practically making an idol of baptism.

I ask all persons who hold these exceedingly high and lofty views of baptism, to consider seriously what warrant they have in the Bible for their opinions. To quote texts in which the greatest privileges and blessings are connected with baptism, is not enough. What we want are plain texts which show that these blessings and privileges are *always and invariably conferred*. The question to be settled is not whether a child may be born again and receive grace in baptism, but whether *all* children are born again, and receive grace when they are baptized.—The question is not whether an adult may "put on Christ" when he goes down into the water, but whether *all* do as a matter of course. Surely these things demand grave and calm consideration!—It is positively wearisome to read the sweeping and illogical assertions which are often made upon this subject. To tell us, for example, that our Lord's famous words to Nicodemus (John iii. 5), teach anything more than the *general necessity* of being "born of water and the spirit," is an insult to common sense. Whether *all* persons baptized are "born of water and the Spirit" is another question altogether, and one which the text never touches at all. To assert that it is taught in the text, is just as illogical as the common assertion of the Baptist, when he tells you that because Jesus said, "He that believeth and is baptized shall be saved,"—therefore nobody ought to be baptized until he believes!

The right position of baptism can only be decided by a careful observation of the language of Scripture about it. Let a man read the New Testament honestly and impartially for himself. Let him come to the reading of it with an unprejudiced, fair, and unbiased mind. Let him not bring with him pre-conceived ideas, and a blind reverence for the opinion of any uninspired writing, of any man, or of any set of men. Let him simply ask the question,—"What does Scripture teach about baptism, and its place in Christian theology?"—and I have little doubt as to the conclusion he will come to. He will neither trample baptism under his feet, nor exalt it over his head.

(*a*) He will find that baptism is frequently mentioned, and yet not so frequently as to lead us to think that it is the very first, chief, and foremost thing in Christianity. In fourteen out of twenty-one Epistles, baptism is not even named. In five out of the remaining seven, it is only mentioned once. In one of the remaining two, it is only mentioned twice. In the two pastoral Epistles to Timothy it is not mentioned at all. There is, in short, only one Epistle, viz., the first to the Corinthians, in which baptism is even named on more than two occasions. And, singularly enough, this is the very Epistle in which St. Paul says, "I thank God that I baptized none of you,"—and "Christ sent me not to baptize, but to preach the Gospel." (1 Cor. i. 14, 17.)

(*b*) He will find that baptism is spoken of with deep reverence, and in close connection with the highest privileges and blessings. Baptized people are said to be "buried with Christ,"—to have "put on Christ,"—to have "risen again,"—and even (by straining a doubtful text) to have the "washing of regeneration." But he will also find that Judas Iscariot, Ananias and Sapphira, Simon Magus, and others, were baptized, and yet gave no evidence of having been born again. He will also see that in the first Epistle of John, people "born of God" are said to have certain marks and characteristics which myriads of baptized persons never possess at any period of their lives. (1 John ii. 29; iii. 9; v. 1, 4, 18.) And not least, he will find St. Peter declaring that the baptism which saves is "not the putting away the filth of the flesh," the mere washing of the body, but the "answer of a good conscience." (1 Peter iii. 21.)

(*c*) Finally, he will discover that while baptism is frequently spoken of in the New Testament, there are other subjects which are spoken of much more frequently. Faith, hope, charity, God's grace, Christ's offices, the work of the Holy Ghost, redemption, justification, the nature of Christian holiness,—all these are points about which he will find far more than about baptism. Above all, he will find, if he marks the language of Scripture about the Old Testament sacrament of circumcision, that the value of God's ordinances depends entirely on the spirit in which they are received, and the heart of the receiver. "In Jesus Christ neither circumcision availeth anything, nor uncircumcision; but faith which worketh by love,—but a new creature." (Gal. v. 6; vi. 15.) "He is not a Jew which is one outwardly; neither is that circumcision which is outward in the flesh; but he is a Jew which is one inwardly; and circumcision is that of the heart, in the spirit, and not in the letter; whose praise is not of men, but of God." (Rom. ii. 28, 29.)

It only remains for me now to say a few words by way of practical conclusion to the whole paper. The nature, manner, subjects, and position of baptism have been severally considered. Let me now show the reader the special lessons to which I think attention ought to be directed.

(1) For one thing, I wish to urge on all who study the much-disputed subject of baptism, the importance of aiming at *simple views* of this sacrament. The dim, hazy, swelling words, which are often used by

writers about baptism, have been fruitful sources of strange and unscriptural views of the ordinance. Poets, and hymn-composers, and
Romish theologians, have flooded the world with so much high-flown
and rhapsodical language on the point, that the minds of many have
been thoroughly swamped and confounded. Thousands have imbibed
notions about baptism from poetry, without knowing it, for which they
can show no warrant in God's Word. Milton's *Paradise Lost* is the sole
parent of many a current view of Satan's agency; and uninspired poetry
is the sole parent of many a man's views of baptism in the present day.

Once for all, let me entreat every reader of this paper to hold no
doctrine about baptism which is not plainly taught in God's Word.
Let him beware of maintaining any theory, however plausible, which
cannot be supported by Scripture. In religion, it matters nothing who
says a thing, or how beautifully he says it. The only question we ought
to ask is this,—"Is it written in the Bible? what saith the Lord?"

(2) For another thing, I wish to urge on many of my fellow Churchmen
the *dangerous tendency* of extravagantly high views of the efficacy of
baptism. I have no wish to conceal my meaning. I refer to those Churchmen who maintain that grace invariably accompanies baptism, and that
all baptized infants are in baptism born again. I ask such persons, in all
courtesy and brotherly kindness, to consider seriously the dangerous
tendency of their views, and the consequences which logically result
from them.

They seem to me, and to many others, to degrade a holy ordinance
appointed by Christ into a mere charm, which is to act mechanically,
like a medicine acting on the body, without any movement of a man's
heart or soul. Surely this is dangerous!

They encourage the notion that it matters nothing in what manner of
spirit people bring their children to be baptized. It signifies nothing
whether they come with faith, and prayer, and solemn feelings, or whether
they come careless, prayerless, godless, and ignorant as heathens! The
effect, we are told, is always the same in all cases! In all cases, we are
told, the infant is born again the moment it is baptized, although it has
no right to baptism at all, except as the child of Christian parents. Surely
this is dangerous!

They help forward the perilous and soul-ruining delusion that a man
may have grace in his heart, while it cannot be seen in his life. Multitudes
of our worshippers have not a spark of religious life or grace about them.
And yet we are told that they must all be addressed as regenerate, or
possessors of grace, because they have been baptized! Surely this is
dangerous!

Now I firmly believe that hundreds of excellent Churchmen have never
fully considered the points which I have just brought forward. I ask
them to do so. For the honour of the Holy Ghost, for the honour of

Christ's holy sacraments, I invite them to consider seriously the *tendency* of their views. Sure am I that there is only one safe ground to take up in stating the effects of baptism, and that is the old ground stated by our Lord: "Every tree is known by his own fruit." (Luke vi. 44.) When baptism is used profanely and carelessly, we have no right to expect a blessing to follow it, any more than we expect it for a careless recipient of the Lord's Supper. When no grace can be seen in a man's life, we have no right to say that he is regenerate and received grace in baptism.

(3) For another thing, I wish to urge on all Baptists who may happen to read this paper, *the duty of moderation* in stating their views of baptism, and of those who disagree with them. I say this with sorrow. I respect many members of the Baptist community, and I believe they are men and women whom I shall meet in heaven. But when I mark the extravagantly violent language which *some* Baptists use against infant baptism, I cannot help feeling that they may be justly requested to judge more moderately of those with whom they disagree.

Does the Baptist mean to say that his peculiar views of baptism are needful to salvation, and that nobody will be saved who holds that infants ought to be baptized? I cannot think that any intelligent Baptist in his senses would assert this. At this rate he would shut out of heaven the whole Church of England, all the Methodists, all the Presbyterians, and all the Independents! At this rate, Cranmer, Ridley, Latimer, Luther, Calvin, Knox, Baxter, Owen, Wesley, Whitfield, and Chalmers, are all lost! They all firmly maintained infant baptism, and therefore they are all in hell! I cannot believe that any Baptist would say anything so monstrous and absurd.

Does the Baptist mean to say that his peculiar views of baptism are necessary to a high degree of grace and holiness? Will he undertake to assert that Baptists have always been the most eminent Christians in the world, and are so at this day? If he does make this assertion, he may be fairly asked to give some proof of it. But he cannot do so. He may show us, no doubt, many Baptists who are excellent Christians. But he will find it hard to prove that they are one bit better than some of the Episcopalians, Presbyterians, Independents, and Methodists, who all hold that infants ought to be baptized.

Now, surely, if the peculiar opinions of the Baptists are neither necessary to salvation nor to eminent holiness, we may fairly ask Baptists to be moderate in their language about those who disagree with them. Let them, by all means, maintain their own peculiar views, if they think they have discovered a "more excellent way." Let them use their liberty and be fully persuaded in their own minds. The narrow way to heaven is wide enough for believers of every name and denomination. But for the sake of peace and charity, let me entreat Baptists to exercise moderation in their judgment of others.

(4) In the last place, I wish to urge on all Christians the immense importance of giving to each part of Christianity its *proper proportion and value*, but nothing more. Let us beware of wresting things from their right places, and putting that which is second first, and that which is first second. Let us give all due honour to baptism and the Lord's Supper, as sacraments ordained by Christ Himself. But let us never forget that, like every outward ordinance, their benefit depends entirely on the manner in which they are received. Above all, let us never forget that while a man may be baptized, like Judas, and yet never be saved, so also a man may never be baptized, like the penitent thief, and yet may be saved.— The things needful to salvation are an interest in Christ's atoning blood, and the presence of the Holy Ghost in the heart and life. He that is wrong on these two points will get no benefit from his baptism, whether he is baptized as an infant or grown up. He will find at the last day that he is wrong for evermore.

VI

REGENERATION

THE subject of Regeneration is a most important one at any time. Those words of our Lord Jesus Christ to Nicodemus are very solemn: "Except a man be born again, he cannot see the kingdom of God." (John iii. 3.) The world has gone through many changes since those words were spoken. Eighteen hundred years have passed away. Empires and kingdoms have risen and fallen. Great men and wise men have lived, laboured, written, and died. But there stands the rule of the Lord Jesus unaltered and unchanged. And there it will stand, till heaven and earth will pass away: "Except a man be born again, he cannot see the kingdom of God."

But the subject is one which is peculiarly important to members of the Church of England in the present day. Things have happened of late years which have drawn special attention to it. Men's minds are full of it, and men's eyes are fixed on it. Regeneration has been discussed in newspapers. Regeneration has been talked of in private society. Regeneration has been argued about in courts of law. Surely it is a time when every true Churchman should examine himself upon the subject, and make sure that his views are sound. It is a time when we should not halt between two opinions. We should try to know what we hold. We should be ready to give a reason for our belief. When truth is assailed, those who love truth should grasp it more firmly than ever.

I propose in this paper to attempt three things:—

I. First, to explain *what Regeneration, or being born again, means.*

II. Secondly, to show *the necessity of Regeneration.*

III. Thirdly, to point out *the marks and evidences of Regeneration.*

If I can make these three points clear, I believe I shall have done my readers a great service.

I. Let me then, first of all, explain *what Regeneration or being born again means.*

Regeneration means, that change of heart and nature which a man goes through when he becomes a true Christian.

I think there can be no question that there is an immense difference among those who profess and call themselves Christians. Beyond all dispute there are always two classes in the outward Church: the class of those who are Christians in name and form only, and the class of those who are Christians in deed and in truth. All were not Israel who were called Israel, and all are not Christians who are called Christians. "In the visible Church," says an Article of the Church of England, "the evil be ever mingled with the good."

Some, as the Thirty-nine Articles say, are "wicked and void of a lively faith;" others, as another Article says, "are made like the image of God's only-begotten Son Jesus Christ, and walk religiously in good works. Some worship God as a mere form, and some in spirit and in truth. Some give their hearts to God, and some give them to the world. Some believe the Bible, and live as if they believed it: others do not. Some feel their sins and mourn over them: others do not. Some love Christ, trust in Him, and serve Him: others do not. In short, as Scripture says, some walk in the narrow way, some in the broad; some are the good fish of the Gospel net, some are the bad; some are the wheat in Christ's field, and some are the tares.*

I think no man with his eyes open can fail to see all this, both in the Bible, and in the world around him. Whatever he may think about the subject I am writing of, he cannot possibly deny that this difference exists.

Now what is the explanation of the difference? I answer unhesitatingly, Regeneration, or being born again. I answer that true Christians are what they are, because they are regenerate, and formal Christians are what they are, because they are not regenerate. The heart of the Christian in deed has been changed. The heart of the Christian in name only, has not been changed. The change of heart makes the whole difference.†

This change of heart is spoken of continually in the Bible, under various emblems and figures.

Ezekiel calls it "a taking away the stony heart, and giving an heart of flesh;"—"a giving a new heart, and putting within us a new spirit." (Ezek. xi. 19; xxxvi. 26.)

The Apostle John sometimes calls it being "born of God,"—sometimes being "born again,"—sometimes being "born of the Spirit." (John i. 13; iii. 3, 6.)

---

* "There be two manner of men. Some there be that be not justified, nor regenerated, nor yet in the state of salvation; that is to say, not God's servants. They lack the renovation or regeneration; they be not come yet to Christ."— *Bishop Latimer's Sermons.* 1552.

† The reader must not suppose there is anything new or modern in this statement. It would be an endless work to quote passages from standard divines of the Church of England, in which the words "regenerate" and "unregenerate" are used to describe the difference which I have been speaking of. The pious and godly members of the Church are called "the regenerate,"—the worldly and ungodly are called "the unregenerate." I think no one, well read in English divinity, can question this for a moment.

The Apostle Peter, in the Acts, calls it "repenting and being converted." (Acts iii. 19.)

The Epistle to the Romans speaks of it as a "being alive from the dead." (Rom. vi. 13.)

The Second Epistle to the Corinthians calls it "being a new creature: old things have passed away, and all things become new." (2 Cor. v. 17.)

The Epistle to the Ephesians speaks of it as a resurrection together with Christ: "You hath He quickened, who were dead in trespasses and sins" (Eph. ii. 1); as "a putting off the old man, which is corrupt,—being renewed in the spirit of our mind,—and putting on the new man, which after God is created in righteousness and true holiness." (Eph. iv. 22, 24.)

The Epistle to the Colossians calls it "a putting off the old man with his deeds; and putting on the new man, which is renewed in knowledge after the image of Him that created him." (Col. iii. 9, 10.)

The Epistle to Titus calls it "the washing of regeneration, and renewing of the Holy Ghost." (Titus iii. 5.)

The First Epistle of Peter speaks of it as "a being called out of darkness into God's marvellous light." (1 Peter ii. 9.) And the second Epistle, as "being made partakers of the Divine nature." (2 Peter i. 4.)

The First Epistle of John calls it "a passing from death to life." (1 John iii. 14.)

All these expressions come to the same thing in the end. They are all the same truth, only viewed from different sides. And all have one and the same meaning. They describe a great radical change of heart and nature,—a thorough alteration and transformation of the whole inner man,—a participation in the resurrection life of Christ; or, to borrow the words of the Church of England Catechism, "A death unto sin, and a new birth unto righteousness."*

This change of heart in a true Christian is thorough and complete, so complete, that no word could be chosen more fitting to express it than the word "Regeneration," or "new birth." Doubtless it is no outward, bodily alteration, but undoubtedly it is an entire alteration of the inner man. It adds no new faculties to a man's mind, but it certainly gives an entirely new bent and bias to all his old ones. His will is so new, his tastes so new, his opinions so new, his views of sin, the world, the Bible, and Christ so new, that he is to all intents and purposes a new man. The change seems to bring a new being into existence. It may well be called being "born again."

This change is *not always given to believers at the same time in their lives.* Some are born again when they are infants, and seem, like Jeremiah and John the Baptist, filled with the Holy Ghost even from their mother's

---

* "All these expressions set forth the same work of grace upon the heart, though they may be understood under different notions."—*Bishop Hopkins.* 1670.

womb. Some few are born again in old age. The great majority of true Christians probably are born again after they grow up. A vast multitude of persons, it is to be feared, go down to the grave without having been born again at all.

This change of heart *does not always begin in the same way* in those who go through it after they have grown up. With some, like the Apostle Paul and the jailer at Philippi, it is a sudden and a violent change, attended with much distress of mind. With others, like Lydia of Thyatira, it is more gentle and gradual: their winter becomes spring almost without their knowing how. With some the change is brought about by the Spirit working through afflictions, or providential visitations. With others, and probably the greater number of true Christians, the Word of God preached or written, is the means of effecting it.*

This change is *one which can only be known and discerned by its effects.* Its beginnings are a hidden and secret thing. We cannot see them. Our Lord Jesus Christ tells us this most plainly: "The wind bloweth where it listeth, and thou hearest the sound thereof, but canst not tell whence it cometh or whither it goeth; so is every one that is born of the Spirit." (John iii. 8.) Would we know if we are regenerate? We must try the question, by examining what we know of the effects of Regeneration. Those effects are always the same. The ways by which true Christians are led, in passing through their great change, are certainly various. But the state of heart and soul into which they are brought at last, is always the same. Ask them what they think of sin, Christ, holiness, the world, the Bible, and prayer, and you will find them all of one mind.

This change is *one which no man can give to himself, nor yet to another.* It would be as reasonable to expect the dead to raise themselves, or to require an artist to give a marble statue life. The sons of God are born "not of blood, nor of the will of the flesh, nor of the will of man, but of God." (John i. 13.) Sometimes the change is ascribed to God the Father: "The God and Father of our Lord Jesus Christ hath begotten us again unto a lively hope." (1 Peter i. 3.) Sometimes it is ascribed to God the Son: "The Son quickeneth whom He will." (John iii. 21.) "If ye know that He is righteousness, ye know that every one that doeth righteousness

---

* "The preaching of the Word is the great means which God hath appointed for Regeneration: 'Faith cometh by hearing, and hearing by the Word of God.' (Rom. x. 17.) When God first created man, it is said that 'He breathed into his nostrils the breath of life,' but when God new creates man, He breathes into his ears. This is the Word that raiseth the dead, calling them out of the grave; this is that Word that opens the eyes of the blind, that turns the hearts of the disobedient and rebellious. And though wicked and profane men scoff at preaching, and count all ministers' words, and God's words too, but so much wind, yet they are such wind, believe it, as is able to tear rocks and rend mountains; such wind as, if ever they are saved, must shale and overturn the foundations of all their carnal confidence and presumption. Be exhorted therefore more to prize and more to frequent the preaching of the Word."—*Bishop Hopkins.* 1670.

is born of Him." (1 John ii. 29.) Sometimes it is ascribed to the Spirit,—and He in fact is the great agent by whom it is always effected: "That which is born of the Spirit is Spirit." (John iii. 6.) But man has no power to work the change. It is something far, far beyond his reach. "The condition of man after the fall of Adam," says the Tenth Article of the Church of England, "is such that he cannot turn and prepare himself, by his own natural strength and good works, to faith and calling upon God." No minister on earth can convey grace to any one of his congregation at his discretion. He may preach as truly and faithfully as Paul or Apollos; but God must "give the increase." (1 Cor. iii. 6.) He may baptize with water in the name of the Trinity; but unless the Holy Ghost accompanies and blesses the ordinance, there is no death unto sin, and no new birth unto righteousness. Jesus alone, the great Head of the Church, can baptize with the Holy Ghost. Blessed and happy are they, who have the inward baptism, as well as the outward.*

I believe the foregoing account of Regeneration to be Scriptural and correct. It is that change of heart which is the distinguishing mark of a true Christian man, the invariable companion of a justifying faith in Christ, the inseparable consequence of vital union with Him, and the root and beginning of inward sanctification. I ask my readers to ponder it well before they go any further. It is of the utmost importance that our views should be clear upon this point,—*What Regeneration really is.*

I know well that many will not allow that Regeneration is what I have described it to be. They will think the statement I have made, by way of definition, much too strong. Some hold that Regeneration only means admission into a state of ecclesiastical privileges, by being made a member of the Church, but does not mean a change of heart. Some tell us that a regenerate man has a certain power within him which enables him to repent and believe if he thinks fit, but that he still needs a further change in order to make him a true Christian. Some say there is a difference between Regeneration and being born again. Others say there is a difference between being born again and conversion.

To all this I have one simple reply, and that is, *I can find no such Regeneration spoken of anywhere in the Bible.* A Regeneration which only means admission into a state of ecclesiastical privilege may be

---

* "The Scripture carries it, that no more than a child can beget itself, or a dead man quicken himself, or a nonentity create itself; no more can any carnal man regenerate himself, or work true saving grace in his own soul."—*Bishop Hopkins.* 1670.
"There are two kinds of baptism, and both necessary: the one interior, which is the cleansing of the heart, the drawing of the Father, the operation of the Holy Ghost; and this baptism is in man when he believeth and trusteth that Christ is the only method of his salvation."—*Bishop Hooper.* 1547.
"It is on all parts gladly confessed, that there may be, in divers cases, life by virtue of inward baptism, where outward is not found."—*Richard Hooker.*
"There is a baptism of the Spirit as of water."—*Bishop Jeremy Taylor.* 1660.

ancient and primitive for anything I know. But something more than this is wanted. A few plain texts of Scripture are needed; and these texts have yet to be found.

Such a notion of Regeneration is utterly inconsistent with that which St. John gives us in his first Epistle. It renders it necessary to invent the awkward theory that there are two Regenerations, and is thus eminently calculated to confuse the minds of unlearned people, and introduce false doctrine. It is a notion which seems not to answer to the solemnity with which our Lord introduces the subject to Nicodemus. When He said, "Verily, verily, except a man be born again, he cannot see the kingdom of God," did He only mean except a man be admitted to a state of ecclesiastical privilege? Surely He meant more than this. Such a Regeneration a man might have, like Simon Magus, and yet never be saved. Such a Regeneration he might never have, like the penitent thief, and yet see the kingdom of God. Surely He must have meant a change of heart. As to the notion that there is any distinction between being regenerate and being born again, it is one which will not bear examination. It is the general opinion of all who know Greek, that the two expressions mean one and the same thing.

To me, indeed, there seems to be much confusion of ideas, and indistinctness of apprehension in men's minds on this simple point,—what Regeneration really is,—and all arising from not simply adhering to the Word of God. That a man is admitted into a state of great privilege when he is made a member of a pure Church of Christ, I do not for an instant deny. That he is in a far better and more advantageous position for his soul, than if he did not belong to the Church, I make no question. That a wide door is set open before his soul, which is not set before the poor heathen, I can most clearly see. *But I do not see that the Bible ever calls this Regeneration.* And I cannot find a single text in Scripture which warrants the assumption that it is so. It is very important in theology to distinguish things that differ. Church privileges are one thing; Regeneration is another. I, for one, dare not confound them.*

I am quite aware that great and good men have clung to that low view of Regeneration, to which I have adverted.† But when a doctrine of the everlasting Gospel is at stake, I can call no man master. The words of the old philosopher are never to be forgotten: "I love Plato, I love Socrates, but I love truth better than either." I say unhesitatingly, that those who

* "The mixture of those things by speech, which by nature are divided, is the mother of all error."—*Hooker.* 1595.

† For instance, Bishop Davenant and Bishop Hopkins frequently speak of a "Sacramental Regeneration," when they are handling the subject of baptism, as a thing entirely distinct from Spiritual Regeneration. The general tenor of their writings is to speak of the godly as the regenerate, and the ungodly as the unregenerate. But with every feeling of respect for two such good men, the question yet remains,—What Scripture warrant have we for saying there are two Regenerations? I answer unhesitatingly,—We have none at all.

hold the view that there are two Regenerations, can bring forward no plain text in proof of it. I firmly believe that no plain reader of the Bible only would ever find this view there for himself; and that goes very far to make me suspect it is an idea of man's invention. The only Regeneration that I can see in Scripture is, not a change of *state*, but a change of *heart*. That is the view, I once more assert, which the Church Catechism takes when it speaks of the "death unto sin, and new birth unto righteousness," and on that view I take my stand.

The doctrine before us is one of vital importance. This is no matter of names, and words, and forms, about which I am writing. It is a thing that we must feel and know by experience, each for himself, if we are to be saved. Let us try to become acquainted with it. Let not the din and smoke of controversy draw off our attention from our own hearts. Are our hearts changed? Alas, it is poor work to wrangle, and argue, and dispute about Regeneration, if after all we know nothing about it within.

II. Let me show, in the second place, *the necessity there is for our being regenerate, or born again.*

That there is such a necessity is most plain from our Lord Jesus Christ's words in the third chapter of St. John's Gospel. Nothing can be more clear and positive than His language to Nicodemus: "Except a man be born again, he cannot see the kingdom of God." "Marvel not that I say unto thee, Ye must be born again." (John iii. 3, 7.)

The reason of this necessity is the exceeding sinfulness and corruption of our natural hearts. The words of St. Paul to the Corinthians are literally accurate: "The natural man receiveth not the things of the Spirit of God, for they are foolishness unto him." (1 Cor. ii. 14.) Just as rivers flow downward, and sparks fly upward, and stones fall to the ground, so does a man's heart naturally incline to what is evil. We love our soul's enemies,—we dislike our soul's friends. We call good evil, and we call evil good. We take pleasure in ungodliness, we take no pleasure in Christ. We not only commit sin, but we also love sin. We not only need to be cleansed from the guilt of sin, but we also need to be delivered from its power. The natural tone, bias, and current of our minds must be completely altered. The image of God, which sin has blotted out, must be restored. The disorder and confusion which reigns within us must be put down. The first things must no longer be last, and the last first. The Spirit must let in the light on our hearts, put everything in its right place, and create all things new.

It ought always to be remembered that there are two distinct things which the Lord Jesus Christ does for every sinner whom He undertakes to save. He washes him from his sins in His own blood, and gives him a free pardon:—*this is his justification.* He puts the Holy Spirit into his heart, and makes him an entirely new man:—*this is his Regeneration.*

The two things are *both absolutely necessary to salvation*. The change of heart is as necessary as the pardon; and the pardon is as necessary as the change. Without the pardon we have no right or title to heaven. Without the change we should not be meet and ready to enjoy heaven, even if we got there.

The two things are *never separate*. They are never found apart. Every justified man is also a regenerate man, and every regenerate man is also a justified man. When the Lord Jesus Christ gives a man remission of sins, He also gives him repentance. When He grants peace with God, He also grants "power to become a son of God." There are two great standing maxims of the glorious Gospel, which ought never to be forgotten. One is: "He that believeth not shall be damned." (Mark xvi. 16.) The other is: "If any man hath not the Spirit of Christ, he is none of His." (Rom. viii. 9.)

The man who denies the universal necessity of Regeneration can know very little of the heart's corruption. He is blind indeed who fancies that pardon is all we want in order to get to heaven, and does not see that pardon without a change of heart would be a useless gift. Blessed be God that both are freely offered to us in Christ's Gospel, and that Jesus is able and willing to give the one as well as the other!

Surely we must be aware that the vast majority of people in the world *see nothing, feel nothing, and know nothing in religion as they ought*. How and why is this, is not the present question. I only put it to the conscience of every reader of this volume,—Is it not the fact?

Tell them of the sinfulness of many things which they are doing continually; and what is generally the reply?—"They see no harm."

Tell them of the awful peril in which their souls are,—of the shortness of time,—the nearness of eternity,—the uncertainty of life,—the reality of judgment. They feel no danger.

Tell them of their need of a Saviour,—mighty, loving, and Divine, and of the impossibility of being saved from hell, except by faith in Him. It all falls flat and dead on their ears. They see no such great barrier between themselves and heaven.

Tell them of holiness, and the high standard of living which the Bible requires. They cannot comprehend the need of such strictness. They see no use in being so very good.

There are thousands and tens of thousands of such people on every side of us. They will hear these things all their lives. They will even attend the ministry of the most striking preachers, and listen to the most powerful appeals to their consciences. And yet when you come to visit them on their death-beds, they are like men and women who never heard these things at all. They know nothing of the leading doctrines of the Gospel by experience. They can render no reason whatever of their own hope.

And why and wherefore is all this? What is the explanation?—What is the cause of such a state of things? It all comes from this,—that man naturally has no sense of spiritual things. In vain the sun of righteousness shines before him: the eyes of his soul are blind, and cannot see. In vain the music of Christ's invitations sound around him: the ears of his soul are deaf, and cannot hear it. In vain the wrath of God against sin is set forth: the perceptions of his soul are stopped up;—like the sleeping traveller, he does not perceive the coming storm. In vain the bread and water of life are offered to him: his soul is neither hungry for the one, nor thirsty for the other. In vain he is advised to flee to the Great Physician: his soul is unconscious of its disease;—why should he go? In vain you put a price into his hand to buy wisdom: the mind of his soul wanders,— he is like the lunatic, who calls straws a crown, and dust diamonds; he says, "I am rich, and increased with goods, and have need of nothing." Alas, there is nothing so sad as the utter corruption of our nature! There is nothing so painful as the anatomy of a dead soul.

Now what does such a man need? He needs to be born again, and made a new creature. He needs a complete putting off the old man, and a complete putting on the new. We do not live our natural life till we are born into the world, and we do not live our spiritual life till we are born of the Spirit.

But we must furthermore be aware that the vast majority of people *are utterly unfit to enjoy heaven in their present state.* I state it as a great fact. Is it not so?

Look at the masses of men and women gathered together in our cities and towns, and observe them well. They are all dying creatures,—all immortal beings,—all going to the judgment-seat of Christ,—all certain to live for ever in heaven or in hell. But where is the slightest evidence that most of them are in the least degree meet and ready for heaven?

Look at the greater part of those who are called Christians, in every part throughout the land. Take any parish you please in town or country. Take that which you know best. What are the tastes and pleasures of the majority of the people who live there? What do they like best, when they have a choice? What do they enjoy most, when they can have their own way? Observe the manner in which they spend their Sundays. Mark how little delight they seem to feel in the Bible and prayer. Take notice of the low and earthly notions of pleasure and happiness which every- where prevail, among young and old,—among rich and poor. Mark well these things,—and then think quietly over this question: "What would these people do in heaven?"

You and I, it may be said, know little about heaven. Our notions of heaven may be very dim and indistinct. But at all events, I suppose we are agreed in thinking that heaven is a very holy place,—that God is there,—and Christ is there,—and saints and angels are there,—that sin is not there in any shape,—and that nothing is said, thought, or done, which God does not like. Only let this be granted, and then I think there

can be no doubt the great majority of people around us are as little fit
for heaven as a bird for swimming beneath the sea, or a fish for living
upon dry land.*

And what is it that they need in order to make them fit to enjoy heaven?
They need to be regenerated and born again. It is not a little changing
and outward amendment that they require. It is not merely the putting
a restraint on raging passions and the quieting of unruly affections. All
this is not enough. Old age,—the want of opportunity for indulgence,
the fear of man, may produce all this. The tiger is still a tiger, even when
he is chained, and the serpent is still a serpent, even when he lies motion-
less and coiled up. The alteration needed is far greater and deeper. Every
one must have a new nature put within him; every one must be made a
new creature; the fountain-head must be purified; the root must be set
right; each one wants a new heart and a new will. The change required
is not that of the snake when he casts his skin and yet remains a reptile
still: it is the change of the caterpillar when he dies, and his crawling life
ceases; but from his body rises the butterfly,—a new animal, with a new
nature.

All this, and nothing less, is required. Well says the Homily of Good
Works: "They be as much dead to God that lack faith as those are to
the world that lack souls."

The plain truth is, the vast proportion of professing Christians in the
world have nothing whatever of Christianity except the name. The reality
of Christianity, the graces, the experience, the faith, the hopes, the life,
the conflict, the tastes, the hungering and thirsting after righteousness,—
all these are things of which they know nothing at all. They need to be
converted as truly as any among the Gentiles to whom Paul preached,
and to be turned from idols, and renewed in the spirit of their minds as
really, if not as literally. And one main part of the message which should
be continually delivered to the greater portion of every congregation on
earth is this: "Ye must be born again." I write this down deliberately.
I know it will sound dreadful and uncharitable in many ears. But I ask
any one to take the New Testament in his hand, and see what it says is
Christianity, and compare that with the ways of professing Christians
and then deny the truth of what I have written, if he can.

* "Tell me, thou that in holy duties grudgest at every word that is spoken;
that thinkest every summons to the public worship as unpleasant as the sound
of thy passing bell; that sayest, 'When will the Sabbath be gone, and the
ordinances be over?' What wilt thou do in heaven! What shall such an unholy
heart do there, where a Sabbath shall be as long as eternity itself; where there
shall be nothing but holy duties; and where there shall not be a spare minute,
so much as for a vain thought, or an idle word? What wilt thou do in heaven
where whatsoever thou shalt hear, see, or converse with, all is holy? And by
how much more perfect the holiness of heaven is than that of the saints on earth,
by so much the more irksome and intolerable would it be to wicked men,—for
if they cannot endure the weak light of a star, how will they be able to endure
the dazzling light of the sun itself?"—*Bishop Hopkins.*

And now let every one who reads these pages remember this grand principle of Scriptural religion: "No salvation without Regeneration,—no spiritual life without a new birth,—no heaven without a new heart."

Let us not think for a moment that the subject of this paper is a mere matter of controversy,—an empty question for learned men to argue about, but not one that concerns us. It concerns us deeply; it touches our own eternal interests, it is a thing that we must know for ourselves, feel for ourselves, and experience for ourselves, if we would ever be saved. No soul of man, woman, or child, will ever enter heaven without having been born again.*

And let us not think for a moment that this Regeneration is a change which people may go through after they are dead, though they never went through it while they were alive. Such a notion is absurd. Now or never is the only time to be saved. Now, in this world of toil and labour, and money-getting, and business,—*now* we must be prepared for heaven, if we are ever to be prepared at all. Now is the only time to be justified, now the only time to be sanctified, and now the only time to be "born again." So sure as the Bible is true, the man who dies without these three things will only rise again at the last day to be lost for ever.

We may be saved and reach heaven without many things which men reckon of great importance,—without riches, without learning, without books, without worldly comforts, without health, without house, without lands, without friends;—but *without Regeneration we shall never be saved at all*. Without our natural birth we should never have lived and moved and read these pages on earth: without a new birth we shall never live and move in heaven. I bless God that the saints in glory will be a multitude that no man can number. I comfort myself with the thought that after all there will be "much people" in heaven. But this I know, and am persuaded of from God's Word, that of all who reach heaven there will not be one single individual who has not been born again.†

III.   Let me, in the third place, point out *the marks of being regenerate, or born again*.

* "Make sure to yourselves this great change. It is no notion that I have now preached unto you. Your nature and your lives must be changed, or, believe it, you will be found at the last day under the wrath of God. For God will not change or alter the word that is gone out of His mouth. He hath said it: Christ, who is the truth and word of God, hath pronounced it,—that without the new birth, or regeneration, no man shall inherit the kingdom of God."—*Bishop Hopkins*. 1670.

† "Regeneration, or the new birth, is of absolute necessity unto eternal life. There is no other change simply necessary, but only this. If thou art poor, thou mayest so continue, and yet be saved. If thou art despised, thou mayest so continue, and yet be saved. If thou art unlearned, thou mayest so continue, and yet be saved. Only one change is necessary. If thou art wicked and ungodly, and continuest so, Christ, Who hath the keys of heaven, Who shutteth and no man openeth, hath Himself doomed thee, that thou shalt in no wise enter the kingdom of God."—*Bishop Hopkins*. 1670.

It is a most important thing to have clear and distinct views on this part of the subject we are considering. We have seen what Regeneration is, and why it is necessary to salvation. The next step is to find out the signs and evidences by which a man may know whether he is born again or not,—whether his heart has been changed by the Holy Spirit, or whether his change is yet to come.

Now these signs and evidences are laid down plainly for us in Scripture. God has not left us in ignorance on this point. He foresaw how some would torture themselves with doubts and questionings, and would never believe it was well with their souls. He foresaw how others would take it for granted they were "regenerate," who had no right to do so at all. He has therefore mercifully provided us with a test and gauge of our spiritual condition, in the First Epistle general of St. John. There he has written for our learning what the regenerate man is, and what the regenerate man does,—his ways, his habits, his manner of life, his faith, his experience. Every one who wishes to possess the key to a right understanding of this subject should thoroughly study the First Epistle of St. John.

I invite the reader's particular attention to these marks and evidences of Regeneration, while I try to set them forth in order. I might easily mention other evidences besides those I am about to mention. But I will not do so. I would rather confine myself to the First Epistle of St. John, because of the peculiar explicitness of its statements about the man that is born of God. He that hath an ear let him hear what the beloved Apostle says about the marks of Regeneration.

(1) First of all, St. John says, "Whosoever is born of God doth not commit sin;" and again, "Whosoever is born of God sinneth not." (1 John iii. 9; v. 18.)

A regenerate man *does not commit sin as a habit*. He no longer sins with his heart and will, and whole inclination, as an unregenerate man does. There was probably a time when he did not think whether his actions were sinful or not, and never felt grieved after doing evil. There was no quarrel between him and sin;—they were friends. Now he hates sin, flees from it, fights against it, counts it his greatest plague, groans under the burden of its presence, mourns when he falls under its influence, and longs to be delivered from it altogether. In one word, sin no longer pleases him, nor is even a matter of indifference: it has become the abominable thing which he hates. He cannot prevent it dwelling within him. "If he said he had no sin, there would be no truth in him" (1 John i. 8); but he can say that he cordially abhors it, and the great desire of his soul is not to commit sin at all. He cannot prevent bad thoughts arising within him, and short-comings, omissions, and defects appearing both in his words and actions. He knows, as St. James says, that "in many things we offend all." (James iii. 2.) But he can say truly, and as in the sight of God, that these things are a daily grief and sorrow to him, and that his whole nature does not consent unto them, as that of the unregenerate man does.

(2) Secondly, St. John says, "whosoever believeth that Jesus is the Christ, is born of God." (1 John v. 1.)

A regenerate man *believes that Jesus Christ is the only Saviour* by whom his soul can be pardoned and justified, that He is the Divine Person appointed and anointed by God the Father for this very purpose, and that beside Him there is no Saviour at all. In himself he sees nothing but unworthiness, but in Christ he sees ground for the fullest confidence, and trusting in Him he believes that his sins are all forgiven, and his iniquities all put away. He believes that for the sake of Christ's finished work and death upon the cross he is reckoned righteous in God's sight, and may look forward to death and judgment without alarm. He may have his fears and doubts. He may sometimes tell you he feels as if he had no faith at all. But ask him whether he is willing to trust in anything instead of Christ, and see what he will say. Ask him whether he will rest his hopes of eternal life on his own goodness, his own amendments, his prayers, his minister, his doings in church and out of church, either in whole or in part, and see what he will reply. Ask him whether he will give up Christ, and place his confidence in any other way of salvation. Depend upon it, he would say, that though he does feel weak and bad, he would not give up Christ for all the world. Depend upon it, he would say he found a preciousness in Christ, a suitableness to his own soul in Christ, that he found nowhere else, and that he must cling to Him.

(3) Thirdly, St. John says, "Every one that doeth righteousness is born of God." (1 John ii. 29.)

The regenerate man is *a holy man*. He endeavours to live according to God's will, to do the things that please God, to avoid the things that God hates. His aim and desire is to love God with heart, and soul, and mind, and strength, and to love his neighbour as himself. His wish is to be continually looking to Christ as his example as well as his Saviour, and to show himself Christ's friend by doing whatsoever Christ commands. No doubt he is not perfect. None will tell you that sooner than himself. He groans under the burden of indwelling corruption cleaving to him. He finds an evil principle within him constantly warring against grace, and trying to draw him away from God. But he does not consent to it though he cannot prevent its presence. In spite of all short-comings, the average bent and bias of his way is holy,—his doings holy,—his tastes holy,—and his habits holy. In spite of all his swerving and turning aside, like a ship beating up against a contrary wind, the general course of his life is in one direction, toward God and for God. And though he may sometimes feel so low that he questions whether he is a Christian at all, in his calmer moments he will generally be able to say with old John

Newton, "I am not what I ought to be; I am not what I want to be; I am not what I hope to be in another world; but still I am not what I once used to be, and by the grace of God I am what I am."*

(4) Fourthly, St. John says, "We know that we have passed from death unto life, because we love the brethren." (1 John iii. 14.)

A regenerate man *has a special love for all true disciples of Christ*. Like his Father in heaven, he loves all men with a great general love, but he has a special love for them who are of one mind with himself. Like his Lord and Saviour, he loves the worst of sinners, and could weep over them; but he has a peculiar love for those who are believers. He is never so much at home as when he is in their company: he is never so happy as when he is among the saints and the excellent of the earth. Others may value learning, or cleverness, or agreeableness, or riches, or rank, in the society they choose. The regenerate man values grace. Those who have most grace, and are most like Christ, are those he most loves. He feels that they are members of the same family with himself,— his brethren, his sisters, children of the same Father. He feels that they are fellow-soldiers, fighting under the same captain, warring against the same enemy. He feels that they are his fellow-travellers, journeying along the same road, tried by the same difficulties, and soon about to rest with him in the same eternal home. He understands them, and they understand him. There is a kind of spiritual freemasonry between them. He and they may be very different in many ways,—in rank, in station, in wealth. What matter? They are Jesus Christ's people: they are His Father's sons and daughters. Then he cannot help loving them.

(5) Fifthly, St. John says, "Whatsoever is born of God, overcometh the world." (1 John v. 4.)

A regenerate man *does not make the world's opinion his rule, of right and wrong*. He does not mind going against the stream of the world's ways, notions, and customs. "What will men say?" is no longer a turning point with him. He overcomes the love of the world. He finds no pleasure in things which most around him call happiness. He cannot enjoy their enjoyments,—they weary him,—they appear to him vain, unprofitable, and unworthy of an immortal being.—He overcomes the fear of the world. He is content to do many things which all around him think unnecessary, to say the least. They blame him: it does not move him. They ridicule him: he does not give way. He loves the praise of God more than the praise of man. He fears offending Him more than giving offence to man. He has counted the cost. He has taken his stand. It is a small thing with him now, whether he is blamed or praised. His eye is upon Him that is

---

* "Let none conclude that they have no grace because they have many imperfections in their obedience. Thy grace may be very weak and imperfect, and yet thou mayest be truly born again to God, and be a genuine son and heir of heaven."—*Bishop Hopkins*. 1670.

invisible. Him he is resolved to follow whithersoever He goeth. It may be necessary in this following to come out from the world and be separate. The regenerate man will not shrink from doing so. Tell him that he is unlike other people, that his views are not the views of society generally, and that he is making himself singular and peculiar. You will not shake him. He is no longer the servant of fashion and custom. To please the world is quite a secondary consideration with him. His first aim is to please God.

(6) Sixthly, St. John says, "He that is begotten of God keepeth himself." (1 John v. 18.)

A regenerate man *is very careful of his own soul.* He endeavours not only to keep clear of sin, but also to keep clear of everything which may lead to it. He is careful about the company he keeps. He feels that evil communications corrupt the heart, and that evil is far more catching than good, just as disease is more infectious than health. He is careful about the employment of his time: his chief desire about it is to spend it profitably. He is careful about the books he reads: he fears getting his mind poisoned by mischievous writings. He is careful about the friendships he forms: it is not enough for him that people are kind and amiable and good-natured,—all this is very well; but will they do good to his soul? He is careful over his own daily habits and behaviour: he tries to recollect that his own heart is deceitful, that the world is full of wickedness, that the devil is always labouring to do him harm, and therefore he would fain be always on his guard. He desires to live like a soldier in an enemy's country, to wear his armour continually, and to be prepared for temptation. He finds by experience that his soul is ever among enemies, and he studies to be a watchful, humble, prayerful man.

Such are the six great marks of Regeneration, which God has given for our learning. Let every one who has gone so far with me, read them over with attention, and lay them to heart. I believe they were written with a view to settle the great question of the present day, and intended to prevent disputes. Once more, then, I ask the reader to mark and consider them.

I know there is a vast difference in the depth and distinctness of these marks among those who are "regenerate." In some people they are faint, dim, feeble, and hardly to be discerned. You almost need a microscope to make them out. In others they are bold, sharp, clear, plain and unmistakable, so that he who runs may read them. Some of these marks are more visible in some people, and others are more visible in others. It seldom happens that all are equally manifest in one and the same soul. All this I am quite ready to allow.

But still, after every allowance, here we find boldly painted the six marks of being born of God. Here are certain positive things laid down by St. John as parts of the regenerate man's character, as plainly and distinctly as the features of a man's face. Here is an inspired Apostle writing one of the last general Epistles to the Church of Christ, telling us that a man born of God does not commit sin,—believes that Jesus is the Christ,—doeth righteousness,—loves the brethren,—overcomes the world, and keepeth himself. And more than once in the very same Epistle, when these marks are mentioned, the Apostle tells us that he who has not this or that mark is "not of God." I ask the reader to observe all this.

Now what shall we say to these things? What they can say who hold that Regeneration is only an admission to outward Church privileges, I am sure I do not know. For myself, I say boldly, I can only come to one conclusion. That conclusion is, that those persons only are "regenerate" who have these six marks about them, and that all men and women who have not these marks are not "regenerate," are not born again. And I firmly believe that this is the conclusion to which the Apostle wished us to come.

I commend what I have been saying to the serious consideration of all my readers. I believe that I have said nothing but what is God's truth. We live in a day of gross darkness on the subject of Regeneration. Thousands are darkening God's counsel by confounding baptism and Regeneration. Let us beware of this. Let us keep the two subjects separate in our mind. Let us get clear views about Regeneration first of all, and then we are not likely to fall into mistakes about baptism. And when we have got clear views let us hold them fast, and never let them go.

VII

PRAYER-BOOK STATEMENTS ABOUT REGENERATION

"Except a man be born again, he cannot see the kingdom of God."—JOHN iii. 3.

"This child is regenerate."—Baptismal Service of the Church of England.

IN this paper I have one simple object in view. I wish to throw light on certain expressions about "Regeneration" in the Baptismal Service of the Church of England.

The subject is one of no slight importance. The minds of many true Christians in the Church of England are troubled about it. They do not see the real meaning of our excellent Reformers in putting such language in a Prayer-book Service. They are perplexed and confounded by the bold and reckless assertions made by opponents of Evangelical Religion within the Church, and of Dissenters outside the Church, and, though not convinced, they find nothing to reply.

I propose in this paper to supply an answer to the common arguments in favour of "Baptismal Regeneration," which are based on the Baptismal Service of the Prayer-book. I wish to show that in this, as in many other questions, the truth is not so entirely on one side, as many seem to suppose. Above all, I wish to show that it is possible to be a consistent, honest, thoughtful member of the Church of England, and yet not to hold the doctrine of Baptismal Regeneration.

In considering this subject, I shall strictly confine myself to the one point at issue. I purposely avoid entering into the general question of the nature of Regeneration and the Scriptural warrant for infant baptism. I shall only make a few preliminary remarks by way of explanation, and to prevent mistakes about the meaning of words.

(1) My first remark is this: I believe that, according to Scripture, Regeneration is that great change of heart and character which is absolutely needful to man's salvation. "Except a man be born again, he cannot see the kingdom of God." (John iii. 3.) Sometimes it is called conversion,—sometimes being made alive from the dead,—sometimes putting off the old man, and putting on the new,—sometimes a new creation,—sometimes being renewed,—sometimes being made partaker of the Divine nature. All these expressions of the Bible come to the same thing. They are all the same truth, only viewed from different

points. They all describe that mighty, radical change of nature, which it is the special office of the Holy Ghost to give,—and without which no one can be saved.

I am aware that many do not allow "Regeneration" to be what I have here described it. They regard it as nothing more than an admission to Church privileges,—a change of state, and not a change of heart. But what plain text of Scripture can they show us in support of this view? I answer boldly,—"Not one."*

(2) My second remark is this. I believe there is only one sure evidence, according to Scripture, of any one being a regenerate person. That evidence is the fruit that he brings forth in his heart and in his life. "Every tree is known by his own fruit." Those fruits are laid down clearly and plainly in the New Testament. The Sermon on the Mount, and the latter part of most of St. Paul's Epistles, contain unmistakable descriptions of the man who is born of the Spirit. But nowhere shall we find the marks of Regeneration so fully given as in the first Epistle of St. John. "Whosoever is born of God sinneth not."† "Whosoever believeth that Jesus is the Christ is born of God." "Every one that doeth righteousness is born of Him." "Whatsoever is born of God overcometh the world." "He that is begotten of God keepeth himself." "In this the children of God are manifest, and the children of the devil: whosoever doeth not righteousness is not of God, neither he that loveth not his brother." (1 John v. 18; 1 John v. 1; 1 John ii. 29; 1 John v. 4; 1 John v. 18; 1 John iii. 10.)

Of course I am aware that many divines maintain that we may call people "regenerate," in whom none of the marks just described are seen, or ever were seen since they were born. They tell us, in short, that people may possess the gift of the Spirit, and the grace of Regeneration, when neither the gift nor the grace can be seen. Such a doctrine appears to me dangerous in the highest degree. It seems to my mind little better than Antinomianism.

(3) My third remark is this. I believe that Regeneration and baptism, according to Scripture, do not necessarily go together. I see that people may be filled with the Holy Ghost, and have new hearts, without baptism, like John the Baptist and the penitent thief. I see also that people may be

---

* I willingly concede that this low view of Regeneration is held by many holy and good men, like Bishop Davenant and Bishop Hopkins, whose doctrinal views are in all other respects Scriptural and sound. But I can call no man master. Warrant of Scripture for drawing a distinction between baptismal and spiritual Regeneration, I can nowhere find.

† "The interpretation of this place that I judge to be the most natural and unforced is this: 'He that is born of God doth not commit sin;' that is, he doth not sin in that malignant manner in which the children of the devil do; he doth not make a trade of sin, nor live in the constant and allowed practice of it. There is a great difference betwixt regenerate and unregenerate persons in the very sins that they commit. All indeed sin; but a child of God cannot sin,— that is, though he doth sin, yet he cannot sin after such a manner as wicked and unregenerate men do."—*Bishop Hopkins.* 1670.

baptized, and yet remain in the gall of bitterness and bond of iniquity, like Simon Magus. Above all, I find St. Peter telling us expressly, that the baptism which "saves," and whereby we are buried with Christ, and put on Christ, is not water-baptism only, whether infant or adult. It is "not" the putting away of the filth of the flesh, but the "answer of a good conscience." (1 Peter iii. 21.)

It is well known that many people hold that baptism and Regeneration are inseparable; but there is a fatal absence of texts in support of this view. Sixteen times, at least, the new birth is mentioned in the New Testament.* "Regeneration" is a word used twice, but only once in the sense of a change of heart. "Born again,"—"born of God,"—"born of the Spirit,"—"begotten of God," are expressions used frequently. Once the word "water" is joined with the words "born of the Spirit;" once the word "washing" is joined with the word "Regeneration;" twice believers are said to be born of the "Word of God," the "Word of truth." But it is a striking fact that there is not one text in Scripture which says distinctly and expressly that we are born again in baptism, and that every baptized person is necessarily regenerate!

(4) My fourth and last remark is this. I believe that according to Scripture, baptism has no more power to confer Regeneration on infants, *ex opere operato*, than it has upon grown-up people. That infants ought to be solemnly and formally admitted into the Church under the New Testament, as well as under the Old, I make no question. The promise to the children of believers, and the behaviour of our Lord Jesus Christ to children, ought to encourage all believing parents to expect the greatest blessings in bringing their infants to be baptized. But beyond this I cannot go.

I am aware that many people think that infants must be regenerated in baptism, as a matter of course, because they put no bar in the way of grace, and must therefore receive the sacrament worthily. Once more I am obliged to say, there is a fatal absence of Scripture in defence of this view. The right of Christian infants to baptism is only through their parents. The precise effect of baptism on infants is never once stated in the New Testament. There is no description of a child's baptism: and to say that children, born in sin, as all are, are in themselves *worthy* to receive grace, appears to me a near approach to the old heresy of Pelagianism.†

I now come to the point which forms the chief subject of this paper. That point is the true interpretation of some expressions in the Baptismal

* John i. 13. John iii. 3. John iii. 5. John iii. 7. John iii. 8. Titus iii. 5. 1 Peter i. 3. 1 Peter i. 23. James i. 18. 1 John ii. 29. 1 John iii. 9. 1 John iv. 7. 1 John v. 1. 1 John v. 4. 1 John v. 18.

† If infants are in themselves worthy to receive grace, because they put no bar in its way, let this question be answered:—"Why do not missionaries to the heathen baptize all the heathen infants whom they can find, without waiting

Service of the Church of England, which appear *at first sight* to contradict the view which I have been endeavouring to set forth on the subject of Regeneration. It is asserted that the Prayer-book decidedly teaches the doctrine of Baptismal Regeneration in the Baptismal Service.—It is said that the words of that service, "Seeing now that this child is regenerate,"— "We yield Thee hearty thanks, that it hath pleased Thee to regenerate this child with Thy Holy Spirit," admit of only one meaning.—They are used, it is said, over every child that is baptized.—They prove, it is said, beyond all question, that the Church of England maintains the doctrine of Baptismal Regeneration.—They settle the point, it is said, and leave no room to doubt. These are the statements I now propose to examine. Can they be proved, or can they not? I say unhesitatingly that they *cannot*, and I will proceed to give my reasons for saying so, if the reader will give me his patient attention.

I desire to approach the whole subject in dispute with a sorrowful recollection of the sad difference of opinion which has long prevailed in my own Church upon the subject which it involves. I am quite aware of the positive assertions so frequently made, that the views of Regeneration I have tried to set forth are not *"Church views,"* and so forth. Such assertions go for very little with me. I have read Bishop Jewel's *Apology*, and I do not forget what he says there about those "who impose upon silly men by vain and useless shows, and seek to overwhelm us with the mere name of the *Church.*" I am thoroughly persuaded that the views of Regeneration I maintain are the views of the Prayer-book, Articles, and Homilies of the Church of England, and I will endeavour to satisfy the reader that I have good reasons for saying so. The more I have searched into the subject, the more thoroughly convinced have I felt in my own mind that those who say the views I advocate are not *"Church views,"* are asserting what they cannot prove.

And now let me proceed to reply to the objection that the invariable Regeneration of all infants in baptism is proved to be the doctrine of the Church of England by the language of her Baptismal Service.

I. I answer then, first of all, that the *mere quotation of two isolated expressions in one particular service in our Liturgy is not of itself sufficient.* It must be proved that the sense in which the objector takes these expressions is the correct one. It must also be shown that this sense will bear comparison with the other Services and formularies of the Church, and does not involve any contradiction. If this last point cannot

for the will of their parents?" No Protestant missionary at any rate thinks of doing so.

If the children of believing and unbelieving parents are sure to receive exactly the same amount of grace in baptism, by virtue of the baptismal water, in whatever state of mind their parents bring them to the font, the whole sacrament becomes nothing but a form.

be shown and proved, it is clear that the objector has put a wrong interpretation on the Baptismal Service, and does not understand the great
principle on which all the Services of our Church are drawn up.

It is a most unsound method of reasoning to take one or two expressions
out of a book which has been written as one great whole, to place a
certain meaning on these expressions, and then refuse to inquire whether
that meaning can be reconciled with the general spirit of the rest of the
book. The beginning of every heresy and erroneous tenet in religion may
be traced up to this kind of reasoning, and to unfair and partial quotations.

This is precisely the *Roman Catholic's argument* when he wants to
prove the doctrine of transubstantiation. "I read," he says, "these plain
words, 'This is My body,—this is My blood.' I want no more. I have
nothing to do with your explanations and quotations from other parts
of the Bible. Here is quite enough for me. The Lord Jesus Christ says,
'This is My body.' This settles the question."

This again is precisely *the Arian's argument*, when he wants to prove
that the Lord Jesus Christ is inferior to the Father. "I read," he says,
"these plain words, 'My Father is greater than I.' " It is in vain you tell
him that there are other texts which show the Son to be equal with the
Father, and give a different meaning to the one he has quoted. It matters
not. He rests on the one single text that he has chosen to rest on, and he
will hear nothing further.

This also is precisely *the Socinian's argument*, when he wants to prove
that Jesus Christ is only a man, and not God. "I read," he tells us, "these
plain words, 'The man, Christ Jesus.'—Do not talk to me about other
passages which contradict my view. All I know is, here are words which
cannot be mistaken,—'The man, Christ Jesus.' "

Now, without desiring to give offence, I must frankly say that I observe
this kind of argument continually used in discussing the Church of
England's doctrine about Regeneration. People quote the words of our
Baptismal Service, "Seeing now that this child is regenerate," etc., as an
unanswerable proof that the Church considers all baptized infants to be
born again. They will not listen to anything else that is brought forward
from other Services and formularies of the Church. They tell you they
take their stand on the simple expression, "This child is regenerate."
The words are plain, they inform us! They settle the question incontro-
vertibly! They seem to doubt your honesty and good sense, if you are
not at once convinced. And all this time they do not see that they are
taking their stand on very dangerous ground, and putting a sword into
the hand of the next Socinian, Arian, or Roman Catholic who happens
to dispute with them.

I warn such people, if this paper falls in their hands, that this favourite
argument will not do. A single quotation dragged out of a Service will

not suffice. They must prove that the meaning they attach to it is consistent with the rest of the Prayer-book, and with the Articles and Homilies. They must not expound one place of the Prayer-book, any more than of the Bible, so as to make it repugnant to another. And this, whether they mean it or not, I firmly believe they are doing.

II. I answer, in the next place, that to say all baptized infants are regenerate, because of the expressions in the Baptismal Service, is to *contradict the great principle on which the whole Prayer-book is drawn up.*

The principle of the Prayer-book is to suppose all members of the Church to be in *reality* what they are in *profession,*—to be true believers in Christ, to be sanctified by the Holy Ghost. The Prayer-book takes the highest standard of what a Christian ought to be, and is all through worded accordingly. The minister addresses those who assemble together for public worship *as believers.* The people who use the words the Liturgy puts into their mouths, are supposed to be *believers.* But those who drew up the Prayer-book never meant to assert that all who were members of the Church of England were actually and really true Christians. On the contrary, they tell us expressly in the Articles, that "in the visible Church the evil be ever mingled with the good." But they held that if forms of devotion were drawn up at all, they must be drawn up on the supposition that those who used them were real Christians, and not false ones. And in so doing I think they were quite right. A Liturgy for unbelievers and unconverted men would be absurd, and practically useless! The part of the congregation for whom it was meant would care little or nothing for any Liturgy at all. The holy and believing part of the congregation would find its language entirely unsuited to them.

Now this general principle of the Prayer-book is the principle on which the Baptismal Service is drawn up. It supposes those who bring their children to be baptized, to bring them as *believers.* As the seed of godly parents and children of believers, their infants are baptized. As believers, the sponsors and parents are exhorted to pray that the child may be born again, and encouraged to lay hold on the promises. And *as the child of believers* the infant when baptized is pronounced "regenerate," and thanks are given for it.

The principle which the Church lays down *as an abstract principle* is this,—that baptism *when rightly and worthily received,* is a means whereby we may receive inward and spiritual grace, even a death unto sin and a new birth unto righteousness.* That an infant may receive baptism

* It may be well to remark that this is also the doctrine of the Church of Scotland. "The efficacy of baptism is not tied to that moment of time wherein it is administered; yet, notwithstanding, by the *right use* of this ordinance, the grace promised is not only offered, but really exhibited and *conferred* by the Holy Ghost, to such (whether of age or infants) as that grace belongeth unto, according to the counsel of God's own will, in His appointed time."—*Scotch Confession of Faith,* chap. 28.

"rightly" the Church of England unquestionably holds, though the way and manner of it may be a hidden thing to us; for as good Archbishop Usher beautifully remarks, "He that hath said of infants, to them belongs the kingdom of God, knows how to settle upon them the kingdom of heaven." Her ministers cannot see the book of God's election. They cannot see the hidden workings of the Holy Ghost. They cannot read the hearts of parents and sponsors. They can never say of any individual child, "This child is certainly receiving baptism unworthily." And this being the case, the Church most wisely leans to the side of *charity*, assumes hopefully of each child that it receives baptism worthily, and uses language accordingly.

The men who drew up our Baptismal Service, held that there was a connection between baptism and spiritual Regeneration, and they were right.* They knew that there was nothing too high in the way of blessing to expect for the child of a believer. They knew that God might of His sovereign mercy give grace to any child before, or in, or at, or by the act of baptism. At all events they dared not undertake the responsibility of denying it in the case of any particular infant, and they therefore took the safer course, to express a *charitable hope of all*.—They could not draw up two Services of baptism, one of a high standard of privilege, the other of a low one. They could not leave it to the option of a minister to decide when one should be used, and when the other. It would have made a minister's position at the baptismal font a most invidious one;—it would have exposed him to the risk of making painful mistakes;—it would have required him to decide points which none but God can decide. They leaned to the side of charity. They drew up a form containing the highest standard of privilege and blessing, and required that in every case of infant baptism that form, and that only, should be used. And in so doing they acted in the spirit of our Lord Jesus Christ's remarkable words to the seventy disciples, "Into *whatsoever* house ye enter, first say, Peace be to this house. And if the son of peace be there, your peace shall rest upon it: if not, it shall turn to you again." (Luke x. 5, 6.)

But as for maintaining that the ministerial act of baptizing a child did always necessarily convey Regeneration, and that every infant baptized was invariably born again, I believe it never entered into the thoughts of those who drew up the Prayer-book. In the judgment of charity and hope they supposed all to be regenerated in baptism, and used language accordingly. Whether any particular child was actually and really regenerated they left to be decided by its life and ways when it grew up. To say that the assertions of the Prayer-book Baptismal Service are to

* "There is in every sacrament a spiritual relation, or sacramental union between the sign and the thing signified; whence it comes to pass that the names and effects of the one are attributed to the other."—*Scotch Confession of Faith*, chap. 27.

be taken for more than a *charitable supposition*, will be found, on close examination, to throw the whole Prayer-book into confusion.*

This is the only principle on which many of the *Collects* can be reasonably explained. The Collect for the Epiphany says, "Grant that we who know Thee now by faith, may after this life have the fruition of Thy glorious God-head."—Will any one tell us that the compilers of the Prayer-book meant to teach, that all who use the Prayer-book do know God by faith? Surely not.—The Collect for Sexagesima Sunday says, "O, Lord God, Who seest that we put not our trust in anything that we do," etc. Will any dare to say that these words could ever be literally true of all members of the Church of England? Are they not manifestly a charitable supposition?—The Collect for the Third Sunday after Trinity says, "We, to whom Thou has given a hearty desire to pray," etc. Who can have a doubt that this is a form of words, which is used by many of whom it could not strictly and truly be said for one minute? Who can fail to see in all these instances one uniform principle, the principle of *charitably assuming* that members of a Church are what they profess to be? The Church puts in the mouth of her worshipping people the sentiments and language they ought to use, and if they do not come up to her high standard, the fault is theirs, not ours. But to say that by adopting such expressions she stamps and accredits all her members as real and true Christians in the sight of God, would be manifestly absurd.

* "What say you of infants baptized that are born in the Church? Doth the inward grace in their baptism always attend upon the outward sign? Surely, no. The sacrament of baptism is effectual in infants only to those and to all those who belong unto the election of grace. Which thing, though we in the *judgment of charity* do judge of every particular infant, yet we have no ground to judge so of all in general: or if we should judge so, yet is it not any judgment of certainty. We may be mistaken."—*Archbishop Usher*. 1620.

"All that receive baptism are called children of God, regenerate, justified: for to us they must be taken for such *in charity*, until they show themselves other. But the author (Bishop Montague, a friend of Archbishop Laud) affirmeth that this is not left to men's charity, as you, saith he, do inform the world, because we are taught in the service book of our Church earnestly to believe that Christ hath favourably received these infants that are baptized, that He hath embraced them with the arms of His mercy, that He hath given them the blessing of everlasting life; and out of that belief and persuasion we are to give thanks faithfully and devoutly for it. All this we receive and make no doubt of it: but when we have said all we must come to this,—that all this is *the charity of the Church*, and what more can you make of it?"—*George Carleton, Bishop of Chichester*. 1619.

"We are to distinguish between the *judgment of charity* and the judgment of certainty. For although in the general we know that not every one that is baptized is justified or shall be saved, yet when we come to particulars, we are to judge of them that are baptized that they are regenerated and justified, and shall be saved, until they shall discover themselves not to be such. And so our book of Common Prayer speaketh of them."—*George Downame, Bishop of Derry*. 1620.

"There is justification for that prayer in our public liturgy, when the congregation gives thanks to God for the child baptized, that it hath pleased Him

This is the only principle on which *the Service for the Churching of Women* can be interpreted. Every woman for whom that Service is used, is spoken of as "the Lord's servant," and is required to answer that she "puts her trust in the Lord." Yet who in his senses can doubt that such words are utterly inapplicable in the case of a great proportion of those who come to be churched? They are not "servants" of the Lord! They do not in any sense "put their trust" in Him! And who would dare to argue that the compilers of the Liturgy considered that all women who were churched did really trust in the Lord, merely because they used this language? The simple explanation is, that they drew up the Service on the same great principle which runs through the whole Prayer-book, the principle of *charitable supposition.*

This is the only principle on which *the Service of Baptism for grown-up people* can be interpreted. In that Service the minister first prays that the person about to be baptized may have the Holy Spirit given to him and be born again. The Church cannot take upon herself to pronounce decidedly that he is born again, until he has witnessed a good confession, and shown his readiness to receive the seal of baptism. Then, after that prayer, he is called upon openly to profess repentance and faith before the minister and congregation, and that being done he is baptized. Then, and not till then, comes the declaration that the person baptized is "regenerate," and he is born again and made an heir of everlasting

to regenerate this infant by His Holy Spirit, etc. For it cannot be denied but that the holy ordinance of baptism, the seal of our sanctification, doth take effect many times immediately in the infusion of present grace into the infant's soul, though many times also it hath not its effect till many years after. But seeing it is questionably true in many, we may and must *charitably suppose* it in every one, for when we come to particulars whom dare we exclude? And this we may do without tying the grace of Regeneration necessarily to baptism, as some complain that we do."—*William Pemble, Magdalen Hall, Oxford.* 1635.

"The office for baptizing infants carries on the supposition of an internal Regeneration."—*Bishop Burnet.* 1689.

"The Apostles always, when they descend to particular men or Churches, PRESUME every Christian to be elect, sanctified, justified, and in the way of being glorified, until he himself shall have proved himself to be wicked, or an apostate."—*Bishop Davenant.* 1627.

"As to what he says, that no one can be a minister of the Church of England, who is not certainly persuaded of the Regeneration of every infant baptized, neither also is that true. The minister truly gives God thanks after each infant has been baptized, that it has pleased God to regenerate him with His Holy Spirit. But it does not then follow that he ought to be certain of the Regeneration of every infant baptized. For it is sufficient if he is persuaded of the Regeneration of some only,—for instance, of elect infants, or if you like, even of some only of their number, that on that account he may be able, nay ought, to give God thanks for each and all baptized. Since who is elect he knows not: and it is but just that he should *by the judgment of charity presume*, that as many as he baptizes are elect,—and if any are regenerated in baptism (which none but a Socinian or other Catabaptist will deny) regenerated."—*Dr. Durel, Dean of Windsor, and Chaplain to the King.* 1677.

"Though the work of grace be not perfectly wrought, yet when the means are used, without something appearing to the contrary, we ought *to presume* of the good effect."—*Bishop Pearson.* 1680.

salvation. But can these words be strictly and literally true if the person baptized is a hypocrite, and has all along professed that which he does not feel? Are not the words manifestly used on the charitable supposition that he has repented and does believe, and in no other sense at all? And is it not plain to every one that in the absence of this repentance and faith, the words used are a mere form,—used, because the Church cannot draw up two forms, but not for a moment implying that inward and spiritual grace necessarily accompanies the outward sign, or that a "death unto sin and a new birth unto righteousness" is necessarily conveyed to the soul? In short, the person baptized is pronounced regenerate upon the broad principle of the Prayer-book, that, in the Church-services people are *charitably supposed* to be what they profess to be.

This is the only intelligible principle on which *the Burial Service* can be interpreted. In that Service the person buried is spoken of as a "dear brother or sister." It is said that it hath "pleased God of His great mercy to take to Himself his soul." It is said, "We give Thee hearty thanks that it hath pleased Thee to deliver this our brother out of the miseries of this sinful world." It is said that "our hope is, this our brother rests in Christ." Now what does all this mean? Did the compilers of the Prayer-book wish us to believe that all this was strictly and literally applicable to every individual member of the Church over whose body these words were read? Will any one look the Service honestly in the face and dare to say so? I cannot think it. The simple explanation of the Service is, that it was drawn up, like the rest, on the presumption that all members of a Church were what they professed to be. The key to the interpretation of it is the same great principle, the principle of *charitable supposition*.

This is the only principle on which *the Catechism* can be interpreted. In it every child is taught to say, "In baptism I was made a member of Christ, a child of God, and an inheritor of the kingdom of heaven;" and a little further on, "I learn to believe in God the Holy Ghost who sanctifieth me and all the elect people of God." Now what does this mean? Did the Prayer-book writers intend to lay it down as an abstract principle that all baptized children are "sanctified" and all "elect"? Will any one in the present day stand forth and tell us that all the children in his parish are actually sanctified by the Holy Ghost? If he can, I can only say, that his parish is an exception, or else Bible words have no meaning. But I cannot yet believe that any one would say so. I believe there is but one explanation of all these expressions in the Catechism. They are the words of *charitable supposition*, and in no other sense can they be taken.

I lay these things before any one who fancies that all children are regenerated in baptism, because of the expressions in the Prayer-book service, and I ask him to weigh them well. I am not to be moved from my ground by hard names, and bitter epithets, and insinuations that I am not a real Churchman. I am not to be shaken by scraps and sentences torn from their places, and thrust isolated and alone upon our notice. What I say is, that in interpreting the Baptismal Service of the Church we must be consistent.

Men say that the view of the Service I maintain is "non-natural and dishonest." I deny the charge altogether. I might retort it on many of those who make it. Whose view is most unnatural, I ask? Is it the view of the man who expounds the Baptismal Service on one principle, and the Burial Service on another?—or is my view, which interprets all on one uniform and the same system?

We must be consistent I repeat. I refuse to interpret one part of the Prayer-book on one principle, and another part on another. The expressions to which I have been calling attention are either abstract dogmatic declarations, or charitable assumptions and suppositions. They cannot be both. And I now call upon those who hold all children to be invariably regenerated, because of strong expressions in the Baptismal Service, to carry out their principles honestly, fairly, fully, and consistently, if they can.

If all children are actually regenerated in baptism, because the Service says, "This child is regenerate," then by parity of reasoning it follows that all people who use the Collect have faith, and a hearty desire to pray!—all women who are churched put their trust in the Lord!—all members of the Church who are buried are dear brethren, and we hope rest in Christ!—and all children who say the Catechism are sanctified by the Holy Ghost and are elect!—Consistency demands it. Fair interpretation of words demands it. There is not a jot of evidence to show that those are not really sanctified and elect who say the Catechism, if you once maintain that those are all actually "regenerated" over whom the words of the Baptismal Service have been used.

But if I am to be told that the children who use the Catechism are not necessarily all elect and sanctified, and that the people buried are not necessarily all resting in Christ, and that the language in both cases is that of *charitable supposition*, then I reply, in common fairness let us be allowed to take the language of the Baptismal Service in the same sense.— I see one uniform principle running through all the Prayer-book, through all the Offices, through all the devotional Formularies of the Church. That principle is the principle of charitable supposition. Following that principle, I can make good sense and good divinity of every Service in the book. Without that principle I cannot. On that principle therefore I take my stand. If I say all baptized children are really, literally, and actually "regenerate," because of certain words in the Baptismal Service, I contradict that principle. I believe our Services were meant to be consistent one with another, and not contradictory. I therefore cannot say so.

III. My next answer to those who say all baptized persons are regenerate, because of the Baptismal Service, is this,—that *such a view would not agree with the Thirty-nine Articles.*

Now I am aware that many have a very low opinion of the Articles. Many seem to know little about them, and to attach little weight to any quotation from them. "The Prayer-book! the Prayer-book!" is the watchword of these people;—"all we have to do with is, what does the Prayer-book say?"—I disagree with such persons entirely. I look upon the Thirty-nine Articles as the Church of England's Confession of faith. I believe the words of the declaration which prefaces them are strictly true, "That the Articles of the Church of England do contain the true doctrine of the Church of England," and that any doctrine which does not entirely harmonize with those Articles is not the doctrine of the Church. I honour and love the book of Common Prayer, but I do not call it the Church's Confession of faith. I delight in it as an incomparable manual of public worship, but if I want to ascertain the deliberate judgment of the Church upon any point of doctrine, I turn first to the Articles. What would a Lutheran or Scotch Presbyterian say of me, if I judged his Church by his minister's prayers, and did not judge it by the Augsburg or Westminster Confessions? I do not say this in order to disparage the Prayer-book, but to point out calmly what it really is. I want to place the Thirty-nine Articles in their proper position before the reader's mind, and so to make him see the real value of what they say. It is a circumstance deeply to be regretted that the Articles are not more read and studied by members of the Church of England.

I will now ask the reader of this paper to observe the striking prominence which the Articles everywhere give to the Bible as the only rule of faith. The Sixth Article says, that "Whatsoever is not read in Holy Scripture, nor may be proved thereby, is not to be required of any man that it should be believed as an article of the faith, or be thought requisite and necessary to salvation."—The Eighth says, that the "Three Creeds ought thoroughly to be believed and received, for they may be proved by most certain warrant of Holy Scripture."—The Twentieth says, that "It is not lawful for the Church to ordain anything that is contrary to God's Word written, neither may it so expound one place of Scripture that it be repugnant to another."—The Twenty-first says, that "things ordained by General Councils as necessary to salvation have neither strength nor authority, unless it may be declared that they be taken out of Holy Scripture."—The Twenty-second condemns certain Romish doctrines, because they "are grounded upon no warranty of Scripture, but are rather repugnant to the Word of God."—The Twenty-eighth condemns transubstantiation, because it "cannot be proved by Holy Writ, but is repugnant to the plain words of Scripture."—The Thirty-fourth says, that traditions and ceremonies of the Church may be changed, so long as "nothing be ordained against God's Word."

All these quotations make it perfectly certain that the Bible is the sole rule of faith in the Church of England, and that nothing is a doctrine of the Church which cannot be entirely reconciled with the Word of God. And I see here a complete answer to those who say we make an idol of the Bible, and tell us we ought to go first to the Prayer-book, or to the opinion of the primitive Church! I see also that any meaning placed upon any part of the Prayer-book which at all disagrees with the Bible, and cannot be proved by the Bible, must be an incorrect meaning. I am not to listen to any interpretation of any Service in the Liturgy, which cannot be thoroughly reconciled with Scripture. It may sound very plausible. It may be defended very speciously. But does it in any way jar with plain texts in the Bible? If it does, there is a mistake somewhere. There is a flaw in the interpretation. On the very face of it, it is incorrect. It is utterly absurd to suppose that the founders of our Church would assert the supremacy of Scripture seven or eight times over, and then draw up a service in the Prayer-book at all inconsistent with Scripture! And unless the doctrine that all children baptized are necessarily regenerated in baptism, can first be shown to be in the Bible, it is a mere waste of time to begin any discussion of the subject by talking of the Prayer-book.

I ask the reader, in the next place, to observe what the Twenty-fifth and Twenty-sixth Articles say. The Twenty-fifth speaks generally of sacraments; and it says of them,—both of baptism and of the Lord's Supper,—"In such only as *worthily* receive the same they have a wholesome effect or operation." The Twenty-sixth speaks of the unworthiness of ministers not hindering the effect of the sacraments. It says, "Neither is the effect of Christ's ordinance taken away by their wickedness, or the grace of God's gifts diminished, from such as *by faith and rightly* do receive the sacraments." Here we have a broad general principle twice asserted. The benefit of either sacrament is clearly confined to such as *rightly, worthily, and with faith* receive it. The Romish notion of all alike getting good from it, *ex opere operato*, is with equal clearness pointed at and rejected. Now can this be reconciled with the doctrine that all who are baptized are at once invariably regenerated? I say decidedly that it cannot.

I ask the reader, in the next place, to observe the language of the Article about baptism, the Twenty-seventh. It says, "Baptism is not only a sign of profession and mark of difference, whereby Christian men are discerned from others that are not christened, but it is also a sign of Regeneration or new birth, whereby, as by an instrument, they that receive baptism *rightly* are grafted into the Church; the promises of forgiveness of sin and of our adoption to be the sons of God by the Holy Ghost, are visibly signed and sealed; faith is confirmed and grace increased by virtue of prayer unto God. The baptism of young children is in any wise to be retained in the Church as most agreeable with the institution of Christ." Nothing can be more striking than the wise caution of all this language, when contrasted with the statements about baptism with which our ears are continually assailed in this day. There is not a word said which might lead us to suppose that a different principle is to be applied to the baptism of infants, from that which has been already laid down about all sacraments, in the Twenty-fifth Article. We are left to the inevitable conclusion that in all cases *worthy reception* is essential to the full efficacy of the sacrament. There is not a word said about a great inward and spiritual blessing invariably and necessarily attending the baptism of an infant. There is a perfect silence on that head, and a most speaking silence too. Surely a doctrine involving such immense and important consequences as the universal spiritual regeneration of all infants in baptism, would never have been passed over in entire silence, if it had been the doctrine of the Church. The authors of the Articles unquestionably knew the importance of the document they were drawing up. Unquestionably they weighed well every word and every statement they put down on paper. And yet they are perfectly silent on the subject! That silence is like the occasional silence of Scripture, a great fact, and one which can never be got over.

I ask the reader, in the next place, to observe what the Thirteenth Article says. It tells us that "Works done before the grace of Christ and the inspiration of His Spirit are not pleasant to God," etc. Here we are plainly taught that works may be done by men *before* grace and the Spirit are given to them, and this too by baptized members of the Church, for it is for them that the Articles are drawn up! But how can this be reconciled with the notion that all baptized persons are necessarily regenerated? How can any person be regenerated without having the "grace of Christ and the inspiration of the Spirit"? There is only one view on which the Article can be reasonably explained. That view is the simple one, that many baptized people are not regenerate, have no grace and no indwelling of the Spirit, and that it is their case before they are born again and converted, which is here described.

The last Article I will ask the reader to observe is the Seventeenth. The subject of that Article is Predestination and Election. It is a subject which many people dislike exceedingly, and are ready to stop their ears whenever it is mentioned. I acknowledge freely that it is a deep subject. But there stands the Article! It cannot be denied that it forms part of our Church's Confession of faith. Whether men like it or not, they must not talk as if it did not exist, in discussing the subject of the Church's doctrines. The Article begins with laying down the great truth that God "hath constantly decreed by His counsel secret to us, to deliver from curse and damnation those whom He hath chosen in Christ out of mankind, and to bring them by Christ to everlasting salvation." It then proceeds to describe the calling of these persons by God's Spirit, and the consequences of that calling;—"They through grace obey the calling: they be justified freely: *they be made sons of God by adoption:* they be made like the image of His only-begotten Son, Jesus Christ; they walk religiously in good works, and at length by God's mercy they attain to everlasting felicity." Now all I ask the reader to consider is this, did the writers of the Articles mean to say that these persons were a separate and distinct class from those who were "regenerated," or not? We must think so, if we consider baptism is always accompanied by Regeneration. The things spoken of in this description are things of which multitudes of baptized persons know nothing at all. I do not, however, believe that such an idea ever entered into the minds of those who wrote the Articles. I believe that they looked on Election, Justification, Adoption, and Regeneration, as the peculiar privileges of a certain number, but not of all members of the visible Church; and that just as all baptized people are not elect, justified, and sanctified, so also all baptized people are not regenerated. Very striking is the difference between the language of the Article which treats of baptism, and the Article which treats of election. In the former we find the cautious general statement, that in baptism "the promises of our adoption to be the sons of God *are visibly signed and sealed.*" In the latter we find the broad assertion that the elect *"be made the sons of God* by adoption."

Such is the doctrine of the Articles. If Regeneration be what the Catechism describes it, "a death unto sin and a new birth unto righteousness," I cannot find the slightest ground in the Articles for the notion that all baptized persons are necessarily regenerate. There is an absence of any direct assertion of such a doctrine. There are several passages which appear completely inconsistent with it. I cannot suppose that the Articles and Liturgy were meant to be contrary one to the other. The men who drew up the Thirty-nine Articles in 1562, were the men who compiled the Prayer-book in 1549. They drew up the Articles with a certain and distinct knowledge of the contents of the Prayer-book. Yet the interpretation of the Baptismal Service I am contending against would make the one formulary contradictory to the other. The conclusion I come to is clear and decided,—such an interpretation cannot be correct.

IV. My last answer to those who say that all baptized persons are necessarily regenerated, because of the wording of the Baptismal Service, is this,—*such a doctrine would make the Prayer-book disagree with the Homilies of the Church of England.*

The Homilies are not liked by some persons any more than the

Thirty-nine Articles. No doubt they are human compositions, and therefore not perfect; no doubt they contain words and expressions here and there which might be amended; but, after all, the members of the Church of England are bound to recollect that the Thirty-fifth Article expressly asserts that the Homilies contain "a godly and wholesome doctrine." Whatever their deficiencies may be, the general tone of *their doctrine* is clear and unmistakable. And any interpretation of the Prayer-book Services which makes those Services inconsistent with the Homilies must, on the very face of it, be an incorrect interpretation.

Let me then call the reader's attention to the following passages in the Homilies:—

In the Homily of Charity there are the following passages: "What thing can we wish so good for us as the heavenly Father to reckon and take us for *His children?* And this shall we be sure of, saith Christ, if we love every man without exception. And if we do otherwise, saith He, we be no better than the Pharisees, publicans, and heathens, and shall have our reward with them, that is to be shut out from the number of God's chosen children, and from His everlasting inheritance in heaven."—And again: "He that beareth a good heart and mind, and useth well his tongue and deeds unto every man, friend or foe, he may know thereby that he hath charity. And then he is sure also that Almighty God taketh him for *His dearly-beloved son;* as Saint John saith, hereby manifestly are known the children of God from the children of the devil; for whosoever doth not love his brother belongeth not unto God."

In the Homily of Almsdeeds there is this passage: "God of His mercy and special favour towards them whom He hath appointed to everlasting salvation, hath so offered His grace especially, and they have so received it faithfully, that, although by reason of their sinful living outwardly they seemed before to have been the children of wrath and perdition,— yet now, the Spirit of God working mightily in them, unto obedience to God's will and commandments, they declare by their outward deeds and life, in the showing of mercy and charity—which cannot come but of the Spirit of God and His especial grace—that they are *the undoubted children of God*, appointed to everlasting life. And so, as by their wickedness and ungodly living they showed themselves, according to the judgment of men, which follow the outward appearance, to be reprobates and castaways, so now by their obedience unto God's holy will, and by their mercifulness and tender pity,—wherein they show themselves to be like unto God, who is the Fountain and Spring of all mercy, they declare openly and manifestly unto the sight of men that they are *the sons of God*, and elect of Him unto salvation."

In the Homily for Whit-Sunday, I read the following passages: "It is the Holy Ghost, and no other thing, that doth quicken the minds of men, stirring up good and godly motions in their hearts, which are agreeable to the will and commandment of God, such as otherwise of their own crooked and perverse nature they should never have. That which is born of the flesh, saith Christ, is flesh, and that which is born of the Spirit is spirit. As who should say, man of his own nature is fleshly and carnal, corrupt and naught, sinful and disobedient to God, without any spark of goodness in him, without any virtuous or godly notion, only given to evil thoughts and wicked deeds. As for the works of the Spirit, the fruits of faith, charitable and godly motions,—if he have any at all in him,—they proceed only of the Holy Ghost, who is the only worker of our sanctification, and maketh us new men in Christ Jesus. Did not God's Holy Spirit work in the child David, when from a poor shepherd he became a princely prophet? Did not God's Holy Spirit miraculously work in Matthew, sitting at the receipt of custom, when of a proud publican he became a humble and lowly evangelist? And who can choose but marvel to consider that Peter should become, of a simple fisher, a chief and mighty Apostle? Paul of a cruel and bloody persecutor, to teach the Gentiles? Such is the power of the Holy Ghost to *regenerate* men, and, as it were, to bring them forth anew, so that they shall be *nothing like the men that they were before.* Neither doth He think it sufficient inwardly to work the spiritual and new birth of man unless He do also dwell and abide in him.—Oh, what comfort is this to the heart of a true Christian, to think that the Holy Ghost dwelleth within him!"

And then comes the following passage, which I request the reader specially to observe: "How shall I know that the Holy Ghost is within me? some men perchance will say: Forsooth, as the tree is known by his fruit, so is also the Holy Ghost. The fruits of the Holy Ghost, according to the mind of St. Paul, are these: love, joy, peace, long-suffering, gentleness, goodness, faithfulness, meekness, temperance, etc. Contrariwise the deeds of the flesh are these: adultery, fornication, uncleanness, wantonness, idolatry, witchcraft, hatred, debate, emulation, wrath, contention, sedition, heresy, envy, murder, drunkenness, gluttony, and such like. Here is now that glass wherein thou must behold thyself, and discern whether thou have the Holy Ghost within thee or the spirit of the flesh. If thou see that thy works be virtuous and good, consonant to the prescribed rule of God's Word, savouring and tasting not of the flesh, but of the Spirit, *then* assure thyself that thou art endued with the Holy Ghost; *otherwise*, in thinking well of thyself, thou dost nothing but deceive thyself."—Once more: "To conclude and make an end, ye shall briefly take this short lesson: wheresoever ye find the spirit of arrogance and pride, the spirit of envy, hatred, contention, cruelty, murder, extortion, witchcraft, necromancy, etc., assure yourselves that there is the spirit of the devil, and not of God, albeit they pretend outwardly to the world never so much holiness. For as the Gospel teacheth us, the Spirit of

Jesus is a good spirit, an holy spirit, a sweet spirit, a lowly spirit, a merciful spirit, full of charity and love, full of forgiveness and pity, not rendering evil for evil, extremity for extremity, but overcoming evil with good, and remitting all offence even from the heart. According to which rule, if any man live uprightly, of him it may safely be pronounced that he hath the Holy Ghost within him: *if not, then it is a plain token that he doth usurp the name of the Holy Ghost in vain.*"

I lay these passages before the reader in their naked simplicity. I will not weary him with long comments upon them. In fact none are needed. Two things, I think, are abundantly evident. One is, that in the judgment of the Homilies, no men are the "undoubted children of God" and "sons of God," and elect unto salvation, unless it is proved by their charity and good works. The other is, that no man has the Holy Ghost within him, in the judgment of the Homilies, except he brings forth the fruits of the Spirit in his life. But all this is flatly contradictory to the doctrine of those who say that all baptized persons are necessarily re-generate. They tell us that all people are made the children of God by virtue of their baptism, whatever be their manner of living, and must be addressed as such all their lives;—and that all people have the grace of the Holy Ghost within them by virtue of their baptism, and must be considered "regenerate," whatever fruits they may be bringing forth in their daily habits and conversation. According to this, the Homilies say one thing and the Prayer-book says another! I leave the reader to judge whether it is in the least degree probable this can be the case. These Homilies were put forth by authority, in the year 1562, and appointed to be read in churches in order to supply the deficiency of good preaching, and when they had been once read, they were to be "repeated and read again." And yet according to the interpretation of the Baptismal Service I am contending against, these Homilies contradict the Prayer-book! Surely it is difficult to avoid the conclusion which I most unhesitatingly come to myself, that a system of interpreting the Baptismal Service which sets the Prayer-book at variance with the Homilies, as well as with the Articles, must be incorrect.

I leave the subject of the Church of England's views about Regeneration here. I wish I could have spoken of it more shortly. But I have been anxious to meet the objections drawn from the Baptismal Service fully, openly, and face to face. I have not a doubt in my own mind as to the true doctrine of the Church in the question. But many, I know, have been troubled and perplexed about it, and few appear to me to see the matter as clearly as they might. And it is to supply such persons with information, as well as to meet the arguments of adversaries, that I have gone into the question so fully as I have.

Other points might easily be dwelt upon, which would serve to throw even more light on the subject, and seem still further to bear out the views that I maintain, as to the real doctrine of the Church of England about Regeneration.

Is it not notorious, for instance, that the Article about baptism in our Confession of faith was entirely altered, and brought into its present form, when Edward the Sixth came to the throne? Our Reformers found an Article drawn up in 1536, in which the doctrine of grace always accompanying the baptism of infants was plainly and unmistakably asserted. The Articles of 1536 say, "By the sacrament of baptism, infants, innocents, and children, do also obtain remission of their sins, the grace and favour of God, and be made thereby the very sons and children of God." The Reformers of our Church, in drawing up the Articles of 1552, entirely abstained from making any such assertion. They framed our present Article on baptism, in which no such unqualified statement can be found. Now, why did they do so? Why did they not adopt the language of the old Article, if they really believed its doctrine? Let any one answer these questions.—Did it not plainly mean that they did not approve of the doctrine of the invariable Regeneration of infants in baptism?

Again, is it not notorious that the Irish Articles of 1615 have never been repealed or disannulled by the Church of Ireland? Subscription to these Articles is undoubtedly not required at Irish ordinations. Subscription to the Thirty-nine Articles only is held sufficient. But it was distinctly understood, when the Thirty-nine Articles were received by the Irish Church, in 1634, that their reception did not imply any slur on the Irish Articles, and only testified the agreement of the Church of Ireland with that of England, both in doctrine and discipline. Now these Irish Articles most plainly declare that the "regenerate" are the elect, the justified, the believers, the true Christians, who persevere unto the end; and no less plainly imply that those who are not true believers are not "regenerate!" There can be no mistake about this. No man, I think, can read these Articles and not see it. And yet there is the closest union between the Church of England and the Church of Ireland, and always has been. How could this be, if the Church of Ireland's views about the "regenerate" had always been considered false and heretical? Why were the Irish Articles not rejected as unsound, when, for uniformity's sake, the Irish Articles were received? How was it, that for many years after 1634, the Irish Bishops always required subscription to both Irish and English Articles at their ordinations? Let these questions also be answered. Did it not show plainly that the two Churches were not thought to be at variance upon the subject of Regeneration?*

* It was Archbishop Usher himself who proposed, in 1634, that the English Articles should be received by the Irish Church. Yet he was the principal author of the Irish Articles of 1615. His biographer says, "He very well understood the Articles of both Churches, and did then know that they were so far from being inconsistent or contradictory to each other, that he thought the Irish

Again, is it not notorious that almost all the Bishops and leading
divines who took part in the Reformation of our Church, were men
who held opinions which, rightly or wrongly, are called Calvinistic, and
in the main were thoroughly agreed with those clergy who are termed
Evangelical in the present day? There is no room for doubt on this
point. It has been allowed by many who do not approve of Evangelical
opinions themselves. They were in frequent communication with the
leading Swiss Reformers. They procured the help of men like Peter
Martyr and Bucer to assist them in carrying on the work of Reformation.
And yet we are asked to believe that our Reformers deliberately framed
a Baptismal Service containing a doctrine which is inconsistent with their
own views! Is it likely, is it reasonable, is it agreeable to common sense,
to suppose they would do such a thing? And is it not an acknowledged
axiom in interpreting all public documents, such as oaths, articles of
faith, and religious formularies, that they are always to be interpreted
in the sense of those who drew them up and imposed them?*

But I leave all these points, and hasten to a conclusion.

It only remains for me now to wind up all I have said with a few words
of solemn appeal to every one into whose hands this paper may happen
to fall.

I say "solemn appeal," and I say it advisedly. I feel strongly the
immense importance of sound and Scriptural views of the whole question
I have been considering. I feel it especially as respects that part of it
which touches the doctrine of the Church of England. Men sometimes
say it makes no difference whether we think all baptized persons are
regenerate or not. They tell us it all comes to the same thing in the long
run. I cannot say so. To my humble apprehension it seems to make an
immense difference. If I tell a man that he has grace in his heart, and
only needs to "stir up a gift," already within him, it is one thing. If I
tell him that he is dead in sins, and must be "born again," it is quite
another. The moral effect of the two messages must, on the very face of
it, be widely different. The one, I contend, is calculated by God's blessing
to awaken the sinner. The other, I contend, is calculated to lull him to
sleep. The one, I maintain, is likely to feed sloth, check self-examination,
and encourage an easy self-satisfied state of soul: he has got some grace
within him whenever he likes to use it,—why should he be in a hurry,
why be afraid?—The other, I maintain, is likely to rouse convictions,

Articles did only contain the doctrine of the Church of England more fully."—
Life of Archbishop Usher, by Dr. Parr, his chaplain. 1686.

* "It is a settled rule with casuists, that oaths are always to be taken in the
sense of the imposers; the same is the case of solemn leagues or covenants.
Without this principle, no faith, trust, or mutual confidence could be kept up
amongst men."—*Waterland on the Arian Subscriptions. Works,* vol. ii., chap. iii.
There is a passage in Bishop Sanderson's Prelections, on the Obligation of
an Oath, to the same effect.

drive him to self-inquiry, and frighten him out of his dangerous security: he has nothing within him to rest upon,—he must find a refuge and remedy, he is lost and perishing,—what must he do to be saved?—The one message, I affirm, is likely to keep men natural men, the other to make them spiritual men,—the one to have no effect upon the conscience, the other to lead to Christ. Let men say what they will, I, for one, dare not say I think it all comes to the same thing.

I see fresh reason continually for dreading the doctrine that all baptized persons are regenerate. I hear of laymen who once did run well, losing their first love, and appearing to make shipwreck of their faith. I hear of ministers, who once bade fair to be pillars in the Church, stumbling at this stumbling-stone, and marring all their usefulness. I see the doctrine leavening and spoiling the religion of many private Christians, and insensibly paving the way for a long train of unscriptural notions. I see it interfering with every leading doctrine of the Gospel;—it encourages men to believe that election, adoption, justification, and the indwelling of the Spirit, are all conferred on them in baptism;—and then, to avoid the difficulties which such a system entails, the fulness of all these mighty truths is pared down, mutilated, and explained away; or else the minds of congregations are bewildered with contradictory and inconsistent statements. I see it ultimately producing in some minds a mere *sacramental Christianity*,—a Christianity in which there is much said about union with Christ, but it is a union begun only by baptism, and kept up only by the Lord's Supper,—a Christianity in which the leading doctrines that the Apostle Paul dwells on in almost all his Epistles, have nothing but a subordinate position,—a Christianity in which Christ has not His rightful office, and faith has not its rightful place. I see all this, and mourn over it unfeignedly. I cannot think that the subject I am urging on the reader's attention is one of secondary importance. And once more I say, I cannot leave him without a solemn appeal to his conscience, whoever he may be, into whose hands this paper may fall.

(*a*) I appeal then to all men who love the Bible, and make it their standard of truth and error; and in saying this, I address myself especially to all members of the Church of England. I ask you to observe the manner of living of multitudes of baptized persons on every side of you,—I ask you to observe how their hearts are entirely set on this world, and buried in its concerns. And I then ask you, Are they born of God? If you say Yes, I answer, How can that be, when your Bible expressly says, "He that is born of God doeth righteousness, and doth not commit sin"? (1 John ii. 29; iii. 9.) Are they children of God? If you say Yes, I answer, How can that be, when the Bible says expressly, "In this the children of God are manifest and the children of the devil; whosoever doeth not righteousness is not of God"? (1 John iii. 10.) Are they sons of God? If you say Yes, I answer, How can that be, when the Bible says expressly,

"As many as are led by the Spirit of God, they are the sons of God"? (Rom. viii. 14.) What will you say to these things? Surely you will not turn your back upon the Bible.

(*b*) I appeal next to all who love the good old rule of the Bible, "Every tree is known by its own fruit." (Luke vi. 44.) I ask you to try the great bulk of professing Christians by the fruits they bring forth, and to say what kind of fruits they are. Is it not perfectly true that many baptized persons know little or nothing of the fruits of the Spirit,—and much, only too much, of the works of the flesh? Is it not certain that they are destitute of those marks of being born of God which the Bible describes? What will you say to these things? Surely if you abide by your old principle you will hardly say that all baptized people have within them the Holy Spirit.

(*c*) I appeal next to all who love the Church Catechism, and profess to be guided by its statements about the sacraments. You are aware that the inward and spiritual grace of baptism is there said to be "a death unto sin and a new birth into righteousness." I ask you, as in the sight of God, to say whether any evidence whatever of this grace can be seen in the lives of many baptized persons. Where is their deadness to sin? They live in it. It is their element. Where is their new birth unto righteousness? They are habitual "servants of sin, and free from righteousness." (Rom. vi. 20.) Sin reigns and rules in their mortal bodies. They are enemies of all righteousness. What will you say to these things? Surely you will not tell us that the outward and visible sign is always attended by the inward and spiritual grace. If so, grace and no grace are the same thing!

(*d*) I appeal, lastly, to all who dread Antinomianism and licentious doctrine. You have heard of those wretched persons who profess to glory in Christ and free grace, and yet think it no shame to live immoral lives, and continue in wilful sin. You think such conduct horrible, an insult to the Lord Jesus, and a disgrace to Christianity. And you are right to think so. But what will you say to the doctrine, that a man may have the Holy Spirit, and yet not bring forth the fruits of the Spirit;—may have grace in his heart, and yet show no sign of it in his life? What will you say to these things? Surely, if you are consistent, you will recoil from the idea of dishonouring the Third Person of the blessed Trinity, no less than you do from dishonouring the Lord Himself. Surely you will shrink from saying that all baptized persons have the Holy Ghost.

Once for all, in concluding this paper, I protest against the charge that I am no true Churchman because I hold the opinions that I do. In the matter of true and real attachment to the Church of England, I will not give place by subjection to those who are called High Church-men, for one moment. Have they signed the Thirty-nine Articles *ex animo* and *bonâ fide*? So have I.—Have they declared their full assent to the

Liturgy and all things contained in it? So have I.—Have they promised obedience to the Bishops? So have I.—Do they think Episcopacy the best form of Church government? So do I.—Do they honour the sacraments? So do I.—Do they think them generally necessary to salvation? So do I.—Do they labour for the prosperity of the Church? So do I.—Do they urge on their congregations the privileges of the Church of England? So do I.—Do they deprecate all needless secession and separation from her ranks? So do I.—Do they oppose the enemies of the Church, both Romish and infidel? So do I.—Do they love the Prayer-book of the Church of England? So do I. I repudiate with indignation the unworthy imputation that I interpret any part of that Prayer-book in a dishonest or unnatural sense. I offer no opinion as to the wisdom and prudence of the Reformers in drawing up a Service in such a way as to admit of its language being misunderstood, as it unhappily is. But I believe with all my heart that the view I hold of the meaning of the Prayer-book is the view of the very men by whom it was compiled.

One thing I cannot see to be essential in order to prove myself a true Churchman. I cannot see that I ought to hold doctrines which make the Prayer-book clash and jar with the Articles and Homilies. I cannot see that I must hold that all baptized persons are necessarily and invariably born again. I protest against the system of making the baptismal register, and not our lives, the great evidence of our Regeneration. I recoil from the idea that a man may have grace, and yet nobody see it in his behaviour, —may have a new heart, and yet none discover it in his conduct,—may have the Holy Spirit, and yet no fruit of the Spirit appear in any of his ways. I consider that such a notion affects the honour of the Holy Ghost and the cause of true holiness, and I dare not allow it. I consider it throws confusion over the whole system of Christ's Gospel, and involves the necessity of calling things in religion by wrong names, and I dare not allow it. I think as highly of baptism as any one when rightly received. I count Churchmanship a high privilege; but I think Regeneration a higher privilege still, and one to which, unhappily, many Churchmen never attain.

I deny that I hold any new doctrine about Regeneration in saying this. I appeal to the Bible; I appeal to the Articles; I appeal to the Prayer-book; I appeal to the Homilies. In all of them, I say unhesitatingly, I see the doctrines I maintain. I appeal to the writings of all the principal Reformers of our Church; I appeal to the works of some of the best and worthiest Bishops who have ever adorned the Bench. I assert confidently that it has been preached in Church of England pulpits ever since the time of the Reformation,—in many at some periods, in some at all. There never has been wanting a succession of faithful men, who have constantly said to the mass of their congregation, "Ye must be born again." There never was an attempt to shut the door against a minister for preaching such doctrine before the case of Mr. Gorham.* In short, if I err, I feel that I err in good company. I err with Bishop Hooper and Bishop Latimer, those faithful martyrs of Christ. I err with Jewel, with Leighton, and Usher, and Hall, and Hopkins, and Carleton, and Davenant, and many others, of whom I have not time to speak particularly. And when I think of this, I am not disturbed by the charge that I do not agree with Archbishop Laud and the Non-jurors, or even with others of later date still.

We are all travelling to a place where controversies will be forgotten, and nothing but eternal realities remain. Would we have a real hope in that day? We must see to it that we have a real Regeneration. Nothing else will do. "Except a man be born again, he cannot see the kingdom of God." (John iii. 3.)

* In 1847 Bishop Philpotts of Exeter refused to institute an Evangelical, the Rev. G. C. Gorham, to the living of Brampford Speke on account of his doctrine of baptism. The case went eventually to the Privy Council, which decided that Gorham's doctrine (he refused to tie regeneration to the moment of baptism and stressed the need for a spiritual response) was in line with Church of England teaching.

The following quotations, bearing on the subject discussed in this paper, are drawn from writers, of whom some are the greatest and most learned divines the world has ever seen. They are specially commended to the attention of members of the Church of England.

"In baptism those that come feignedly, and those that come unfeignedly, both be washed with the sacramental water, but both be not washed with the Holy Ghost, and clothed with Christ."
"All that be washed with water be not washed with the Holy Spirit."—*Archbishop Cranmer. 1553.*

"Good and evil, clean and unclean, holy and profane, must needs pass by the sacrament of baptism, except you will indeed in more ample and large measure tie the grace of God unto it than ever did the Papists, and say all that be baptized be also saved."—*Archbishop Whitgift. 1583.*

"Are all they that are partakers of the outward washing of baptism, partakers also of the inward washing of the Spirit? Doth this sacrament seal up their spiritual ingrafting into Christ to all who externally receive it. Surely no! Though God hath ordained these outward means for the conveyance of grace to our souls, yet there is no necessity that we should tie the working of God's Spirit to the sacraments more than to the Word."—*Archbishop Usher. 1624.*

"In baptism, as the one part of that holy mystery is Christ's blood, so is the other part the material water. Neither are these parts joined together in place, but in mystery; and therefore they be oftentimes severed, and the one is received without the other."—*Bishop Jewel. 1559.*

"Christ said, 'Except a man be born again from above, he cannot see the kingdom of God.' Ye must have a Regeneration: and what is this Regeneration? It is not to be christened in water as these fire-brands (the Roman Catholics) expound it, and nothing else."—*Bishop Latimer. 1540.*

"All receive not the grace of God which receive the sacraments of His grace."—*Richard Hooker. 1597.*

"Not all are regenerated who are washed with the baptismal water."—*Dr. Whittaker, Regius Professor of Divinity at Cambridge. 1590.*

"Grace sometimes precedes the sacrament, sometimes follows it, and sometimes does not even follow it."—*Theodoret. 450 A.D.*

"All did drink the same spiritual drink, but not with all was God well pleased, and when the sacraments were all common, the grace was not common to all, which constitutes the virtue of the sacraments. So also now, when faith is revealed which was then veiled, the laver of Regeneration is common to all who are baptized in the name of the Father, and of the Son, and of the Holy Ghost; but the grace itself of which they are sacraments, and by which the members of the body of Christ are regenerated with their Head, is not common to all."—*Augustine on the 77th Psalm.* 390 A.D.

"Outward baptism may be administered, where inward conversion of the heart is wanting; and, on the other hand, inward conversion of the heart may exist, where outward baptism has never been received."—*Augustine's Treatise on Baptism.* 390 A.D.

"Some have the outward sign, and not the inward grace. Some have the inward grace, and not the outward sign. We must not commit idolatry by deifying the outward element."—*Archbishop Usher.* 1624.

"We must not glory because we are made partakers of the external sacrament, unless we obtain besides the internal and quickening work of Christ. For if this be wanting, as was said heretofore to Jews, 'O ye uncircumcised in heart,' so it may be justly said to us, 'O ye unbaptized in heart.' "—*Bishop Davenant.* 1627.

"If outward baptism were a cause in itself possessed of that power, either natural or supernatural, without the present operation whereof no such effect could possibly grow, it must then follow that, seeing effects do never precede the necessary causes out of which they spring, no man could ever receive grace before baptism, which is apparently both known and confessed to be otherwise in many particulars."—*Richard Hooker.* 1597.

"The sacrament hath no grace included in it; but to those that receive it well it is turned to grace. After that manner the water in baptism hath grace promised, and by that grace the Holy Spirit is given; not that grace is included in water, but that grace cometh by water."—*Bishop Ridley.* 1547.

"What is so common as water?—what is so common as bread and wine? Yet Christ promiseth it to be found there, when He is sought with a faithful heart."—*Bishop Latimer.* 1540.

"That baptism hath a power, is clear, in that it is so expressly said, 'it doth save us.' What kind of power is equally clear from the way it is here expressed;—not by a natural power of the element;—though adapted and sacramentally used, it only can wash away the filth of the body;—its physical efficacy or power reached no further; but it is in the hand of the Spirit of God as other sacraments are, and as the Word itself is, to purify the conscience, and convey grace and salvation to the soul, by the reference it hath to, and union with that which it represents. Sacraments are neither empty signs to them who believe, nor effectual causes of grace to them that believe not. Sacraments do not save all who partake of them, yet they do really and effectually save believers, for whose salvation they are means, as the other external ordinances of God do. Though they have not that grace which is peculiar to the author of them, yet a power they have such as befits their nature, and by reason of which they are truly said to sanctify and justify, and so to save, as the Apostle here avers of baptism."—*Archbishop Leighton.* 1680.

"Is Christ and the cleansing power of His blood only barely signified in the sacrament of baptism? Nay, more. The inward things are really exhibited to the believer as well as the outward. There is that sacramental union between them that the one is conveyed and sealed up by the other. Hence are those phrases of being 'born again of water and the Holy Ghost,' etc., etc. The sacraments being rightly received do effect that which they do represent."—*Archbishop Usher.* 1624.

"What is the advantage or benefit of baptism to the common Christian? The same as was the benefit of circumcision to the Jew, outward. (Rom. ii. 28.) There is a general grace of baptism which all the baptized partake of as a common favour; and that is their admission into the visible body of the Church; their matriculation and outward incorporation into the number of the worshippers of God by external communion. And so as circumcision was not only a seal of the righteousness which is by faith, but as an overplus, God appointed it to be a wall of separation between Jew and Gentile: so is baptism a badge of an outward member of the Church, a distinction from the common sort of the brethren. And God thereby seals a right upon the party baptized to His ordinances, that He may use them as His privileges, and wait for an inward blessing by them. Yet this is but the porch, the shell, and outside. All that are outwardly received into the visible Church, are not spiritually ingrafted into the mystical body of Christ. Baptism is attended upon always by that general grace, but not always by that special."—*Archbishop Usher.* 1624.

"Let us learn not to confide with Papists in the *opus operatum*, but inquire whether we possess all the other things, without which the inward effects of baptism are not secured."—*Bishop Davenant.* 1627.

"Many ignorant people among us, for want of better teaching, harbour in their minds such Popish conceits, especially that baptism doth confer grace upon all by the work done, for they commonly look no higher: and they conceive a kind of inherent virtue and Christendom, as they call it, necessarily infused into children, by having the water cast upon their faces."—*Archbishop Usher.* 1624.

"It is a pitiful thing to see the ignorance of the most professing Christianity, and partaking of the outward seals of it, yet not knowing what they mean; not appreciating the spiritual dignity and virtue of them. A confused fancy they have of some good in them, and this rising to the other extreme to a superstitious confidence in this simple performance and participation of them, as if that carried some inseparable virtue with it, which none could miss of who are sprinkled with the water of baptism and share in the element of bread and wine in the Lord's Supper."—*Archbishop Leighton.* 1680.

"Wicked is that Popish doctrine, that original sin is forgiven by baptism; and for all actual offences after baptism, partly by Christ's blood, and partly by our own satisfaction, we attain and get pardon of them."—*Bishop Babington, Bishop of Exeter.* 1594.

"Let us consider how corruptly the Church of Rome teacheth us touching this sacrament (baptism), and how horribly they have abused it. First, they teach that baptism doth confer grace and wash away our sins *ex opere operto*; that is, even by the very washing only of the water, though there be no good motion of faith or belief in the heart of him that is baptized."—*Bishop Cooper.* 1570.

"The Papists maintain that grace is conferred upon little children in the sacrament of the New Testament, without faith or any good motive. This is to attribute a power to sacraments of themselves, and by a virtue of their own, in the case of little children: which we say is false. For we assert that grace is not conferred by the sacraments even upon little children from the work wrought, so that all necessarily have grace that receive the sacraments."—*Dr. Whittaker.* 1580.

"If there be that cure that they speak of in the baptized, how is it that there is so little effect or token thereof? How is it that after baptism there remaineth so great crookedness and perverseness of nature, which we find to be no less than men from the beginning have complained of? How is it that it is so rare and hard a matter to be trained to goodness, and so easy and ready a matter to become nought?"—*Bishop Robert Abbot.* 1615.

"From those who are baptized in infancy subsequent faith is required; which if they exhibit not afterward, they retain only the outward sanctification of baptism, the inward effect of sanctification they have not."—*Bishop Davenant.* 1627.

"The true way of judging whether the Spirit of God be in us, is to consider our own deeds. Righteousness and holiness are the only certain marks of regeneration."—*Bishop Sherlock.* 1740.

"As for those who are visibly reclaimed from a notorious wicked course, in them we likewise frequently see this change gradually made by strong impressions made upon their minds, most frequently by the Word of God, sometimes by His providence,—till at length, by the grace of God, they come to a fixed purpose and resolution of forsaking their sins and turning to God; and after many strugglings and conflicts with their lusts, and the strong bias of their evil habits, this resolution, assisted by the grace of God, doth effectually prevail, and make a real change both in the temper of their minds, and course of their lives; and when this is done, and not before, they are said to be regenerate."—*Archbishop Tillotson.* 1691.

"The only certain proof of Regeneration is victory."—*Bishop Wilson.* 1697.

VIII

THE LORD'S SUPPER

THE sacrament of the Lord's Supper is a point in the Christian religion which requires very careful handling. I approach it with reverence, fear, and trembling. I cannot forget that I tread on very delicate ground. There is much connected with the subject which is alike painful, humbling, and difficult.

It is *painful* to think that an ordinance appointed by Christ for our benefit should have been defiled by the din and smoke of theological controversy. It is undeniable that no ordinance has called forth so much passion and strife, and has become such a bone of contention among polemical divines. Such is the corruption of fallen man that the thing which was "ordained for our peace" has become "an occasion of falling."

It is *humbling* to remember that men of opposite opinions have written folios about the Lord's Supper without producing the slightest effect on the minds of their adversaries. Cart-loads of books about it have been published during the last three centuries, and poured into the open gulf between the disputants in vain. Like the "Slough of Despond" in *Pilgrim's Progress*, it is a yawning gulf still. I ask no stronger proof that the fall of Adam has affected the understanding as well as the will of man, than the present divided state of Christendom about the Lord's Supper.

It is *difficult* to know how to handle such a subject without exhausting the patience of readers. It is difficult to know what to say, and what to leave unsaid. The field has been so thoroughly exhausted by the labours of many masters in Israel, that it is literally impossible to bring forward anything that is new. The utmost that I can hope to attain is the condensation of old arguments. If I can only bring together a few ancient things, and present them to my readers in a portable and compact form, I shall be content.

In the present paper I shall content myself with two points, and two only.

I.   *I will show the original intention of the Lord's Supper.*

II. *I will show the position which the Lord's Supper was meant to occupy.*

One thing, at any rate, is very clear to my mind: it is impossible to overrate the importance of the subject. I own to a strong and growing conviction that error about the Lord's Supper is one of the commonest and most dangerous errors of the present day. I suspect we have little idea of the extent to which unsound views of this sacrament prevail, both among clergy and laity. They are the hidden root of nine-tenths of the extravagant Ritualism which, like a fog, is overspreading our Church. Here, if anywhere, all Christian ministers have need to be very jealous for the Lord God of hosts. Our witness must be clear, distinct, and un-mistakable. Our trumpets must give no uncertain sound. The Philistines are upon us. The ark of God is in danger. If we love the truth as it is in Jesus, if we love the Church of England, we must contend earnestly for the faith once delivered to the saints in the matter of the Lord's Supper.

I.   In the first place, *what was the original intention of the Lord's Supper?*

This question can never receive a better general answer than that of our well-known Church Catechism. Wanting in simplicity, as that famous formulary certainly is, and sadly too full of hard words and scholastic metaphysical terms, it is worthy of all honour for its statements about the sacraments. Our Sunday-school teachers may fail to understand the Catechism, and complain justly that it needs another Catechism to explain it. But, after all, there is a logical preciseness and theological accuracy about its definitions, which every well-read divine must acknowledge and appreciate. Rightly used, I hold the Church Catechism to be a most powerful weapon against semi-Romanism. Fairly interpreted, it is utterly subversive of the "Ritualistic" system.

The very first question of the Catechism about the Lord's Supper is as follows: "Why was the sacrament of the Lord's Supper ordained?" The answer supplied is this: "For the continual remembrance of the sacrifice of the death of Christ, and of the benefits which we receive thereby." This is sound speech that cannot be condemned. Founded on plain language of Holy Scripture, it contains the truth, the whole truth, and nothing but the truth. (Luke xxii. 19; 1 Cor. xi. 24.)

The Lord Jesus Christ intended the Lord's Supper to be continual *remembrance** to the Church of His atoning death on the Cross. The bread, broken, given, and eaten, was intended to remind Christians of

* The doctrine of the Communion Service, let me remind the reader, is in precise harmony with that of the Catechism. Let us mark the following expressions:—
"To the end that we should always *remember* the exceeding great love of our Master and only Saviour Jesus Christ, thus dying for us, and the innumerable benefits which by His blood-shedding He hath obtained to us: He hath instituted and ordained holy mysteries as pledges of His love, and for a continual *remembrance* of His death, to our great and endless comfort."—"He did institute, and in His holy Gospel command us to continue, a perpetual *memory* of that His precious death until His coming again."—"Take and eat this in *remembrance* that Christ died for thee."—"Drink this in *remembrance* that Christ's blood was shed for thee."

His body given for our sins. The wine, poured out and drunk, was intended to remind Christians of His blood shed for our sins.

The Lord Jesus knew what was in man. He knew full well the darkness, slowness, coldness, hardness, stupidity, pride, self-conceit, self-righteousness, slothfulness, of human nature in spiritual things. Therefore He took care that His death for sinners should not merely be written in the Bible,—for then it might have been locked up in libraries;—or left to the ministry to proclaim in the pulpit,—for then it might soon have been kept back by false teachers;—but that it should be exhibited in visible signs and emblems, even in bread and wine at a special ordinance. The Lord's Supper was a standing provision against man's forgetfulness. So long as the world stands in its present order, the thing which is done at the Lord's Table shows forth the Lord's death till He comes. (1 Cor. xi. 26.)

The Lord Jesus Christ knew full well the unspeakable importance of His own death for sin as the great corner-stone of Scriptural religion. He knew that His own satisfaction for sin as our Substitute,—His suffering for sin, the Just for the unjust,—His payment of our mighty debt in His own Person,—His complete redemption of us by His blood,—He knew that this was the very root of soul-saving and soul-satisfying Christianity. Without this He knew His incarnation, miracles, teaching, example, and ascension could do no good to man; without this He knew there could be no justification, no reconciliation, no hope, no peace between God and man. Knowing all this, He took care that *His death*, at anyrate, should never be forgotten. He carefully appointed an ordinance, in which, by lively figures, His sacrifice on the Cross should be kept in perpetual remembrance.

The Lord Jesus Christ well knew the weakness and infirmity even of the holiest believers. He knew the absolute necessity of keeping them in intimate communion with His own vicarious sacrifice, as the Fountain of their inward and spiritual life. Therefore, He did not merely leave them promises on which their memories might feed, and words which they might call to mind, He mercifully provided an ordinance in which true faith might be quickened by seeing lively emblems of His body and blood, and in the use of which believers might be strengthened and refreshed. The strengthening of the faith of God's elect in Christ's atonement was one great purpose of the Lord's Supper.

I turn from the positive to the negative side of the subject with real pain and reluctance. But it is plain duty to do so. Ministers, like physicians, must study disease as well as health, and exhibit error as well as truth. Let me then try to show what are not the intentions of the Lord's Supper.

(1) It was never meant to be regarded as a *sacrifice*. We were not intended to believe that there is any change in the elements of bread and wine, or any corporal presence of Christ in the sacrament. These things can never be honestly and fairly got out of Scripture. Let the three accounts

of the institution, in the Gospels of Matthew, Mark, and Luke, and the one given by St. Paul to the Corinthians, be weighed and examined impartially, and I have no doubt as to the result. They teach that there is no sacrifice, no altar, no change in the substance of the elements: that the bread after consecration is still literally and truly bread,—and the wine after consecration is literally and truly wine. In no part of the New Testament do we find the Christian minister called a priest; and in no part do we find any mention of a sacrifice, except that of prayer, and praise, and good works. The last literal sacrifice, we are repeatedly told in the Epistle to the Hebrews, is the once for all finished sacrifice of Christ on the Cross.

No doubt it may satisfy Roman controversialists to adduce such texts as "This is My body," and "This is My blood," as proofs that the Lord's Supper is a sacrifice. But a man must be easily satisfied if such texts content him. The quotation of a single isolated phrase is a mode of arguing that would establish Arianism or Socinianism. The context of these famous expressions shows clearly that those who heard the words used, understood them to mean, "This *represents* My body," and "This *represents* My blood." The analogy of other places proves that "is" and "are" frequently mean "represent" in Scripture. St. Paul, in writing on the sacrament, expressly calls the consecrated bread, "bread," and not the body of Christ, no less than three times. (1 Cor. xi. 26, 27, 28.) Above all, there remains the unanswerable argument, that if our Lord was actually holding His own body in His hands, when He said of the bread, "This is My body," His body must have been a different body to that of ordinary men. Of course if His body was not a body like ours, His real and proper humanity is at an end. At this rate the blessed and comfortable doctrine of Christ's entire sympathy with His people, as very man, would be completely overthrown, and fall to the ground.*

Again, it may please some to regard the sixth chapter of St. John, where our Lord speaks of "eating His flesh and drinking His blood," as a proof that there is a literal bodily presence of Christ in the bread and wine at the Lord's Supper. But there is an utter absence of conclusive proof that this chapter refers to the Lord's Supper at all. The man who maintains that it does refer to the Lord's Supper, will find himself involved in very awkward consequences. He sentences to everlasting death all who do not receive the Lord's Supper. He raises to everlasting life all who do receive it. Enough to say that the great majority of Protestant commentators altogether deny that the chapter refers to the Lord's Supper, and that even some Romish commentators on this point agree with them.†

* That our Lord's body was not a real body like our own, was the favourite doctrine of the ancient heretics called "Apollinarians," in the early Church.
† On this point I venture to refer my readers to my own *Expository Thoughts on St. John's Gospel*, where they will find a condensed summary of opinions, in my notes on the sixth chapter.

(2) I pass on to another negative view of the subject. The Lord's Supper was never meant to confer benefit on communicants *ex opere operato*, or by virtue of a mere formal reception of the ordinance.* We were not intended to believe that it does good to any but those who receive it with faith and knowledge. It is not a medicine or a charm which works mechanically, irrespectively of the state of mind in which it is received. It cannot of itself confer grace, where grace does not already exist. It does not convert, justify, or convey blessings to the heart of an unbeliever. It is an ordinance not for the dead but for the living,—not for the faithless but for the believing,—not for the unconverted but the converted,—not for the impenitent sinner but for the saint. I am almost ashamed to take up time with such trite and well-known statements as these. The Word of God testifies distinctly that a man may go to the Lord's Table, and "eat and drink unworthily,"—may "eat and drink damnation to himself." (1 Cor. xi. 27, 29.) To such testimony I shall not add a word.

(3) I will only mention one more point on the negative side of the subject. The Lord's Supper was *not meant to be a mere social feast*, indicating the love that should exist among believers. We were never intended to regard it in this cold and tame light. The notion of the author of *Ecce Homo*, that "the Christian communion is a club dinner," is not only a degrading one, but one that cannot be reconciled with the language of its Founder at the time of institution. "Feeding on the character of Christ" (I quote this notorious book) is an idea which may satisfy a Socinian, or any one who rejects the doctrine of the atonement. But the true Christian who feeds especially on the vicarious death of Christ, and not His character, will see that death prominently exhibited in the Lord's Supper, and find his faith in that death quickened by the use of it. It was meant to carry his mind back to the sacrifice once made on Calvary, and not merely to the incarnation; and no lower view will ever satisfy a true Christian's heart.

I have now stated the ground that I believe we are meant to take up about the sacrament of the Lord's Supper. Negatively, it was not intended to be a mere social meeting,—nor yet a sacrifice,—nor yet an ordinance conferring grace *ex opere operato*. Positively, it was intended to be a "continual remembrance of the sacrifice of Christ's death," and a strengthener and refresher of true believers. This ground may seem to some very simple, so simple that it is below the truth. Be it so: I am not ashamed of it. Whether men will hear, or whether they will forbear, I am convinced that this is the only view that is in harmony with Scripture and the formularies of the Church of England.

I grant most freely that a large and increasing school within our own Church entirely disagree with the view I have given of the Lord's Supper.

* These three Latin words, be it remembered, mean simply, "out of," or "by means of, the work done."

Hundreds of clergy, both in high places and low, consider that there is
not only a real presence of Christ in the Lord's Supper, which I hold as
strongly as they do, but that there is also a real presence of Christ in
the elements of bread and wine after consecration,* which I entirely
deny.

Let us hear how Archdeacon Denison,† no mean authority, states
this view. He says, "Christ's body and blood are really present in the
holy Eucharist, under the form of bread and wine, *i.e.* present things,—
though they be present after a manner ineffable, incomprehensible by
man, and not cognizable by the senses. The real presence of Christ in
the Eucharist is therefore not, as I believe it is very generally supposed
to be, the presence of an influence emanating from a thing absent, but
the invisible and supernatural presence of a thing present; of His body
and His blood present under the forms of bread and wine." ‡ (Sermon II.,
p. 80.) Let us hear him again. "Worship is due to the real, though
invisible and supernatural, presence of the body and blood of Christ in
the holy Eucharist, under the forms of bread and wine." (Sermon II, p. 81.)
Let us hear him again. "The act of consecration makes the real presence.
Oh, priests of the Church of God! to us it is given to be the channels
and agents, whereby the Holy Ghost doth there make the body and blood
of Christ to be really, though invisibly and supernaturally, present, under
the form of bread and wine in the Lord's Supper; to us it is given to
give His body and His blood unto His people. Oh, priests and people of
the Church of God! to us it is given to take and eat, under the form of

* It is extremely difficult to make some people see the immense importance
of strict accuracy in stating terms, in this unhappy controversy about the Lord's
Supper. The point in dispute is not whether there is a "real presence" of Christ
in the Lord's Supper. This we all hold.—The point is not whether Christ's
presence is a spiritual presence. Even Harding, the well-known antagonist of
Jewel, admits that Christ's body is present, "not after a corporal, or carnal,
or natural wise, but invisibly, unspeakably, miraculously, supernaturally,
spiritually, divinely, and in a manner by Him known."—*Harding's Reply to
Jewel.*—The true point is, whether Christ's real body and blood are really
present in the elements of bread and wine, as soon as they are consecrated in
the Lord's Supper, and independently of the faith of him who receives it.
Romanists and semi-Romanists say that they are so present. We say that they
are not.

† G. A. Denison was Archdeacon of Taunton and a strenuous defender of
the most rigid Anglo-Catholic principles. He figured in several legal actions
between 1854 and 1858.

‡ The antagonism between these sentences of Archdeacon Denison and
Bishop Ridley's views of the same subject, is so singularly strong, that I ask
the reader not to pass on without noticing it. Bishop Ridley, in his Disputation
at Oxford, says of the Romish doctrine of the Real Presence: "It destroyeth
and taketh away the Institution of the Lord's Supper, which was commanded
only to be used and continued until the Lord Himself should come. If, therefore,
He be now really present in the body of His flesh, then must the Supper cease:
for a remembrance is not of a thing present, but of a thing past and absent.
And, as one of the Fathers saith,—'A figure is vain where the thing figured is
present'."—See *Foxe's Martyrs, in loco.*

bread and wine in the Lord's Supper, the body and blood of Christ."
(Sermon II., p. 107.)

Now I shall not multiply quotations of this kind. It would be easy to
show you that the doctrine laid down by Archdeacon Denison is the
doctrine of a large and growing section of the Church of England.* It
would be no less easy to show that the doctrine is substantially one and
the same with that of the Romish Church, and that for refusing this very
doctrine our martyred Reformers laid down their lives. But time would
not allow me to do this. I shall content myself with trying to show that
the doctrine of Archdeacon Denison and his school cannot be reconciled
with the authorized formularies of the Church of England, and that the
simpler and, as some falsely call it, lower view of the intention of the
Lord's Supper, is in entire harmony with those formularies.

Let me turn first to the Thirty-nine Articles. We have no right to appeal
to any formulary before this. The Church's Confession of faith is the
Church's first standard of doctrine. The Twenty-eighth Article says as
follows:—

"The Supper of the Lord is not only a sign of the love that Christians
ought to have among themselves one to another, but rather is a Sacrament
of our Redemption by Christ's death; insomuch that to such as rightly,
worthily, and with faith, receive the same, the Bread which we break is
a partaking of the Body of Christ; and likewise the Cup of Blessing is a
partaking of the Blood of Christ.

"Transubstantiation (or the change of the substance of bread and
wine) in the Supper of the Lord, cannot be proved by holy Writ; but is
repugnant to the plain words of Scripture, overthroweth the nature of a
Sacrament, and hath given occasion to many superstitions.

* In a devotional work, entitled "The Little Prayer-book, intended for
Beginners in Devotion, revised and corrected by three Priests," the following
passages will be found:—"When you enter the church, before you go to your
place, bow reverently to the holy altar, for it is the throne of Christ, and the
most sacred part of the church."—"Bow reverently to the altar, before you
leave the altar."—"At the words 'this is My body, this is My blood,' you must
believe that the bread and wine become the real body and blood with the Soul
and God-head of Jesus Christ. Bow down your heart and body in deepest
adoration when the priest says those awful words, *and worship your Saviour*,
there, verily, and indeed present on His altar."

In a "Catechism on the Office of the Holy Communion, edited by a Committee of Clergymen," will be found the following statement:—"The Holy
Communion is a sacrifice, an offering made on an altar to God."—"We offer
bread and wine; these afterwards become the body and blood of Christ."—
"The Lord Jesus Christ Himself as our High Priest, and the Priests of His
Church whom He hath appointed here on earth, alone have power to offer this
sacrifice."—"The sacrifice is the true body and blood of our Lord Jesus Christ,
and is presented as a sin-offering to obtain pardon for our offences."—The body
and blood of our Lord Jesus Christ are really and truly present on the altar
under the forms of the bread and wine, and the priest offers the sacrifice to
God the Father."—"We should worship our Lord, present in His sacrament
as we should do if we could see Him bodily."

"The Body of Christ is given, taken, and eaten, in the Supper, only after an heavenly and spiritual manner. And the mean whereby the Body of Christ is received and eaten in the Supper is Faith.

"The Sacrament of the Lord's Supper was not by Christ's ordinance received, carried about, lifted up, or worshipped."

I shall make no remark on these words. I only ask plain Churchmen to put them side by side with High Church statements about the Lord's Supper, and to observe the utter contrariety that exists between them. I appeal to the common sense of all impartial and unprejudiced Englishmen. Let them be the judges. If one view is right, the other is wrong. If the language of the Twenty-eighth Article can be reconciled with the doctrine of Archdeacon Denison and his school, I can only say that words have no meaning at all. I shall content myself with quoting the comment of Bishop Beveridge on this Twenty-eighth Article, and pass on.

He says,—"If the bread be not really changed into the body of Christ, then the body of Christ is not really there present; and if it be not really there present, it is impossible that it should be really taken and received into our bodies, as bread is."

Again, he says,—"I cannot see how it can possibly be denied, that Christ ate of the bread whereof He said, 'This is My body;' and if He ate it, and ate it corporally (that is, ate His body as we eat bread), then He ate Himself, and made one body two, and then crowded them into one again, putting His body into His body, even His whole body into part of His body, His stomach. And so He must be thought not only to have two bodies, but two bodies one within another; yea, so as to be one devoured by another: the absurdity of which, and of like assertions, he that hath but half an eye may easily discover. So that it must needs be granted to be in a *spiritual* manner that the Sacrament was instituted, and by consequence that it is in a *spiritual* manner the sacrament must be received."—*Beveridge on the Articles.* Ed. Oxford, 1846. Pp. 482–486.

The Liturgy of the Church of England on this subject is entirely in accordance with the Articles. The word "altar" is not to be found once in our Prayer-book. The idea of a "sacrifice" is most carefully excluded from our Communion Office. However much men may twist and distort the words of the Baptismal Service, they cannot make anything out of the Communion Service, to prove Romish views. Even the famous Nonjuror, Dr. Brett, was obliged to confess that he "knew not how to reconcile the Consecration Prayer in the present established Liturgy with the real presence; for," says he, "it makes a plain distinction betwixt the bread and wine and our Saviour's body and blood, when it says,—'Grant that we receiving these Thy creatures of bread and wine, may be partakers of Christ's body and blood.' Which manifestly implies the bread and wine to be distinct and different things from the body and blood."—*Brett's*

Discourse on discerning the Lord's Body in the Communion. London, 1720. Pref., pp. 19–21.

But the rubric at the end of the Communion Service makes it mere waste of time to say anything more on the subject of the Prayer-book's view of the Lord's Supper. That rubric says,—"Whereas it is ordained in this Office for the Administration of the Lord's Supper, that the communicants should receive the same kneeling (which order is well meant, for a signification of our humble and grateful acknowledgment of the benefits of Christ therein given to all worthy receivers; and for the avoiding of such profanation and disorder in the Holy Communion, as might otherwise ensue); yet, lest the same kneeling should by any persons, either out of ignorance and infirmity, or out of malice and obstinacy, be misconstrued and depraved,—It is thereby declared, That thereby no adoration is intended, or ought to be done, either unto the sacramental bread or wine there bodily received, or unto any Corporal Presence of Christ's natural flesh and blood. For the sacramental bread and wine remain still in their very natural substances, and therefore may not be adored (for that were idolatry, to be abhorred of all faithful Christians); and the natural body and blood of our Saviour Christ are in heaven, and not here; it being against the truth of Christ's natural body to be at one time in more places than one." If that rubric does not flatly condemn the teaching of Archdeacon Denison and his school, about the presence of Christ in the sacrament, under the forms of bread and wine, I am very certain that words have no meaning at all.*

The Catechism of the Church of England is in direct accordance with the Articles and Liturgy. Though it states distinctly that "Christ's body and blood are verily and indeed taken and received by the *faithful* in the Lord's Supper," it carefully avoids saying one word to sanction the idea that the body and blood are locally present in the consecrated elements of bread and wine. In fact, a spiritual presence of Christ in the Lord's Supper to every faithful communicant, but no local corporal presence in the bread and wine to any communicant, is evidently the uniform doctrine of the Church of England.

But I will not pass on without quoting Waterland's interpretation of the doctrine of the Catechism. He says,—"The words *verily and indeed*

---

* The rubric at the end of the Communion of the Sick is another strong evidence of the views of those who drew up our Prayer-book in its present form. It says, "If a man by reason of extremity of sickness, or for want of warning in due time to the curate, or for lack of company to receive with him, or by any other just impediment, do not receive the sacrament of Christ's body and blood, the curate shall instruct him, that if he do truly repent him of his sins, and steadfastly believe that Jesus Christ hath suffered death on the Cross for him, and shed His blood for his redemption, earnestly remembering the benefits he hath thereby, and giving him hearty thanks therefor, he *doth eat and drink the body and blood* of our Saviour Christ profitably to his soul's health, although he do not receive the sacrament with his mouth."

taken and received by the faithful, are rightly interpreted of a real participation of the benefits purchased by Christ's death. The body and blood
of Christ are taken and received by the faithful, not corporally, not
internally, but verily and indeed, that is *effectually.* The sacred symbols
are no bare signs, no untrue figures of a thing absent; but the force,
the grace, the virtue, and benefit of Christ's body broken and blood shed,
that is of His passion, are really and effectually present with all them
that receive worthily. This is *all the real presence* that our Church
teaches."—*Waterland's Works.* Oxford, 1843. Vol. vi., p. 42.

Once more I say that if Waterland's view of the Catechism can be
reconciled with that of Archdeacon Denison and his school, words have
no meaning at all.

The Homily of the Church of England about the sacrament is in
complete harmony with the Articles, Liturgy, and Catechism. It says,
"Before all things this we must be sure of especially, that this Supper
be in such wise done and ministered as our Lord and Saviour did, and
commanded to be done; as His holy Apostles used it; and the good
Fathers in the Church frequented it. For, as that worthy man St. Ambrose
saith, he is unworthy of the Lord that doth celebrate this mystery otherwise than it was delivered by Him. Neither can he be devout that doth
presume otherwise than it was given by the Author. We must then take
heed, *lest of the memory it be made a sacrifice,* lest of a communion it be
made a private eating; lest of two parts we have but one; lest, applying
it for the dead, we lose the fruit that be alive."—Again, it says, after
pressing the necessity of knowledge and faith in communicants: "This is
to stick fast to Christ's promise made in His institution: to make Christ
thine own, and to apply His merits unto thyself. Herein thou needest no
other man's help, no other sacrifice or oblation, no sacrificing priest,
no mass, no means established by man's invention."—Again, it says:
"It is well known that the meat we seek for in this Supper is spiritual
food, the nourishment of our soul, a heavenly refection and not earthly,
an invisible meat and not bodily, a ghostly substance and not carnal.
So that to think that without faith we really enjoy the eating and drinking
thereof, or that that is the fruition of it, is but to dream a gross carnal
feeling, basely objecting and binding ourselves to the elements and
creatures. Whereas by the order of the Council of Nicene, we ought to
lift up our minds by faith, and leaving these inferior and earthly things,
there seek it where the Sun of Righteousness ever shineth. Take then
this lesson, O thou that art desirous of this table, of Emissenus, a godly
Father,—that when thou goest up to the reverend communion to be
satisfied with spiritual meat, thou look up with faith upon the holy body
and blood of thy God, thou marvel with reverence, thou touch it with
thy mind, thou receive it with the hand of thy heart, and thou take it
fully with thy inward man."

Now it would be easy to multiply quotations in support of the view of the Lord's Supper which I advocate, from leading divines of the Church of England. But I forbear. Time is precious in these latter days of hurry, bustle, and excitement. Quotations are wearisome, and too often are not read. Those who wish to follow up the subject should study Dean Goode's unanswerable, but much neglected, book on the Eucharist.

Two quotations only I will give, from two men of no mean authority, though differing widely on some points.

The first is the well-known Jeremy Taylor. In his book on *The Real Presence* (Edit. 1654, pp. 13–15) he says: "We say that Christ's body is in the sacrament really, but spiritually. The Roman Catholics say that it is there really, but spiritually. For so Bellarmine is bold to say that the word may be allowed in this question. Where now is the difference? Here by *spiritually*, they mean spiritual after the manner of a spirit. We by *spiritually*, mean present to our spirit only. They say that Christ's body is truly present there as it was upon the Cross, but not after the manner of all or anybody, but after that manner of being as an angel is in a place. That's their *spiritually.*—But we by the real spiritual presence of Christ do understand Christ to be present, as the Spirit of God is present, in the hearts of the faithful by blessing and grace; and this is all which we mean beside the tropecal and figurative presence."

The other divine whom I will quote is one who was a very giant in theology, and as remarkable for his soundness in the faith as for his prodigious learning. I mean Archbishop Usher. In his sermon before the House of Commons, he says: "In the sacrament of the Lord's Supper, the bread and wine are not changed in substance from being the same with that which is served at ordinary tables; but in respect of the sacred use whereunto they are consecrated, such a change is made that now they differ as much from common bread and wine as heaven from earth. Neither are they to be accounted barely significative, but truly exhibitive also of those heavenly things whereunto they have relation; as being appointed by God to be a means of conveying the same to us, and putting us in actual possession thereof. So that in the use of this holy ordinance, as verily as a man with his bodily hand and mouth receiveth the earthly creatures of bread and wine, so verily with his spiritual hand and mouth, *if he have any*, doth he receive the body and blood of Christ. And this is that real and substantial presence which we affirm to be in the inward part of this sacred action."

I cannot leave this part of the subject without entering my indignant protest against the often-repeated sneer that learning, reasoning, and research are not to be found among the supporters of Evangelical Religion in the Church of England! The work of Dean Goode, on the nature of Christ's presence in the Eucharist, containing 986 pages of masterly argument in defence of sound Protestant views of the Lord's Supper,

has now been for many years before the public. It stands to this day
unanswered hitherto and unanswerable. Where is the honesty, where the
fairness, of neglecting to refute that book if it can be refuted, and yet
clinging obstinately to views which it triumphantly subverts?—I unhesitatingly commend that book to the patient and diligent study of all
my younger brethren in the ministry, if they want their minds established
and confirmed about the sacrament of the Lord's Supper. Let them
read it carefully, and I think they will find it impossible to arrive at any
but one conclusion. That conclusion is, that the Church of England
holds that there is no sacrifice in the Lord's Supper, no oblation, no
altar, no corporal presence of Christ in the bread and wine; and that
the true intention of the Lord's Supper is just what the Catechism states,
and neither less nor more:—"It was ordained for the continual remembrance of the sacrifice of the death of Christ, and of the benefits that we
receive thereby."

II. The second point which I propose to handle in this paper is so
completely bound up with the first, that I shall not dwell upon it at
length. He that can answer the question—"What is the true intention"
of the Lord's Supper?—will find no difficulty in discerning "*what is
its rightful position in the Church of Christ.*"

Like the ark of God in the Old Testament, this blessed sacrament has
a proper position and rank among Christian ordinances, and, like the
ark of God, it may easily be put in the wrong one. The history of that ark
will readily recur to our minds. Put in the place of God, and treated like
an idol, it did the Israelites no good at all. In the days of Eli, it could
not save them out of the hand of the Philistine. Their armies were
defeated, and the ark itself was taken.—Defiled and dishonoured by being
placed in an idol's temple, it was the cause of God's wrath falling on a
whole nation, till the Philistines said with one voice, "Send it away."—
Treated with carelessness and levity, it brought down God's judgment
on the men of Bethshemesh, and on Uzza.—Treated with reverence and
respect, it brought a blessing on Obed-edom and all his house.—It is
even so with the Lord's Supper.—Placed in its right position, it is an
ordinance full of blessing. The great question to be settled is,—What is
that position?

(1) The Lord's Supper is not in its right place, *when it is made the first,
foremost, principal, and most important thing in Christian worship.* That
it is so in many quarters, we all must know. The well-known "masses"
of the Romish Church, the increasing importance attached to "Holy
Communion," as it is called, by many in our own Church, are plain
evidence of what I mean. The sermon, the mode of conducting prayer,
the reading of "holy Scripture," in many churches are made second to
this one thing,—the administration of the Lord's Supper.—We may well

ask, "What warrant of Scripture is there for this extravagant honour? but we shall get no answer. There are at most but five books in the whole canon of the New Testament in which the Lord's Supper is even mentioned. About grace, faith, and redemption; about the work of Christ, the work of the Spirit, and the love of the Father; about man's ruin, weakness, and spiritual poverty; about justification, sanctification, and holy living;— about all these mighty subjects we find the inspired writers giving us line upon line, and precept upon precept. About the Lord's Supper, on the contrary, we may observe in the great bulk of the New Testament a speaking silence. Even the Epistles to Timothy and Titus, containing much instruction about a minister's duties, do not contain a word about it. This fact alone surely speaks volumes! To thrust the Lord's Supper forward, till it towers over and overrides everything else in religion, is giving it a position for which there is no authority in God's Word.*

(2) Again, the Lord's Supper is not in its right place, *when it is administered with an extravagent degree of outward ceremony and veneration*. In saying this I should be sorry to be misunderstood. God forbid that I should countenance anything like carelessness or irreverence in the use of any ordinance of Christ. By all means let us give honour where honour is due. But I ask all who read this paper, whether there is not something painfully suspicious about the enormous amount of pomp and bodily reverence with which the Lord's Supper is now administered in many of our churches? The ostentatious treatment of the Communion table as an altar,—the lights, ornaments, flowers, millinery, gestures, postures, bowings, crossings, incensing, processions, which are connected with the so-called altar,—the mysterious and obsequious veneration with which the bread and wine are consecrated, given, taken, and received,— what does it all mean?† Where is there in all this the simplicity of the first institution, as we find it recorded in the Bible? Where is the simplicity which our Protestant Reformers both preached and practised? Where is the simplicity which any plain reader of the English Prayer-book might justly expect? We may well ask, Where? The true Lord's Supper is no longer there. The whole thing savours of Romanism. A plain man can only see in it an attempt to introduce into our worship the doctrine of sacrifice, the "blasphemous fable and dangerous deceit" of the mass, the

---

* I take occasion to say that I view with strong dislike the modern practice of substituting the Lord's Supper for a sermon at Episcopal and Archidiaconal visitations. No doubt it saves Bishops and Archdeacons much trouble. It delivers them from the invidious responsibility of selecting a preacher. But the thing has a very suspicious and unsatisfactory appearance. Preaching the Word, in my judgment, is a far more important ordinance than the Lord's Supper. The subject is one about which Evangelical Churchmen would do well to awake and be on their guard. This studied attempt to thrust in the Lord's Supper on all occasions has a most unfortunate tendency to make men remember the Popish mass.

† It is truly lamentable to observe how many young men and women, of whom better things might have been expected, fall away into semi-Romanism

Popish real presence, and transubstantiation. It is impossible to avoid feeling that a deadly heresy underlies this pompous ceremonial, and that we have not to do merely with a childish love of show and form, but with a deep-laid design to bring back Popery into the Church of England, and to subvert the Gospel of Christ. One thing at any rate is very plain to my mind: the sacrament of the Lord's Supper, administered as it is now in many places, is not in its rightful position. It is so disguised, and painted, and daubed, and overlaid, and bloated, and swollen, and changed by this new treatment, that I can hardly see in it any Lord's Supper at all.

(3) Again, the Lord's Supper is not in its right place, *when it is pressed on all worshippers indiscriminately*, as a means of grace which all, as a matter of course, ought to use. Once more I ask that no one will misunderstand me. I feel as strongly as any one, that to go to church as a worshipper, and yet not be a communicant, is to be a most inconsistent Christian, and that to be unfit for the Lord's Table is to be unfit to die. But it is one thing to teach this, and quite another to urge all men to receive the sacrament as a matter of course, whether they are qualified to receive it or not.—I should be sorry to raise a false accusation. I do not for a moment suppose that any High Church clergyman recommends, in naked language, wicked people to come to the Lord's Supper that they may be made good. But I cannot forget that from many pulpits people are constantly taught that they are born again, and have grace, by virtue of their baptism; and that if they want to stir up the grace within them, and get more religion, they must use all means of grace, and specially the Lord's Supper! And I cannot help fearing that thousands in the present day are practically substituting attendance at the Lord's Supper for repentance, faith, and vital union with Christ, and flattering themselves that the more often they receive the Sacrament, the more they are justified, and the more fit they are to die. My own firm conviction is that the Lord's Supper should on no account be placed before Christ, and that men should always be taught to come to Christ by faith *before* they draw near to the Lord's Table. I believe that this order can never be inverted without bringing in gross superstition, and doing immense harm to men's souls. Those parts of Christendom where "the mass" is

in the present day, under the attraction of a highly ornamental and sensuous ceremonial. Flowers, crucifixes, processions, banners, incense, gorgeous vestments, and the like, never fail to draw such young persons together, just as honey attracts flies. I will not insult the common sense of those who find these things attractive, by asking them whether they really believe they get any food from them for heart, and conscience, and soul. But I should like them to consider seriously what these things mean. Do they really know that the doctrines of the mass and transubstantiation are the root of the whole system? Are they prepared to swallow these awful heresies? I suspect many are playing with Ritualism without the least idea what it covers over. They see an attractive bait, but they do not see the hook.

made everything, and the Word of God hardly ever preached, are precisely those parts where there is the most entire absence of vital Christianity. I wish I could say there was no fear of our coming to this state of things in our own land. But when we hear of hundreds crowding the Lord's Table on Sundays, and then plunging into every dissipation on weekdays, there is grave reason for suspecting that the Lord's Supper is pressed on many congregations in a manner utterly unwarranted by Scripture.

Does any one ask now what is the rightful position of the Lord's Supper? I answer that question without any hesitation. I believe its rightful position, like that of holiness, is between grace and glory,—between justification and heaven,—between faith and paradise,—between conversion and the final rest,—between the wicket-gate and the celestial city. It is not Christ; it is not conversion; it is not a passport to heaven. It is for the strengthening and refreshing of those who have come to Christ already, who know something of conversion, who are already in the narrow way, and have fled from the city of destruction.

We cannot read hearts, I am well aware. We must not be too strict and exclusive in our terms of communion, and make those sad whom God has not made sad. But we must never shrink from telling the unconverted and the unbelieving that, in their present condition, they are not fit to come to the Lord's Table. A faithful clergyman, at any rate, need never be ashamed of taking up the ground marked out for him in the Church Catechism. The last question in that well-known formulary is as follows: "What is required of them that come to the Lord's Supper?" The answer to that question is weighty and full of meaning. Those who come to the Lord's Supper must "examine themselves whether they repent them truly of their former sins, steadfastly purposing to lead a new life,—have a lively faith in God's mercy through Christ, and a thankful remembrance of His death,—and are in charity with all men." Does any one feel these things in his own heart? Then we may boldly tell him that the Lord's Supper is placed before him by a merciful Saviour, to help him in running the race set before him.—Higher than this we must not place the ordinance. A communicant was not expected to be an angel, but a sinner who feels his sins, and trusts in his Saviour.—Lower than this we have no right to place the ordinance. To encourage people to come up to the Table without knowledge, faith, repentance, or grace, is to do them positive harm, promote superstition, and displease the Master of the feast. He desires to see at His Table not dead guests, but living ones,—not the dead service of formal eating and drinking, but the spiritual sacrifice of feeling and loving hearts.

I pause here. I trust I have said enough to make clear the views I hold of the true intention and rightful position of the sacrament of the Lord's Supper. If, in expounding these views, I have said anything that grates on the feelings of any reader, I can assure him that I am unfeignedly sorry. Nothing could be further from my desire than to hurt the feelings of a brother.

But it is my firm conviction that the state of the Church of England requires great plainness of speech and distinctness of statement about the sacraments. There is nothing, I am persuaded, which the times so imperatively demand of Evangelical Churchmen, as a bold, manly, and explicit assertion of the great principles held by our forefathers, and specially about baptism and the Lord's Supper. If we would "strengthen the things that remain which are ready to die," we must resolutely go back to the old paths, and maintain old truths in the old way. We must give up the vain idea that we can ever make the Cross of Christ acceptable by polishing, and varnishing, and painting, and gilding it, and sawing off its corners. We must cease to suppose that we can ever lure men into being Evangelical by a trimming, temporizing, half-and-half, milk-and-water mode of exhibiting the doctrines of the Gospel,—or by wearing borrowed plumes, and dabbling with High Churchism,—or by loudly proclaiming that we are not "party-men,"—or by laying aside plain Scriptural phrases, and praising up "earnestness,"—or by adroitly keeping back truths that are likely to give offence. The plan is an utter delusion. It wins no enemy: it disgusts many a true friend. It makes the worldly bystander sneer, and fills him with scorn. We may rest assured that the right line and the wisest course for the Evangelical body to pursue, is to adhere steadily to the old plan of maintaining the truth, the whole truth, and nothing but the truth, as it is in Jesus, and specially the truth about the two sacraments of baptism and the Lord's Supper. Let us be courteous, amiable, charitable, affable, considerate for the feelings of others, by all means, but let no consideration make us keep back any part of God's truth.

Let me close this paper with a few practical suggestions. Assuming, for a moment, that we have made up our minds, what is the intention and rightful position of the Lord's Supper, let us just consider what the times demand at our hands.

(1) For one thing let us *cultivate a godly simplicity* in all our statements about the Lord's Supper, and a godly jealousy in all our practices about it.

If we are ministers, let us often remind our people that there is no sacrifice in the Lord's Supper,—no real presence of Christ's body and blood in the bread and wine,—no change of the elements,—no grace conferred *ex opere operato*,—no altar at the east end of our churches,—no sacrificing priesthood in the Church of England. Let us tell them these things again, and again, and again, till our congregations have them ingrained into their very minds and memories and souls, and let us charge them, as they love life, not to forget them.

Whether we are clergymen or laymen, let us beware of countenancing or tolerating any practices in connection with the Lord's Supper which either exceed or contradict the rubrics of our Prayer-book, and imply any belief in a Romish view of this sacrament. Let us protest in every possible way against any extravagant veneration of the Communion Table and the bread and wine, as if Christ's body and blood were in these elements, or on the Table; and let us never forget what the Prayer-book says about "idolatry to be abhorred of all faithful Christians."

We cannot be too particular on these points. The times are changed. Things that we might have borne with in past years as matters of indifference, and comparative trifles in ceremonial, ought not to be borne with any longer. A few years ago I would have turned to the east in repeating the Creed in any parish church, rather than offend a neighbour's feelings. I can do so no longer, for I see great principles at stake. Let our protest on all these matters be firm, unflinching, and universal all over the country, and we may do much good.

(2) For another thing, *let us not be shaken or troubled by the common charge that we are not Churchmen*, because we do not agree with many of our brethren on the subject of the sacraments. Such charges are easily made, but not so easily established. I trust my younger brethren especially will treat them with perfect indifference and unconcern. I know not which to admire most, the impudence or the ignorance of those who make them.

Do those who coolly say that Evangelical Churchmen are not true Churchmen, suppose that we cannot read? Do they fancy we cannot understand the meaning of plain English? Do they think to persuade us that our doctrinal views are not to be found in the Articles, the Liturgy, and the Homilies, and in the writings of all the leading divines of our Church, up to the days of Charles the First?—Do they fancy, for example, that we do not know that the Communion Table was seldom to be found at the east end of the Church, till the time of Laud, but generally stood in the chancel, like a table, and that Ridley specially called it "the Lord's Board"?* Alas, I fear they presume on the non-reading propensities of the day. They know too well that the reading of many Evangelical people is seldom carried beyond newspapers and magazines.

I am bold to say that in the matter of true, honest, conscientious membership of the Church of England, the Evangelical body need fear no comparison with any other section within the Church's pale. We may

* It is a fact that the Communion Table in Gloucester Cathedral was first placed altar-wise against the east end of the chancel by Laud himself, when he was Dean of Gloucester, in the year 1616. It is also a fact that Bishop Miles Smith, then Bishop of Gloucester, was so pained and annoyed by this change, that he declared he would not enter the Cathedral again till the table was brought back to its former position. He kept his word, and never went within the walls of the Cathedral, till he was buried there in 1624.

Let us observe the language used by Bishop Ridley in his injunctions to the clergy of the See of London. Assigning reasons for the removal of altars and safely challenge any amount of fair investigation and inquiry. Have others signed the Thirty-nine Articles "*ex animo et bonâ fide*"? so have we. Have others declared their full assent to the Liturgy? so have we. Do others use the Liturgy, adding nothing and omitting nothing, reverently, solemnly, and audibly? so do we. Are others obedient to Bishops? so are we. Do others labour for the prosperity of the Church of England? so do we. Do others value the privileges of the Church of England, and deprecate needless separation? so do we. Do others honour the Lord's Supper, and press it on the attention of all believing hearers? so do we. But we will not concede that a man must follow Archbishop Laud, and be half a Romanist, in order to be a Churchman. We are true High Churchmen and not Romish High Churchmen. And the best proof of our Churchmanship is the fact that for every one of *our body* who has left the Church of England and gone over to Dissent, we can point to ten *High Churchmen* who have left the Church of England and gone over to Rome.

No! Evangelical Churchmen never need be moved by the charge that they are not true Churchmen. Ignorant and impudent men may make such charges, but none except shallow and ill-read men will ever believe them. When those who make them have answered Dean Goode's work on the Eucharist, as well as his other works on Baptism and the Rule of Faith, it will be time for us to pay attention to what they say. But till then we may safely act on the advice given to the Jews by Hezekiah about Rabshakeh's railing accusations,—"Answer them not."

(3) In the last place, let me express an *earnest hope that no one who reads this paper will ever let himself be driven out of the Church of England* by the rise of the present tide of extreme Ritualism, and the seeming decay of the Evangelical body. I lament that there should be a need for uttering this warning, but I am sure there is a cause.

I can well understand the feelings which actuate many in this day. They live perhaps in a parish where the Gospel is never preached at all, where Romish doctrines and practices about the Lord's Supper carry all before them,—where, in fact, they stand alone. Week after week, and month after month, and year after year, they hear nothing but the same dreary round of phrases about "holy Church, holy baptism, holy communion, holy priests, holy altars, holy sacrifice," until they are almost sick of the word "holy," and Sunday becomes a positive weariness to their souls. And then comes up the thought, "Why not leave the Church

the substitution of tables, he says: "The use of an altar is to sacrifice upon; the use of a table is to serve men to eat upon. Now when we come to the Lord's Board, what do we come for? To sacrifice Christ again, and to crucify Him again, or to feed upon Him that was once only crucified and offered up for us? If we come to feed upon Him, spiritually to eat His body, and spiritually to drink His blood, which is the true use of the Lord's Supper, then no man can deny that the form of a table is more meet than the form of an altar."—See *Foxe's Acts and Mon.* Vol. vi. Seeley's Edition, p. 6.

of England altogether? What good can there be in such a Church as this? Why not become a Dissenter or a Plymouth Brother?"

Now I desire to offer an affectionate warning to all who are in this frame of mind. I ask them to consider well what they do, and to take the advice of the town-clerk of Ephesus,—"To do nothing rashly." I entreat them to call faith and patience into exercise, and at any rate to wait long before they secede, to pray much, to read their Bibles much, and to be very sure that they have done everything that can be done to amend what is wrong.

It is a cheap and easy remedy to secede from a Church when we see evils round us, but it is not always the wisest one. To pull down a house because the chimney smokes, to chop off a hand because we have cut our finger, to forsake a ship because she has sprung a leak and makes a little water,—all this we know is childish impatience. But is it a wise man's act to forsake a Church because things in our own parish, and under our own minister in that Church, are wrong? I answer decidedly and unhesitatingly, No!

It is not so sure as it seems that we mend matters by leaving the Church of England. Every man knows the faults of his own house, but he never knows the faults of another till he moves into it, and then perhaps he finds he is worse off than he was before his move. There are often smoky chimneys, and bad drains, and draughts, and doors that will not shut, and windows that will not open, in No. 2 as well as in No. 1. All is not perfect among Dissenters and Plymouth Brethren. We may find to our cost, if we join them in disgust with the Church of England, that we have only changed one sort of evil for another, and that the chimney smokes in chapel as well as in church.

It is very certain that a sensible and well-instructed layman can do an immense deal of good to the Church of England,—can check much evil and promote Christ's truth,—if he will only hold his ground and use all lawful means. Public opinion is very powerful. Exposure of extreme malpractice has a great effect. Bishops cannot altogether ignore appeals from the laity. By much importunity even the most cautious occupants of the Episcopal bench may be roused to action. The press is open to every man. In short, there is much to be done, though, like anything else that is good, it may give much trouble. And as for a man's own soul, he must be in a strange position if he cannot hear the Gospel in some Church near him. At the worst he has the Bible, the throne of grace, and the Lord Jesus Christ always near him at his own home.

I say these things as one who is called a Low Churchman, and as one who feels a righteous indignation at the Romanizing proceedings of many clergymen in our own day. I mourn over the danger done to the Church of England by the Ritualism of this day. I mourn over the many driven in disgust out of the pale of our Zion. But Low Churchman as I am called, I am a Churchman, and I am anxious that no one should be goaded into doing rash and hasty things by the proceedings to which I have alluded. So long as we have truth, liberty, and an unaltered Confession of faith in the Church of England, so long I am convinced that the way of patience is much better than the way of secession.

When the Thirty-nine Articles are altered,—when the Prayer-book is revised on Romish principles and filled with Popery,—when the Bible is withdrawn from the reading desk,—when the pulpit is shut against the Gospel,—when the mass is formally restored in every parish church by Act of Parliament,—when, in fact, our present order of things in the Church of England is altered by statute, and Queen, Lords, and Commons command that our parish churches shall be given over to processions, incense, crosses, images, banners, flowers, gorgeous vestments, idolatrous veneration of the sacrament of the Lord's Supper, mumbled prayers, gabbled-over apocryphal lessons, short, dry, sapless sermons, histrionic gestures and postures, bowings, crossings, and the like,—when these things come to pass by law and rule, then it will be time for us all to leave the Church of England. Then we may arise and say with one voice, "Let us depart, for God is not here."

But till that time,—and God forbid it should ever come: till that time,—and when it does come, there will be a good many seceders: till that time let us stand fast, and fight for the truth. Let us not desert our post to save trouble, and move out to please our adversaries, and spike our guns to avoid a battle. No! in the name of God, let us fight on, even if we are like the 300 at Thermopylæ,—few with us, many against us, and traitors on every side. Let us fight on, and contend earnestly for the faith once delivered to the saints.

The good ship of the Church of England may have some rotten planks about her. The crew may, many of them, be useless and mutinous, and not trustworthy. But there are still some faithful ones among them. There is still hope for the good old craft. The Great Pilot has not yet left her. Let us therefore stick by the ship.

The following quotations may be interesting to some readers.

(1) Archbishop Cranmer, in the Preface to his *Answer to Gardiner*, says:—
"They (the Romanists) say that Christ is corporally under or in the form of bread and wine; we say that Christ is not there, neither corporally nor spiritually. But in them that worthily eat and drink the bread and wine He is spiritually, and corporally He is in heaven.—I mean not that Christ is spiritually, either in the table, or in the bread and wine that be set on the table, but I mean that He is present in the ministration and receiving of that Holy Supper, according to His own institution and ordinance."—See *Goode on the Eucharist*, vol. ii., p. 772.

(2) Bishop Ridley, in his *Disputation at Oxford*, says:—
"The circumstances of the Scripture, the analogy and proportion of the sacraments, and the testimony of the faithful Fathers, ought to rule us in taking the meaning of the Holy Scripture touching the sacraments.

"But the words of the Lord's Supper, the circumstances of the Scripture, the analogy of the sacraments, and the sayings of the Fathers, do most effectually and plainly prove a figurative speech in the words of the Lord's Supper.

"Therefore a figurative sense and meaning is specially to be received in these words, 'This is My body.' "—See *Goode on the Eucharist*, vol. ii., p. 766.

(3) Bishop Hooper, in his *Brief and Clear Confession of the Christian Faith*, says:—

"I believe that all this sacrament consisteth in the use thereof; so that without the right use the bread and wine in nothing differ from other common bread and wine that is commonly used: and, therefore, I do not believe that the body of Christ can be contained, hid, or inclosed in the bread, under the bread, or with the bread,—neither the blood in the wine, under the wine, or with the wine. But I believe and confess the only body of Christ to be in heaven, on the right hand of the Father; and that always, and as often as we use this bread and wine according to this ordinance and institution of Christ, we do verily and indeed receive His body and blood."—*Hooper's Works*. Parker Society's Edition, vol. ii., p. 48.

(4) Bishop Jewel says:—

"Let us examine what difference there is between the body of Christ and the sacrament of His body.

"The difference is this: a sacrament is a figure or token; the body of Christ is figured or tokened. The sacramental bread is bread, it is not the body of Christ; the body of Christ is flesh, it is not bread. The bread is beneath; the body is above. The bread is on the table; the body is in heaven. The bread is in the mouth; the body is in the heart. The bread feedeth the body; the body feedeth the soul. The bread shall come to nothing; the body is immortal, and shall not perish. The bread is vile; the body of Christ is glorious. Such a difference is there between the bread which is a sacrament of the body, and the body of Christ itself. The sacrament is eaten as well of the wicked as of the faithful. The body is only eaten of the faithful. The sacrament may be eaten unto judgment; the body cannot be eaten but unto salvation. Without the sacrament we may be saved; but without the body of Christ we have no salvation: we cannot be saved."—*Jewel on the Sacrament*. Parker Society's Edition, vol. iv., p. 1121.

(5) Richard Hooker, in his *Ecclesiastical Polity*, says:—

"The real presence of Christ's most blessed body and blood is not to be sought for in the sacrament, but in the worthy receiver of the sacrament.

"And with this the very order of our Saviour's words agreeth. First, 'take and eat;' then, 'this is My body which is broken for you.' First, 'drink ye all of this;' then followeth, 'this is My blood of the New Testament, which is shed for many for the remission of sins.' I see not which way it should be gathered by the words of Christ,—when and where the bread is His body, or the wine His blood, but only in the very heart and soul of him which receiveth them. As for the sacraments, they really exhibit, but for aught we can gather out of that which is written of them, they *are* not really nor do really *contain* in themselves that grace which with them or by them it pleaseth God to bestow."
—*Hooker, Eccl. Pol.*, book v., p. 67.

(6) Waterland says:—

"The Fathers well understood that to make Christ's natural body the real sacrifice of the Eucharist, would not only be absurd in reason but highly presumptuous and profane: and that to make the outward symbols a proper sacrifice, a material sacrifice, would be entirely contrary to Gospel principles, degrading the Christian sacrifice into a Jewish one, yea, and making it much lower and meaner than the Jewish one, both in value and dignity. The right way, therefore, was to make the sacrifice spiritual, and it could be no other upon Gospel principles."—*Works*, vol. iv., p. 762.

"No one has any authority or right to offer Christ as a sacrifice, whether really or symbolically, but Christ Himself; such a sacrifice is His sacrifice, not ours,—offered for us, not by us, to God the Father."—*Works*, vol. iv., p. 753.

IX

THE REAL PRESENCE

"If Thy presence go not with me, carry us not up hence."—
Exod. xxxiii. 15.

THERE is a word in the text that heads this page which demands the attention of all English Christians in this day. That word is "presence." There is a religious subject bound up with that word, on which it is most important to have clear, distinct, and Scriptural views. That subject is the "presence of God," and specially the "presence of our Lord Jesus Christ" with Christian people. What is that presence? Where is that presence? What is the nature of that presence? To these questions I propose to supply answers.

  I.   I shall consider, first, *the general doctrine of God's presence in the world.*

 II.   I shall consider, secondly, *the special doctrine of Christ's real spiritual presence.*

III.   I shall consider, thirdly, *the special doctrine of Christ's real bodily presence.*

The whole subject deserves serious thought. If we suppose that this is a mere question of controversy, which only concerns theological partisans, we have yet much to learn. It is a subject which lies at the very roots of saving religion. It is a subject which is inseparably tied up with one of the most precious articles of the Christian faith. It is a subject about which it is most dangerous to be wrong. An error here may first lead a man to the Church of Rome, and then land him finally in the gulf of infidelity. Surely it is worth while to examine carefully the doctrine of the "presence" of God and of His Christ.

I.   The first subject we have to consider, is *the general doctrine of God's presence in the world.*

The teaching of the Bible on this point is clear, plain, and unmistakable. God is everywhere. There is no place in heaven or earth where He is not. There is no place in air or land or sea, no place above ground or under ground, no place in town or country, no place in Europe, Asia, Africa, or America, where God is not always present. Enter into your closet and

151

F

lock the door: God is there. Climb to the top of the highest mountain, where not even an insect moves: God is there. Sail to the most remote island in the Pacific Ocean, where the foot of man never trod: God is there. He is always near us,—seeing, hearing, observing, knowing every action, and deed, and word, and whisper, and look, and thought, and motive, and secret of every one of us, and everywhere.

What saith the Scripture? It is written in Job, "His eyes are upon the ways of man, and He seeth all his goings. There is no darkness, nor shadow of death, where the workers of iniquity may hide themselves." (Job xxxiv. 21.) It is written in Proverbs, "The eyes of the Lord are in every place, beholding the evil and the good." (Prov. xv. 3.) It is written in Jeremiah, "Thine eyes are open upon all the ways of the sons of men: to give every one according to the fruit of his doings." (Jer. xxxii. 19.) It is written in the Psalms, "Thou knowest my down-sitting and mine up-rising: Thou understandest my thought afar off. Thou compassest my path, and my lying down, and art acquainted with all my ways. For there is not a word in my tongue, but, lo, O Lord, Thou knowest it altogether. Whither shall I go from Thy Spirit? or whither shall I flee from Thy presence? If I ascend up into heaven, Thou art there: if I make my bed in hell, behold, Thou art there. If I take the wings of the morning, and dwell in the uttermost parts of the sea; even there shall Thy hand lead me, and Thy right hand shall hold me. If I say, Surely the darkness shall cover me; even the night shall be light about me. Yea, the darkness hideth not from Thee; but the night shineth as the day: the darkness and the light are both alike to Thee." (Psalm cxxxix. 2–12.)

Such language as this confounds and overwhelms us. The doctrine before us is one which we cannot fully understand. Precisely so. David said the same thing about it almost three thousand years ago. "Such knowledge is too wonderful for me: it is high, I cannot attain unto it." (Psalm cxxxix. 6.) But it does not follow that the doctrine is not true, because we cannot understand it. It is the weakness of our poor minds and intellects that we must blame, and not the doctrine.

There are scores of things in the world around us, which few can understand or explain, yet no sensible man refuses to believe. How this earth is ever rolling round the sun with enormous swiftness, while we feel no motion,—how the moon affects the tides, and makes them rise and fall twice very twenty-four hours,—how millions of perfectly organized living creatures exist in every pint of pond-water, which our naked eye cannot see,—all these are things well known to men of science, while most of us could not explain them for our lives. And shall we, in the face of such facts, presume to doubt that God is everywhere present, for no better reason than this, that we cannot understand it? Let us never dare to say so again.

How many things there are about God Himself which we cannot

possibly understand, and yet we must believe them, unless so senseless as to be atheists! Who can explain the eternity of God, the infinite power and wisdom of God, or the works of God in creation and providence? Who can comprehend a Being who is a Spirit, without body, parts, or passions? How can a material creature, who can only be in one place at one time, take in the idea of an immaterial Being, who existed before creation, who formed this world by His word out of nothing, and who can be everywhere and see everything at one and the same time? Where, in a word, is there a single attribute of God that mortal man can thoroughly comprehend? Where, then, is the common sense or wisdom of refusing to believe the doctrine of God being present everywhere, merely because our minds cannot take it in? Well says the Book of Job, "Canst thou by searching find out God? canst thou find out the Almighty unto perfection? It is high as heaven; what canst thou do? deeper than hell; what canst thou know?" (Job xi. 7, 8.)

Let us have high and honourable thoughts of the God with whom we have to do while we live, and before whose bar we must stand when we die. Let us seek to have just notions of His power, His wisdom, His eternity, His holiness, His perfect knowledge, His "presence" everywhere. One half the sin committed by mankind arises from wrong views of their Maker and Judge. Men are reckless and wicked, because they do not think that God sees them. They do things they would never do if they really believed they were under the eyes of the Almighty. It is written, "Thou thoughtest that I was altogether such an one as thyself." (Psalm l. 21.) It is written again, "They say the Lord shall not see, neither shall the God of Jacob regard it. Understand, ye brutish among the people: and ye fools, when will ye be wise? He that planted the ear, shall He not hear? He that formed the eye, shall He not see?" (Psalm xciv. 7–9.) No wonder that holy Job said in his best moments, "When I consider, I am afraid of Him." (Job xxiii. 15.)

"What is your God like?" said a sneering infidel one day to a poor Christian. "What is this God of yours like: this God about whom you make such ado? Is He great or is He small?" "My God," was the wise reply, "is a great and a small God at the same time: so great that the heaven of heavens cannot contain Him, and yet so small that He can dwell in the heart of a poor sinner like me."—"Where is your God, my boy?" said another infidel to a child whom he saw coming out of a school where the Bible was taught. "Where is your God about whom you have been reading? Show Him to me, and I will give you an orange." "Show me where He is not," was the answer, "and I will give you two. My God is everywhere."—Well is it said in a certain place, "God hath chosen the weak things of the world to confound the things that are mighty." "Out of the mouth of babes and sucklings Thou hast perfected praise." (2 Cor. i. 27; Matt. xxi. 16.)

However hard to understand this doctrine may be, it is one which is most useful and wholesome for our souls. To keep continually in mind that God is always present with us, to live always as in God's sight, to act and speak and think as under His eye,—all this is eminently calculated to have a good effect upon our souls. Wide, and deep, and searching, and piercing is the influence of that one thought, "Thou God seest me."

(*a*) The thought of God's presence is a loud call to humility. How much that is evil and defective must the All-seeing eye see in every one of us! How small a part of our character is really known by man! "Man looketh on the outward appearance, but the Lord looketh on the heart." (1 Sam. xvi. 7.) Man does not always see us, but the Lord is always looking at us, morning, noon, and night. Who has not need to say, "God be merciful to me a sinner"?

(*b*) The thought of God's presence is a crushing proof of our need of Jesus Christ. What hope of salvation could we have if there was not a Mediator between God and man? Before the eye of an ever-present God, our best righteousness is filthy rags, and our best doings are full of imperfection. Where should we be if there was not a Fountain open for all sin, even the blood of Christ? Without Christ, the prospect of death, judgment, and eternity would drive us to despair.

(*c*) The thought of God's presence teaches the folly of hypocrisy in religion. What can be more silly and childish than to wear a mere cloak of Christianity while we inwardly cleave to sin, when God is ever looking at us and sees us through and through? It is easy to deceive ministers and fellow-Christians, because they often see us only upon Sundays. But God sees us morning, noon, and night, and cannot be deceived. Oh, whatever we are in religion, let us be real and true!

(*d*) The thought of God's presence is a check and curb on the inclination to sin. The recollection that there is One always near us and observing us, who will one day have a reckoning with all mankind, may well keep us back from evil. Happy are those sons and daughters who, when they leave the family home, and launch forth into the world, carry with them the abiding remembrance of God's eye. "My father and mother do not see me, but God does." This was the feeling that preserved Joseph when tempted in a foreign land: "How can I do this great wickedness, and sin against God?" (Gen. xxxix. 9.)

(*e*) The thought of God's presence is a spur to the pursuit of true holiness. The highest standard of sanctification is to "walk with God" as Enoch did, and to "walk before God" as Abraham did. Where is the man who would not strive to live so as to please God, if he realized that God was always standing at his right hand? To get away from God is the secret aim of the sinner; to get nearer to God is the longing desire of the saint. The real servants of the Lord are "a people near unto Him." (Psalm cxlviii. 14.)

(*f*) The thought of God's presence is a comfort in time of public trouble. When war and famine and pestilence break in upon a land, when the nations are rent and torn by inward divisions, and all order seems in peril, it is cheering to reflect that God sees and knows and is close at hand,—that the King of kings is near and not asleep. He that saw the Spanish Armada sail to invade England, and scattered it with the breath of His mouth,—He that looked on when the schemers of the Gunpowder Plot were planning the destruction of Parliament,—this God is not changed.

(*g*) The thought of God's presence is a strong consolation in private trial. We may be driven from home and native land, and placed at the other side of the world; we may be bereaved of wife and children and friends, and left alone in our family, like the last tree in a forest: but we can never go to any place where God is not, and under no circumstances can we be left entirely alone.

Such thoughts as these are useful and profitable for us all. That man must be in a poor state of soul who does not feel them to be so. Let it be a settled principle in our religion never to forget that in every condition and place we are under the eye of God. It need not frighten us if we are true believers. The sins of all believers are cast behind God's back, and even the all-seeing God sees no spot in them. It ought to cheer us, if our Christianity is genuine and sincere. We can then appeal to God with confidence, like David, and say, "Search me, O God, and know my heart: try me, and know my thoughts: and see if there be any wicked way in me, and lead me in the way everlasting." (Psalm cxxxix. 23, 24.) Great is the mystery of God's presence everywhere; but the true man of God can look at it without fear.

II.   The second thing which I propose to consider, is *the real spiritual presence of our Lord Jesus Christ.*

In considering this branch of our subject, we must carefully remember that we are speaking of One who is God and man in one Person. We are speaking of One who in infinite love to our souls, took man's nature, and was born of the Virgin Mary, was crucified, dead, and buried, to be a sacrifice for sins, and yet never ceased for a moment to be very God. The peculiar "presence" of this blessed Person, our Lord Jesus Christ, with His Church, is the point which I want to unfold in this part of my paper. I want to show that He is really and truly present with His believing people, spiritually or after the manner of a spirit, and that His presence is one of the grand privileges of a true Christian. What then is the real spiritual "presence" of Christ, and wherein does it consist? Let us see.

(*a*) There is a real spiritual presence of Christ with that Church which is His mystical body,—the blessed company of all faithful people. This is the meaning of that parting saying of our Lord to His Apostles, "I am with you alway, even unto the end of the world." (Matt. xxviii. 20.) To the visible Church of Christ that saying did not strictly belong. Rent by divisions, defiled by heresies, disgraced by superstitions and corruptions, the visible Church has often given mournful proof that Christ does not always dwell in it. Many of its branches in the course of years, like the Churches of Asia, have decayed and passed away. It is the Holy Catholic Church, composed of God's elect, the Church of which every member is truly sanctified, the Church of believing and penitent men and women,— this is the Church to which alone, strictly speaking, the promise belongs. This is the Church in which there is always a real spiritual "presence" of Christ.

There is not a visible Church on earth, however ancient and well ordered, which is secure against falling away. Scripture and history alike testify that, like the Jewish Church, it may become corrupt, and depart from the faith, and departing from the faith, may die. And why is this? Simply because Christ has never promised to any visible Church that He will be with it always, even unto the end of the world. The word that He inspired St. Paul to write to the Roman Church is the same word that He sends to every visible Church throughout the world, whether Episcopal, Presbyterian, or Congregational: "Be not high-minded, but fear:—continue in God's goodness: otherwise thou also shalt be cut off."* (Rom. xi. 20-22.)

On the other hand, the perpetual presence of Christ with that Holy Catholic Church, which is His body, is the great secret of its continuance and security. It lives on, and cannot die, because Jesus Christ is in the midst of it. It is a ship tossed with storm and tempest; but it cannot sink, because Christ is on board. Its members may be persecuted, oppressed, imprisoned, robbed, beaten, beheaded, or burned; but His true Church is never extinguished. It lives on through fire and water. When crushed in one land, it springs up in another. The Pharaohs, the Herods, the Neros, the Julians, the bloody Marys, the Charles the Ninths, have laboured in vain to destroy this Church. They slay their thousands, and then go to their own place. The true Church outlives them all. It is a bush that is often burning, and yet is never consumed. And what is the reason of all this? It is the perpetual "presence" of Jesus Christ.

(b) There is a real spiritual "presence" of Christ in the heart of every

---

* "Whatsoever we read in Scripture concerning the endless love and the saving mercy which God showeth towards His Church, the only proper subject thereof is this Church which is the mystical body of Christ. Concerning this flock it is that our Lord and Saviour hath promised, 'I give unto them eternal life, and they shall never perish, neither shall any pluck them out of My hand."— *Hooker, Eccl. Polity*, book iii., ch. i., p. 2.

These are wise words, and words that all Hooker's professed admirers would do well to ponder and digest. Few things are so mischievous as the common habit of applying to such mixed and corrupt bodies as visible Churches those blessed promises of perpetuity and preservation which belong to none but the company of true believers.

true believer. This is what St. Paul meant when he speaks of "Christ dwelling in the heart by faith." (Eph. iii. 17.) This is what our Lord meant when He says of the man that loves Him and keeps His Word, "We will come unto him, and make our abode with him." (John xiv. 23.) In every believer, whether high or low, or rich or poor, or young or old, or feeble or strong, the Lord Jesus dwells, and keeps up His work of grace by the power of the Holy Ghost. As He dwells in the whole Church, which is His body,—keeping, guarding, preserving, and sanctifying it,—so does He continually dwell in every member of that body, in the least as well as in the greatest. This "presence" is the secret of all that peace, and hope, and joy, and comfort, which believers feel. All spring from their having a Divine tenant within their hearts. This "presence" is the secret of their continuance in the faith, and perseverance unto the end. In themselves they are weak and unstable as water. But they have within them One who is "able to save to the uttermost," and will not allow His work to be overthrown. Not one bone of Christ's mystical body shall ever be broken. Not one lamb of Christ's flock shall ever be plucked out of His hand. The house in which Christ is pleased to dwell, though it be but a cottage, is one which the devil shall never break into and make his own.

(c) There is a real spiritual "presence" of Christ wherever His believing people meet together in His name. This is the plain meaning of that famous saying, "Wherever two or three are gathered together in My name, there am I in the midst of them." (Matt. xviii. 20.) The smallest gathering of true Christians for the purposes of prayer or praise, or holy conference, or reading God's Word, is sanctified by the best of company. The great or rich or noble may not be there, but the King of kings Himself is present, and angels look on with reverence. The grandest buildings that men have reared for religious uses are often no better than whitened sepulchres, destitute of any holy influence, because given up to super-stitious ceremonies, and filled to no purpose with crowds of formal worshippers, who come unfeeling, and go unfeeling away. No worship is of any use to souls at which Christ is not present. Incense, banners, pictures, flowers, crucifixes, and long processions of richly-dressed ecclesi-astics are a poor substitute for the great High Priest Himself. The meanest room where a few penitent believers assemble in the name of Jesus is a consecrated and most holy place in the sight of God. They that worship God in spirit and truth never draw near to Him in vain. Often they go home from such meetings warmed, cheered, stablished, strengthened, comforted, and refreshed. And what is the secret of their feelings? They have had with them the great Master of assemblies, even Christ Himself.

(d) There is a real spiritual "presence" of Christ with the hearts of all true-hearted communicants in the Lord's Supper. Rejecting as I do, with all my heart, the baseless notion of any bodily presence of Christ on the Lord's Table, I can never doubt that the great ordinance appointed by

Christ has a special and peculiar blessing attached to it. That blessing, I believe, consists in a special and peculiar presence of Christ, vouchsafed *to the heart* of every believing communicant. That truth appears to me to lie under those wonderful words of institution, "Take, eat: this is My body." "Drink ye all of this: this is My blood." Those words were never meant to teach that the bread in the Lord's Supper was literally Christ's body, or the wine literally Christ's blood. But our Lord did mean to teach that every right-hearted believer, who ate that bread and drank that wine in remembrance of Christ, would in so doing find a special presence of Christ in his heart, and a special revelation of Christ's sacrifice of His own body and blood to his soul. In a word, there is a special spiritual "presence" of Christ in the Lord's Supper, which they only know who are faithful communicants, and which they who are not communicants miss altogether.

After all, the experience of all the best servants of Christ is the best proof that there is a special blessing attached to the Lord's Supper. You will rarely find a true believer who will not say that he reckons this ordinance one of his greatest helps and highest privileges. He will tell you that if he was deprived of it, he would find the loss of it a great drawback to his soul. He will tell you that in eating that bread, and drinking that cup, he realizes something of Christ dwelling in him; and finds his repentance deepened, his faith increased, his knowledge enlarged, his graces strengthened. Eating the bread with faith, he feels closer communion with the body of Christ. Drinking the wine with faith, he feels closer communion with the blood of Christ. He sees more clearly what Christ is to him, and what he is to Christ. He understands more thoroughly what it is to be one with Christ and Christ with him. He feels the roots of his spiritual life insensibly watered, and the work of grace within him insensibly built up and carried forward. He cannot explain or define it. It is a matter of experience, which no one knows but he who feels it. And the true explanation of the whole matter is this,—there is a special and spiritual "presence" of Christ in the ordinance of the Lord's Supper. Jesus meets those who draw near to His Table with a true heart, in a special and peculiar way.

(e) Last, but not least, there is a real spiritual "presence" of Christ vouchsafed to believers in special times of trouble and difficulty. This is the presence of which St. Paul received assurance on more than one occasion. At Corinth, for instance, it is written, "Then spake the Lord to Paul in the night by a vision, Be not afraid, but speak, and hold not thy peace: for I am with thee, and no man shall set on thee to hurt thee." (Acts xviii. 9, 10.) At Jerusalem, again, when the apostle was in danger of his life, it is written, "The night following the Lord stood by him, and said, Be of good cheer, Paul; for as thou hast testified of Me in Jerusalem, so must thou bear witness also in Rome." (Acts xxiii. 11.) Again, in the last Epistle St. Paul wrote, we find him saying, "At my first answer no man stood with me, but all men forsook me: I pray God that it may not be laid to their charge. Notwithstanding the Lord stood with me and strengthened me." (2 Tim. iv. 16, 17.)

This is the account of the singular and miraculous courage which many of God's children have occasionally shown under circumstances of unusual trial, in every age of the Church. When the three children were cast into the fiery furnace, and preferred the risk of death to idolatry, we are told that Nebuchadnezzar exclaimed, 'Lo, I see four men loose, walking in the midst of the fire, and they have no hurt; and the form of the fourth is like the Son of God." (Dan. iii. 25.) When Stephen was beset by bloody-minded enemies on the very point of stoning him, we read that he said, "Behold, I see heaven opened, and the Son of man standing on the right hand of God." (Acts vii. 56.) Nor ought we to doubt that this special presence was the secret of the fearlessness with which many early Christian martyrs met their deaths, and of the marvellous courage which the Marian martyrs, such as Bradford, Latimer, and Rogers, displayed at the stake. A peculiar sense of Christ being with them is the right explanation of all these cases. These men died as they did because Christ was with them. Nor ought any believer to fear that the same helping presence will be with him, whenever his own time of special need arrives. Many are over-careful about what they shall do in their last sickness, and on the bed of death. Many disquiet themselves with anxious thoughts as to what they would do if husband or wife died, or if they were suddenly turned out of house and home. Let us believe that when the need comes the help will come also. Let us not carry our crosses before they are laid upon us. He that said to Moses, "Certainly I will be with thee," will never fail any believer who cries to Him. When the hour of special storm comes, the Lord who walks upon the waters will come and say, "Peace: be still." There are thousands of doubting saints continually crossing the river, who go down to the water in fear and trembling, and yet are able at last to say with David, "Though I walk through the valley of the shadow of death, I will fear no evil; for Thou art with me." (Psa. xxiii. 4.)

This branch of our subject deserves to be pondered well. This spiritual presence of Christ is a real and true thing, though a thing which the children of this world neither know nor understand. It is precisely one of those matters of which St. Paul writes, "The natural man receiveth not the things of the Spirit of God, for they are foolishness unto him." (1 Cor. ii. 14.) But for all that, I repeat emphatically, the spiritual presence of Christ,—His presence after the manner of a Spirit with the spirits of His own people,—is a thing real and true. Let us not doubt it. Let us hold it fast. Let us seek to feel it more and more. The man who feels nothing whatever of it in his own heart's experience, may depend on it that he is not yet in a right state of soul.

III. The last point which I propose to consider, is the *real bodily presence of our Lord Jesus Christ*. Where is it? What ought we to think about it? What ought we to reject, and what ought we to hold fast?

This is a branch of my subject on which it is most important to have clear and well-defined views. There are rocks around it on which many are making shipwreck. No doubt there are deep things and difficulties connected with it. But this must not prevent our examining it as far as possible by the light of Scripture. Whatever the Bible teaches plainly about Christ's bodily presence, it is our duty to hold and believe. To shrink from holding it because we cannot reconcile it with some human tradition, some minister's teaching, or some early prejudice inbibed in youth, is presumption, and not humility. To the law and to the testimony! What says the Scripture about Christ's bodily presence? Let us examine the matter step by step.

(a) There was a bodily presence of our Lord Jesus Christ during the time that He was upon earth at His first advent. For thirty-three years, at least, between His birth and His ascension, He was present in a body in this world. In infinite mercy to our souls the eternal Son of God was pleased to take our nature on Him, and to be miraculously born of a woman, with a body just like our own. He was made like unto us in all things, sin only excepted. Like us He grew from infancy to boyhood, and from boyhood to youth, and from youth to manhood. Like us He ate, and drank, and slept, and hungered, and thirsted, and wept, and felt fatigue and pain. He had a body which was subject to all the conditions of a material body. While, as God, He was in heaven and earth at the same time; as man, His body was only in one place at one time. When He was in Galilee He was not in Judæa, and when He was in Capernaum He was not in Jerusalem. In a real, true human body He lived; in a real, true human body He kept the law, and fulfilled all righteousness; and in a real, true human body He bore our sins on the Cross, and made satisfaction for us by His atoning blood. He that died for us on Calvary was perfect man, while at the same time He was perfect God. This was the first real bodily presence of Jesus Christ.

The truth before us is full of unspeakable comfort to all who have an awakened conscience, and know the value of their souls. It is a heart-cheering thought that the "One Mediator between God and man is the man Jesus Christ:" real Man, and so able to be touched with the feeling of our infirmities; Almighty God, and so able to save to the uttermost all who come to the Father by Him. The Saviour in whom the labouring and heavy-laden are invited to trust, is One who had a real body when He was working out our redemption on earth. It was no angel, nor spirit, nor ghost, that stood in our place and became our Substitute, that finished the work of redemption, and did what Adam failed to do. No: it was One who was real man! "By man came death, and by man came also the resurrection of the dead." (1 Cor. xv. 21.) The battle was fought for us, and the victory was won by the eternal Word made flesh,—by the real bodily presence among us of Jesus Christ. For ever let us praise God that Christ did not remain in heaven, but came into the world and was made flesh to save sinners; that in the body, He was born for us, lived for us, died for us, and rose again. Whether men know it or not, our whole hope of eternal life hinges on the simple fact, that eighteen hundred years ago there was a real bodily presence of the Son of God for us on the earth.

(b) Let us now go a step further. There is a real bodily presence of Jesus Christ in heaven at the right hand of God. This is a deep and mysterious subject, beyond question. What God the Father is, and where He dwells, what the nature of His dwelling-place who is a Spirit,—these are high things which we have no minds to take in. But where the Bible speaks plainly it is our duty and our wisdom to believe. When our Lord rose again from the dead, He rose with a real human body,—a body which could not be in two places at once,—a body of which the angels said, "He is not here, but is risen." (Luke xxiv. 6.) In that body, having finished His redeeming work on earth, He ascended visibly into heaven. He took His body with Him, and did not leave it behind, like Elijah's mantle. It was not laid in the grave at last, and did not become dust and ashes in some Syrian village, like the bodies of saints and martyrs. The same body which walked in the streets of Capernaum, and sat in the house of Mary and Martha, and was crucified on Golgotha, and was laid in Joseph's tomb,—that same body,—after the resurrection glorified undoubtedly, but still real and material,—was taken up into heaven, and is there at this very moment. To use the inspired words of the Acts, "While they beheld, He was taken up, and a cloud received Him out of their sight." (Acts i. 11.) To use the words of St. Luke's Gospel, "While He blessed them, He was parted from them, and carried up into heaven." (Luke xxiv. 51.) To use the words of St. Mark, "After the Lord had spoken to them, He was received up into heaven, and sat on the right hand of God." (Mark xvi. 19.) The Fourth Article of the Church of England states the whole matter fully and accurately: "Christ did truly rise again from death, and took again His body, with flesh, bones, and all things appertaining to the perfection of man's nature: wherewith He ascended into heaven, and there sitteth, until He return to judge all men at the last day." And thus, to come round to the point with which we started, there is in heaven a real bodily presence of Jesus Christ.

The doctrine before us is singularly rich in comfort and consolation to all true Christians. That divine Saviour in heaven, on whom the Gospel tells us to cast the burden of our sinful souls, is not a Being who is Spirit only, but a Being who is man as well as God. He is One who has taken up to heaven a body like our own; and in that body sits at the right hand of God, to be our Priest and our Advocate, our Representative and our

Friend. He can be touched with the feeling of our infirmities, because He
has suffered Himself in the body being tempted. He knows by experience
all that the body is liable to from pain, and weariness, and hunger, and
thirst, and work; and has taken to heaven that very body which endured
the contradiction of sinners and was nailed to the tree. Who can doubt
that that body in heaven is a continual plea for believers, and renders
them ever acceptable in the Father's sight? It is a perpetual remembrance
of the perfect propitiation made for us upon the Cross. God will not
forget that our debts are paid for, so long as the body which paid for them
with life-blood is in heaven before His eyes. Who can doubt that when
we pour out our petitions and prayers before the throne of grace, we
put them in the hand of One whose sympathy passes knowledge? None
can feel for poor believers wrestling here in the body, like Him who in
the body sits pleading for them in heaven. For ever let us bless God that
there is a real bodily presence of Christ in heaven.

(c) Let us now go a step further. There is no real bodily presence of
Christ in the sacrament of the Lord's Supper or in the consecrated
elements of bread and wine.

This is a point which it is peculiarly painful to discuss, because it has
long divided Christians into two parties, and defiled a very solemn subject
with sharp controversy. Nevertheless, it is one which cannot possibly be
avoided in handling the question we are considering. Moreover, it is a
point of vast importance, and demands very plain speaking. Those amiable
and well-meaning persons who imagine that it signifies little what opinion
people hold about Christ's presence in the Lord's Supper,—that it is a
matter of indifference, and that it all comes to the same thing at last,—
are totally and entirely mistaken. They have yet to learn that an unscriptural view of the subject may land them at length in a very dangerous
heresy. Let us search and see.

My reason for saying that there is no bodily presence of Christ in the
Lord's Supper or in the consecrated bread and wine, is simply this: there
is no such presence taught anywhere in holy Scripture. It is a presence
that can never be honestly and fairly got out of the Bible. Let the three
accounts of the institution of the Lord's Supper, in the Gospels of St.
Matthew, St. Mark, and St. Luke, and the one given by St. Paul to the
Corinthians, be weighed and examined impartially, and I have no doubt
as to the result. They teach that the Lord Jesus, in the same night that He
was betrayed, took bread and gave it to His disciples, saying, "Take, eat:
this is My body;" and also took the cup of wine, and gave it to them,
saying, "Drink ye all of this: this is My blood." But there is nothing in
the simple narrative, or in the verses which follow it, which shows that
the disciples thought their Master's body and blood were really *present
in the bread and wine* which they received.—There is not a word in the
Epistles to show that after our Lord's ascension into heaven the Christians

believed that His body and blood were present in an ordinance celebrated on earth, or that the bread in the Lord's Supper, after consecration, was not truly and literally bread, and the wine truly and literally wine.

Some persons, I am aware, suppose that such texts as "This is My body," and "This is My blood," are proofs that Christ's body and blood, in some mysterious manner, are locally present in the bread and wine at the Lord's Supper, after their consecration. But a man must be easily satisfied if such texts content him. The quotation of a single isolated phrase is a mode of arguing which would establish Arianism or Socianism. The context of these famous expressions shows clearly that those who heard the words used, and were accustomed to our Lord's mode of speaking, understood them to mean, "This *represents* My body," and "This *represents* My blood."

The comparison of other places proves that there is nothing unfair in this interpretation. It is certain that the words "is" and "are" frequently mean "represent" in Scripture. The disciples no doubt remembered their Master saying such things as "The field *is* the world,—the good seed *are* the children of the kingdom." (Matt. xiii. 38.)—St. Paul, in writing on the sacrament, confirms this interpretation by expressly calling the consecrated bread, "bread," and not the body of Christ, no less than three times. (1 Cor. xi. 26–28.)

Some persons, again, regard the sixth chapter of St. John, where our Lord speaks of "eating His flesh and drinking His blood," as a proof that there is a literal bodily presence of Christ in the bread and wine at the Lord's Supper. But there is an utter absence of conclusive proof that this chapter refers to the Lord's Supper at all! The Lord's Supper had not been instituted, and did not exist, till at least a year after these words were spoken. Enough to say that the great majority of Protestant commentators altogether deny that the chapter refers to the Lord's Supper, and that even some Romish commentators on this point agree with them. The eating and drinking here spoken of are the eating and drinking of faith, and not a bodily action.

Some people fancy that St. Paul's words to the Corinthians, "The bread that we eat, is it not the communion of the body of Christ?" (1 Cor. x. 16) are enough to prove a bodily presence of Christ in the Lord's Supper. But unfortunately for their argument, St. Paul does not say, "The bread is the body," but the "communion of the body." And the obvious sense of the words is this,—"The bread that a worthy communicant eats in the Lord's Supper, is a means whereby his soul holds communion with the body of Christ." Nor do I believe that more than this can be got out of the words.

Above all, there remains the unanswerable argument that if our Lord was actually holding His own body in His hands, when He said of the bread, "This is My body," His body must have been a different body to that of ordinary men. Of course if His body was not a body like ours, His real and proper "humanity" is at an end. At this rate the blessed and comfortable doctrine of Christ's entire sympathy with His people, arising from the fact that He is really and truly man, would be completely overthrown and fall to the ground.

Finally, if the body with which our blessed Lord ascended up into heaven can be in heaven, and on earth, and on ten thousand communion tables at one and the same time, it cannot be a real human body at all. Yet that He did ascend with a real Human body, although a glorified body, is one of the prime articles of the Christian faith, and one that we ought never to let go! Once admit that a body can be present in two places at once, and you cannot prove that it is a body at all. Once admit that Christ's body can be present at God's right hand and on a communion table at the same moment, and it cannot be the body which was born of the Virgin Mary and crucified upon the Cross. From such a conclusion we may well draw back with horror and dismay. Well says the Prayer-book of the Church of England: "The sacramental bread and wine remain still in their very natural substances, and therefore may not be adored (for that were idolatry, to be abhored of all faithful Christians); and the natural body and blood of our Saviour Christ are in heaven, and *not here;* it being against the truth of Christ's natural body to be at one time in more places than one." This is sound speech that cannot be condemned. Well would it be for the Church of England if all Churchmen would read, mark, learn, and inwardly digest what the Prayer-book teaches about Christ's presence in the Lord's Supper.

If we love our souls and desire their prosperity, let us be very jealous over our doctrine about the Lord's Supper. Let us stand fast on the simple teaching of Scripture, and let no one drive us from it under the pretence of increased reverence for the ordinance of Christ. Let us take heed, lest under confused and mystical notions of some inexplicable presence of Christ's body and blood under the form of bread and wine, we find ourselves unawares heretics about Christ's human nature. Next to the doctrine that Christ is not God, but only man, there is nothing more dangerous than the doctrine that Christ is not man, but only God. If we would not fall into that pit, we must hold firmly that there can be no literal presence of Christ's body in the Lord's Supper; because His body is in heaven, and not on earth, though as God He is everywhere.*

(*d*) Let us now go one step further, and bring our whole subject to a

---

* The following sentence from Hooker, on the subject of Christ's body, deserves special attention:—

"It behoveth us to take great heed, lest while we go about to maintain the glorious deity of Him which is man, we leave Him not the true bodily substance of a man. According to Augustine's opinion, that majestical body which we make to be everywhere present, doth thereby cease to have the substance of a true body."—*Hooker, Eccles. Polity*, book v., ch. 55.

conclusion. There will be a real bodily presence of Christ when He comes again the second time to judge the world. This is a point about which the Bible speaks so plainly that there is no room left for dispute or doubt. When our Lord had ascended up before the eyes of His disciples, the angels said to them, "This same Jesus which is taken up from you into heaven, shall so come in like manner as ye have seen Him go into heaven." (Acts i. 11.) There can be no mistake about the meaning of these words. Visibly and bodily our Lord left the world, and visibly and bodily He will return in the day which is emphatically called the day of "His appearing." (1 Peter i. 7.)

The world has not yet done with Christ. Myriads talk and think of Him as of One who did His work in the world and passed on to His own place, like some statesman or philosopher, leaving nothing but His memory behind Him. The world will be fearfully undeceived one day. That same Jesus who came eighteen centuries ago in lowliness and poverty, to be despised and crucified, shall come again one day in power and glory, to raise the dead and change the living, and to reward every man according to his works. The wicked shall see that Saviour whom they despised, but too late, and shall call on the rocks to fall on them and hide them from the face of the Lamb. Those solemn words which Jesus addressed to the High Priest the night before His crucifixion shall at length be fulfilled: "Ye shall see the Son of man sitting on the right hand of power, and coming in the clouds of heaven." (Matt. xxvi. 64.) The godly shall see the Saviour whom they have read of, heard of, and believed, and find, like the Queen of Sheba, that the half of His goodness had not been known. They shall find that sight is far better than faith, and that in Christ's actual presence is fulness of joy.

This is the real bodily presence of Christ, for which every true-hearted Christian ought daily to long and pray. Happy are those who make it an article of their faith, and live in the constant expectation of a second personal advent of Christ. Then, and then only, will the devil be bound, the curse be taken off the earth, the world be restored to its original purity, sickness and death be taken away, tears be wiped from all eyes, and the redemption of the saint, in body as well as soul, be completed. "It doth not yet appear what we shall be; but we know that when He shall appear we shall be like Him, for we shall see Him as He is." (1 John iii. 2.) The highest style of Christian is the man who desires the real presence of his Master, and "loves His appearing." (2 Tim. iv. 8.)

I have now unfolded, as far as I can in a short paper, the truth about the presence of God and His Christ. I have shown (1) the general doctrine of God's presence everywhere; (2) the Scriptural doctrine of Christ's real, spiritual presence; (3) the Scriptural doctrine of Christ's real, bodily presence. I now leave the whole subject with a parting word of application, and commend it to serious attention. In an age of hurry and bustle about secular things, in an age of wretched strife and controversy about religion, I entreat men not to neglect the great truths which this paper contains.

(1) What do we know of Christ ourselves? We have heard of Him thousands of times. We call ourselves Christians. But what do we know of Christ experimentally, as our own personal Saviour, our own Priest, our own Friend, the Healer of our conscience, the Comfort of our heart, the Pardoner of our sins, the Foundation of our hope, the Confidence of our souls? How is it?

(2) Let us not rest till we feel Christ "present" in our own hearts, and know what it is to be one with Christ and Christ with us. This is real religion. To live in the habit of looking backward to Christ on the Cross, upward to Christ at God's right hand, and forward to Christ coming again,—this is the only Christianity which gives comfort in life and good hope in death. Let us remember this.

(3) Let us beware of holding erroneous views about the Lord's Supper, and especially about the real nature of Christ's "presence" in it. Let us not so mistake that blessed ordinance, which was meant to be our soul's meat, as to turn it into our soul's poison. There is no sacrifice in the Lord's Supper, no sacrificing priest, no altar, no bodily "presence" of Christ in the bread and wine. These things are not in the Bible, and are dangerous inventions of man, leading on to superstition. Let us take care.

(4) Let us keep continually before our minds the second advent of Christ, and that real "presence" which is yet to come. Let our loins be girded, and our lamps burning, and ourselves like men daily waiting for their Master's return. Then, and then only, shall we have all the desires of our souls satisfied. Till then the less we expect from this world the better. Let our daily cry be, "Come, Lord Jesus."

NOTE

Controversy about the Lord's Supper and the real presence of Christ, we all know, is at this moment one of the chief causes of division and disturbance in the Church of England. At such a crisis, it may not be uninteresting to some readers to hear the opinions of some of our well-known English divines about the points in dispute, in addition to those which I have already given, at the end of the paper on the "Lord's Supper."

I will give four quotations from four men of no mean authority, and ask the reader to consider them.

(1) Waterland says,—

"The words of the Church Catechism, *verily and indeed taken and received by the faithful*, are rightly interpreted of a real participation of the benefits purchased by Christ's death. The body and blood of Christ are taken and received by the faithful, not corporally, not internally, but verily and indeed, that is *effectually*. The sacred symbols are no bare signs, no untrue figures of a thing absent; but the force, the grace, the virtue, and benefit of Christ's body broken and blood shed, that is, of His passion, are really and effectually present with all them that receive worthily. This is *all the real presence* that our Church teaches."—*Waterland's Works*. Oxford, 1843. Vol. vi., p. 42.

(2) Dean Aldrich, of Christ Church, says,—

"The Church of England has wisely forborne to use the term of 'Real Presence' in all the books that are set forth by her authority. We neither find it recommended in the Liturgy, nor the Articles, nor the Homilies, nor the Church's Catechism, nor Nowell's. For although it be seen in the Liturgy, and once more in the Articles of 1552, it is mentioned in both places as a phrase of the Papists, and rejected for the abuse of it. So that *if any Church of England man use it, he does more than the Church directs him. If any reject it, he has the Church's example to warrant him; and it would very much contribute to the peace of Christendom if all men would write after so excellent a copy."—Dean Aldrich's Reply to Two Discourses.* Oxford, 1682. 4to, pp. 13–18.

(3) Henry Philpotts, Bishop of Exeter, in his letter to Charles Butler, says,—

"The Church of Rome holds that the body and blood of Christ are present under the accidents of bread and wine; the Church of England holds that their real presence is in the *soul of the communicant* at the sacrament of the Lord's Supper.

"She holds, that after the consecration of the bread and wine they are changed not in their nature but in their *use;* that instead of nourishing our bodies only, they now are instruments by which, when worthily received, God gives to our souls the body and blood of Christ to nourish and sustain them: that this is not a fictitious, or imaginary exhibition of our crucified Redeemer to us, but a real though spiritual one, more real, indeed, because more effectual, than the carnal exhibition and manducation of Him could be (for the flesh profiteth nothing).

"In the same manner, then, as our Lord Himself said, 'I am the *true* bread that came down from heaven' (not meaning thereby that He was a lump of baked dough, or manna, but the true means of sustaining the true life of man, which is spiritual, not corporeal), so in the sacrament, to the worthy receiver of the consecrated elements, though in their nature mere bread and wine, are yet given, truly, really, and effectively, the crucified body and blood of Christ; that body and blood which were the instruments of man's redemption, and upon which our spiritual life and strength solely depend. It is in this sense that the crucified Jesus is present in the sacrament of His Supper, not in, nor with, bread and wine, nor under their accidents, but in the souls of communicants; not carnally, but effectually and faithfully, and therefore most really."—*Philpott's Letter to Butler.* 8vo Edition. 1825. Pp. 235, 236.

(4) Archbishop Longley says, in his last Charge, printed and published after his death in 1868:—

"The doctrine of the Real Presence is, *in one sense*, the doctrine of the Church of England. She asserts that the body and blood of Christ are 'verily and indeed taken and received by the faithful in the Lord's Supper.' And she asserts equally that *such presence is not material or corporal*, but that Christ's body 'is given, taken, and eaten in the Supper, only after a heavenly and spiritual manner.' (Article xxviii.) Christ's presence is effectual for all those intents and purposes for which His body was broken and His blood shed. *As to a presence elsewhere than in the heart of a believer, the Church of England is silent*, and the words of Hooker therefore represent her views: 'The real presence of Christ's most blessed body and blood is not to be sought in the sacrament, but in the worthy receiver of the sacrament.' "

I will now conclude the whole subject with the following remarkable quotation, which I commend to the special attention of all my readers. It is taken from the elaborate judgment delivered by the Judicial Committee of the Privy Council, the highest Court of the realm, in the famous case of Sheppard *v.* Bennett:—

"Any presence of Christ in the Holy Communion, which is not *a presence* to the soul of the faithful receiver, the Church of England does not by her Articles and Formularies affirm, or require her ministers to accept." This cannot be stated too plainly.

X

THE CHURCH

THERE is perhaps no subject in religion which is so much misunderstood as the subject of the "Church." There is certainly no misunderstanding which has done more harm to professing Christians than the misunderstanding of this subject.

There are few words in the New Testament which are used in such a variety of meanings, as the word "Church."* It is a word which we hear constantly, and yet we cannot help observing that different people use it in different senses. The English politician in our days talks of "the Church." What does he mean? You will generally find he means the Episcopal Church established in his own country.—The Roman Catholic talks of "the Church." What does he mean? He means the Church of Rome, and tells you that there is no other Church in the world except his own.—The Dissenter talks of "the Church." What does he mean? He means the communicants of that chapel of which he is a member.— The members of the Church of England talk of "the Church." What do they mean? One means the building in which he worships on a Sunday. Another means the clergy,—and when any one is ordained, tells you that he has gone into the Church! A third has some vague notions about what he is pleased to call apostolical succession, and hints mysteriously that the Church is made up of Christians who are governed by Bishops, and of none beside. There is no denying these things. They are all patent and notorious facts. And they all help to explain the assertion with which I started,—that there are few subjects so much misunderstood as that of the "Church."

I believe that to have clear ideas about the Church is of the first importance in the present day. I believe that mistakes on this point are one grand cause of the religious delusions into which so many fall. I wish to direct attention to that great primary meaning in which the word "Church" is used in the New Testament, and to clear the subject of that

---

* There seem to be four meanings of the word Church in the New Testament. (1) It is applied to the whole body of the elect. (Heb. xii. 23.) (2) It is applied to the baptized Christians of a particular place or district. (Acts viii. 1.) (3) It is applied to a small number of professing Christians, in a particular family. (Rom. xvi. 5.) (4) It is applied to the whole body of baptized people throughout the world, both good and bad. (1 Cor. xii. 28.) In the fourth sense the word is used very seldom indeed. The first and second senses are the most common.

misty vagueness by which it is surrounded in so many minds. It was a most true saying of Bishop Jewel the Reformer, *"There never was anything yet so absurd or so wicked, but it might seem easy to be covered and defended by the name of the Church."* * (Jewel's *Apol.*, sec. xx.)

I. Let me then show, first of all, *what is that one true Church, out of which no man can be saved.*

II. Let me explain, in the second place, *what is the position and value of all visible professing Churches.*

III. And let me, in the third place, draw from the subject *some practical counsels and cautions for the times in which we live.*

I. First of all, let me show *that one true Church out of which no man can be saved.*

There is a Church outside of which there is no salvation,—a Church to which a man must belong, or be lost eternally. I lay this down without hesitation or reserve. I say it as strongly and as confidently as the strongest advocate of the Church of Rome. But what is this Church? Where is this Church? What are the marks by which this Church may be known? This is the grand question.

The one true Church is well described in the Communion Service of the Church of England, as "the mystical body of Christ, which is the blessed company of all faithful people." It is composed of all believers in the Lord Jesus.—It is made up of all God's elect,—of all converted men and women,—of all true Christians. In whatsoever we can discern the election of God the Father, the sprinkling of the blood of God the Son, the sanctifying work of God the Spirit, in that person we see a member of Christ's true Church.†

* "The adversaries of the truth defend many a false error under the name of the holy Church.

"Beware of deceit, when thou hearest the name of the Church. The verity is then assaulted. They call the Church of the devil the holy Church many times."—*Bishop Hooper.* 1547. *Parker Edit.*, pp. 83, 84.

† "The Church is the body of Christ.—It is the whole number and society of the faithful, whom God through Christ hath before the beginning of time appointed to everlasting life."—*Dean Nowell's Catechism, sanctioned by Convocation.* 1572.

"That Church which is Christ's body, and of which Christ is the head, standeth only of living stones, and true Christians, not only outwardly in name and title, but inwardly in heart and in truth."—*Bishop Ridley.* 1556. *Parker Edit.*, p. 126.

"Unto this Church pertain so many as from the beginning of the world until this time have unfeignedly believed in Christ, or shall believe unto the very end of the world. Against this Church the gates of hell shall not prevail."—*Thomas Becon, chaplain to Archbishop Cranmer,* 1550. *Parker Edit.*, vol. i., p. 294.

"The Holy Catholic Church is nothing else but a company of saints. To this Church pertain all they that since the beginning of the world have been saved, and that shall be saved unto the end thereof."—*Bishop Coverdale.* 1550. *Parker Edit.*, p. 461.

It is a Church of which all the members have the same marks. They are all born again of the Spirit.—They all possess "repentance towards God, faith towards our Lord Jesus Christ," and holiness of life and conversation.—They all hate sin, and they all love Christ.—They worship differently, and after various fashions. Some worship with a form of prayer, and some with none. Some worship kneeling, and some standing. But they all worship with one heart.—They are all led by one Spirit.—They all build upon one foundation.—They all draw their religion from one single book.—They are all joined to one great centre, that is Jesus Christ. They all, even now, can say with one heart,"Hallelujah!"—and they all can respond with one heart and voice, "Amen and amen."

It is a Church which is dependent upon no ministers upon earth, however much it values those who preach the Gospel to its members. The life of its members does not hang on Church-membership and baptism and the Lord's Supper, although they highly value these things, when they are to be had. But it has only one Great Head,—one Shepherd,—one chief Bishop,—and that is Jesus Christ. He alone, by His Spirit, admits the members of this Church, though ministers may show the door. Till He opens the door, no man on earth can open it,—neither bishops, nor presbyters, nor convocations, nor synods. Once let a man repent and believe the Gospel, and that moment he becomes a member of this Church. Like the penitent thief, he may have no opportunity of being baptized. But he has that which is far better than any water-baptism,—the baptism of the Spirit. He may not be able to receive the bread and wine in the Lord's Supper,—but he eats Christ's body and drinks Christ's blood by faith every day he lives, and no minister on earth can prevent him. He may be excommunicated by ordained men, and cut off from the outward ordinances of the professing Church,—but all the ordained men in the world cannot shut him out of the true Church.*

"The Catholic Church which is called the body of Christ, consists of such as are truly sanctified and united to Christ by an internal alliance, so that no wicked person, or unbeliever, is a member of this body, solely by the external profession of faith and participation of the sacraments."—*Bishop Davenant on Coloss.*, vol. i., p. 18. 1627.

"They who are indeed holy and obedient to Christ's laws of faith and manners, these are truly and perfectly the Church. These are the Church of God in the eyes and heart of God. For the Church of God is the body of Christ. But the mere profession of Christianity makes no man a member of Christ,—nothing but a new creature, nothing but a faith working by love, and keeping the commandments of God."—*Bishop Jeremy Taylor's Dissuasive from Popery,* part ii., book i., sec. 1. 1660.

"That Church which is Christ's mystical body consisteth of none but only true Israelites, true sons of Abraham, true servants and saints of God."—*Hooker, Eccles. Polity,* book iii., sec. 1. 1600.

* "A man may be a true and visible member of the Holy Catholic Church, and yet be no actual member of any visible Church."

"Many there be, or may be in most ages, which are no members of the visible Church, and yet better members of the true Church than the members of the Church visible for the present are."—*Jackson on the Church.* 1670.

It is a Church whose existence does not depend on forms, ceremonies, cathedrals, churches, chapels, pulpits, fonts, vestments, organs, endowments, money, kings, governments, magistrates, or any favour whatsoever from the hand of man. It has often lived on and continued when all these things have been taken from it. It has often been driven into the wilderness, or into dens and caves of the earth, by those who ought to have been its friends. But its existence depends on nothing but the presence of Christ and His Spirit, and so long as they are with it the Church cannot die.

This is the Church to which the titles of present honour and privilege, and the promises of future glory especially belong.* This is the body of Christ.—This is the bride.—This is the Lamb's wife.—This is the flock of Christ.—This is the household of faith and family of God.—This is God's building, God's foundation, and the temple of the Holy Ghost. This is the Church of the first-born, whose names are written in heaven. This is the royal priesthood, the chosen generation, the peculiar people, the purchased possession, the habitation of God, the light of the world, the salt and the wheat of the earth. This is the "holy Catholic Church" of the Apostle's Creed.—This is the "One Catholic and Apostolic Church" of the Nicene Creed.—This is that Church to which the Lord Jesus promises "the gates of hell shall not prevail against it," and to

---

* "Whatsoever we read in Scripture concerning the endless love and saving mercy which God showeth towards His Church, the only proper subject thereof is this Church, which we properly term the mystical body of Christ."—*Hooker, Eccles. Pol.*, book iii., sec. 1. 1600.

"If any will agree to call the universality of professors by the title of the Church, they may if they will. Any word by consent may signify anything. But if by a Church we mean that society which is really joined to Christ, which hath received the Holy Ghost, which is heir of the promises and of the good things of God, which is the body of which Christ is the head, then the invisible part of the visible Church, that is the true servants of Christ, only are the Church."—*Bishop Jeremy Taylor's Dissuasive from Popery.* 1660.

"The Catholic Church in the prime sense consists only of such men as are actual and indissoluble members of Christ's mystical body, or of such as have the Catholic faith not only sown in their brains and understandings, but thoroughly rooted in their hearts.—All the glorious prerogatives, titles, or promises, annexed to the Church in Scripture, are in the first place and principally meant of Christ's live and mystical body."—*Jackson on the Church.* 1670.

"What is meant in the Creed by the Catholic Church? That whole universal company of the elect, that ever were, are, or shall be gathered together in one body, knit together in one faith, under one head, Jesus Christ."—*Archbishop Usher.* 1650.

"In the Creed we do believe in the Church, but not in this or that Church, but the Catholic Church,—which is no particular assembly of men, much less the Roman synagogue, tied to any one place, but the body of the elect which hath existed from the beginning of the world, and shall exist unto the end."—*Whittaker's Disputations.* 1610. *Parker Edit.* Vol. i., p. 199.

"The Holy Catholic Church, a number that serve God here, and enjoy Him in eternity.—Universal, diffused through the various ages, places, and nations of the world.—Holy, washed in the blood of Christ, and sanctified by His Spirit."—*Archbishop Leighton on the Creed.* 1680.

which He says, "I am with you alway, even unto the end of the world."
(Matt. xvi. 18, xxviii. 20.)

This is the only Church which possesses true *unity*. Its members are
entirely agreed on all the weightier matters of religion, for they are all
taught by one Spirit. About God, and Christ, and the Spirit, and sin,
and their own hearts, and faith, and repentance, and the necessity of
holiness, and the value of the Bible, and the importance of prayer, and
the resurrection, and judgment to come,—about all these points they see
eye to eye. Take three or four of them, strangers to one another, from
the remotest corners of the earth. Examine them separately on these
points. You will find them all of one mind.*

This is the only Church which possesses true *sanctity*. Its members
are all holy. They are not merely holy by profession, holy in name, and
holy in the judgment of charity. They are all holy in act, and deed, and
reality, and life, and truth. They are all more or less conformed to the
image of Jesus Christ. They are all more or less like their great Head.
No unholy man belongs to this Church.†

This is the only Church which is truly *Catholic*. It is not the Church
of any one nation or people. Its members are to be found in every part
of the world where the Gospel is received and believed. It is not confined
within the limits of any one country, nor pent up within the pale of any
particular forms or outward government. In it there is no difference
between Jew and Greek, black man and white, Episcopalian and Presbyterian;—but faith in Christ is all. Its members will be gathered from
north, and south, and east, and west, in the last day, and will be of every
name, and denomination, and kindred, and people, and tongue, but all
one in Christ Jesus.

This is the only Church which is truly *Apostolic*. It is built on the
foundation laid by the Apostles, and holds the doctrines which they
preached. The two grand objects at which its members aim, are aspostolic
faith and apostolic practice; and they consider the man who talks of
following the Apostles without possessing these two things, to be no
better than sounding brass and a tinkling cymbal.‡

This is the only Church which is *certain to endure* unto the end. Nothing

* "To the mystical and invisible Church belongs peculiarly that unity which
is often attributed unto the Church."—"This is the society of those for whom
Christ did pray that they might be one."—*Barrow on the Unity of the Church.*
1670.

† "To this Holy Catholic Church, which forms the mystical body of Christ,
we deny that the ungodly, hypocrites, or any belong, who are not partakers
of spiritual life, and are void of inward faith, charity, and holiness. The most
learned Augustine has denied it as well, giving it as his opinion that all such
should be ranked among the members of Antichrist."—*Bishop Davenant's
Determinations.* 1634. Vol. ii., p. 475.

‡ "They are the successors of the Apostles that succeed in virtue, holiness,
truth, and so forth; not they that sit upon the same stool."—*Bishop Babington.*
1615. *Folio edition,* p. 307.

can altogether overthrow and destroy it. Its members may be persecuted, oppressed, imprisoned, beaten, beheaded, burned.—But the true Church is never altogether extinguished. It rises again from its affliction.—It lives on through fire and water.—When crushed in one land, it springs up in another. The Pharaohs, the Herods, the Neros, the Julians, the Diocletians, the bloody Marys, the Charles the Ninths have laboured in vain to put down this Church. They slay their thousands, and then pass away and go to their own place. The true Church out-lives them all, and sees them buried each in his turn. It is an anvil that has broken many a hammer in this world, and will break many a hammer still. It is a bush which is often burning, and yet is not consumed.*

This is the only Church *of which no one member can perish.* Once enrolled in the lists of this Church, sinners are safe for eternity.—They are never cast away. The election of God the Father,—the continual intercession of God the Son,—the daily renewing and sanctifying power of God the Holy Ghost, surround and fence them in like a garden enclosed. Not one bone of Christ's mystical body shall ever be broken. Not one lamb of Christ's flock shall ever be plucked out of His hand.†

This is the Church which *does the work of Christ* upon earth. Its members are a little flock, and few in number compared with the children of the world:—one or two here, and two or three there,—a few in this parish, and a few in that. But these are they who shake the universe.—These are they who change the fortunes of kingdoms by their prayers.—These are they who are the active workers for spreading the knowledge of pure religion and undefiled.—These are the life-blood of a country,—the shield, the defence, the stay and the support of any nation to which they belong.

This is the Church which *shall be truly glorious* at the end of all things. When all earthly glory is passed away, then shall this Church be presented without spot, before God the Father's throne. Thrones, principalities, and powers upon earth shall come to nothing.—Dignities and offices and endowments shall all pass away.—But the Church of the first-born shall shine as the stars at the last, and be presented with joy before the Father's throne, in the day of Christ's appearing. When the Lord's

---

* "The Holy Catholic Church is built upon a rock, so that not even the gates of hell can prevail against it. This is the privilege of the elect and believers. All the ungodly and hypocrites are built upon the sand, are overcome by Satan, and are sunk at last into hell. How then can they form a part of the mystical body of Christ, which admits not condemned members?"—*Bishop Davenant's Determinations.* 1634. Vol. ii., p. 478.

"The preservation of the Church is a continuing miracle. It resembles Daniel's safety among the hungry lions, but prolonged from one age to another. The ship wherein Christ is may be weather-beaten, but shall not perish."—*Archbishop Leighton on the Creed.* 1680.

† "Of all such as are effectually called, or authentically admitted into this society, none will revolt again to the Synagogue of Satan or to the world."—*Jackson on the Church.* 1670.

jewels are made up, and the manifestation of the sons of God takes place, Episcopacy, and Presbyterianism, and Congregationalism will not be mentioned. One Church only will be named, and that is the Church of the elect.

This is the Church for *which a true minister of the Lord Jesus Christ's Gospel chiefly labours.* What is it to a true minister to fill the building in which he preaches? What is it to him to see communicants come up more and more to his table? What is it to him to see his party grow? It is all nothing, unless he can see men and women "born again,"—unless he can see souls converted and brought to Christ,—unless he can see here one and there another, "coming out from the world," "taking up the cross and following Christ," and thus increasing the numbers of the one true Church.

This is the Church *to which a man must belong, if he would be saved.* Till we belong to this, we are nothing better than lost souls. We may have the form, the husk, the skin, and the shell of religion, but we have not got the substance and the life. Yes! we may have countless outward privileges,—we may enjoy great light and knowledge and opportunities; —but if we do not belong to the body of Christ, our light, and knowledge, and privileges, and opportunities, will not save our souls. Alas, for the ignorance that prevails on this point! Men fancy if they join this Church or that Church, and become communicants, and go through certain forms, that all must be right with their souls. It is an utter delusion: it is a gross mistake. All were not Israel who were called Israel, and all are not members of Christ's body who profess themselves Christians. Never let us forget that we may be staunch Episcopalians, or Presbyterians, or Independents, or Baptists, or Wesleyans, or Plymouth Brethren,—and yet not belong to the true Church. And if we do not, it will be better at last if we had never been born.*

II.   Let me pass on now to the second point I proposed to speak of. Let me explain *the position and value of all visible professing Churches.*

No careful reader of the Bible can fail to observe that many separate Churches are mentioned in the New Testament. At Corinth, at Ephesus, at Thessalonica, at Antioch, at Smyrna, at Sardis, at Laodicea, and several other places; at each we find a distinct body of professing Christians,—a body of people baptized in Christ's name, and professing the faith of Christ's Gospel. And these bodies of people we find spoken of as "the Churches" of the places which are named. Thus St. Paul says

* "We insist that Christians do certainly become members of particular Churches,—such as the Roman, Anglican, or Gallican, by outward profession; yet do not become true members of the Holy Catholic Church, which we believe, unless they are sanctified by the inward gift of grace, and are united to Christ the Head, by the bond of the spirit,"—*Bishop Davenant's Determinations.* 1634. Vol. ii., p. 474.

to the Corinthians, "But we have no such custom, neither the Churches of Christ." (1 Cor. xi. 16.) So also we read of the Churches of Judea, the Churches of Syria, the Churches of Galatia, the Churches of Asia, the Churches of Macedonia. In each case the expression means the bodies of baptized Christians in the countries mentioned.

Now, we have but little information given us in the New Testament about these Churches;—but that little is very clear and plain, so far as it goes.

We know, for one thing, that these Churches were all mixed bodies. They consisted not only of converted persons, but of many unconverted persons also. They contained not only believers, but members who fell into gross errors and mistakes, both of faith and practice. This is clear from the account we have of the Churches at Corinth, at Ephesus, and at Sardis. Of Sardis the Lord Jesus Himself says, that there were "a few," a few only, in it, who had not "defiled their garments." (Rev. iii. 4.)

We know, moreover, that even in the Apostles' times Churches received plain warnings, that they might perish and pass away altogether. To the Church at Rome the threat was held out that it should be "cut off;" to the Church at Ephesus, that its "candlestick should be taken away;" to the Church at Laodicea, that it should be utterly rejected. (Rom. xi. 22; Rev. ii. 5, and iii. 16.)

We know, moreover, that in all these Churches there was public worship, preaching, reading of the Scriptures, prayer, praise, discipline, order, government, the ministry, and the sacraments. What kind of governments some Churches had it is impossible to say positively. We read of officers who were called angels, of bishops, of deacons, of elders, of pastors, of teachers, of evangelists, of prophets, of helps, of governments. (1 Cor. xii. 28; Ephes. iv. 11; Phil. i. 1; 1 Tim. iii.; Rev. i. 20.) All these are mentioned. But the particulars about most of these officers are kept from us by the Spirit of God. As to the standard of doctrine and practice in the Churches, we have the fullest and most distinct information. On these points the language of the New Testament is clear and unmistakable. But as to government and outward ceremonies, the information given to us is strikingly small. The contrast between the Church of the Old Testament and the Churches of the New, in this respect, is very great. In the one, we find little, comparatively, about doctrine, but much about forms and ordinances. In the other, we have much about doctrine, and little about forms. In the Old Testament Church the minutest directions were given for the performance of every part of the ceremonies of religion. In the New Testament Churches we find the ceremonies expressly abolished, as no longer needed after Christ's death, and nothing hardly, except a few general principles, supplying their place. The New Testament Churches have got no book of Leviticus. Their two chief principles seem to be, "Let all things be done decently and in order;—Let all things be done unto edification." (1 Cor. xiv. 26, 40.) But as to the application of these general principles, it seems to have been left to each particular Church to decide.*

We know, finally, that the work begun by the missionary preaching of the Apostles was carried on through the instrumentality of the professing Churches. It was through the means of grace used in their public assemblies that God added to the number of His people, converted sinners, and built up saints. Mixed and imperfect as these Churches plainly were, within their pale were to be found nearly all the existing believers and members of the body of Christ. Everything in the New Testament leads us to suppose that there could have been few believers, if any, who were not members of some one or other of the professing Churches scattered up and down the world.

Such is about the whole of the information the New Testament gives us concerning visible Churches in the apostolic times. How shall we use this information? What shall we say of all the visible Churches in our own time? We live in days when there are many Churches:—the Church of England, the Church of Scotland, the Church of Ireland, the Church of Rome, the Greek Church, the Syrian Church, the Armenian Church, the Lutheran Church, the Genevan Church, and many others. We have Episcopalian Churches. We have Presbyterian Churches. We have Independent Churches. In what manner shall we speak of them? Let me put down a few general principles.†

(a) For one thing, no visible Church on earth has a right to say, "We are the true Church, and except men belong to our communion they cannot be saved." No Church whatever has a right to say that;—whether it be the Church of Rome, the Church of Scotland, or the Church of England;—whether it be an Episcopalian Church, a Presbyterian, or an Independent. Where is the text in the Bible that ties admission into the kingdom of God to the membership of any one particular visible Church upon earth?—I say confidently, not one.

---

* "I find no one certain and perfect kind of government prescribed or commanded in the Scriptures to the Church of Christ.

"I do deny that the Scriptures do express particularly everything that is to be done in the Church, or that it doth put down any one sort of form and kind of government of the Church to be perpetual for all times, persons, and places, without alteration."—*Archbishop Whitgift*. 1574. *Folio edition*, p. 84.

"I for my part do confess that, in revolving the Scriptures, I could never find but that God hath left the like liberty to the Church government as He hath done to the Civil government;—to be varied according to time, place, and accidents. So likewise in Church matters, the substance of doctrine is immutable, and so are the general rules of government. But for rites and ceremonies, and the particular hierarchies, policies, and discipline of the Churches, they be left at large."—*Lord Bacon's Works*, vol. vii., p. 68.

† For convenience sake these Churches collectively are often spoken of as "The Church," in contradistinction to the Heathen and Mahometan part of mankind. Only let us remember, that this is a very mixed Church, and one to which no special promises belong.

(b) Furthermore, no visible Church has a right to say, "We alone have the true form of worship, the true Church government, the true way of administering the sacraments, and the true manner of offering up united prayer; and all others are completely wrong." No Church, I repeat, has a right to say anything of the kind. Where can such assertions be proved by Scripture? What one plain, positive word of revelation can men bring forward in proof of any such affirmations? I say confidently, not one. There is not a text in the Bible which expressly commands Churches to have one special form of government, and expressly forbids any other. If there is, let men point it out. There is not a text which expressly confines Christians to the use of a Liturgy, or expressly enjoins them only to have extempore prayer. If there is, let it be shown. And yet for hundreds of years Episcopalians and Presbyterians and Independents have contended with each other, as if these things had been settled as minutely as the Levitical ceremonies, and as if everybody who did not see with their eyes was almost guilty of a deadly sin! It seems wonderful that in a matter like this, men should not be satisfied with the full persuasion that they themselves are right, but must also go on to condemn everybody who disagrees with them as utterly wrong! And yet this groundless theory, that God has laid down one particular form of Church government and ceremonies, has often divided men who ought to have known better. It has caused even good men to speak and write very unadvisedly. It has been made a fountain of incessant strife, intolerance, and bigotry by men of all parties, even among Protestants, from the times of Cartwright, Travers, and Laud, down to the present day.

(c) Furthermore, no visible Church on earth has a right to say, "We shall never fall away. We shall last for ever." There is no promise in the Bible to guarantee the continuance of any professing Church upon earth. Many have fallen completely, and perished already. Where are the Churches of Africa, in which Augustine and Cyprian used once to preach? Where are most of the Churches of Asia Minor, which we read of in the New Testament?—They are gone. They have passed away, and left hardly a wreck behind. Other existing Churches are so corrupt that it is a plain duty to leave them, lest we become partakers of their sins, and share in their plagues.

(d) Furthermore, no visible Church is in a sound and healthy state, which has not the marks we see in all the New Testament Churches. A Church in which the Bible is not the standard of faith and practice,—a Church in which repentance, faith, and holiness, are not prominently put forward as essential to salvation,—a Church in which forms, and ceremonies, and ordinances not commanded in the Bible, are the chief things urged upon the attention of the members,—such a Church is in a very diseased and unsatisfactory condition. It may not formally deny any article of the Christian faith. It may have been founded originally by

the Apostles. It may boast that it is Catholic. But if the Apostles were to
rise from the dead, and visit such a Church, I believe they would command
it to repent, and have no communion with it till it did.

(e) Furthermore, no mere membership of any visible Church will avail
a man anything " in the hour of death and in the day of judgment." No
communion with a visible Church will stand in the place of direct personal
communion with the Lord Jesus. No attendance whatever on its ordinances is a substitute for personal faith and conversion. It will be no
consolation when we lay our heads upon a dying pillow, if we can say
no more than this,—that we have belonged to a pure Church. It will be
no answer in the last great day, when the secrets of all hearts are revealed,
if we can only say that we worshipped in the Church in which we were
baptized, and used its forms.

(f) After all, what is the great use and purpose for which God has
raised up and maintained visible Churches upon earth? They are useful
as witnesses, keepers, and librarians of Holy Scripture. They are useful
as maintainers of a regular succession of ministers to preach the Gospel.
They are useful as preservers of order among professing Christians. But
their great and principal use is to train up, to rear, to nurse, to keep
together, members of that one true Church which is the body of Jesus
Christ. They are intended to "edify the body of Christ." (Ephes. iv. 12.)

Which is the best visible Church upon earth? That is the best, which
adds most members to the one true Church, which most promotes
"repentance towards God, faith towards the Lord Jesus Christ," and
good works among its members. These are the true tests and tokens of a
really good and flourishing Church. Give me that Church which has
evidence of this kind to show.

Which is the worst visible Church on earth? That is the worst which
has the fewest members of the one true Church to show in its ranks.
Such a Church may possess excellent forms, pure orders,—venerable
customs, ancient institutions. But if it cannot point to faith, repentance,
and holiness of heart and life among its members, it is a poor Church
indeed. "By their fruits" the Churches upon earth must be judged, as
well as individual Christians.*

We shall do well to remember these things. On the one side, a visible
professing Church is a true thing, and a thing according to the mind of
God. It is not, as some would tell us in these days, a mere human device,—
a thing which God does not speak of in the Word. It is amazing, to my

* "That which makes every visible Church to be more or less the true Church
of God, is the greater or less efficacy or conformity of its public doctrines and
discipline for adapting or fashioning the visible members of it, that they may
become live members of the Holy Catholic Church, or living stones of the new
Jerusalem. Every true visible Church is as an inferior free school or nursery
for training up scholars, that they may be fit to be admitted into the celestial
academy."—*Jackson on the Church.* 1670.

mind, that any one can read the New Testament, and then say that visible Churches are not authorized in the Bible.—On the other side, something more is needed than merely belonging to this Church, or that Church, to take a man to heaven. Are we born again? Have we repented of our sins? Have we laid hold of Christ by faith? Are we holy in life and conversation?—These are the grand points that a man must seek to ascertain. Without these things, the highest, the strictest, and the most regular member of a visible Church, will be a lost Churchman in the last great day.

Let us look upon visible Churches, with their outward forms and ordinances, as being to the one true Church what the husk is to the kernel of the nut. Both grow together,—both husk and kernel. Yet one is far more precious than the other. Just so the true Church is far more precious than the outward and visible.—The husk is useful to the kernel. It preserves it from many injuries, and enables it to grow. Just so the outward Church is useful to the body of Christ; it is within the pale of its ordinances that believers are generally born again, and grow up in faith, hope, and charity.—The husk is utterly worthless without the kernel. Just so the outward Church is utterly worthless except it guards and covers over the inward and the true.—The husk will die, but the kernel has a principle of life in it. Just so the forms and ordinances of the outward Church will all pass away, but that which lives and lasts for ever is the true Church within.—To expect the kernel without the husk, is expecting that which is contrary to the common order of the laws of nature. To expect to find the true Church, and members of the true Church, without having an orderly and well-governed and visible Church, is expecting that which God, in the ordinary course of things, does not give.*

Let us seek a right understanding upon these points. To give to the visible Church the names, attributes, promises, and privileges which belong to the one true Church,—the body of Christ; to confound the two things, the visible and the inward Church,—the Church professing and the Church of the elect,—is an immense delusion. It is a trap into which only too many fall. It is a great rock, on which many, in these days, unhappily make shipwreck.

Once confirmed the body of Christ with the outward professing Church, and there is no amount of error into which you may not at last fall. Nearly all perverts to Romanism begin with getting wrong here.†

Once get hold of the idea that Church government is of more importance than sound doctrine, and that a Church with bishops teaching falsehood

---

* "The invisible Church is ordinarily and regularly part of the visible, but yet that only part that is the true one."—*Bishop Jeremy Taylor.* 1670.

† "For lack of diligent observing the difference first between the Church of God, mystical and visible,—then between the visible sound and the visible corrupted,—the oversights are neither few nor light that have been committed." —*Hooker, Eccles. Pol.,* book iii. 1600.

is better than a Church without bishops teaching truth, and none can say what we may come to in religion.

III.   Let me now pass on to the third and last thing I proposed to do. Let me *draw from the subject some practical counsels and cautions for the times in which we live.*

I feel deeply that I should neglect a duty if I did not do this. The errors and mistakes connected with the subject of the Church are so many and so serious, that they need to be plainly denounced, and men need to be plainly put upon their guard against them. I have laid down some general principles about the one true Church, and about the visible professing Churches. Now let me go on to make some particular application of these general principles to the times in which we live.

(1) First of all, *let no reader suppose, because I have said that no membership of a visible Church can be the saving of a soul, that it does not signify to what visible Church a man belongs.* It does signify to what visible Church a man belongs;—and it signifies very much. There are Churches in which the Bible is practically lost sight of altogether. There are Churches in which Jesus Christ's Gospel is buried, and lies completely hidden. There are Churches in which a man may hear God's service performed in an unknown tongue, and never hear of "repentance towards God, faith towards Christ," and the work of the Holy Ghost, from one end of the year to the other. Such are the Armenian and Greek Churches, and such, above all others in corruption, is the Church of Rome. To belong to such Churches brings tremendous peril upon anybody's soul. They do not help men to the one true Church. They are far more likely to keep men out, and put barriers in their way for ever. A wise man should beware of ever being tempted to belong to such Churches himself, or of ever thinking lightly of the conduct of those who join such Churches, as if they had only committed a little sin.*

(2) In the next place, *let us not be moved by the argument of the Roman Catholic, when he says, "There is only one true Church and that one true Church is the Church of Rome, and you must join us if you mean to be saved."* Let no reader be entrapped by such miserable sophistry as this. A more preposterous and unwarrantable assertion was never made, if the question is simply tried by the Bible. It is a wonderful proof of the

* "If it be possible to be there, where the true Church is not, then is it at Rome."—*Church of England Homily for Whit-Sunday.*

"We have forsaken a Church in which we could neither hear the pure Word of God nor administer the sacraments, nor invoke the name of God as we ought,—and in which there was nothing to retain a prudent man who thought seriously of his salvation."—*Bishop Jewel's Apology.*

"Such adherence to the visible or representative Church of Rome, as Jesuits and others now challenge, doth induce a separation from the Holy Catholic Church, and is more deadly to the soul than to be bedfellow to one sick of the pestilence is to the body."—*Jackson on the Catholic Church. 1670.*

fallen condition of man's understanding that so many people are taken in by it. Tell the man who uses this argument, that there is indeed only one true Church, but it is not the Church of Rome, or the Church of England, or the Church of any other nation upon earth. Defy him boldly to show a single text which says that the Church of Rome is that one true Church to which men must belong. Tell him that to quote texts of Scripture which merely speak of "the Church," is no proof on his side at all, and that such texts might just as well refer to the Church of Jerusalem, or to the Church of Antioch, as to Rome. Point out to him the eleventh chapter of the Epistle to the Romans, which foretells Romish arrogance, and Romish presumption, and the possibility of Rome itself being cut off. Tell him that the Church's proud claim to be the one true Church is a mere baseless assumption,—a house built upon sand, which has not a tittle of Scripture to rest upon. Alas, how awful it is to think that many in this day of light and knowledge should be completely carried away by this miserable argument: "There must be one true Church; that one true Church must be a visible, professing Church: the Church of Rome is that one true Church;—therefore join it, or you will not be saved!"

(3) In the next place, *let us not be shaken by those persons who talk of "the voice of the Church," and the "Catholic Church," when we disagree with them, as if the very mention of these words ought to silence us.* There are many in these days of theological warfare, whose favourite weapon, when the Bible is appealed to, is this: "The Church says it;—the Church has always so ruled it;—the voice of the Church has always so pronounced it." I warn my readers never to be put down by arguments of this kind. Ask men what they mean when they talk in this vague way about "the Church." If they mean the whole professing Church throughout the world, call upon them to show when and where the whole Church has met to decide the matter about which they speak. Or ask them, if the Church had met, what right its decision would have to be listened to, except it could be shown to be founded upon the Word of God? Or, if they mean by "the voice of the Church," the voice of the Church of England, ask them to show you in the Thirty-nine Articles the doctrine which they want you to receive, and are pressing upon you. Point out to them that the Church of England says in those Articles, that "nothing is to be required of men, as necessary for salvation, except it can be read in, or proved by, the Holy Scriptures." Point out to them that it says furthermore, that although the Church has power to decree rites and ceremonies, and authority in controversies of faith, yet "it is not lawful for the visible Church to ordain anything contrary to God's Word written, or so to expound one place of Scripture as to make it repugnant to another." Show them also what the Church of England says when it speaks of the three creeds,—the Apostles' Creed, the Nicene Creed, and the Athanasian Creed. It does not say they are to be received and believed because the

Primitive Church put them forth,—but because "they may be proved by most certain warrants of Holy Scripture." (Arts. vi., xx., viii.)

Tell men, when they talk mysteriously to you about "hearing the Church," that our Lord was not speaking of matters of faith at all when He said, "Hear the Church." (Matt. xviii. 17.) Tell them that your rule of faith and practice is the Bible only, and that if they will show you their views in the Bible, you will receive them, but not otherwise. Tell them that their favourite arguments, "the voice of the Church," and the "Catholic Church," are nothing but high-sounding phrases, and mere meaningless terms. They are great swelling words, which make a noise in the distance, but in reality have neither substance nor power.

Alas, that it should be needful to say all this. But I fear there are only too many to whom "the voice of the Church" has been like the fabled Medusa's head. It seems to have petrified their common sense.*

(4) In the next place, *let me warn members of the Church of England never to take up ground on behalf of their Church which cannot be defended from the Holy Scriptures.* I love the Church of which I am a minister, and I delight to take up high ground on its behalf. But I do not call that ground really high which is not also Scripturally safe. I think it foolish and wrong to take up ground from which we are sure to be driven when we come to argue closely with those who differ from us.

Now there are many in this day who would have us tell all Presbyterians and Independents that the only true Church is always an Episcopal Church,—that to this belong the promises of Christ, and to no other kind of Church at all,—that to separate from an Episcopal Church is to leave the Catholic Church, to be guilty of an act of schism, and fearfully to peril the soul. This is the argument made use of by many. Let us beware of ever taking up such ground. It cannot be maintained. It cannot be shown to be tenable by plain, unmistakable texts of Scripture.

When the Scripture says, "Except a man be born again, he cannot see the kingdom of God,"—when the Scripture says, "Except ye repent, ye shall all likewise perish,"—when the Scripture says, "Without holiness no man shall see the Lord,"—when the Scripture says, "He that believeth not on the Lord Jesus Christ shall be damned;"—when the Scripture so speaks, such doctrines cannot be proclaimed too plainly by us. But never anywhere does Scripture say, from Matthew down to Revelation,

---

* The only case in which an appeal to the testimony of the Church seems allowable is where it is made in order to establish an historical fact. For instance, the Sixth Article of the Church of England says, that of the "Authority of the Canonical Books of the New Testament there never was any doubt in the Church," that is, in the whole body of professing Churches. Only let it be remembered that receiving the testimony of the Church to a fact does not for a moment imply that the Church has any authoritative power to interpret doctrine infallibly. A man may be a very competent witness to the fact that a book has been faithfully printed, and yet know little or nothing about the meaning of its contents.

"Except a man belong to a Church governed by bishops, he cannot be saved." There is not a text in Scripture which says anything of the kind, from first to last. It is in vain for us to argue as if Scripture had spoken in this way. Once begin to require things in religion which are not required of men in the Bible, and where are we to stop?*

Let no one misunderstand my meaning in saying this. I am deeply convinced of the excellency of my own Church,—I would even say, if it were not a proud boast,—its superiority over any other Church upon earth. I see more for Episcopacy in the Bible than I do for any other form of Church government. I consider the historical fact that there were bishops in most of the professing Churches at the beginning of Christianity, deserves much weight. I believe it is far wiser to have a regular, settled Liturgy, for the use of congregations, than to make a congregation dependent upon its minister's frames and feelings for the tone of its regular prayers. I think that endowments settled and established by law, are a way of paying ministers far preferable to the voluntary system. I am satisfied that, *well administered*, the Church of England is more calculated to help souls to heaven than any Church on earth. But I never can take up the ground that some men do in this day, who say that the Episcopal Church is the only true Church in Great Britain, and that all outside that Church are guilty schismatics. I cannot do it, because I am sure such ground as this never can be maintained.

No doubt the opinions I am expressing on this point are utterly opposed to those which many members of the Church of England hold in the present day. Such men will say that I am no sound Churchman,—that I am ignorant of true Church principles,—and so forth. Such charges weigh very little with me. I have found that those who talk loudest about the Church are not always its most faithful friends, and often end with leaving it altogether. I am not to be put down by such vague talk as this. I should like men who tell me my views are not "Church" views, to consider calmly what authority they have for such an assertion. I appeal confidently to the authorized Formularies of the Church of England, and

---

* "You shall not find in all the Scripture this your essential point of succession of bishops."—*John Bradford, Reformer and Martyr, Chaplain to Bishop Ridley.*

"I conceive that the power of ordination was restrained to bishops rather by Apostolical practice, and the perpetual custom and Canons of the Church, than by any absolute precept that either Christ or His Apostles gave concerning it. Nor can I yet meet with any convincing argument to set it upon a more high and divine institution."—*Bishop Cosin.* 1660.

"We have found neither any express commandment, nor any example, which prescribes as universal and unchangeable one particular system for the regulation of the Church and its ministers. Our argument consists only of inferences.— The conclusions in favour of Episcopacy from the New Testament are intimations rather than proofs.—We can produce no single text so clear as to compel us to conclude that the Apostles deemed any one peculiar form of government to be indispensable, and unalterable in the Church."—*Discourses by the Rev. C. Benson, Master of the Temple.*

o

I defy them to meet me on that ground. What do these Formularies say of the visible Church? Hear the Nineteenth Article: "It is a congregation of faithful men, in which the pure Word of God is preached, and the sacraments be duly ministered." What do they say of the ministry? Hear the Twenty-third Article: "We ought to judge those lawfully called and sent, which be chosen and called to this work by men who have public authority given unto them, in the congregation, to call and send ministers into the Lord's vineyard." What do they say of ceremonies? Hear the Thirty-fourth Article: "They may be changed, according to the diversities of countries, times, and men's manners, so that nothing be ordained against God's Word." What do they say of bishops, priests, and deacons? Hear the Preface to the Ordination Service: "It is evident unto all men diligently reading the Holy Scriptures and ancient authors, that from the Apostles' times there have been these orders of ministers in Christ's Church: bishops, priests, and deacons." What do they say of ministers ordained according to this service? Hear the Thirty-sixth Article: "We decree all such to be rightly, orderly, and lawfully consecrated and ordered."

Now to all this I heartily and cordially subscribe. The Church of England calmly asserts that its own ministers are Scripturally ordained. But this is a very different thing from saying that those who are not ordained in like manner are not ordained at all.—It calmly asserts that there always have been bishops, priests, and deacons. But this is very different from saying that where these orders are not there is no true Church.—It calmly asserts that a man must be lawfully called and sent, in order to be a minister. But it nowhere says that none but bishops have power to call.*

I believe the Church of England has been graciously guided by God's mercy to adopt the language of true Scriptural moderation. It is a moderation strikingly in contrast with the bold, decided language which it uses when speaking in the Doctrinal Articles about things essential to salvation. But it is the only true ground which can ever be maintained. It is the only ground on which we ought to stand. Let us be satisfied that our own communion is Scriptural; but let us never pretend to unchurch all other communions beside our own. For my own part, I abhor the

---

* "It might have been expected that the defenders of the English Hierarchy against the first Puritans should take the highest ground, and challenge for the bishops the same unreserved submission, on the same plea of exclusive Apostolical prerogative, which their adversaries feared not to insist on for their elders and deacons. It is notorious, however, that such was not in general the line preferred by Jewel, Whitgift, Bishop Cooper, and others, to whom the management of that controversy was intrusted during the early part of Elizabeth's reign.—It is enough with them to show that the government by archbishops and bishops is ancient and allowable. They never venture to urge its exclusive claims, or to connect the succession with the validity of the sacraments."— *Keble's Preface to Hooker's Works*, page 59.

idea of saying that men like Carey, and Rhenius, and Williams, and Campbell, the missionaries, were not real ministers of Jesus Christ. I loathe the idea of handing over the communions to which such men as Matthew Henry, and Doddridge, and Robert Hall, and M'Cheyne, and Chalmers belonged, to the uncovenanted mercies of God, or saying that such men as these were not really and truly ordained. Hard language is sometimes used about them. People dare to talk of their not belonging to the "Catholic Church," and of their being guilty of schism! I cannot for a moment hold such views. I deeply lament that any one should hold them. I would to God that we had many Episcopalians like the men I have named. People may shut them out from what they call the "Catholic Church," but I am firmly persuaded they will not shut them out from the kingdom of God. Surely those whom God hath not excluded, we should take care not to exclude.

(5) In the next place, *let us not set down men as no Christians, because they do not agree with us in our manner of worshipping God*. In saying this, I would have it distinctly understood that I am not speaking now of those who deny the doctrine of the Trinity, and the sufficiency of Scripture to make men wise unto salvation. I speak with especial reference to the great body of Protestant Dissenters in England, who hold the leading doctrines of the Gospel as set forth at the time of the Reformation. I wish every member of the Church of England to take broad, charitable, and Scriptural views of such persons, and to dismiss from his mind the wretched, narrow-minded, bigoted prejudices which are so unhappily common on the subject. Are they members of the one true Church?— Do they love the Lord Jesus Christ?—Are they born again of God's Spirit?—Are they penitent, believing, holy people?—If they are, they will get to heaven, I firmly believe, as certainly as any Episcopalian on earth. Men must tolerate them,—if such a word may be used,—men must tolerate them, see them, and love them too, in heaven and the kingdom of Christ. Surely if we expect to meet men of different denominations from our own at the right hand of the Lord Jesus, and to spend eternity in their company, we ought not to look coldly on them upon earth. Surely it were far better to begin something like union and co-operation with them, and to cultivate a spirit of love and kind feeling towards them while we can.

We may think our Dissenting brethren mistaken in many of their views. We may believe they miss privileges and lose advantages by being separated from our own Church. We may be fully satisfied that Episcopacy is that form of government which is most agreeable to God's Word, and most in harmony with what we read of in the history of the early Church. We may feel persuaded that, taking human nature as it is, it is far better, both for ministers and hearers, to have a Liturgy, or settled form of prayer. We may feel persuaded, from observation of the working of the voluntary system, and of the state of religion among Dissenters generally, that the way of the Church of England is the "more excellent way." But, after all, we must not speak positively where the Bible does not speak positively. Where, in all the compass of Scripture, can we point out that text which says that Episcopacy and a Liturgy are things *absolutely needful to salvation?* I say, without fear of contradiction, nowhere at all.

We may regret the divisions among professing Christians in our own country. We may feel that they weaken the holy cause of Christ's Gospel. We may feel that people have often, and do often, become Dissenters in England from very insufficient reasons, and from motives by no means of the highest order. But, after all, we must not forget by whom the greater part of these divisions were primarily occasioned. Who obliged the bulk of English Nonconformists to secede? Who drove them out of the fold of the Church of England? We of the Church of England did it ourselves, by not properly providing for their souls' wants. Who, in reality, built the Dissenting chapels, the Bethels, the Bethesdas, which so often offend the eyes of many members of the Church of England in these days? We did ourselves! We did it by gross neglect of the people's souls,—by the grossly unscriptural kind of preaching which prevailed in the pulpits of our churches a century ago. I believe the plain truth is, that the vast majority of Dissenters in England did not leave the Church of England at *first* from any abstract dislike to the principle of Episcopacy, or Liturgies, or establishments.—But they did dislike the moral essays and inconsistent lives of the clergy; and we must confess, with shame, that they had only too much reason. Some may think it strange that they did not see the beauties of our Prayer-book and Episcopacy more clearly. But there was one thing they saw far more clearly,—and that was, that men wholly taken up with field sports and the world, and never preaching Christ, were not likely to teach them the way to be saved. Surely when these things are so we have no right to speak harshly about Dissenters. We have no right to wonder at secession and separations. If sheep are not fed, who can wonder if they stray? If men found out that the Gospel was not preached by the clergy of the Church of England, who can blame them if they cared more for the Gospel than for the clergy, and went to hear that Gospel wherever it could be heard?

I know well that such opinions as these are very offensive to many people. Many will think I am taking very low ground in speaking as I have done about Dissenters. It is easy to think so, and to fancy higher ground might be found. It is not quite so easy to point out higher ground in Scripture, or to justify the language frequently used in speaking of English Dissenters. We must consider calmly the conduct of the Church of England for the last two hundred years. We must not forget that "he is the schismatic who causes the schism." We must confess that the

Church of England caused most of the dissent that has taken place. However much we may regret divisions, we must take the greater part of the blame to ourselves. Surely we ought to feel very tenderly towards our separating brethren. We should never forget that many of them hold the essence of Jesus Christ's Gospel. Justice and fairness demand that we should treat them with kindness. Whatever their mistakes may be, we of the Church of England made the vast majority of them what they are at the present day. Granting for a moment that they are wrong, we are not the men who can, with any face, tell them so.

(6) Let me pass on now to another warning of a different kind. Let me warn men *not to fancy that divisions and schisms are unimportant things*. This also is a great delusion, and one into which many fall, when they find there is no visible Church which can be called the only true Church on earth. So weak are our understandings, that if we do not fall over upon the one side, we are disposed at once to fall over on the other. Let us settle it down then in our minds that all divisions among Christians are an immense evil. All divisions strengthen the hands of infidels, and help the devil.—The great maxim of Satan is, "Divide and conquer." If he can set professing Christians by the ears, and make them spend their strength in contending one with another, our spiritual enemy has gained a great point. We may be very sure that union is strength, and we may be no less sure that discipline and uniformity are one great aid to union. Order is a vast help to efficient working in Christ's cause as well as in other things, and "God is not the Author of confusion, but of peace, as in all Churches of the saints." (1 Cor. xiv. 33.)

I would not be misunderstood in saying this. I fully admit that separation is justifiable under some circumstances, beyond a question. But it is absurd to say on that account that there is no such thing as schism. I for one cannot say so. Men ought to tolerate much,—I say it confidently, —men ought to tolerate and put up with much, before they think of separating and dividing, and leaving one Church for another. It is a step which nothing but the deliberate teaching of false doctrine can really justify. It is a step that should never be taken without much consideration, much waiting, and much prayer. It is a step that seems to me more than questionable, except it can be clearly proved that the salvation of the soul is really at stake. It is a step that in England is often taken far too lightly, and with an evident want of thought as to its serious nature and tendency. It is a common opinion of ignorant people, "It is no matter where we go. It is no matter if we first join one denomination and then join another; first worship with this people and then with that. It is all the same where we go, if we do but go to some place of worship." I say this common opinion is an enormous evil, and ought to be denounced by all true-hearted Christians. This Athenian kind of spirit, which ever wants something new,—which must have something different in religion from what

it had a little time ago,—is a spirit which I cannot praise. I believe it to
be the mark of a very diseased and unhealthy state of soul.

(7) In the next place, let me warn men *not to be shaken by those who
say that all visible Churches are necessarily corrupt, and that no man can
belong to them without peril to his soul.* There never have been wanting
men of this kind, men who have forgotten that everything must be
imperfect which is carried on by human agency, and have spent their
lives in a vain search after a perfectly pure Church. Members of all
Churches must be prepared to meet such men, and especially members
of the Church of England. Fault-finding is the easiest of all tasks. There
never was a system upon earth, in which man had anything to do, in
which faults, and many faults, too, might not soon be found. We must
expect to find imperfections in every visible Church upon earth. There
always were such in the New Testament Churches. There always will be
such now. There is only one Church without spot or blemish. That is
the one true Church, the body of Christ, which Christ shall present to
His Father in the last great day.

With regard to the Church of England, I will only remark that men
ought not to confound the bad working of a system with the system
itself. It may be quite true that many of its ministers are not what they
ought to be. It may be true that some of its revenues are misapplied, and
not properly spent. This does not prove that the whole machinery of the
Church of England is rotten and corrupt, and the whole Church an
institution which ought to be cast down. Surely there is many a good
machine on earth at this moment which works badly, simply because it
is in hands that know not in what way it ought to be worked.

I will only ask those who advise men to leave the Church of England,
what they have got better to show us?—Where is the visible Church,—
where is the denomination of Christians upon earth,—which is perfect,
without spot, and without blemish? None, I say confidently,—none is
to be found at all. Many people of scrupulous consciences, I firmly believe,
have found this to their cost already.—They left the Church of England
because of alleged imperfections. They thought they could better their
condition. What do they think now? If the truth were really told, I
believe they would confess that in getting rid of one kind of imperfection,
they have met with another; and that in healing one sore, they have
opened two more, far worse than the first.

I advise the members of the Church of England not to leave that
Church lightly, and without good reason. Numerous forms and ceremonies
may be attended with evil consequences, but there are also evils in the
absence of them. Episcopacy may have its disadvantages, but Presbyterianism and Congregationalism have their disadvantages too. A Liturgy
may possibly cramp and confine some highly gifted ministers, but the
want of one sadly cramps and confines the public devotions of many

congregations. The Church of England Prayer-book may not be perfect, and may be capable of many improvements. It would be strange if this was not the case, when we remember that its compilers were not inspired men. Still, after all, the Prayer-book's imperfections are few, compared to its excellencies. The testimony of Robert Hall, the famous Baptist, on this subject is very striking. He says,—"The evangelical purity of its sentiments, the chastened fervour of its devotion, and the majestic simplicity of its language, have combined to place it in the very first rank of uninspired compositions."

(8) In the last place, let me advise men *to try to understand thoroughly the principles and constitution of the Church of England.* I say that advisedly. I say it to Churchmen and Dissenters alike. The ignorance which prevails in our country about the Church of England is great and deplorable. There are thousands of members of that Church who never studied the Thirty-nine Articles of Religion,—who hardly know of their existence,—and who have often found fault with the very doctrines that these Articles contain, and especially the Seventeenth. Yet those Articles are the Church's Confession of faith. They show what is the Church's view of doctrine. No man, I say, is a true member of the Church of England who does not thoroughly agree, in heart and in truth, with the Thirty-nine Articles of his own Church.

So also there are thousands who have never read the Homilies which the Church of England has provided. Many have never heard of them, much less read them. Yet those Homilies are declared by the Thirty-fifth Article to contain "godly and wholesome doctrine," and they condemn thousands of so-called Churchmen in this day.

So also there are hundreds of thousands who do not know that the laity might prevent many improper ministers from being ordained in the Established Church. No man can be ordained a deacon in the Church of England, without notice being read in the parish church to which he belongs, and without people being invited to tell the bishop if they know of any just cause or impediment why he should not be ordained. But the laity hardly ever raise any impediment against the ordination of a young man.—Surely when this is the case, if men utterly unfit for the ministerial office get into the ministry of the Church of England, the blame out not to be borne only by the bishops who ordain them, but to be shared by the laity who never objected to their being ordained.

If we belong to the Church of England, let us wipe off this reproach. Let us try to understand our own Church.—Let us study the Articles of Religion regularly, and make ourselves master of them.—Let us read the Homilies with care, and see in them what the Reformers taught as true. Surely I may well come round to the point with which I started. I may well say that ignorance covers the whole subject as with a cloud. As to the true Church,—as to the visible professing Churches,—as to the real doctrines and constitution of the Established Church of England,—as to all these subjects, it is painful to see the ignorance which prevails. Surely it ought not to be so.

And now, let me conclude this paper by saying a few words of practical application to the conscience of every one who reads it.

(*a*) First of all, let me advise every reader to ask himself, solemnly and seriously, whether he belongs to that one true Church of Christ which I began by describing.

Oh, that men would but see that salvation turns upon this question! Oh, that men would but see that it shall profit nothing to say, "I have always gone to my Church," or "always gone to Meeting," if they have not gone to Christ by faith, and been born again, and been made one with Christ, and Christ with them! Oh, that men would understand that "the kingdom of God is not meat and drink, but righteousness, and peace, and joy in the Holy Ghost,"—that true religion does not turn on Episcopacy, or Presbyterianism,—on churches or chapels,—on liturgies or extempore prayer,—but on justification and sanctification, on saving faith, and new hearts!* Oh, that men would set their minds more upon these points, and leave off their miserable squabbling about unprofitable controversies, and settle down to this one great question,—Have I come to Christ and laid hold of Him, and been born again?

(*b*) Last of all, if we can say that we belong to the one true Church, we may rejoice. Our Church shall never fall.—Our Church shall never come to an end. The world and all its greatness will pass away. The works of statesmen shall vanish and come to nothing. The cathedrals and churches of man's erecting shall all crumble into dust. But the one true Church shall never perish.—It is built upon a rock.—It shall stand for ever.—It shall never fall.—It shall wax brighter and brighter to the end, and never be so bright as when the wicked shall be separated from it, and it shall stand alone.

If we belong to the true Church, let us not waste our time in controversies about outward things. Let us say to them all, "Get ye behind me." Let us care for nothing so much as the heart and marrow of Christianity. Let the grand point to which we give our attention be the essence of true religion,—the foundations of the one true Church.

If we belong to the true Church, let us see that we love all its members.

---

* "I cannot be so narrow in my principles of Church communion as many are,—that are so much for a Liturgy, or so much against it,—so much for ceremonies, or so much against them, that they can hold communion with no Church that is not of their mind and way.

"I cannot be of their mind who think God will not accept him that prayeth by the Common Prayer-book; and that such forms are a self-invented worship which God rejecteth; nor yet can I be of their mind that say the like of extempore prayers."—*Baxter, in Orme's Life*, page]385.

Let our principle be, "Grace be with all that love the Lord Jesus Christ in sincerity." (Ephes. vi. 24.) Wherever we find a man that has grace and faith, let us hold out our right hand to him. Let us not stop to ask him where he was baptized, and what place of worship he attends?—Has he been with Jesus?—Is he born again?—Then let us say to ourselves, "This is a brother. We are to be with him in heaven by-and-by for ever. Let us love him upon earth. If we are to be in the same home, let us love each other even now upon the road."*

Finally, if we belong to the true Church, let us try to increase the number of members of that Church. Let us not work merely for a party, or labour only to get proselytes to our own professing visible Church. Let our first care be to pluck brands from the fire,—to awaken sleeping souls—to rouse those who are in darkness and ignorance, and to make them acquainted with Him who is "the light of the world," and "Whom to know is life eternal." Never let us forget, that he who has helped to turn one sinner from his sins and make him a temple of the Holy Ghost, has done a far more glorious and lasting work than if he had built York Minster, or St. Peter's at Rome.

* "Wherever my Lord has a true believer, I have a brother.—*Bishop M'Ilvaine*

XI

THE PRIEST

"We have a great High Priest."—HEB. iv. 14

HE that wishes to have any comfort in religion must have a priest. A religion without a priest is a poor, unhappy, useless thing. Now what is our religion? *Have we a Priest?*

We are all such sinful, corrupt creatures, that we are unfit, by ourselves, to have anything to do with God. God is so holy a Being that He cannot bear that which is evil, and so high a Being that His majesty makes us afraid. We are so fallen, and defective, and guilty, that we naturally shrink from God, and dare not speak to Him or look Him in the face. We need an almighty Friend between us. We need a Mediator and Advocate, able, willing, loving, commissioned, tried, proved, and ready to help us. Have we found this out? Have we got a Friend? *Have we a Priest?*

The Christian religion provides the very thing that man's soul and conscience require. It is the glory of God's Word that it reveals to man the very Friend and Mediator that he needs,—the God-man Christ Jesus. It tells us of the very Priest that meets our wants,—even Jesus the Son of God. It sets Him fully before us, in the Epistle to the Hebrews, as the very Person that our longing hearts could desire. To open up this great subject is the simple purpose of this paper.

I think it will clear our way, and throw broad light on the matter in hand, if I state three plain questions, and try to supply answers to them.

    I. *Where is Jesus Christ now?*
   II. *What is Jesus Christ doing now?*
 III. *What is Jesus Christ going to do before the end of the world?*

When we have considered these three questions, we shall perhaps be better able to answer the inquiry, Have we a Priest?

I. In the first place, *Where is Jesus Christ now?*
Let us take care that we understand the drift of this inquiry. He about whom we are now asking is no common person. He is God as well as man, and man as well as God. The words of the Creed ought to be carefully remembered. Jesus Christ is—"God of the substance of the Father,

192

begotten before the worlds; and Man of the substance of His mother, born in the world: perfect God and perfect Man, of a reasonable soul and human flesh subsisting."—This, at any rate, is sound speech that cannot be condemned. This is one of the foundation doctrines of Christianity.

Where is Jesus Christ, *as God?* That is not the question I want to consider. As God He is everywhere. He fills heaven and earth. There is no secret corner, there is no height above or depth beneath where He is not. Wherever two or three are met together on earth in His name, there is He in the midst of them.—"Show me where your God is," said an infidel to a Christian. "Show me where your God is, and I will give you a penny."—"Show me where He is not," was the crushing reply. I am not asking where Christ is as God.

But where is Christ, *as Man?* That is the point. Where is the body that was born of the Virgin Mary? Where is the head that was crowned with thorns? Where are the hands that were nailed to the cross, and the feet that walked by the sea of Galilee? Where are the eyes that wept tears at the grave of Lazarus? Where is the side that was pierced with a spear? Where is the "visage that was marred more than any man, and the form more than the sons of men?" (Isa. lii. 14.) Where, in a word, is the Man Christ Jesus? That is the question.

I answer in the words of Scripture, that "Christ is passed into the heavens,"—that He "has entered into the holy place,"—that "He has entered into heaven itself, now to appear in the presence of God for us,"—and that "the heavens must receive Him until the time of restitution of all things." (Heb. iv. 14; ix. 12–24; Acts iii. 21.)

Let us mark this well. Christ, as Man, is *in heaven, and not in the grave.* The Jews pretended to deny that He rose from the dead. The infidels of modern times profess to believe that the ashes of Jesus of Nazareth are still lying, like the remains of any other man, in some Syrian town. What is this but kicking against the pricks? If ever there was a fact proved by unanswerable evidence in this world, it is the fact that Jesus rose from the dead!—That He died on a Friday, is certain. That He was buried in a sepulchre hewn out of rock that night, is certain. That the stone over the place was sealed, and a guard of soldiers set around it, is certain. That the grave was opened and the body gone on Sunday morning, is certain. That the soldiers could give no account of it, is certain. That the disciples themselves could hardly believe that their Master had risen, is certain. That after seeing Him several times for forty days, they at last were convinced, is certain. That, once convinced, they never ceased to teach and hold, even to death, that their Master had risen, is certain. That the unbelieving Jews could neither shake the disciples out of their belief, nor show Christ's dead body, nor give any satisfactory account of what had become of it, is equally certain. All this is certain, certain,

certain! The resurrection of Christ is a great, unanswerable, undeniable fact. There are none so blind as those that will not see.

Once more let us mark this point. Christ, as man, is *in heaven and not on the Communion Table*, at the celebration of the Lord's Supper. He is not present at that holy sacrament under the form of bread and wine, as the Roman Catholics, and some Anglicans, say. The consecrated bread is not the body of Christ, and the consecrated wine is not the blood of Christ. Those sacred elements are the emblem of something *absent*, and not of something *present*. The words of the Prayer-book state this fact with unmistakable clearness: "The sacramental bread and wine remain still in their very natural substance, and therefore may not be adored (for that were idolatry to be abhorred of all faithful Christians); and the natural body and blood of our Saviour Christ are in heaven and not here, it being against the truth of Christ's natural body to be at one time in more places than one."—*Rubric at the end of the Communion Service.*

Let these things sink down into our hearts. It is a point of vast importance in this day, to see clearly where Christ's natural body and blood are. Right knowledge of this point may save our souls from many ruinous errors.

Let us not be moved, for a moment, by the infidel, when he sneers at miracles, and tries to persuade us that a religion based on miracles cannot be true. Tell him not to waste his time in talking about the flood, or the sun standing still, or Balaam's ass speaking, or the whale swallowing Jonah, or the ravens feeding Elijah. Ask him to grapple, like a man, with the greatest miracle of all,—the resurrection of Christ from the dead. Ask him to explain away the evidence of that miracle, if he can. Remind him that, long before He died, Jesus Christ staked the truth of His Messiahship on His resurrection, and told the Jews not to believe Him if He did not rise from the dead. Remind him that the Jews remembered this, and did all they could to prevent any removal of our Lord's body, but in vain. Tell him, finally, that when he has overthrown the evidence of Christ's resurrection, it will be time to listen to his argument against miracles in general, but not till then. The Man Christ Jesus is in heaven, and not on earth. The mere fact that His natural body and blood are in heaven, is one among many proofs of the truth of Christianity.

Let us not be moved by the Roman Catholic, any more than by the infidel. Let us not listen to his favourite doctrine of Christ's body and blood being "really present" in the elements of bread and wine at the Lord's Supper. It is his common argument that we should believe the doctrine, though we cannot understand it; and that it is a pleasant, comfortable, and reverent thought, that Christ's natural body and blood are in the bread and wine in some mysterious way, though we know not how. Let us beware of the argument. It is not only without foundation of Scripture, but full of dangerous heresy. Let us stand fast on the old doctrine, that Christ's natural body and blood "cannot be in more places than one at one time." Let us maintain firmly that Christ's human nature is like our own, sin only excepted, and cannot therefore be at once in heaven and on the Communion Table. He that overthrows the doctrine of Christ's real, true, and proper humanity, is no friend to the Gospel, any more than he that denies His divinity. Tell me that my Lord is not really Man, and you rob me of one half of my soul's comfort. Tell me that His body can be on earth and yet in heaven at the same time, and you tell me that He is not Man. Let us resist this mischievous doctrine. Christ, as Man, is in heaven, and in heaven alone.

So much for the first question which I proposed to answer. Christ is in heaven, and not in the grave. Miserable indeed is that religion which is content to honour Him as nothing more than a moral teacher, who died like Plato or Socrates, and saw corruption.—Christ is in heaven, and not in the bread and wine at the Lord's Supper. They do Him little real honour who in fancied reverence try to persuade us that His body is a body unlike that of man.—Christ is in heaven, alive, and not dead. For ever let us glory in His atoning death, and the life-blood that He shed for us on the cross. But never let us forget that He was "raised again for our justification." His life is as important to us as His death. What saith the Scripture? "If, when we were enemies, we were reconciled to God by the death of His Son, much more, being reconciled, we shall be saved by His life." (Rom. v. 10.)

II. Let us next consider the second question which I propose to examine: *What is Jesus Christ doing now?*

That He is doing some great thing for man we need not doubt for a moment. The Bible account of all His dealings with man makes it impossible to arrive at any other conclusion. In abounding mercy and grace He has always been taking thought for our poor fallen race, and caring for our best interests. He has been ever caring and working for our souls. And "His mercy endureth for ever." He never changes.

Do we not read that Christ was "the Lamb slain from the foundation of the world?" (Rev. xiii. 18.) Do we not hear Him saying, "When the Lord gave to the sea His decree, that the waters should not pass His commandment: when He appointed the foundations of the earth: then I was by Him, as one brought up with Him: and I was daily His delight, rejoicing always before Him; rejoicing in the habitable part of the earth; and my delights were with the sons of men." (Prov. viii. 29–31.) Are we not taught everywhere in Scripture that for 4000 years He was trusted for salvation by all saved souls, though seen dimly and afar off through figures and sacrifices?—Do we not learn that Christ, and Christ alone, was the only hope of Abel, and Enoch, and Noah, and Abraham, and Isaac, and Jacob, and Moses, and Samuel, and David, though they only

saw "through a glass darkly" what we see face to face?—Do we not
know that in the fulness of time Christ came into the world born of a
woman, lived for us, suffered for us, wrought righteousness for us, made
satisfaction for us, died for us, rose again for us, and purchased eternal
redemption for sinners at the cost of His own blood?—And can we doubt
for a moment that Christ is still doing great things for us? No, indeed!
He said Himself in a certain place, "My Father worketh hitherto, and
I work." (John v. 17.) We may take up the expression, and say, "Christ
has worked for us, and Christ is working for us at this very day."

But what is that special thing that Christ is doing now? The question
demands our best attention. This is no light and speculative matter. It
lies near the foundation of all comfortable Christianity. Let us see.

Christ is now carrying on in heaven the work of a Priest, which He
began upon earth. He took our nature on Him in the fulness of time,
and became a man, that He might be perfectly fitted to be the Priest that
our case required. As a Priest, He offered up His body and soul as a
sacrifice for sin upon the cross, and made a complete atonement for us
with His own blood. As a Priest, He ascended up on high, passed within
the veil, and entered into the presence of God. As a Priest, He is now
sitting on our behalf at the right hand of God; and what He began
actively on earth He is carrying on actively in heaven. This is what Christ
is doing.

How and in what manner does Christ exercise His priestly office?
This is a deep subject, and one about which it is easy to make rash statements. The action of one of the Persons of the blessed Trinity in heaven
is a high thing, and passes man's understanding. The place whereon we
stand is holy ground. The thing we are handling must be touched with
reverence, like the ark of God. Nevertheless, there are some things about
Christ's priestly office which even our weak eyes may boldly look at;
and God has caused them to be written plainly for our learning. "The
secret things belong unto the Lord our God: but those things which are
revealed belong unto us and to our children." (Deut. xxix. 29.) Let us see.

(1) We need not doubt that Christ, as our Priest, is *ever presenting the
merits of His sacrifice for us before God*. Of course He has no need to
repeat that sacrifice. "By one offering He has perfected for ever those
that are sanctified." (Heb. x. 14.) But in some ineffable manner He is
ever in God's presence as the Bearer of the sins of His people. The atonement made on the cross for us is kept continually in remembrance by
the appearance of Him who made it. Twenty-seven times the visions of
heaven in Revelation describe Christ as the "Lamb." Twice they call
Him "the Lamb slain." Twice they speak of His "blood." The Priest
who offered the sacrifice is always in heaven: the sacrifice is never forgotten
in heaven: and so they that trust in it are always acceptable in heaven.
This is one thing.

(2) Again: we need not doubt that Christ, as our Priest, is *ever interceding for us* in heaven. It is written, "He is able to save them to the uttermost who come unto God by Him, because He ever liveth to make intercession for them." (Heb. vii. 25.) It is asked by St. Paul, "Who is he that condemneth?" and one reason he gives why there is no condemnation for believers, is the fact that "Christ maketh intercession for us."(Rom. viii. 34.) Of the manner of that intercession we cannot of course speak particularly: we may not intrude into things unseen. But it may suffice us to remember how our Lord prayed for His people in the seventeenth chapter of John, and how He told Peter He prayed for him, that his faith might not fail. (Luke xxii. 32.) Our great High Priest knows how to intercede. This is another thing.

(3) Again: we need not doubt that Christ, as our Priest, *presents the names of His people continually before His Father*. The Jewish high priest had the names of the tribes of Israel engraved on the ornaments he wore upon his head and shoulders. That this was the figure of something which Christ is ever doing for Christians in heaven, is clear and plain as the day. He "appears in the presence of God for us." (Heb. ix. 24.) He acts as the Representative of His people. Through Him they are known and thought for in heavenly places, long before they go there. The interests and safety of the body are secured and provided for, because the Head is already in heaven. This is another thing.

(4) Again: we need not doubt that Christ, as our Priest, *presents the prayers and services of His people before God*, and obtains for them hearing, acceptance, and favour. Like the Jewish Priest, He offers incense within the veil (Lev. xvi. 12, 13), and that incense is mingled with the prayers of His saints. (Rev. viii. 3.) This is a great mystery, no doubt, but one full of consolation. It is hard at any time to understand how any word or deed of sinful creatures like us can ever come into the presence of God, and do us any good. But the Priesthood of Christ explains all. Placed in His hands and endorsed by Him, our petitions, like bank-notes duly signed, obtain a value which they have not in themselves. A young Christian once said to an old one, "My prayers are so poor and weak, that I cannot think they are of any use." The old Christian replied, with deep wisdom, "Only place them in Christ's hands, and He makes them look so different in heaven that you would hardly know them again."— Prayers that are worth nothing in themselves are effectual, when offered "through Christ,—for the sake of Christ,—through the mediation of Christ." Expressions like these are so common, that few duly weigh their meaning. But rightly considered, they are full of deep doctrine, even the doctrine of the priestly office of Jesus. This is another thing.

(5) Again: we need not doubt that Christ, as our Priest in heaven, *is ever doing the work of a Friend*, a Protector, a Counsellor, and Advocate, on behalf of His people. It is not for nothing that we are told that He is

"at God's right hand" (Rom. viii. 34), and that He "sitteth at the right hand of God." (Coloss. iii. 1; 1 Peter iii. 22.) These words have a deep meaning. They teach that Christ is ever watching over the interests of His people, and providing a continual supply of all that they need.—"He that keepeth Israel neither slumbers nor sleeps." "We have an Advocate with the Father,—Jesus Christ, the righteous." (Psalm cxxi. 4; 1 John ii. 1.)—To hear the daily confessions of His saints, and grant them daily absolution; to sympathize with them in all their troubles, guide them in their perplexities, strengthen them for their duties, preserve them in their temptations,—all this is part of Christ's priestly office. What else can be the meaning of St. Paul's words, when he says to the Hebrews, "Let us come boldly to the throne of grace, that we may obtain mercy and find grace to help in time of need"? (Heb. iv. 16.) The Priesthood of Jesus is the very hinge and pivot on which that whole exhortation turns. This is another thing.

(6) Finally, we need not doubt that Christ as a Priest in heaven is continually *doing the work of a Receiver of sinners, and a Mediator between God and man.* The priest was the person to whom the Israelite was bidden to go, when he was ceremonially unclean and wanted forgiveness. The command was distinct: "Go to the priest." The Heavenly Priest is the person to whom labouring and heavy-laden souls ought always to be directed when they want pardon and rest. He that feels the burden of sin on his conscience and wants it taken away, ought to be told that there is One appointed by the Father for the very purpose of taking it away, and that the first step he must take is to go to Him. When the frightened jailer of Philippi cried out in agony of spirit, "What must I do to be saved?" he got, to all appearance, a very simple answer: "Believe on the Lord Jesus Christ, and thou shalt be saved." (Acts xvi. 30, 31.) Yet simple as that answer seems, it contains the whole doctrine of Christ's priestly office. It was as good as saying, "There is a Priest ready to receive, confess, and absolve you: Jesus Christ the Lord. Go and put your soul into His hands, and you shall have full pardon."—The power of absolving every sinner that comes to Him is one grand part of Christ's priestly office. "Thou hast given him power over all flesh, that He should give eternal life to as many as Thou hast given Him." (John xvii. 3.) "Jesus whom ye slew and hanged on a tree, Him hath God exalted with His right hand to be a Prince and a Saviour, for to give repentance unto Israel, and forgiveness of sins." (Acts v. 31.) This is another thing.

Such is the manner in which Christ exercises the work of a Priest in heaven. It is a vast and wide subject. I feel deeply that I have only touched the surface of it, and the half of it is left untold. Who can describe fully the singular fitness of our Lord Jesus Christ to be the Priest of man?— His possession of all power in heaven and earth, so that He is able to save to the uttermost, and no case is too hard for Him, and no sinner too bad to be saved,—His tenderness and sympathy, so that He can be touched with the feeling of our infirmities,—His long-suffering and patience, so that He can bear with our weaknesses and pity our mistakes,—His wisdom, His faithfulness, His readiness to aid,—who can describe or number up these things? None know them but those who know them by experience: and even they know very little of their extent. Of all the offices that Christ exercises on behalf of His people, none will so richly repay thought and study as that of His Priesthood.

Let us thank God daily that Christ is doing the work of a Priest for us in heaven. Let us glory in His death, but let us not glory less in His life. Let us praise God daily that Jesus "died for our sins according to the Scriptures;" but let us never forget to praise Him that He "rose again for us, and sat down at the right hand of God." Let us be thankful for the precious blood of Christ; but let us not be less thankful for His precious intercession.

Christ's Priesthood is the great secret of *daily comfort* in Christianity. It is hard to do our duty in that place of life which God has appointed us, and not to become absorbed in it. We are such poor weak creatures that we cannot do two things at once. The cares, and business, and occupations of life, however innocent and sinless, often seem to drink up all our thoughts, and swallow up all our attention. But, oh, what an unspeakable comfort it is to remember that we have an High Priest in heaven, who never forgets us night or day, and is continually interceding for us, and providing for our safety. Happy is that man who knows how to begin and end each day with his Priest! This is, indeed, to live the life of faith.

Christ's Priesthood is the great secret of a saint's *perseverance to the end*. Left to ourselves there would be little likelihood of our getting safe home. We might begin well and end ill. So weak are our hearts, so busy the devil, so many the temptations of the world, that nothing could prevent our making shipwreck. But, thanks be to God, the Priesthood of Christ secures our safety.—He who never slumbers and never sleeps is continually watching over our interests, and providing for our need. While Satan pours water on the fire of grace, and strives to quench it, Christ pours on oil, and makes it burn more brightly. Start us in the narrow way of life, with pardon, grace, and a new heart, and leave us to ourselves, and we should soon fall away. But grant us the continual intercession of an Almighty Priest in heaven,—God as well as Man, and Man as well as God,—and we shall never be lost. "Because I live," says our Lord, "ye shall live also." (John xiv. 19.)

Let us ever beware of any doctrine which interferes with the Priesthood of Christ. Any system of religion which teaches that we need other mediators besides Jesus,—other priests besides Jesus,—other intercessors besides Jesus,—is unscriptural and dangerous to men's souls. What greater folly can be conceived than to flee to the Virgin Mary or the saints, or to put our souls in the hands of clergymen and ministers, when we have such a Priest as Jesus Christ in heaven? What can a woman, who herself needed a "Saviour," do for the souls of others? (Luke i. 47.) What has she done to prove her love to sinners, compared to the Great High Priest,—Christ the Lord? What single example have we in all the New Testament of any one using a minister as a priest, even in the days of Peter and Paul? This modern system, which is not satisfied with Christ's Priesthood, but must have mortal men as priests besides, bears the mark of its origin on its face. It is from beneath, and not from above. "There is no office of Christ," said John Owen, "that Satan labours so hard to obscure and overthrow as His priestly one." Satan cares little, comparatively, for Christ the Prophet, and Christ the King, so long as he can persuade man to forget Christ the Priest. For ever let us stand fast on this point. That Christ is carrying on the office of a Priest in heaven, is the crown and glory of Christian theology.

III. Last of all, let us consider the third question which I propose to examine: *What is Jesus Christ going to do before the end of the world?*

I will answer that inquiry in the words of Scripture. In speaking of things to come, the safest plan is to go to the Book. Let us hear what St. Paul says to the Hebrews: "Christ was once offered to bear the sins of many; and unto them that look for Him shall He appear the second time, without sin, unto salvation." (Heb. ix. 28.) Let us hear what the angel said to the Apostles on the Mount of Olives, in the day of the ascension: "Ye men of Galilee, why stand ye gazing up into heaven? This same Jesus which is taken up from you into heaven, shall so come in like manner as ye have seen Him go into heaven." (Acts i. 11.) Let us hear what St. Peter preached to the Jews at Jerusalem: "Times of refreshing shall come from the presence of the Lord; and He shall send Jesus Christ, which before was preached unto you: whom the heavens must receive until the times of restitution of all things." (Acts iii. 19–21.) Let us hear what St. Paul writes to the Thessalonians: "The Lord Himself shall descend from heaven with a shout, with the voice of the archangel, and with the trump of God: and the dead in Christ shall rise first." (1 Thess. iv. 16.) Let us hear what Enoch prophesied 5000 years ago: "Behold, the Lord cometh with ten thousands of His saints." (Jude 14.)

The world has not done with Jesus Christ yet. The wicked, and worldly, and unbelieving, and sceptical, who flatter themselves that Christianity, as a system, is worn out and dying away, will find themselves fearfully mistaken one day. The philosophers and admirers of science, falsely so called, who talk of "modern progress" and "free thought," and sneer at "old world creeds," as they term them, will have their eyes rudely opened by and by. That same Jesus of Nazareth of whom they speak so lightly now, will appear to their confusion, and set up a kingdom over all the earth. He shall rise up from that seat at God's right hand, which He now occupies as Priest, and come down to this sin-burdened world to rule over it as King. Every eye shall see Him, and every knee shall bow before Him, and every tongue which has spoken against Him shall be silenced for ever. The great High Priest shall come forth from within the veil, and sit upon His throne as a King. This is what Christ is going to do before the end of the world.

How will Jesus come the second time? Not spiritually and figuratively, as some say; but really, literally, truly, and in the body, as He came the first time. He came with a real material body, when He came the first time to suffer and be crucified. He will come back with a real material body, when He returns to be glorified and to reign. There will be a *"real presence"* at length on earth of that holy body which was born of the Virgin Mary and crucified under Pontius Pilate. But it will be a very different "presence" from that which is now ignorantly talked of by the Church and the world!

In what fashion will Jesus Christ return the second time? Not as He came the first time, in weakness and humiliation. He shall come, as He told Caiaphas in the judgment-hall, "in the clouds of heaven," with power and great glory. He shall come attended by thousands of ministering angels, with all the pomp and majesty that becomes the King of kings. Before His face the frame of this world shall be shaken to the very centre. It was shaken when the law was given on Mount Sinai. It was shaken again when Christ offered Himself for our sins on the cross. How much more shall it be shaken when the throne of mercy shall be taken down, and the great High Priest shall return in power to reign! The earth quaked, and the rocks were rent, and the sun was darkened, when the great High Priest of our profession shed His atoning blood for us on Calvary. Much more then may we expect signs and wonders when He "appears the second time, without sin, unto salvation." (Heb. ix. 28.)

For what purpose is Christ coming the second time? He is coming to set up His throne of judgment, and to wind up the affairs of this sin-laden and bankrupt world. He is coming to raise the dead, and change the living; to gather all mankind before His bar, and to hold a last assize. He is coming to reckon with His professing Churches, and to punish with everlasting destruction the impenitent, the unbelieving, and the ungodly. They will find to their cost that there is such a thing as "the wrath of the Lamb." He is coming to bless and reward His own believing people, to gather them into one happy home, to wipe away all their tears, and to give them a crown of glory that fadeth not away. (Rev. vi. 16.)

When is the Lord Jesus Christ coming the second time? We do not know the precise season. "Of that day and hour knoweth no man: no, not the angels in heaven." (Matt. xxiv. 36.) The time is wisely withheld

from us in order that we may be kept in a watchful frame of mind. We
know the fact, but we do not know the date. When the iniquity of Christ's
enemies is full,—when the number of His elect is complete,—when the
last sinner in the mystical company of His people has been brought to
repentance,—then, and not till then, the Lord will return. He will not
send the plough of judgment into the field till the last sheaf has been
gathered into the barn. Come when He may, His advent will be a very
sudden and unexpected one. It will take a sleeping world by surprise,
like a thief in the night. It will startle a drowsy Church from its slumber,
and make myriads cry, "Give us of your oil; for our lamps are gone out."
(Matt. xxv. 8.) As it was in the days of Noah, so shall it be at the second
coming of the Son of Man. Blessed, indeed, is that servant whom the Lord,
when He cometh, shall find watching!

Great indeed are the things which our great High Priest shall do at
His second coming. He did great things when He came the first time,
and spoiled principalities and powers by His sacrifice on the cross. He
is doing great things now, by carrying believers from grace to glory, by
His almighty intercession. But He will put the crown on all His doings
for His Church, when He comes forth from within the veil the second
time, to confound His enemies and reward His friends. Never will our
great High Priest appear so glorious as when He presents His people
before the Father's throne, saying, for the last time, "Of them whom
thou gavest Me, have I lost none." (John xviii. 9.) He did thoroughly
the work He came to do, when He made His soul a sacrifice for sin, and
died upon the cross as our substitute. He is doing thoroughly the work
He undertook when He ascended up to heaven, and sat down on the right
hand of God to be the Priest and Advocate of His people. He will yet
do thoroughly His last great work, when He shall come again to complete
our salvation, and to present us "without spot, or wrinkle, or any such
thing," before His Father's throne. (Eph. v. 27.)

Let us lean back our souls, if we know anything of saving religion,
on Christ's coming again, as well as Christ dying and Christ interceding.
Let the comfortable thought of our Lord's return sustain us in public
troubles, and cheer us in private trials. When the governments of the
world are reeling and tottering,—when the air is filled with rumours of
wars and revolutions,—when the nations of the earth are heaving up
and down and ill at ease,—when faith is faint and love is waxing cold,
and the best of Churches seem running to seed and decay,—when men's
hearts are failing for fear and looking after the things coming on the
earth,—in times like these let us fix our eyes steadily on the second advent
of our Lord Jesus Christ. That great High Priest who died for us and
intercedes for us, will never forget His people, or allow one lamb of His
flock to perish. The disciples on the sea of Galilee, when tossed by storm
and worn with toil, were ready perhaps to think their Lord had forgotten

them. Yet, just when it was the darkest hour of the night, Jesus came to them "walking on the water," and they heard His welcome voice, saying, "It is I: be not afraid." Let us not cast away our confidence, however dark the horizon may seem around us. Let us look *back* to the cross. Let us look *upward* to the right hand of God. Let us look *forward* to the day of the promised return. Let experience of the past give lessons for the future. The merciful and faithful High Priest who began a work for us on the cross, will bring that work to a triumphant conclusion. He will never forsake the work of His own hands. "Yet a little while, and He that shall come will come, and will not tarry." (Heb. x. 37.)

It only remains to wind up the whole subject with a few words of practical application. Living in a world full of uncertainty, I commend the following words to the attention of all who may read these pages.

(1) First of all, have we a Priest in our religion? Is there any one whom we employ as our Mediator and Advocate with God? Is the person we employ the one true appointed and anointed Priest, Jesus Christ the Lord? Can we lay our hand on our heart and say, "Christ is mine and I am His? I have come to Him, poured out my heart to Him, received absolution from Him, cast all my burden on Him, placed my soul in His hands." We may be sure, if we have a religion without a Priest, or any Priest except Christ, we are in awful danger: we are yet unpardoned, unforgiven, unfit to die, unprepared to meet God. If we die without Christ as our Priest, we shall awake to find we had better never have been born. It is not enough to talk of "God," and "mercy," and "providence," and "trying all we can," and "saying our prayers," and "going to church or chapel," and being "a member" here and there. It will not do. This will not save us. We need far more than this. We must lay hold on Christ as our Mediator and Advocate, or else we shall never be saved. Have we done this? Is Christ our Priest?

(2) In the second place, if Christ is really the Priest of our souls, let us use Him regularly, and keep back nothing from Him. It is a sorrowful fact that many believers enjoy the Gospel far less than they ought to do, for lack of boldness in using the priestly office of Jesus Christ. They go mourning and weeping along the way to heaven, perplexing themselves by poring over their infirmities and sins, and carrying ten times as much weight on their backs as Christ ever meant them to bear. Ignorance, sad ignorance, is too often the simple account of the condition of these people. They think only of the death of Christ, and not of the life of Christ. They think of His finished work on the cross, but forget His priestly intercession. If this be our case, let us turn over a new leaf, and change our plan this very day. Let us think of Jesus Christ as a loving Friend, to whom we may go morning, noon, and night, and get relief from Him every day. "Cast they burden on the Lord, and He will sustain thee."

(Psalm lv. 22.) Let us live the life of faith in the Son of God, and hold communion with Him continually. Let us use Him every morning as a Fountain of grace and help, and drink freely of that Fountain. Let us use Him every evening as a Fountain of absolution and refreshment, and draw out of Him living water. He that tries this plan will find it for the health of his soul.

(3) In the third place, if Christ is the Priest of our souls, let us beware of ever giving His office to another. Let no man delude us into supposing that we need any clergyman, or minister, or priest of any Church on earth, to be our spiritual director and soul's confessor.

I am sure this warning is greatly needed in this day. One of the most mischievous delusions of this age, I firmly believe, is the attempt that is widely made to teach the benefit of habitual private confession to a clergyman. Occasional private conference with a minister is one thing; habitual confession if sin, with habitual absolution, is quite another. The first practice, under proper restriction, may do good; the last is a practice fraught with danger, dishonouring to our Lord Jesus Christ, and calculated to do infinite harm to souls.

(a) Where is the warrant of Scripture for habitual private confession and private absolution? I answer, Nowhere at all. Not a single case can be shown in the New Testament where any one confessed sin in private to a minister, or was privately absolved. Not a single word did Paul say in the Epistles which he wrote to his two young friends in the ministry, Timothy and Titus, to justify habitual private confession and absolution.

(b) Where is the man upon earth who is really fit to be an habitual hearer of confessions? He only is fit for such an office who has perfect knowledge, and knows that the person confessing is telling all the truth.— He only is fit who will receive no damage himself by hearing others constantly confess and unbosom their secret sins.—He only is fit who is sure to use the knowledge He possesses of others' sins rightly, and can always feel rightly for those who confess.—He only is fit who has full power to pardon the sins he hears confessed, and to set the conscience of the confessing entirely free.—Where shall we find such a man upon earth? I answer boldly, Nowhere at all! There is but one Person fit to be our Confessor, and that one is Christ Jesus the Lord.

(c) Where is the wisdom of ignoring the lessons of history and experience? If there is any fact in Church history which is clearly established, it is the fact that the confessional has led to a flood of wickedness and immorality. I challenge any well-informed reader of history to deny this, if he can. He that desires to re-introduce the practice of private confession into the Church of England may be a devout and well-meaning man, but he is ignorantly seeking to bring back among us a fountain of the worst kind of sins.

(d) Where is the sense or reason of going to an earthly confessor, so long as we can have the best of all Priests,—the commissioned and appointed Priest, the perfect Mediator between God and man, the man Christ Jesus! When His ear is deaf, and His heart is cold,—when His hand is feeble, and His power to heal is exhausted,—when the treasure-house of His sympathy is empty, and His love and goodwill have become cold,—then, and not till then, it will be time to turn to earthly priests and earthly confessionals. Thank God, that time is not yet come!

Let us stand fast in the old paths. Let no man deceive us with vain words. Away with the plausible idea that habitual private confession tends to "deepen spiritual life." We may be sure it does nothing of the kind. Nothing really "deepens spiritual life" which interposes anything between our souls and Christ. Ministers are useful just so far as they promote private communion between Jesus Christ and our souls. But the moment a minister begins to stand between our soul and Christ, even in the slightest degree, he becomes an enemy and not a friend to our peace.

Once more I repeat my warning. No priest but Christ! No confessor but Christ! No absolver but Christ! No habitual private submission or bowing down in religion to any one but Christ! No spiritual director but Christ! No putting of our conscience in the power of any one but Christ! If we love peace and wish to honour Christ, let us beware of the confessional, or the slightest approach to it. I declare I had almost rather hear my sons and daughters had gone to the grave, than hear they had adopted the habit of going to a confessional.

(4) In the last place, if Christ is the Priest of our souls, let us live always like men who look for His second coming. Let us live like men who long to see face to face the Saviour in whom they believe. Let us live like men who would be found ready at any moment,—like good servants prepared for their master. Happy is the Christian who lives the life of faith in Christ's dying, interceding, and coming again! There is a crown laid up for "all that love His appearing." (2 Tim. iv. 8.) Let us give diligence that this crown may be ours!

XII

CONFESSION

"If we confess our sins, He is faithful and just to forgive us our sins, and to cleanse us from all unrighteousness."—1 JOHN i. 9.

THERE are occasions when circumstances give a peculiar importance to particular doctrines in religion. The assaults of enemies sometimes make it needful to exhibit some special truth with special distinctness. The plausible assertion of some error sometimes requires to be met by more than ordinary carefulness in showing "the thing as it is" in the Word. A doctrine may perhaps be in the rear rank to-day, and to-morrow may be thrust forward by the force of events into the very front of the battle. This is the case at the present time with the subject of "Confession." Many years have passed away since men thought and talked so much as they do now about "the confession of sins."

I desire in this paper to lay down a few plain Scriptural principles about "Confession of sin." The subject is one of primary importance. Let us beware, in the din of controversy and discussion, that we do not lose sight of the mind of Holy Scripture, and injure our own souls.—There is a confession which is needful to salvation, and there is a confession which is not needful at all.—There is a confessional to which all men and women ought to go, and there is a confessional which ought to be denounced, avoided, and abhorred. Let us endeavour to separate the wheat from the chaff, and the precious from the vile.

   I.   In the first place,—*Who are they who ought to confess sin?*
  II.   In the second place,—*To whom ought confession of sin to be made?*

Once let a man have clear views on these two points, and he will never go far wrong on the subject of confession.

   I.   In the first place,—*Who are they that ought to confess sins?*
I answer this question in one plain sentence. All men and women in the world! All are born in sin and children of wrath. All have sinned and come short of the glory of God. Before God all are guilty. There is not a just man upon earth that dieth good and sinneth not. There is not a child of Adam that ought not to confess sin. (Eph. ii. 3; Rom. iii. 23, 19; Eccles. vii. 20.)

There is no exception to this rule. It does not apply only to murderers, and felons, and the inmates of prisons: it applies to all ranks, and classes, and orders of mankind. The highest are not too high to need confession; the lowest are not too low to be reached by God's requirement in this matter. Kings in their palaces and poor men in their cottages,—preachers and hearers,—teachers and scholars,—landlords and tenants,—all, all are alike summoned in the Bible to confession. None are so moral and respectable that they need not confess that they have sinned. All are sinners in thought, word, and deed, and all are commanded to acknowledge their transgressions. Every knee ought to bow, and every tongue ought to confess to God. "Behold," saith the Lord, " I will plead with thee because thou sayest, I have not sinned." (Jer. ii. 35.) "If we say that we have no sin, we deceive ourselves, and the truth is not in us." (1 John i. 8.)

Without confession there is *no salvation*. The love of God towards sinners is infinite. The readiness of Christ to receive sinners is unbounded. The blood of Christ can cleanse away all sin. But we must "plead guilty", before God can declare us innocent. We must acknowledge that we surrender at discretion, before we can be pardoned and let go free. Sins that are known and not confessed, are sins that are not forgiven: they are yet upon us, and daily sinking us nearer to hell. "He that covereth his sins shall not prosper: but whoso confesseth and forsaketh them shall find mercy." (Prov. xxviii. 13.)

Without confession there is *no inward peace*. Conscience will never be at rest, so long as it feels the burden of unacknowledged transgression. It is a load of which man must get rid if he means to be really happy. It is a worm at the root of all comfort. It is a blight on joy and mirth. The heart of the little child is not easy, when he stands in his parents' presence and knows that he has been doing something wrong. He is never easy till he has confessed.—The heart of the grown-up man is never really easy, until he has unburdened himself before God and obtained pardon and absolution. "When I kept silence," says David, "my bones waxed old through my roaring all the day long. For day and night Thy hand was heavy upon me: my moisture is turned into the drought of summer. I acknowledged my sin unto Thee, and mine iniquity have I not hid. I said, I will confess my transgression unto the Lord; and Thou forgavest the iniquity of my sin." (Psalm xxxii. 3–5.)

There is no gainsaying these things. They stand out plainly on the face of Scripture, as if they were written with a sunbeam: they are so clear that he who runs may read. Confession of sin is absolutely necessary to salvation: it is a habit which is an essential part of repentance unto life. Without it there is no entrance into heaven. Without it we have no part or lot in Christ. Without it we shall certainly go to hell. All this is undoubtedly true. And yet in the face of all this, it is a melancholy and appalling fact that few people confess their sins!

Some people have *no thought* or feeling about their sins: the subject is one which hardly crosses their minds. They rise in the morning and go to bed at night; they eat, and drink, and sleep, and work, and get money, and spend money, as if they had no souls at all. They live on as if this world was the only thing worth thinking of. They leave religion to parsons, and old men and women. Their consciences seem asleep, if not dead. Of course they never confess!

Some people are *too proud* to acknowledge themselves sinners. Like the Pharisee of old, they flatter themselves they are "not as other men." They do not get drunk like some, or swear like others, or live profligate lives like others. They are moral and respectable! They perform the duties of their station! They attend church regularly! They are kind to the poor! What more would you have? If they are not good people and going to heaven, who can be saved?—But as to habitual confession of sin, they do not see that they need it. It is all very well for wicked people, but not for them. Of course, when sin is not really *felt*, sin will never be confessed!

Some people are *too indolent* and slothful to take any step in religion so decided as confession. Their Christianity consists in meaning, and hoping, and intending, and resolving. They do not positively object to anything that they hear upon spiritual subjects. They can even approve of the Gospel. They hope one day to repent, and believe, and be converted, and become thorough Christians, and go to heaven after death. But they never get beyond "hoping." They never come to the point of making a business of religion. Of course they never confess sin.

In one or other of these ways thousands of persons on every side are ruining their souls. In one point they are all agreed. They may sometimes call themselves "sinners," in a vague, general way, and cry out, "I have sinned," like Pharaoh, and Balaam, and Achan, and Saul, and Judas Iscariot (Exod. ix. 27; Num. xxii. 34; Josh. vii. 20; Matt. xxvii. 4); but they have no real sense, or sight, or understanding of sin. Its guilt, and vileness, and wickedness, and consequences, are utterly hid from their eyes. And the result, in each case, is one and the same. They know nothing practically of confession of sins.

Shall I say what seems to me the clearest proof that man is a fallen and corrupt creature? It is not open vice or unblushing profligacy. It is not the crowded public-house, or the murderer's cell in a jail. It is not avowed infidelity, or gross and foul idolatry. All these are proofs, and convincing proofs indeed, that man is fallen;—but there is to my mind a stronger proof still. That proof is the wide-spread "spirit of slumber" in which most men lie chained and bound about their souls. When I see that multitudes of sensible men, and intelligent men, and decent-living men, can travel quietly towards the grave, and feel no concern about their sins, I want no more convincing evidence that man is "born in sin," and that his heart is alienated from God. There is no avoiding the conclusion. Man is naturally asleep, and must be awakened. He is blind, and must be made to see. He is dead, and must be made alive. If this was not the case there would be no need for our pressing the duty of confession. Scripture commands it. Reason assents to it. Conscience, in its best moments, approves of it. And yet, notwithstanding this, the vast majority of men have no practical acquaintance with confession of sin!— No disease of body is so desperate as mortification. No heart is in so bad a state as the heart that does not feel sin.

Shall I say what is my first and foremost wish for men's souls, if they are yet unconverted? I can wish them nothing better than thorough *self-knowledge*. Ignorance of self and sin is the root of all mischief to the soul. There is hardly a religious error or a false doctrine that may not be traced up to it. Light was the first thing called into being. When God created the world, He said, "Let there be light." (Gen. i. 3.) Light is the first thing that the Holy Ghost creates in a man's heart, when He awakens, converts, and makes him a true Christian. (2 Cor. iv. 6.) For want of seeing sin men do not value salvation. Once let a man get a sight of his own heart, and he will begin to cry, "God be merciful to me a sinner."

If a man has learned to feel and acknowledge his sinfulness, he has great reason to thank God. It is a real symptom of health in the inward man. It is a mighty token for good. To know our spiritual disease is one step towards a cure. To feel bad and wicked and hell-deserving, is the first beginning of being really good.

What though we feel ashamed and confounded at the sight of our own transgressions! What though we are humbled to the dust, and cry, "Lord, I am vile. Lord, I am the very chief of sinners!" It is better a thousand times to have these feelings and be miserable under them, than to have no feelings at all. Anything is better than a dead conscience, and a cold heart, and a prayerless tongue!

If we have learned to feel and confess sin, we may well thank God and take courage. Whence came those feelings? Who told you that you were a guilty sinner? What moved you to begin acknowledging your transgressions? How was it that you first found sin a burden, and longed to be set free from it?—These feelings do not come from man's natural heart. The devil does not teach such lessons. The schools of this world have no power to impart them. These feelings came down from above. They are the precious gifts of God the Holy Ghost. It is His special office to convince of sin. The man who has really learned to feel and confess his sins, has learned that which millions never learn, and for want of which millions die in their sins, and are lost to all eternity.

II. I now turn to the second branch of my subject: *To whom ought confession of sin to be made?*

I enter on this branch of the subject with sorrowful feelings. I approach it as a sailor would approach some rock on which many gallant ships have made shipwreck. I cannot forget that I have arrived at a point on which millions of so-called Christians have erred greatly, and millions are erring at the present day. But I dare not keep back anything that is Scriptural, for fear of giving offence. The errors of millions must not prevent a minister of the Gospel speaking the truth. If multitudes are hewing out broken cisterns that can hold no water, it becomes the more needful to point out the true fountain. If countless souls are turning aside from the right way, it becomes the more important to show clearly to whom confession ought to be made.

Sin, to speak generally, ought to be confessed to God. He it is whom we have chiefly offended: His are the laws which we have broken. To Him it is that all men and women will one day give account: His displeasure is that which sinners have principally to fear. This is what David felt: "Against Thee, Thee only, have I sinned, and done this evil in Thy sight." (Psalm li. 4.) This is what David practised: "I said I will confess my transgressions unto the Lord." (Psalm xxxii. 5.) This is what Joshua advised Achan to do: "My son, give glory to God, and make confession to Him." (Josh. vii. 19.) The Jews were right when they said, "Who can forgive sins but God only?" (Mark ii. 7.)

But must we leave the matter here? Can vile sinners like us ever dare to confess our sins to a holy God? Will not the thought of His infinite purity shut our mouths and make us afraid? Must not the remembrance of His holiness make us afraid? Is it not written of God, that He is "of purer eyes than to behold evil, and cannot look on iniquity"? (Hab. i. 13.) Is it not said, that He "hates all workers of iniquity"? (Psalm v. 5.) Did he not say to Moses, "There shall no man see My face and live"? (Exod. xxxiii. 20.) Did not Israel say of old, "Let not God speak with us, lest we die"? (Exod. xx. 19.) Did not Daniel say, "How can the servant of my Lord talk with this my Lord"? (Dan. x. 17.) Did not Job say, "When I consider, I am afraid of Him"? (Job xxiii. 15.) Did not Isaiah say, "Woe is me, for I am undone:—for mine eyes have seen the King, the Lord of hosts"? (Isa. vi. 5.) Does not Elihu say, "Shall it be told Him that I speak? If a man speak, surely he shall be swallowed up"? (Job xxxvi. 20.)

These are serious questions. They are questions which must and will occur to thoughtful minds. There are many who know what Luther meant, when he said, "I dare not have anything to do with an absolute God." But I thank God they are questions to which the Gospel supplies a full and satisfactory answer. The Gospel reveals One who is exactly suited to the wants of souls which desire to confess sin.

I say then that sin ought to be confessed to God in Christ.—I say that sin ought specially to be confessed to God manifest in the flesh,—to

Christ Jesus the Lord,—to that Jesus who came into the world to save sinners,—to that Jesus who died for our sins, and rose again for our justification, and now lives at the right hand of God to intercede for all who come to God by Him. He that desires to confess sin should apply direct to Christ.

Christ is a great High Priest. Let that truth sink down into our hearts and never be forgotten. He is sealed and appointed by God the Father for that very purpose, to be the Priest of Christians. It is His peculiar office to receive, and hear, and pardon, and absolve sinners. It is His place to receive confessions, and to grant plenary absolutions. It is written in Scripture, "Thou art a Priest for ever."—"We have a great High Priest that is passed into the heavens."—"Having an High Priest over the house of God, let us draw near with a true heart, in full assurance of faith." (Heb. iv. 14; v. 6; vi. 20; x. 21, 22.)

(*a*) Christ is a High Priest of Almighty *power*. There is no sin that He cannot pardon, and no sinner that He cannot absolve. He is very God of very God. He is "over all, God blessed for ever." He says Himself, "I and my Father are one." He has "all power in heaven and earth." He has "power on earth to forgive sins." He has complete authority to say to the chief of sinners, "Thy sins are forgiven. Go in peace." He has "the keys of death and hell." When He opens no one can shut. (Rom. ix. 5; John x. 30; Matt. xxviii. 18; ix. 6; Luke vii. 48–50; Rev. i. 18; iii.7.)

(*b*) Christ is a High Priest of infinite *willingness* to receive confession of sin. He invites all who feel their guilt to come to Him for relief. "Come unto Me," He says, "all ye that labour and are heavy laden, and I will give you rest."—"If any man thirst, let him come unto Me and drink."— When the penitent thief cried to Him on the cross, He at once absolved him fully, and gave him an answer of peace. (Matt. xi. 28; John vii. 37.)

(*c*) Christ is a High Priest of perfect *knowledge*. He knows exactly the whole history of all who confess to Him: from Him no secrets are hid. He never errs in judgment: He makes no mistakes. It is written that "He is of quick understanding. He shall not judge after the sight of His eyes, neither reprove after the hearing of His ears." (Isa. xi. 3.) He can discern the difference between the hypocritical professor who is full of words, and the broken-hearted sinner who can scarce stammer out his confession. People may deceive ministers by "good words and fair speeches," but they will never deceive Christ.

(*d*) Christ is a High Priest of matchless *tenderness*. He will not afflict willingly, or grieve any soul that comes to Him. He will handle delicately every wound that is exposed to Him. He will deal tenderly even with the vilest sinners, as He did with the Samaritan woman. Confidence reposed in Him is never abused: secrets confided to Him are completely safe. Of Him it is written, that "He will not break the bruised reed, nor quench the smoking flax." He is one that "despiseth not any." (Isaiah xlii. 3; Job xxxvi. 5.)

(e) Christ is a High Priest who *can sympathize* with all that confess to Him. He knows the heart of a man by experience, for He had a body like our own, and was made in the likeness of man. "We have not a High Priest who cannot be touched with the feeling of our infirmities; but was in all points tempted like as we are, yet without sin." (Heb. iv. 15.) To Him the words can most truly be applied, which Elihu applied to himself, "Behold, I am according to thy wish in God's stead: I also am formed out of the clay. Behold, my terror shall not make thee afraid, neither shall my hand be heavy upon thee." (Job xxxiii. 6, 7.)

This great High Priest of the Gospel is the person whom we ought specially to employ in our confession of sin. It is only through Him and by Him that we should make all our approaches to God. In Him we may draw near to God with boldness, and have access with confidence. (Ephes. iii. 12.) Laying our hand on Him and His atonement, we may "come boldly to the throne of grace, that we may obtain mercy and find grace to help in time of need." (Heb. iv. 16.) We need no other Mediator or Priest. We can find no better High Priest. To whom should the sick man disclose his ailment, but the physician? To whom should the prisoner tell his story, but to his legal advocate? To whom should the sinner open his heart and confess his sins, but to Him who is the "Advocate with the Father, Jesus Christ the righteous"? (1 John ii. 1.)

Why should we confess our sins to angels and dead saints, while we have Christ for a High Priest? Why should we confess to the Virgin Mary, Michael the Archangel, John the Baptist, St. Paul, or any other creature in the unseen world! The Church of Rome enjoins such confession as this on her millions of members, and many members of the Church of England seem half-disposed to think the Church of Rome is right! But when we ask a Scriptural reason for the practice, we may ask long without getting an answer.

There is *no need* for such a confession. Christ has not given up His office, and ceased to be a Priest. The saints and angels cannot possibly do more for us than Christ can. They certainly have not more pity or compassion, or more good-will towards our souls.

There is *no warrant of Scripture* for such a confession. There is not a text in the Bible that bids us confess to dead saints and angels. There is not an instance in Scripture of any living believer taking his sins to them.

There is not the slightest proof that there is *any use* in such a confession. We do not even know that the saints in glory can hear what we say; much less do we know that they could help us if they heard. They were all sinners saved by grace themselves:—where is the likelihood that they could do anything to aid our souls?

The man who turns away from Christ to confess to saints and angels is a deluded robber of his own soul. He is following a shadow, and forsaking the substance. He is rejecting the bread of life, and trying to satisfy his spiritual hunger with sand.

But why, again, should we confess our sins to living priests or ministers, while we have Christ for a High Priest? The Church of Rome commands her members to do so. A party within the Church of England approves the practice as useful, helpful, and almost needful to the soul. But, again, when we ask for Scripture and reason in support of the practice, we receive no satisfactory answer.*

---

* The only passages in the Prayer-book of the Church of England, which appear at first sight to favour the Romish view of confession and absolution, are to be found in the Exhortation in the Communion Service, and in the Visitation of the Sick.

In both these cases I am entirely satisfied that the Reformers never *intended* to give any countenance to the Romish doctrine, and that the true and honest interpretation of the language used affords no help to those who hold that doctrine.

In the Exhortation in the Communion Service, the case is supposed of some person who "cannot quiet his conscience." The advice then follows: "Let him come to me, or to some other discreet and learned minister of God's holy Word, and open his grief; that by the ministry of God's holy Word he may receive the benefit of absolution, together with ghostly counsel and advice."

If men are determined to twist this passage into a sanction of the Romish doctrine of habitual confession and absolution, it is useless to reason with them. To my own eyes the exhortation seems nothing more than advice to people who are troubled with some special difficulties, to go and speak to a minister in private about them, and to get them cleared up by texts from the Bible.

But I can see nothing in the passage like Romish auricular confession and priestly absolution.

In the Visitation of the Sick, the language used about absolving the sick man, "if he humbly and heartily desire it," is undoubtedly very strong, and the direction to "move" the sick person to "make a special confession of his sins, if he feel his conscience troubled with any mighty matter," is unmistakable.

Yet, even here, it is hard to prove that this confession means more than any faithful minister of the Gospel would press on any sick and dying person, if he saw him "troubled," or distressed about "some weighty matter." It is only in this case, be it remembered, that he is to be "moved to make" it.

As to the absolution, the most that can be made of it is that it is *declaratory*. It is a very strong and authoritative declaration of the forgiveness of the Gospel, addressed to a dying person, in need of special comfort. It is the custom of the Prayer-book to call any ministerial declaration of God's willingness to pardon those who repent and believe, an "absolution." We see this very plainly in the beginning of the morning and afternoon service. After the general confession, the minister reads what is called "an absolution."

The language of the absolution in the Visitation of the Sick is undoubtedly very strong. But still it must be observed that it only declares a person absolved, who is already absolved by God. The very form itself says that the Church's absolution is to be given to "all sinners who truly repent and believe in Jesus Christ." Now all such are of course pardoned the very moment they repent and believe. When, therefore, the minister says, "I absolve thee," he can only mean, "I declare thee absolved."

When I add to this explanation the striking fact that the Homily of Repentance contains a long passage most strongly condemning auricular confession, I can see no fair ground for the charge that the Church of England sanctions auricular confession, as a practice of general utility to the soul. At the same time I deeply regret that the formularies of the Church contain any expressions which are capable of being twisted into an argument in defence of the doctrine, and I should rejoice to see them removed.

Is there *any need* for confessing to priests or ministers? There is none. There is nothing they can do for a sinner that Christ cannot do a thousand times better. When Christ has failed the soul that cried to Him, it may be time to turn to ministers. But that time will never come.

Is there *any Scriptural warrant* for confessing to priests or ministers? There is none. There is not a passage in the New Testament which commands it. St. Paul writes three Epistles to Timothy and Titus about ministerial duty. But he says nothing about receiving confessions.—St. James bids us "confess our faults to one another," but he says nothing about confessing to ministers.—Above all, there is not a single example in Scripture of any one confessing to a minister and receiving absolution. We see the Apostles often declaring plainly the way of forgiveness, and pointing men to Christ. But we nowhere find them telling men to confess to them, and offering to absolve them after confession.

Finally, is *any good likely to result* from confessing to priests or ministers? I answer boldly, There is none. Ministers can never know that those who confess to them are telling the truth. Those who confess to them will never feel their consciences really satisfied, and will never feel certain that what they confess will not be improperly used. Above all, the experience of former times is enough to condemn "auricular confession" for ever, as a practice of most vile and evil tendency. Facts, stubborn facts, abound to show that the practice of confessing to ministers has often led to the grossest and most disgusting immorality. A living writer has truly said, "There is no better school of wickedness on earth than the confessional. History testifies that for every offender whom the confessional has reclaimed it has hardened thousands; for one it may have saved it has destroyed millions."—*Wylie on Popery*, p. 329.*

The man who turns away from Christ to confess his sins to ministers, is like a man who chooses to live in prison when he may walk at liberty, or to starve and go in rags in the midst of riches and plenty, or to cringe for favours at the feet of a servant, when he may go boldly to the Master and ask what he will. A mighty and sinless High Priest is provided for him, and yet he prefers to employ the aid of mere fellow-sinners like himself! He is trying to fill his purse with rubbish, when he may have fine gold for the asking. He is insisting on lighting a rush-light, when he may enjoy the noon-day light of God's sun!

If we love our souls, let us beware of giving to ministers the honour that belongs to Christ alone. He is the true High Priest of the Christian's

* Those who wish for more information on this painful subject will find it fully supplied in Elliott's *Delineation of Romanism* (p. 210), under the head "Confession." Those who take a favourable view of auricular confession, and wish to see it introduced into the English Church, would do well to study Elliott's account of the Bull of Pope Paul IV. against those Spanish confessors who were called "Solicitants." If then they are not convinced of the immoral tendency of the confessional, I shall be surprised.

profession. He ever lives to receive confessions, and to absolve sinners. Why should we turn away from Him to man? Above all, let us beware of the whole system of the Romish confessional. Of all practices that were ever devised by man in the name of religion, I firmly believe that none was ever devised so mischievous and objectionable as the confessional. It overthrows Christ's office, and places man in the seat which should only be occupied by the Son of God.—It puts two sinners in a thoroughly wrong position: it exalts the confessor far too high; it places those who confess far too low. It gives the confessor a place which it is not safe for any child of Adam to occupy. It imposes on those who confess a bondage to which it is not safe for any child of Adam to submit. It sinks one poor sinner into the degrading attitude of a serf; it raises another poor sinner into a dangerous mastery over his brother's soul. It makes the confessor little less than a god: it makes those who confess little better than slaves.— If we love Christian liberty, and value inward peace, let us beware of the slightest approach to the Romish confessional!

Those who tell us that Christian ministers were intended to receive confessions, and that Evangelical teaching makes light of the ministerial office, and strips it of all authority and power, are making assertions which they cannot prove. We honour the minister's office highly, but we refuse to give it a hair's breadth more dignity that we find given in the Word of God. We honour ministers as Christ's ambassadors, Christ's messengers, Christ's watchmen, helpers of believers' joy, preachers of the Word, and stewards of the mysteries of God. But we decline to regard them as priests, mediators, confessors, and rulers over men's faith, both for the sake of their souls and of our own.*

The common notion that Evangelical teaching is opposed to the exercise of soul-discipline, or heart-examination, or self-humiliation, or mortification of the flesh, or true contrition, is a mere invention of man's. Opposed to it! There never was a more baseless assertion. We are entirely favourable to it. This only we require,—that it shall be carried on in the right way. We approve of a confessional; but it must be the only true one, —the throne of grace. We approve of going to a confessor; but it must be the true One,—Christ the Lord. We approve of submitting consciences to a priest; but it must be to the great High Priest,—Jesus the Son of God. We approve of unbosoming our secret sins, and seeking absolution; but it must be at the feet of the great Head of the Church, and not at the feet of one of His weak members. We approve of kneeling to receive ghostly counsel; but it must be at the feet of Christ, and not at the feet of man.

Let us beware of ever losing sight of Christ's priestly office. Let us glory in His atoning death, honour Him as our Substitute and Surety on

* It should always be remembered that the word "priest" in the Prayer-book, was not intended to mean a sacrificing priest, like the Old Testament priests. It signifies the same as presbyter or elder.

H

the cross, follow Him as our Shepherd, hear His voice as our Prophet, obey Him as our King. But in all our thoughts about Christ, let it be often before our minds that He alone is our High Priest, and that He has deputed His priestly office to no order of men in the world.* This is the office of Christ, which Satan labours above all to obscure. It is the neglect of this office which leads to every kind of error. It is the remembrance of this office which is the best safe-guard against the plausible teaching of the Church of Rome. Once right about this office we shall never greatly err in the matter of the confession of sin. We shall know to whom confession ought to be made; and to know that rightly is no slight thing.

I shall conclude this paper with two words of practical application. (a) We have seen who ought to confess sin. (b) We have seen to whom confession ought to be made. Let us try to bring the subject nearer to our hearts and consciences. Time flies very fast. Writing and preaching,— reading and working,—doubting and speculating,—discussion and controversy,—all, all will soon be past and gone for ever. Yet a little while and there will remain nothing but certainties, realities, and eternity.

Let us then ask ourselves honestly and conscientiously, Do we CONFESS?

(1) If we never confessed sin before, let us go this very day to the throne of grace, and speak to the great High Priest, the Lord Jesus Christ, about our souls. Let us pour out our hearts before Him, and keep nothing back from Him. Let us acknowledge our iniquities to Him, and entreat Him to cleanse them away. Let us say to Him, in David's words, "For Thy name's sake, pardon my iniquity; for it is great." "Hide Thy face from my sins, and blot out all my iniquities." Let us cry to Him as the publican did in the parable, "God be merciful to me a sinner." (Ps. xxv. 11; li. 9; Luke xviii. 13.)

Are we afraid to do this? Do we feel unworthy and unfit to begin?

* The passage, "Whosoever sins ye remit they are remitted unto them; and whosoever sins ye retain they are retained" (John xx. 23), is often quoted in defence of the Romish view of priestly absolution, but I am firmly persuaded, in entire contradiction to our Lord's intention.

I believe that in these words our Lord conferred on His apostles, and all those disciples who were present with them at the same time (Luke xxiv. 33), the power of authoritatively declaring whose sins are forgiven, and whose sins are not forgiven, but nothing more.—I believe, moreover, that from their peculiar gift of discerning spirits, the Apostles were fitted and enabled to exercise this power of declaring, in a way that no minister, since the apostolic times, ever can or ever did.

But that the Apostles ever took on themselves to "remit or retain sins," in the way that the Romish Church enjoins on her priests to do, is not to be traced out in any passage in the whole New Testament.

The reader who wishes to investigate this subject further, will find it fully discussed in my *Expository Thoughts on St. John's Gospel* (vol. iii., pp. 444–453), together with many valuable quotations from eminent divines elucidating the whole matter. The passage is too long for insertion in this place.

Let us resist such feelings, and begin without delay. There are glorious Bible examples to encourage us: there are rich Bible promises to lure us on. In all the volume of Scripture there are no passages so encouraging as those which are about confession of sin. "If we confess our sins, He is faithful and just to forgive us our sins, and to cleanse us from all unrighteousness." (1 John i. 8.) "If any say, I have sinned, and perverted that which is right, and it profited me not; He will deliver his soul from going into the pit, and his life shall see the light." (Job xxxiii. 27.) "Father," said the prodigal son, "I have sinned against heaven and in thy sight, and am no more worthy to be called thy son. But the father said to his servant, Bring forth the best robe, and put it on him, and put a ring on his hand, and shoes on his feet; and bring hither the fatted calf and kill it, and let us eat and be merry." (Luke xv. 21–23.) If Christ had never died for sinners, there might be some excuse for doubting. But Christ having suffered for sin, there is nothing that need keep us back.

(2) If we have been taught by the Holy Ghost to confess our sins, and know the subject of this paper by inward experience, let us keep up the habit of confession to the last day of our lives.

We shall never cease to be sinners as long as we are in the body. Every day we shall find something to deplore in our thoughts, or motives, or words, or deeds. Every day we shall find that we need the blood of sprinkling, and the intercession of Christ. Then let us keep up daily transactions with the throne of grace. Let us daily confess our infirmities at the feet of our merciful and faithful High Priest, and seek fresh absolution. Let us daily cast ourselves under the shadow of His wings, and cry, "Surely in me dwelleth no good thing: Thou art my hiding-place, O Lamb of God!"

May every day find us more humble and yet more hopeful,—more sensible of our own unworthiness, and yet more ready to rejoice in Christ Jesus, and have no confidence in the flesh!—May our prayers become every day more fervent, and our confessions of sin more real;—our eye more single, and our walk with God more close:—our knowledge of Jesus more clear, and our love to Jesus more deep;—our citizenship in heaven more manifest, and our separation from the world more distinct!

So living, we shall cross the waves of this troublesome world with comfort, and have an abundant entrance into God's kingdom. So living, we shall find that our light affliction, which is but for a moment, works for us a far more exceeding and eternal weight of glory. Yet a few more years, and our prayers and confessions shall cease for ever. We shall begin an endless life of praise. We shall exchange our daily confessions for eternal thanksgivings.*

---

* The attention of all members of the Church of England is particularly requested to the following passages from the "HOMILY OF REPENTANCE":—
"Whereas the adversaries [Roman Catholics] wrest this place [in St. James—

(James v.)—], for to maintain their auricular confession withal, they are greatly deceived themselves and do shamefully deceive others; for if this text ought to be understood of auricular confession, then the priests are as much bound to confess themselves unto the lay-people, as the lay-people are bound to confess themselves to them. And if to pray is to absolve, then the laity by this place as great authority to absolve the priests, as the priests have to absolve the laity.

"And where that they do allege this saying of our Saviour Jesus Christ unto the leper, to prove auricular confession to stand on God's Word, '*Go thy way, and show thyself unto the priest*' (Matt. viii.), do they not see that the leper was cleansed from his leprosy before he was by Christ sent unto the priest, for to show himself unto Him? By the same reason we must be cleansed from our spiritual leprosy, I mean our sins must be forgiven us, before that we come to confession. What need we then to tell forth our sins into the ear of the priest, sith that they be already taken away! Therefore holy Ambrose, in his second sermon upon the hundred-and-nineteenth Psalm, doth say full well, '*Go, show thyself unto the priest*.' Who is the true priest, but He which is the Priest for ever, after the order of Melchisedec? Whereby this holy Father doth understand that, both the priesthood and the law being changed, we ought to acknowledge none other Priest for deliverance from our sins but our Saviour Jesus Christ: who being Sovereign Bishop, doth with the sacrifice of His body and blood, offered once for ever upon the altar of the cross, most effectually cleanse the spiritual leprosy, and wash away the sins of all those that with true confession of the same do flee unto Him.

"It is most evident and plain that this auricular confession hath not the warrant of God's Word, else it had not been lawful for Nectarius, Bishop of Constantinople, upon a just occasion to have put it down. (*Nectarius Sozomen Eccles. Hist.*, lib. vii, cap. 16.) For when anything ordained of God is by the lewdness of men abused, the abuse ought to be taken away, and the thing itself suffered to remain. Moreover, these are St. Augustine's words (*Confessionum*, lib. x., cap. 3):—'What have I to do with men, that they should hear my confession, as though they were able to heal my diseases? A curious sort of men to know another man's life, and slothful to correct and amend their own. Why do they seek to hear of me what I am, which will not hear of Thee what they are? And how can they tell, when they hear by me of myself, whether I tell the truth, or not; sith no mortal man knoweth what is in man, but the spirit of man which is in him?' Augustine would not have written thus if auricular confession had been used in his time.

"Being, therefore, not led with the conscience thereof, let us with fear and trembling, and with a true contrite heart, use that kind of confession that God doth command in His Word; and then doubtless, as He is faithful and righteous, He will forgive us our sins, and make us clean from all wickedness. I do not say but that, if any do find themselves troubled in conscience, they may repair to their learned curate or pastor, or to some other godly learned man, and show the trouble and doubt of their conscience to them, that they may receive at their hand the comfortable salve of God's Word; but it is against the true Christian liberty that any man should be bound to the numbering of his sins, as it hath been used heretofore in the time of blindness and ignorance."

XIII

WORSHIP

"God is a Spirit: and they that worship Him must worship Him in spirit and in truth."—JOHN iv. 24.
"We are the circumcision, which worship God in the spirit."—PHIL. iii. 3.
"In vain they do worship Me."—MATT. xv. 9.
"A show of wisdom in will-worship."—COL. ii. 23.

WE live in times when there is a vast quantity of public religious worship. Most English people who have any respect for appearances go to some church or chapel on Sundays. To attend no place of worship in this country, whatever may be the case abroad, is at present the exception and not the rule. But we all know that quantity is of little value without quality. It is not enough that we worship sometimes. There remains behind a mighty question to be answered,—"How do we worship?"

Not all religious worship is right in the sight of God. I think this is as clear as the sun at noon-day to any honest reader of the Bible. The Bible speaks of worship which is "in vain," as well as worship which is true,— and of "will-worship," as well as spiritual worship. To suppose, as some thoughtless persons do, that it signifies nothing where we go on Sundays, and matters nothing *how* the thing is done, provided it is done, is mere childish folly. Merchants and tradesmen do not carry on their business in this fashion. They look at the way their work is done, and are not content with work done anyhow. Let us not be deceived. God is not mocked. The question, "How do we worship?" is a very serious one.

I propose to unfold the subject of worship, and to lay down some Scriptural principles about it. In a day of profound ignorance in some quarters, and of systematic false teaching in others, I hold it to be of primary importance to have clear ideas about all disputed points in religion. I fear that thousands of English men and women can render no reason of their faith and practice. They do not know why they believe, or what they believe, or why they do what they do. Like children, they are tossed to and fro by every wind of doctrine, and are liable to be led astray by the first clever heretic who meets them. In a day like this let us try to get hold of some distinct notions about Christian worship.

I. *I will show the general importance of public worship.*
II. *I will show the leading principles of public worship.*

219

III. *I will show the essential parts of complete public worship.*

IV. *I will show the things to be avoided in public worship.*

V. *I will show the tests by which our public worship should be tried.*

I purposely confine my attention to public worship. I purposely pass over all private religious habits, such as praying, Bible-reading, self-examination, and meditation. No doubt they lie at the very root of personal Christianity, and without them all public religion is utterly in vain. But they are not the subject I want to handle to-day.

I.   I have first *to show the general importance of public worship.*

I trust I need not dwell long on this part of my subject. This paper is not likely to fall into the hands of any who do not at least call themselves Christians. There are few, except downright infidels, who will dare to say that we ought not to make some public profession of religion. Most people, whatever their own practice may be, will admit that we ought to meet other Christians at stated times and in stated places, and unitedly and together to worship God.*

Public worship, I am bold to say, has always been one mark of God's servants. Man, as a general rule, is a social being, and does not like to live separate from his fellows. In every age God has made use of that mighty principle, and has taught His people to worship Him publicly as well as privately, together as well as alone. I believe the last day will show that wherever God has had a people He has always had a congregation. His servants, however few in number, have always assembled themselves together, and approached their Heavenly Father in company. They have been taught to do it for many wise reasons,—partly to bear a public testimony to the world,—partly to strengthen, cheer, help, encourage, and comfort one another,—and above all, to train and prepare them for the general assembly in heaven. "As iron sharpeneth iron, so doth the countenance of a man his friend." That man can know little of human nature who does not know that to see others doing and professing the

---

* "To deny God a worship is as great a folly as to deny His being. He that renounceth all homage to his Creator, envies Him the being of which he cannot deprive Him. The natural inclination to worship is as universal as the notion of a God; else idolatry had never gained a footing in the world. The existence of God was never owned in any nation without a worship of God being appointed; and many people who have turned their backs upon some other parts of the law of nature, have paid a continual homage to some superior and invisible Being. The Jews gave a reason why man was created in the evening of the Sabbath, because he should begin his being with the worship of his Maker. As soon as ever he found himself to be a creature, his first solemn act should be a particular respect to his Creator. To fear God and keep His commandment, is the whole of man (Eccles. xii. 13), or is 'whole man:' he is not a man, but a beast, without observance of God. Religion is as requisite as reason to complete a man. He were not reasonable, if he were not religious, because by neglecting religion he neglects the chiefest dictate of reason."— *Charnock's Works.* Nichol's Edition. Vol. i., p. 182.

same things that we do in religion, is an immense help and encouragement to our souls.

From the beginning of the Bible down to the end, you may trace out a line of public worship in the history of all God's saints. You see it in the very first family that lived on earth. The familiar story of Cain and Abel hinges entirely on acts of public worship.—You see it in the history of Noah. The very first thing recorded about Noah and his family, when they came forth from the ark, was a solemn act of public worship.—You see it in the history of Abraham, Isaac, and Jacob. Wherever the patriarchs had a tent they always had an altar. They not only prayed in private, but worshipped in public.—You see it throughout the whole Mosaic economy, from Sinai downward, till our Lord appeared. The Jew who was not a public worshipper in the tabernacle or the temple, would have been cut off from the congregation of Israel.—You see it throughout the whole New Testament. The Lord Jesus Himself gives a special promise of His presence wherever two or three are assembled in His name. The Apostles, in every Church they founded, made the duty of assembling together a first principle in their list of duties. Their universal rule was, "Forsake not the assembling of yourselves together." (Heb. x. 25.) These are ancient things, I know; but it is well to be reminded of them. Just as you may lay it down, as a certainty, that where there is no private prayer there is no grace in a man's heart, so you may lay it down, as the highest probability, that where there is no public worship there is no Church of God, and no profession of Christianity.*

Turn now from the Word of God to the pages of Church history, and what will you find? You will find that from the days of the Apostles down to this hour, public worship has always been one of God's great instruments in doing good to souls. Where is it that sleeping souls are generally awakened, dark souls enlightened, dead souls quickened, doubting souls brought to decision, mourning souls cheered, heavy-laden souls relieved? Where, as a general rule, but in the public assembly of Christian worshippers, and during the preaching of God's Word? Take away public worship from a land, shut up the churches and chapels, forbid people to meet together for religious services, prohibit any kind of religion except that which is private,—do this, and see what the result would be. You would inflict the greatest spiritual injury on the country which was so treated. You could do nothing so likely to help the devil and stop the progress of Christ's cause, except the taking away of the Bible. Next to the Word of God there is nothing which does so much good to mankind

* The reader will of course understand that I fully admit the impossibility of public worship being kept up in times of persecution. When the Roman Emperors persecuted the early Church, and all Christians were proscribed, there could of necessity have been no public worship. But these are evidently exceptional cases.

as public worship. "Faith cometh by hearing." (Rom. x. 7.) There is a special presence of Christ in religious assemblies.

I grant freely that public worship may become a mere act of formality. Thousands of so-called Christians, no doubt, are continually going to churches and chapels, and getting no benefit from their attendance. Like Pharaoh's lean kine, they are nothing bettered, but rather worse, more impenitent, and more hardened. No wonder that the ignorant Sabbath-breaker defends himself by saying,—"For anything I can see, those who go nowhere on Sundays are just as good people as church-goers and chapel-goers." But we must never forget that the misuse of a good thing is no argument against the use of it. Once begin to refuse everything that is misused in this sinful world, and there is hardly anything left for you that is good. Take a broader view of the question before you. Look at any district you like in England, and divide people into two great parties,—worshippers and non-worshippers. I will engage you will find that there is far more good among those that worship than among those that do not. It does make a difference, whatever men may say. It is not true that worshippers and non-worshippers are all alike.

We ought never to forget the solemn words of St. Paul: "Forsake not the assembling of yourselves together, as the manner of some is; but exhort one another." (Heb. x. 25.) Let us act upon that exhortation, as long as we live, and through evil report and good report continue regular attendants at public worship. Let us not care for the bad example of many around us who rob God of His Day, and never go up to His House from one end of the year to the other. Let us go on worshipping in spite of every discouragement, and let us not doubt that in the long run of life it does us good. Let us prove our own meetness for heaven by our feelings toward the earthly assemblies of God's people. Happy is that man who can say with David, "I was glad when they said unto me, Let us go into the house of the Lord;"—"I had rather be a door-keeper in the house of my God, than to dwell in the tents of wickedness." (Psalm cxxii. 1; lxxxiv. 10.)

II. I proceed, in the second place, to show *the leading principles of public worship.*

These leading principles are so plain and obvious to any thoughtful reader of the Bible, that I need not dwell on them at any length. But for the sake of some who may not hitherto have given much attention to the subject, I feel it best to state them in order.

(*a*) For one thing, true public worship must be *directed to the right object.* It is written plainly, both in the Old and New Testament: "Thou shalt worship the Lord thy God, and Him only shalt thou serve." (Deut. vi. 13; Matt. iv. 10.) All adoration and prayers addressed to the Virgin Mary, the saints and angels, is utterly useless, and unwarranted by

Scripture. It is worship that is mere waste of time. There is not the slightest proof that the departed saints or the angels can hear our worship, or that if they did hear it they could do anything for us. It is worship that is most offensive to God. He is a jealous God, and has declared that He will not give His glory to another. Of all His Ten Commandments there is none more stringent and sweeping than the Second. It forbids us not only to worship, but even to "bow down" to anything beside God.

(b) For another thing, true public worship must be directed to God *through the mediation of Christ.* It is written plainly, "I am the way, the truth, and the life: no man cometh unto the Father, but by Me." (John xiv. 6.) It is written of Christians, that they are a people who "come unto God by Christ." (Heb. vii. 25.) The mighty Being with whom we have to do, without controversy, is a God of infinite love, kindness, mercy, and compassion. "God is love." But it is no less true that He is a Being of infinite justice, purity, and holiness, that He has an infinite hatred of sin, and cannot bear that which is evil. He is the same God that cast down the angels from heaven, drowned the world with a flood, and burned up Sodom and Gomorrah. He who carelessly presumes to draw near to Him without an atonement and a mediator, or by any other mediator than the one Mediator whom He has appointed, will find that he worships in vain. "Our God is a consuming fire." (Heb. xii. 29.)

(c) For another thing, true public worship must be either directly *Scriptural,* or deducible from Scripture, or in harmony with Scripture. It is written plainly concerning the Jews of our Lord's time, "In vain do they worship Me, teaching for doctrines the commandments of men." (Matt. xv. 9.) No doubt there is a conspicuous absence of particular injunctions about New Testament worship. No doubt there is a reasonable liberty allowed to Churches and congregations in their arrangements about worship. But still the rule must never be forgotten: "Nothing must be required of men contrary to God's Word." Well says the Twentieth Article of the Church of England: "The Church hath power to decree rites and ceremonies, and authority in controversies of faith. And yet it is not lawful for the Church to ordain anything that is contrary to God's Word written." Well says the Thirty-fourth Article: "Ceremonies at all times have been divers, and may be changed according to the diversities of countries, times, and men's manners, so that nothing be ordained against God's Word." I say therefore that any man who tells us that there are seven sacraments, when the Bible only mentions two,—or that any man-made ordinance is as binding on our consciences and as needful to salvation as an ordinance appointed by Christ, is telling us what he has no right to tell. We must not listen to him. He is committing not only a mistake, but a sin. St. Paul distinctly tells us that there is such a thing as "will-worship," which has a "show of wisdom," but is in reality useless, because it only "satisfies the flesh." (Col. ii. 23.)

(d) For another thing, true public worship must be an *intelligent* worship. I mean by that expression that worshippers must know what they are doing. It is written plainly as a charge against the Samaritans, "Ye worship ye know not what: we know what we worship." (John iv. 22.) It is written of the heathen Athenians, that they ignorantly worshipped an "unknown god." It is utterly false that ignorance is the mother of devotion. The poor Spanish Papists, not knowing a chapter in the Bible, may appear extremely devout and sincere, as they kneel in crowds before the image of the Virgin Mary, or hear Latin prayers which they do not understand. But it is utterly preposterous to suppose that their worship is acceptable to God. He who made man at the beginning made him an intelligent being, with mind as well as body. A worship in which the mind takes no part is useless and unprofitable. It might suit a beast as well as a man.

(e) For another thing, true public worship must be the worship *of the heart*. I mean by this, that the affections must be employed as well as our intellect, and our inward man must serve God as well as our body. It is written plainly in the Old Testament, and the saying is quoted by Jesus Christ Himself: "This people draweth nigh to Me with their mouth, and honoureth Me with their lips; but their heart is far from Me. But in vain do they worship Me." (Isa. xxix 13; Matt. xv. 8.) It is written of the Jews in Ezekiel's time: "They come unto thee as the people cometh, and they sit before thee as My people, and they hear thy words, but they will not do them: for with their mouth they show much love, but their heart goeth after their covetousness." (Ezek. xxxiii. 31.) The heart is the principal thing that God asks man to bring in all his approaches to Him, whether public or private. A church may be full of worshippers who may give God an immense amount of bodily service. There may be abundance of gestures, and postures, and turnings to the East, and bowings, and crossings, and prostrations, and grave countenances, and upturned eyes, and yet the hearts of the worshippers may be at the end of the earth. One may be thinking only of coming or past pleasures, another of coming or past business, and another of coming or past sins. Such worship, we may be very sure, is utterly worthless in God's sight. It is even worse than worthless: it is abominable hypocrisy. God is a Spirit, and He cares nothing for man's bodily service without man's heart. Bodily service profiteth little. "Man looketh on the outward appearance; but the Lord looketh on the heart." The broken and contrite heart is the true sacrifice, the sacrifice which "God will not despise."* (1 Sam. xvi. 7; Psalm li. 17.)

---

* "Men may attend on worship all their days with a juiceless heart and unquickened frame, and think to compensate the neglect of the manner, with the abundance of the matter of the service. Outward expressions are only the badges and liveries of service, not the service itself. As the strength of sin lies in the inward frame of the heart, so the strength of worship lies in the inward complexion and temper of the soul. What do a thousand services avail, without

(*f*) In the last place, true public worship must be a *reverent* worship. It is written, "Keep they foot when thou goest to the house of God, and be more ready to hear than to give the sacrifice of fools: for they consider not that they do evil." (Eccles. v. 1.) It is recorded that our Lord Jesus Christ began and ended His ministry with two practical protests against irreverent worship. On two distinct occasions He cast out of the temple the buyers and sellers who were profaning its courts by their traffic, and justified His act by the weighty words, "It is written, My house shall be called the house of prayer, but ye have made it a den of thieves." (Matt. xxi. 13.) People who call themselves Christians, and go to churches and chapels to stare about, whisper, fidget, yawn, or sleep, but not to pray, or praise, or listen, are not a whit better than the wicked Jews. They do not consider that God detests profaneness and carelessness in His presence, and that to behave before God as they would not dare to behave before their sovereign at a levée or a drawing-room, is a very grave offence indeed. We must beware that we do not rush from one extreme into another. It does not follow, because "bodily service" alone is useless, that it does not matter how we behave ourselves in the congregation. Surely even nature, reason, and common sense should teach us that there is a manner and demeanour suitable to mortal man, when he draws nigh to his Almighty Maker. It is not for nothing that it is written, "God is greatly to be feared in the assembly of the saints, and to be had in reverence of all them that are about Him." (Psalm lxxxix. 7.) If it is worth while to attend public worship at all, it is worth while to do it carefully and well. God is in heaven, and we are on earth. Let us not be rash and hasty. Let us mind what we are about. "Let us have grace, whereby we may serve God acceptably with reverence and godly fear." (Heb. xii. 28, 29.)

I ask the reader's special attention to the five leading principles which I have just laid down. I fear they strike at the root of the worship of myriads in our own land, to say nothing of Papists, Mahometans, and heathens abroad. Thousands of English people, I fear, are regularly spending their Sundays in a worship which is utterly useless. It is a worship without Scripture, without Christ, without the Holy Spirit, without

cutting the throat of carnal affections? What are loud prayers, but as sounding brass and tinkling cymbals, without divine charity? A Pharisaical diligence in outward forms had no better title vouchsafed by our Saviour than that of hypocrisy. God desires not sacrifices nor delights in burnt-offerings. Shadows are not to be offered instead of substance. God required the heart of man for itself, but commanded outward ceremonies, as subservient to inward worship, and goads and spurs unto it. They were never appointed as the substance of religion, but as auxiliaries to it.

"Could the Israelites have been called worshippers of God according to His order, if they had brought Him a thousand lambs that had died in a ditch or been killed at home? They were to be brought to the altar living, and the blood shed at the foot of it. A thousand sacrifices killed without had not been so valuable as one brought alive to the place of offering."—*Charnock*, vol. i,. p. 323.

knowledge, without heart, and without the slightest benefit to the wor-shippers. For any good they get from it, they might just as well be sitting at home, and not worship at all. Let us take heed that this is not our condition. Let us remember, as long as we live, that it is not the quantity of worship, but the quality that God regards. The inward and spiritual character of the congregation is of far more importance in His sight than the number of the worshippers, or the outward and visible signs of devotion which they exhibit. Children and fools, who admire poppies more than corn, may think all is right when there is a great external show of religion. But it is not so with God. His all-seeing eye looks at the inner man.

III. I proceed, in the third place, to show the *essential parts of Christian public worship.*

I will suppose the case of a man who has never given the subject of religion any sincere attention, and has never gone regularly to any place of worship at all. I will suppose such a man to be awakened to a sense of the value of his soul, and to be desirous of information about things in religion. He is puzzled by finding that all Christians do not worship God in the same way, and that one neighbour worships God in one fashion, and another in another. He hears one man saying that there is no road to heaven excepting through his Church, and another replying that all will go to hell who do not join his Chapel. Now what is he to think? Are there not certain things which are essential parts of Christian worship? I answer without hesitation that there are. It shall be my next business to exhibit them in order.

I freely grant that there is little said on the nature of public worship in the New Testament. There is a wide difference in this respect between the law of Moses and the law of Christ. The Jew's religion was full of strict and minute directions about worship: the Christian's contains very few directions, and those of the simplest and most general description. The Jew's religion was full of types, emblems, and figures: the Christian's only contains two,—viz. Baptism and the Lord's Supper. The Jew's religion approached the worshipper chiefly through the eye: the New Testament religion appeals directly to the heart and conscience. The Jew's religion was confined to one particular nation: the Christian's was meant for the whole world. The Jew could turn to the writings of Moses, and see at a glance every item of his worship: the Christian can only point to a few isolated texts and passages, which are to be applied by every Church according to circumstances. In a word, there is nothing answering to Exodus or Leviticus in the New Testament. Yet a careful reader of the Christian Scriptures can hardly fail to pick out of them the essential parts and principles of Christian worship. Where these essential parts are present, there is Christian worship. Where they are absent, the worship is, to say the least, defective, imperfect, and incomplete.

(*a*) In complete public worship *the Sabbath* should always be honoured. That blessed day was appointed for this very purpose, among others, to give men an opportunity of meeting together in God's service. A Sabbath was given to man even in Paradise. The observance of a Sabbath was made part of the Ten Commandments. The worship of God on the Sabbath was observed by our Lord Jesus Christ Himself. To meet together on one day in the week at least was a practice of the early Christians, though they met on the first day instead of the seventh. (Acts xx. 7; 1 Cor. xvi. 2.) To assemble in God's house on the Christian Sabbath has been the custom of all professing Christians for eighteen hundred years. The best and holiest of God's saints have always pressed on others most strongly the value of Sabbath worship, and borne witness to its usefulness. It sounds very fine and spiritual, no doubt, to say that every day should be a Sabbath to a Christian, and that one day should not be kept more holy than another. But facts are stronger than theories. Experience proves that human nature requires such helps as fixed days, and hours, and seasons for carrying on spiritual business, and that public worship never prospers unless we observe God's order. "The Sabbath was made for man" by Him who made man at the beginning, and knew what flesh and blood is. As a general rule, it will always be found that where there is no Sabbath there is no public worship.

(*b*) In complete public worship there should *be a ministry*. I do not for a moment say that it is of absolute necessity that it must be an Episcopal ministry. I am not so narrow-minded and uncharitable as to deny the validity of Presbyterian or Congregational orders. I only maintain that it is the mind of God that ministers of some kind should conduct the worship of Christian congregations, and be responsible for its decent and orderly conduct in approaching God. I am at a loss to understand how any one can read the Acts of the Apostles, and the Epistles to the Corinthians, Ephesians, Timothy, and Titus, and deny that the ministry is an appointment of God. I say this with every feeling of respect for the Quakers and Plymouth Brethren, who have no ordained ministers: I simply say that I cannot understand their views on this subject. Reason itself appears to me to tell us that business which is left to nobody in particular to attend to, is a business which is soon entirely neglected. Order is said to be heaven's first law. Once let a people begin with no Sabbath and no ministry, and it would never surprise me if they ended with no public worship, no religion, and no God.

(*c*) In complete public worship there should be the *preaching of God's Word*. I can find no record of Church assemblies in the New Testament in which preaching and teaching orally does not occupy a most prominent position. It appears to me to be the chief instrument by which the Holy Ghost not only awakens sinners, but also leads on and establishes saints. I observe that in the very last words that St. Paul wrote to Timothy, as a young minister, he especially enjoins on him to "preach the Word." (2 Tim. iv. 2.) I cannot, therefore, believe that any system of worship in which the sermon is made little of, or thrust into a corner, can be a Scriptural system, or one likely to have the blessing of God. I have no faith in the general utility of services composed entirely of prayer-reading, hymn-singing, sacrament-receiving, and walking in procession. I hold firmly with Bishop Latimer, that it is one of Satan's great aims to exalt ceremonies and put down preaching. There is a deep meaning in the words, "Despise not prophesying." (1 Thess. v. 20.) A contempt for sermons is a pretty sure mark of a decline in spiritual religion.

(d) In complete public worship there should be united *public prayer*. I can find no account of religious assemblies in the New Testament in which prayer and supplication do not form a principal business. I find St. Paul telling Timothy, "I exhort, first of all, that supplications, prayers, intercessions, and giving of thanks, be made for all men." (1 Tim. ii. 1.) Such prayers should be plain and intelligible, that all the worshippers may know what is going on, and be able to go along with him who prays. They should as far as possible be the joint act of all the assembly and not the act of one man's mind alone. A congregation of professing Christians which only meets to hear a grand sermon, and takes no part or interest in the prayers, seems to me to fall far short of the standard of the New Testament. Public worship does not consist only of hearing.*

(e) In complete public worship there should be the public *reading of the Holy Scriptures*. This was evidently a part of the service of the Jewish synagogue, as we may learn from what happened at Nazareth, and at Antioch in Pisidia. (Luke iv. 16; Acts xiii. 15.) We cannot doubt that the Christian Church was intended to honour the Bible as much as the Jewish. To my eye St. Paul points to this when he says to Timothy, "Till I come give attention to reading." (1 Tim. iv. 13.) I do not believe that "reading"

---

* The reader is requested to observe that I purposely abstain from saying anything about the vexed question, whether public prayers in the congregation should be liturgical and pre-composed, or extemporaneous. I say nothing, because nothing is said about it in Scripture. Neither liturgies nor extemporaneous prayers are expressly sanctioned, or expressly prohibited, in God's Word. A large liberty is mercifully given to the Churches. I think the Christian (so-called) who anathematises and abuses his brother because he uses a liturgy, is an ignorant, narrow-minded bigot on one side. I think the Christian (so-called) who anathematises and excommunicates his brother because he does not use a liturgy, is a narrow-minded, ignorant bigot on the other side. Both are wrong. My own mind has been long made up. If all ministers prayed extempore always, as some ministers pray sometimes, I should be against a liturgy. But considering what human nature is, I decidedly think it better both for minister and people, in the regular, habitual, and stated assemblies of the Church to have a liturgy. With all its imperfections I am very thankful for the Book of Common Prayer. It may have defects, because it was not compiled by inspiration. But for all that, it is an admirable and matchless manual of public devotion. I would not impose the use of it on a brother's conscience for a thousand worlds. But I claim the right to use it myself undisturbed.

in that text means "private study." Reason and common sense alike teach the usefulness of the practice of publicly reading the Scriptures. A visible Church will always contain many professing members who either cannot read, or have no will or time to read at home. What safer plan can be devised for the instruction of such people than the regular reading of God's Word? A congregation which hears but little of the Bible is always in danger of becoming entirely dependent on its minister. God should always speak in the assembly of His people as well as man.*

(*f*) In complete public worship there should be united *public praise*. That this was the custom among the first Christians, is evident from St. Paul's words to the Ephesians and Colossians, in which he commended the use of "psalms and hymns and spiritual songs." (Ephes. v. 19; Coloss. iii. 16.) That it was a custom so widely prevalent as to be a mark of the earliest Christians, is simply matter of history. Pliny records that when they met they "used to sing a hymn to Christ as God." No one indeed can read the Old Testament and not discover the extremely prominent place which praise occupied in the temple service. What man in his senses can doubt that the "service of song" was meant to be highly esteemed under the New Testament? Praise has been truly called the flower of all devotion. It is the only part of our worship which will never die. Preaching and praying and reading shall one day be no longer needed. But praise shall go on for ever. A congregation which takes no part in praise, or leaves it all to be done by deputy through a choir, can be hardly thought in a satisfactory state.

(*g*) Finally, in complete public worship there should be the *regular use of the two sacraments* which Christ appointed in His Church. By baptism new members should be continually added to the congregation, and publicly enrolled in the list of professing Christians. By the Lord's Supper believers should be continually offered an opportunity of confessing their Master, and continually strengthened and refreshed, and put in remembrance of His sacrifice on the cross. I believe, with every feeling of respect for Quakers and Plymouth Brethren, that no one who neglected these two sacraments would have been regarded as a Christian by St. Paul and St. Peter, St. James and St. John. No doubt, like every other good thing, they may be painfully misused and profaned by some, and superstitiously idolized by others. But after all there is no getting over the fact that baptism and the Lord's Supper were ordained by Christ Himself as means of grace, and we cannot doubt He meant them to be reverently and duly used. A man who preferred to worship God for many years without ever

---

* There is nothing in the public worship of the Church of England which I admire so much as the large quantity of Scripture which it orders to be read aloud to its members. Every Churchman who goes to church twice on Sunday hears two chapters of the Old Testament and two of the New, beside the Psalms, the Epistle, and the Gospel. I doubt if the members of any other Church in Christendom hear anything like the same proportion of God's Word.

receiving the sacrament of the Lord's Supper, is a man, I am firmly persuaded, that would not have been thought in a right state in the days of the Apostles.

I commend these seven points to the serious attention of my readers, and invite them to consider them well. I can easily believe that I may have said things about them with which some Christians may not agree. I am not their judge. To their own Master they must stand or fall. I can only tell my readers, as an honest man, what appears to me the teaching of Holy Scripture. I do not for a moment say that no man will be saved who does not see public worship precisely with my eyes. I say nothing of the kind. But I do say that any regular system of public worship which does not give a place to the Sabbath, the ministry, preaching, prayers, Scripture-reading, praise, and the two sacraments, appears to me deficient and incomplete. If we attend a place of worship where any of these seven points is neglected, I think we suffer loss and damage. We may be doing well; but I think we might be doing better. To my mind these seven parts of public worship appear to stand out plainly on the face of the New Testament; and I plainly say so.

IV. I proceed, in the fourth place, to show *some things which ought to be avoided in public worship.*

I am well aware that there is no perfection in this world. There is no visible Church, I am sure, in whose public worship it would not be easy to show faults, defects, and shortcomings. The best service in the best visible Church on earth will always be infinitely below the standard of the glorified Church in heaven. I admit with sorrow and humiliation, that the faith, and hope, and life, and worship of God's people are all alike full of imperfections. To be continually separating and seceding from Churches, because we detect blemishes in their administration, is not the act of a wise man. It is to forget the parable of the wheat and tares.

But I cannot forget, for all this, that we have fallen on dangerous times in the matter of worship. There are things going on in many English churches and chapels in the present day so highly objectionable, that I feel it a plain duty to offer some cautions about them. Plain speaking about them is imperatively demanded at a minister's hands. If the watchmen hold their peace, how shall the city take alarm? "If the trumpet give an uncertain sound, who shall prepare himself for the battle?" (1 Cor. xiv. 8.)

There are three great and growing evils in public worship, which require special watching in the present day. I feel it a positive duty to direct attention to them. We have need to stand on our guard about these evils, and to take heed that they do not infect and damage our souls.

(a) Let us beware, for one thing, of any worship in which a *disproportionate honour* is given to any one ordinance of Christ, to the neglect of another. There are Churches at this moment, in which baptism and the Lord's Supper, like Aaron's rod, swallow up everything else in religion. Nothing beside receives much attention. The honour done to the font and the Lord's Table meet you at every turn. All else, in comparison, is jostled out of its place, overshadowed, dwarfed, and driven into a corner. Worship of this sort, I hesitate not to say, is useless to man's soul. Once alter the proportions of a doctor's prescription, and you may turn his medicine into a poison. Once bury the whole of Christianity under baptism and the Lord's Supper, and the real idea of Christian worship is completely destroyed.

(b) Let us beware, for another thing, of any worship in which an *excessive quantity of decoration* and ornament is used. There are many Churches at this moment, in which Divine service is carried on with such an amount of gaudy dressing, candle-lighting, and theatrical ceremonial, that it defeats the very purpose of worship. Simplicity should be the grand characteristic of New Testament worship. Ornament at any time should be employed with a very sparing hand. Neither in the Gospels nor in the Epistles shall we find the slightest warrant for a gorgeous and decorated ceremonial, or for any symbols except water, bread, and wine. Above all, the inherent wickedness of human nature is such that our minds are only too ready to turn away from spiritual things to visible things. Whether men like it or not, what the heart of man needs teaching, is the uselessness of outward ornaments without inward grace.*

(c) Let us beware, above all things, of any worship in which ministers wear the dress, or act in the manner of *sacrificing priests*. There are hundreds of English Churches at this moment in which the Lord's Supper

---

* "Pompous rites have been the great engine whereby the devil hath deceived the souls of men, and wrought them to a nauseating simplicity of Divine worship as if unworthy the majesty and excellency of God. (2 Cor. xi. 3.) But the Jews would not understand the glory of the second temple in the presence of the Messiah, because it had not the pompous grandeur of the temple erected by Solomon.

"Hence in all ages men have been forward to disfigure God's models and to dress up a brat of their own; as though God had been defective in providing for His own honour in His institutions without the assistance of His creature. This hath always been in the world; the old world had their imaginations, and the new world hath continued them. The Israelites, in the midst of miracles and under the memory of a famous deliverance, would erect a calf. The Pharisees who sat in Moses' chair, would coin new traditions, and enjoin them to be as current as the law of God. Papists will be blending Christian appointments with Pagan ceremonies, to please the carnal fancies of the common people.

"How often hath the practice of the Primitive Church, the custom wherein we are bred, the sentiments of our ancestors, been owned as a more authentic rule, in matters of worship, than the mind of God delivered in His Word. It is natural by creation to worship God; and it is as natural by corruption for man to worship Him in a human way, and not in a divine. Is not this to impose laws upon God?—to reckon ourselves wiser than He? To think Him negligent of His own services, and that our feeble brains can find out ways to accommodate His honour better than Himself hath done."—*Charnock*, vol. i., p. 222.

is administered as a sacrifice and not as a sacrament, and the clergy are practically acting as mediators between God and man. The real presence of our Lord's body and blood under the form of bread and wine is openly taught. The Lord's Table is called an altar. The consecrated elements are treated with an idolatrous reverence, as if God Himself was in them, under the form of bread and wine. The habit of private confession to clergymen, is encouraged and urged on the people. I find it impossible to believe that such worship as this can be anything but offensive to God. He is a jealous God, and will not give His honour to another. The sacrifice of our Lord Jesus Christ on the cross once offered, can in no sense or way ever be repeated. His mediatorial and priestly office He has never deputed to any man, or any order of men. There is not a word in the Acts or Epistles to show that the Apostles ever pretended to be sacrificing priests, or to make any oblation in the Lord's Supper, or to hear private confessions, and confer judicial absolutions. Surely that simple fact ought to make men think. Let us beware of Sacrificialism, the Mass, and the Confessional!

Against the three evils of which I have just been speaking, I desire to lift up a warning voice. Such worship is not acceptable in God's sight. It may be pressed upon us most plausibly by clever men. It may be very attractive to the eye, and ear, and the sensual part of our nature. But it has one fatal defect about it: it cannot be defended and maintained by plain texts of Scripture. Sacramentalism, Ceremonialism, Sacrificialism, will never be found in Bibles fairly read and honestly interpreted.

We should search the pages of English history, if nothing else will open our eyes, and see what those pages tell us. Of worship in which Sacraments, Ceremonies, Sacerdotalism, and the Mass made the principal part,—of such worship England has surely had enough. Such worship was tried by the Church of Rome in the days of our forefathers, for centuries before the Protestant Reformation, and utterly failed. It filled the land with superstition, ignorance, formalism, and immorality. It comforted no one, sanctified no one, elevated no one, helped no one toward heaven. It made the priests overbearing tyrants, and the people cringing slaves. And shall we go back to it? God forbid! Shall we once more be content with services in which baptism, the Lord's Supper, the power of the priesthood, the real presence of Christ in the Eucharist, the necessity of symbolical decorations, the value of processions, banners, pictures, altar lights, are incessantly pressed on our minds? Once more I say, God forbid! Let every one that loves his soul come out from such worship and be separate. Let him avoid it and turn away from it, as he would from poison.

V. I proceed, in the last place, to show *some tests by which our public worship should be tried.*

This is a point of vast importance, and one which every professing Christian should look fairly in the face. Too many are apt to cut the knot of all difficulties about the subject before us, by referring to their own feelings. They will tell us that they are not theologians, that they do not pretend to understand the difference between one school of divinity and another. But they do know that the worship in which they take part makes them *feel* so much better, that they cannot doubt it is all right.

I am not disposed to let such people turn away from the subject of this paper quite so easily. I cannot forget that religious feelings are very deceitful things. There is a sort of gentle animal excitement produced in some minds by hearing religious music and seeing religious spectacles, which is not true devotion at all. While it lasts, such excitement is very strong and very contagious; but it soon comes and soon goes, and leaves no permanent impression behind it. It is a mere sensuous animal influence, which even a Romanist may feel at seasons, and yet remain a Romanist both in doctrine and practice.

(a) True spiritual worship will affect a man's *heart and conscience*. It will make him feel more keenly the sinfulness of sin, and his own particular personal corruption. It will deepen his humility. It will render him more jealously careful over his inward life. False public worship, like dram-drinking and opium-eating, will every year produce weaker impressions. True spiritual worship, like wholesome food, will strengthen him who uses it, and make him grow inwardly every year.

(b) True spiritual worship will draw a man into close *communion with Jesus Christ* Himself. It will lift him far above Churches, and ordinances, and ministers. It will make him hunger and thirst after a sight of the King. The more he hears, and reads, and prays, and praises, the more he will feel that nothing but Christ Himself will feed the life of his soul, and that heart communion with Him is "meat indeed and drink indeed." The false worshipper in the time of need will turn to external helps, to ministers, ordinances, and sacraments. The true worshipper will turn instinctively to Christ by simple faith, just as the compass-needle turns to the pole.

(c) True spiritual worship will continually extend a man's *spiritual knowledge*. It will annually give bone, and sinew, and muscle, and firmness to his religion. A true worshipper will every year know more of self, and God, and heaven, and duty, and doctrine, and practice, and experience. His religion is a living thing, and will grow. A false worshipper will never get beyond the old carnal principles and elements of his theology. He will annually go round and round like a horse in a mill, and though labouring much will never get forward. His religion is a dead thing, and cannot increase and multiply.

(d) True spiritual worship will continually increase the *holiness* of a man's life. It will make him every year more watchful over tongue, and temper, and time, and behaviour in every relation of life. The true worshipper's conscience becomes annually more tender. The false worshipper's becomes annually more seared and more hard.

Give me the worship that will stand the test of our Lord's great principle "By their fruits ye shall know them." Give me the worship that sanctifies the life,—that makes a man walk with God and delight in God's law,—that lifts him above the fear of the world and the love of the world,—that enables him to exhibit something of God's image and God's likeness before his fellow-men,—that makes him just, loving, pure, gentle, good-tempered, patient, humble, unselfish, temperate. This is the worship that comes down from heaven, and has the stamp and seal and superscription of God.

Whatever men may please to say, the grand test of the value of any kind of worship is the effect it produces on the lives of the worshippers. A man may tell us that what is called Ritualism now-a-days is the best and most perfect mode of worshipping God. He may despise the simple and unadorned ceremonial of Evangelical congregations. He may exalt to the skies the excellence of ornament, decoration, and pageantry in our service of God. But I take leave to tell him that Christian men will try his favourite system by its results. So long as Ritualistic worshippers can turn from matins and early communions to races and operas, and can oscillate between the confessional and the ball-room, so long the advocates of Ritualism must not be surprised if we think little of the value of Ritualistic worship.

Let us hear the conclusion of the whole matter. The best public worship is that which produces the best private Christianity. The best Church Services for the congregation are those which make its individual members most holy at home and alone. If we want to know whether our own public worship is doing us good, let us try it by these tests. Does it quicken our conscience? Does it send us to Christ? Does it add to our knowledge? Does it sanctify our life? If it does, we may depend on it, it is worship of which we have no cause to be ashamed.

The day is coming when there shall be a congregation that shall never break up, and a Sabbath that shall never end, a song of praise that shall never cease, and an assembly that shall never be dispersed. In that assembly shall be found all who have "worshipped God in spirit" upon earth. If we are such, we shall be there.

Here we often worship God with a deep sense of weakness, corruption, and infirmity. There, at last, we shall be able, with a renewed body, to serve Him without weariness, and to attend on Him without distraction.

Here, at our very best, we see through a glass darkly, and know the Lord Jesus Christ most imperfectly. It is our grief that we do not know Him better and love Him more. There, freed from all the dross and defilement of indwelling sin, we shall see Jesus as we have been seen, and know as we have been known. Surely, if faith has been sweet and peace-giving, sight will be far better.

Here we have often found it hard to worship God joyfully, by reason of the sorrows and cares of this world. Tears over the graves of those we loved have often made it hard to sing praise. Crushed hopes and family sorrows have sometimes made us hang our harps on the willows. There every tear shall be dried, every saint who has fallen asleep in Christ shall meet us once more, and every hard thing in our life-journey shall be made clear and plain as the sun at noon-day.

Here we have often felt that we stand comparatively alone, and that even in God's house the real spiritual worshippers are comparatively few. There we shall at length see a multitude of brethren and sisters that no man can number, all of one heart and one mind, all free from blemishes, weaknesses, and infirmities, all rejoicing in one Saviour, and all prepared to spend an eternity in His praise. We shall have worshipping companions enough in heaven.

Armed with such hopes as these, let us lift up our hearts and look forward! The time is very short. The night is far spent. The day is at hand. Let us worship on, pray on, praise on, and read on. Let us contend earnestly for the faith once delivered to the saints, and resist manfully every effort to spoil Scriptural worship. Let us strive earnestly to hand down the light of Gospel worship to our children's children. Yet a little time and He that shall come will come, and will not tarry. Blessed in that day will be those, and those only, who are found true worshippers, "worshippers in spirit and truth!"

XIV

THE CHRISTIAN SABBATH, OR LORD'S DAY

"Remember the Sabbath Day, to keep it holy."—Exodus xx. 8.

THERE is a subject in the present day which demands the serious attention of all professing Christians in Great Britain. That subject is the Christian Sabbath, or Lord's Day.

It is a subject which is forced upon our notice, whether we like it or not. The minds of Englishmen are agitated by questions arising out of it. "Is the observance of a Sabbath binding on Christians? Have we any right to tell a man that to do his business or seek his pleasure on a Sunday is a sin? Is it desirable to open places of public amusement on the Lord's Day?" All these are questions which are continually asked. They are questions to which we ought to be able to give a decided answer.

The subject is one on which "divers and strange doctrines" abound. Statements are continually made about Sunday, both by speakers and writers, which plain unsophisticated readers of the Bible find it impossible to reconcile with the Word of God. If these statements proceeded only from the ignorant and irreligious part of the world, the defenders of the Sabbath would have no reason to be surprised. But they may well wonder when they find educated and religious persons among their adversaries. It is a melancholy truth that in some quarters the Sabbath is wounded by those who ought to be its best friends.

The subject is one which is of immense importance. It is not too much to say that the prosperity or decay of English Christianity depends on the maintenance of the Christian Sabbath. Break down the fence which now surrounds the Sunday, and our Sunday schools will soon come to an end. Let in the flood of worldliness and dissipation on the Lord's Day, without check or hindrance, and our congregations will soon dwindle away. There is not too much religion in the land now. Destroy the sanctity of the Sabbath, and there would soon be far less. Nothing, in short, I believe, would so thoroughly advance the kingdom of Satan in England, as to withdraw legal protection from the Lord's Day. It would be a joy to the infidel; but it would be an insult and offence to God.

I ask the attention of all professing Christians, while I try to say a few plain words on the subject of the Sabbath. I have no new argument to advance. I can say nothing that has not been said, and said better too,

236

a hundred times before. But at a time like this it becomes every Christian writer to cast in his mite into the treasury of truth. As a minister of Christ, a father of a family, and a lover of my country, I feel bound to plead in behalf of the old English Sunday. My sentence is emphatically expressed in the words of Scripture,—let us "keep it holy." My advice to all Christians is to contend earnestly for the whole day against all enemies, both without and within. It is worth a struggle. Let our united cry be, "We do not want the Sabbath law of England to be changed."

There are four points in connection with the Sabbath which require examination. On each of these I wish to offer a few remarks.

    I.   *The authority on which the Sabbath stands.*

    II. *The purpose for which the Sabbath was appointed.*

    III. *The manner in which the Sabbath ought to be kept.*

    IV. *The ways in which the Sabbath may be profaned.*

    I.   Let me, in the first place, consider *the authority on which the Sabbath stands.*

I hold it to be of primary importance to have this point clearly settled in our minds. Here is the very rock on which many of the enemies of the Sabbath make shipwreck. They tell us that the day is "a mere Jewish ordinance," and that we are no more bound to keep it holy than to offer sacrifice. They proclaim to the world that the observance of the Lord's Day rests upon nothing but Church authority, and cannot be proved by the Word of God.

Now I believe that those who say such things are entirely mistaken. Amiable and respectable as many of them are, I regard them in this matter as being thoroughly in error. Names go for nothing with me in such a case. It is not the assertion of a hundred divines, whether living or dead, that will make me believe black is white, or reject the evidence of plain texts of Scripture. I care little to be told what Jeremy Taylor, or Paley, or Arnold have thought. The grand question is, "Were their thoughts worth credit?—were they right or wrong?"

My own firm conviction is, that the observance of a Sabbath Day is *part of the eternal law of God.* It is not a mere temporary Jewish ordinance. It is not a man-made institution of priestcraft. It is not an unauthorized imposition of the Church. It is one of the everlasting rules which God has revealed for the guidance of all mankind. It is a rule that many nations without the Bible have lost sight of, and buried, like other rules, under the rubbish of superstition and heathenism. But it was a rule intended to be binding on all the children of Adam.

What saith the Scripture? This is the grand point after all. What public opinion says, or newspaper writers think, matters nothing. We are not going to stand at the bar of man when we die. He that judgeth us is the Lord God of the Bible. What saith the Lord?

(*a*) I turn to *the history of creation.* I there read that "God blessed the seventh day and sanctified it." (Gen. ii. 3.) I find the Sabbath mentioned in the very beginning of all things. There are five things which were given to the father of the human race, in the day that he was made. God gave him a dwelling-place, a work to do, a command to observe, a help-meet to be his companion, and a Sabbath Day to keep. I am utterly unable to believe that it was in the mind of God that there ever should be a time when Adam's children should keep no Sabbath.*

(*b*) I turn to *the giving of the Law* on Mount Sinai. I there read one whole commandment out of ten devoted to the Sabbath Day, and that the longest, fullest, and most minute of all. (Exod. xx. 8–11.) I see a broad, plain distinction between these Ten Commandments and any other part of the Law of Moses. It was the only part spoken in the hearing of all the people, and after the Lord had spoken it, the Book of Deuteronomy expressly says, "He added no more." (Deut. v. 22.) It was delivered under circumstances of singular solemnity, and accompanied by thunder, lightning, and an earthquake. It was the only part written on tables of stone by God Himself. It was the only part put *inside* the ark. I find the law of the Sabbath side by side with the law about idolatry, murder, adultery, theft, and the like. I am utterly unable to believe that it was meant to be only of temporary obligation.†

(*c*) I turn to *the writings of the Old Testament Prophets.* I find them repeatedly speaking of the breach of the Sabbath side by side with the most heinous transgressions of the moral law. (Ezek. xx. 13, 16, 24; xxii. 8, 26.) I find them speaking of it as one of the great sins which brought judgments on Israel and carried the Jews into captivity. (Nehem. xiii. 18; Jer. xvii. 19–27.) It seems clear to me that the Sabbath, in their judgment, is something far higher than the washings and cleansings of the ceremonial law. I am utterly unable to believe, when I read their language, that the Fourth Commandment was one of the things one day to pass away.

(*d*) I turn to *the teaching of our Lord Jesus Christ when He was upon earth.* I cannot discover that our Saviour ever let fall a word in discredit of any one of the Ten Commandments. On the contrary, I find Him

---

* "The text (Gen. ii. 3) is so clear for the ancient institution of the Sabbath, that I see no reason on earth why any man should make doubt thereof; especially considering that the very Gentiles, both civil and barbarous, both ancient and of late days, as it were by an universal kind of tradition, retained the distinction of the seven days of the week."—*Letter to Twiss by Archbishop Usher.* 1650.

† The learned Bishop Andrews wisely remarks that it is a dangerous thing to make the Fourth Commandment ceremonial, and of mere temporary obligation: "The Papists will then have the Second Commandment also to be ceremonial; and there is no reason why there may not be as well three as two, and so four and five, and so all."—"We hold that all ceremonies are ended and abrogated by Christ's death: but the Sabbath is not."—*Bishop Andrews on the Moral Law.* 1642.

declaring at the outset of His ministry, "that He came not to destroy
the law but to fulfil," and the context of the passage where He uses these
words, satisfies me that He was not speaking of the ceremonial law, but
the moral. (Matt. v. 17.) I find Him speaking of the Ten Commandments
as a recognized standard of moral right and wrong: "Thou knowest the
Commandments." (Mark x. 19.) I find Him speaking eleven times on the
subject of the Sabbath, but it is always to correct the superstitious additions which the Pharisees had made to the Law of Moses about observing
it, and never to deny the holiness of the day.* He no more abolishes the
Sabbath, than a man destroys a house when he cleans off the moss or
weeds from its roof. Above all, I find our Saviour taking for granted the
continuance of the Sabbath, when He foretells the destruction of Jerusalem. "Pray ye," He says to the disciples, "that your flight be not on
the Sabbath Day." (Matt. xxiv. 20.) I am utterly unable to believe, when
I see all this, that our Lord did not mean the Fourth Commandment to
be as binding on Christians as the other nine.

(e) I turn to *the writings of the Apostles*. I there find plain speaking
about the temporary nature of the ceremonial law and its sacrifices and
ordinances. I see them called "carnal" and "weak." I am told they are
a "shadow of good things to come,"—"a schoolmaster to bring us to
Christ," and "ordained till the time of reformation." But I cannot find a
syllable in their writings which teaches that any one of the Ten Commandments is done away. On the contrary, I see St. Paul speaking of
the moral law in the most respectful manner, though he teaches strongly
that it cannot justify us before God. When he teaches the Ephesians the
duty of children to parents, he simply quotes the Fifth Commandment:
"Honour thy father and mother, which is the first commandment with
promise." (Rom. vii. 12; xiii. 8; Eph. vi. 2; 1 Tim. i. 8.) I see St. James
and St. John recognizing the moral law, as a rule acknowledged and
accredited among those to whom they wrote. (James ii. 10; 1 John iii. 4.)
Again I say that I am utterly unable to believe that when the Apostles
spoke of the law, they only meant nine commandments, and not ten.†

(f) I turn to *the practice of the Apostles*, when they were engaged in
planting the Church of Christ. I find distinct mention of their keeping
one day of the week as a holy day. (Acts xx. 7; 1 Cor. xvi. 2.) I find the
day spoken of by one of them as "the Lord's Day." (Rev. i. 10.) Undoubtedly the day was changed:—it was made the first day of the week
in memory of our Lord's resurrection, instead of the seventh:—but I

* See Bishop Daniel Wilson of Calcutta's *Seven Sermons on the Lord's Day*,
pp. 60, 61.

† It is only fair to mention that many great and learned divines have held that
the text (Heb. iv. 9) distinctly teaches the authority of the Christian Sabbath. The
marginal reading is, "there remaineth the keeping of a Sabbath." I offer no
opinion on the point. I only remark that Owen, Edwards, and Dwight all held
this view.—See Bishop of Calcutta's *Sermons on the Lord's Day*, pp. 92, 93.

believe the Apostles were divinely inspired to make that change, and at the same time wisely directed to make *no public decree* about it. The decree would only have raised a ferment in the Jewish mind, and caused needless offence: the change was one which it was better to effect gradually, and not to force on the consciences of weak brethren. The spirit of the Fourth Commandment was not interfered with by the change in the smallest degree: the Lord's Day, on the first day of the week, was just as much *a day of rest after six days' labour*, as the seventh-day Sabbath had been. But why we are told so pointedly about the "first day of the week" and the "Lord's Day," if the Apostles kept no one day more holy than another, is to my mind wholly inexplicable.

(*g*) I turn, in the last place, to *the pages of unfulfilled Prophecy*. I find there a plain prediction that in the last days, when the knowledge of the Lord shall cover the earth, there shall still be a Sabbath. "From one Sabbath to another shall all flesh come to worship before Me, saith the Lord." (Isa. lxvi. 23.) The subject of this prophecy no doubt is deep. I do not pretend to say that I can fathom all its parts: but one thing is very certain to me,—and that is that in the glorious days to come on the earth there is to be a Sabbath, and a Sabbath not for the Jews only, but for "all flesh." And when I see this I am utterly unable to believe that God meant the Sabbath to cease between the first coming of Christ and the second. I believe He meant it to be an everlasting ordinance in His Church.

I ask serious attention to these arguments from Scripture. To my own mind it appears very plain that wherever God has had a Church, in Bible times, God has also had a Sabbath Day. My own firm conviction is, that a Church without a Sabbath would not be a Church on the model of Scripture.*

---

* The following quotations from Baxter, Lightfoot, Horsley, and Wells, need no apology. They speak for themselves. In a day like the present, when we are so often told that learned divines deny the Divine authority of the Lord's Day, it may be well to show the reader that there are other divines, and some eminently learned, who take an entirely different view.

Let us hear what Baxter says: "It hath been the constant practice of all Christ's Churches in the whole world ever since the days of the Apostles to this day, to assemble for public worship on the Lord's Day, as a day set apart thereto by the Apostles. Yea, so universal was this judgment and practice, that there is no one Church, no one writer, or one heretic that I remember to have read of, that can be proved even to have dissented or gainsaid it till of late times."

"If any will presume to say that men properly endued with the Spirit for the work of His commission, did notwithstanding do such a great thing as to appoint the Lord's Day for Christian worship, without the conduct of the Spirit, they may by the same way of proceeding, pretend it to be as uncertain of every particular book and chapter in the New Testament, whether or no they wrote it by the Spirit."—*Baxter on the Divine Appointment of the Lord's Day.* 1680.

Let us next hear Lightfoot: "The first day of the week was everywhere celebrated for the Christian Sabbath, and which is not to be passed over without observing, as far as appears from Scripture, there is nowhere any dispute about the matter. There was controversy concerning circumcision, and other points

Let me close this part of the subject by offering two cautions, which I consider are eminently required by the temper of the times.

For one thing, *let us beware of under-valuing the Old Testament.* There has arisen of late years a most unhappy tendency to slight and despise any religious argument which is drawn from an Old Testament source, and to regard the man who uses it as a dark, benighted, and old-fashioned person. We shall do well to remember that the Old Testament is just as much inspired as the New, and that the religion of both Testaments is in the main, and at the root, one and the same. The Old Testament is the Gospel in the bud: the New Testament is the Gospel in full flower. The Old Testament is the Gospel in the blade: the New Testament is the Gospel in full ear. The Old Testament saints saw many things through a glass darkly: but they looked to the same Christ by faith, and were led by the same Spirit as ourselves. Let us, therefore, never listen to those who sneer at Old Testament arguments. Much infidelity begins with an ignorant contempt of the Old Testament.

For another thing, *let us beware of despising the law of the Ten Commandments.* I grieve to observe how exceedingly loose and unsound the opinions of many men are upon this subject. I have been astonished at the coolness with which even clergymen sometimes speak of them as a part of Judaism,

of the Jewish religion, whether they were to be retained or not, but nowhere do we read concerning the changing of the Sabbath. There were indeed some Jews converted to the Gospel, who as in some other things they retained a smack of their old Judaism, so they did in the observance of days (Rom. xiv. 5; Gal. iv. 10), but yet not rejecting or neglecting the Lord's Day. They celebrated it and made no manner of scruple, it appears, concerning it; but they would have their old festival days too; and they disputed not at all, whether the Lord's Day were to be celebrated, but whether the Jewish Sabbath ought not to be celebrated also."—*Lightfoot's Works,* vol. xii., p. 556. 1670.

Let us next hear Bishop Horsley: "The Sabbath Days of which St. Paul speaks to the Colossians (Col. ii. 16) were not the Sundays of the Christians, but the Saturdays and other Sabbaths of the Jewish calendar. The Judaizing heretics, with whom St. Paul was all his life engaged, were strenuous advocates for the observation of the Jewish festivals in the Christian Church, and St. Paul's admonition to the Colossians is that they should not be disturbed by the censure of those who reproached them for neglecting to observe the Jewish Sabbaths with Jewish ceremonies. It appears from the First Epistle to the Corinthians that the Sunday was observed in the Church of Corinth with St. Paul's own approbation. It appears from the Apocalypse that it was generally observed in the time when that book was written by St. John; and it is mentioned by the earliest apologists of the Christian faith as a necessary part of Christian worship." —*Bishop Horsley's Sermons.*

Let us hear Wells: "Darkness and division there hath been enough in the Church to quarrel with institutions and appointments of former times. But the perpetual silence of the Church on this particular infallibly shows the Divine right of the Lord's Day. And the Churches are so silent, because they dare not attempt such an enterprise as to raze the foundations of a Divine institution."— *Well's Practical Sabbatarian,* p. 587.

The whole subject of the change from the seventh-day Sabbath to the Lord's Day is one which the reader will find admirably handled in the Sermons of Daniel Wilson, Bishop of Calcutta, *on the Lord's Day.* Those sermons, and Willison *on the Lord's Day,* are by far the two best works on the Sabbath question.

which may be classed with sacrifices and circumcision. I wonder how such men can read them to their congregations every week! For my own part, I believe that the coming of Christ's Gospel did not alter the position of the Ten Commandments one hair's breadth. If anything, it rather exalted and raised their authority. I believe, that in due place and proportion, it is just as important to expound and enforce them, as to preach Christ crucified. By them is the knowledge of sin. By them the Spirit teaches men their need of a Saviour. By them the Lord Jesus teaches His people how to walk and please God. I suspect it would be well for the Church if the Ten Commandments were more frequently expounded in the pulpit than they are. At all events, I fear that much of the present ignorance on the Sabbath question is attributable to erroneous views about the Fourth Commandment.

II. The second point I propose to examine, is *the purpose for which the Sabbath was appointed.*

I feel it imperatively necessary to say something on this point. There is no part of the Sabbath question about which there are so many ridiculous misstatements put forward. Many are raising a cry in the present day, as if we were inflicting a positive injury on them in calling on them to keep the Sabbath holy. They talk as if the observance of the day were a heavy yoke, like circumcision and the washings and purifications of the ceremonial law. They rail at ministers of religion for defending the Sabbath, as if they only wanted it kept for their own selfish ends. They insinuate that our motives are not pure, and that we feel "our craft in danger." And all this sounds very plausible in the ears of ignorant persons.

Once for all, let us understand that all such statements are founded in entire misconception, and are rank delusions. The Sabbath is God's merciful appointment for *the common benefit of all mankind.* It was "made for man." (Mark ii. 27.) It was given for the good of all classes, for the laity quite as much as for the clergy. It is not a yoke, but a blessing. It is not a burden, but a mercy. It is not a hard wearisome requirement, but a mighty public benefit. It is not an ordinance which man is bid to use in faith, without knowing why he uses it. It is one which carries with it its own reward. It is good for man's body and mind. It is good for nations. Above all, it is good for souls.

(*a*) The Sabbath is *good for man's body.* We all need a day of rest. On this point, at any rate, all medical men are agreed. Curiously and wonderfully made as the human frame is, it will not stand incessant work without regular intervals of repose. The first gold-diggers of California soon found out that! Reckless and ungodly as many of them probably were,—urged on as they were, no doubt, by the mighty influence of the hope of gain,—they still found out that a seventh day's rest was absolutely needful to keep themselves alive. Without it they discovered that in digging for gold they were only digging their own graves. I firmly believe that one reason why the health of working clergymen so frequently fails, is the great difficulty they find in getting a day of rest. I am sure if the body could tell us its wants, it would cry loudly, "Remember the Sabbath Day."*

(b) The Sabbath is *good for man's mind*. The mind needs rest quite as much as the body: it cannot bear an uninterrupted strain on its powers; it must have its intervals to unbend and recover its force. Without them it will either prematurely wear out, or fail suddenly, like a broken bow. The testimony of the famous philanthropist, Mr. Wilberforce, on this point is very striking. He declared that he could only attribute his own power of endurance to his regular observance of the Sabbath Day. He remembered that he had observed some of the mightiest intellects among his contemporaries fail suddenly at last, and their possessors come to melancholy ends; and he was satisfied that in every such case of mental shipwreck the true cause was neglect of the Fourth Commandment.

(c) The Sabbath is *good for nations*. It has an enormous effect both on the character and temporal prosperity of a people. I firmly believe that a people which regularly rests one day in seven will do more work, and better work, in a year, than a people which never rest at all. Their hands will be stronger; their minds will be clearer; their power of attention, application, and steady perseverance will be far greater.

(d) Last, but not least, the Sabbath is *an unmixed good for man's soul*. The soul has its wants just as much as the mind and body. It is in the midst of a hurrying, bustling world, in which its interests are constantly in danger of being jostled out of sight. To have those interests properly attended to, there must be a special day set apart; there must be a regularly recurring time for examining the state of our souls; there must be a day to test and prove us, whether we are prepared for an eternal heaven. Take away a man's Sabbath, and his religion soon comes to nothing. As a general rule, there is a regular flight of steps from "no Sabbath" to "no God."

I know well that many say that *"religion does not consist in keeping days and seasons."* I agree with them. I am quite aware that it needs something more than Sabbath observance to save our souls. But I would like such persons to tell us plainly what kind of religion that is which teaches people to keep no days holy at all. It may be the religion of poor corrupt human nature, but I am sure it is not the religion of revelation:

* "During the excesses of the first French Revolution, at the close of last century, Christianity and the Sabbath were abolished in France, but the mere necessities of man's nature compelled the Atheistical government to institute a day of rest of their own, which they called a decade, occurring every tenth day. What a confession of the reasonableness of the Divine command!"—*Bishop of Calcutta's Sermons*, p. 163.

There is an admirable tract on this subject, by that eminent man, the late Professor Miller, of Edinburgh, entitled *Physiology in Harmony with the Bible*.

it is not the religion which tells us that we "must be born again," and believe in Christ, and live holy lives. Revealed religion teaches me that it is not quite so cheap and easy a thing to go to heaven, as many now-a-days seem to fancy, and that it is essential to our soul's prosperity that in every week we give God a day.

I know well that there are some good people who contend that "*every day ought to be holy*" to a true Christian, and on this ground deprecate the special sanctification of the first day of the week. I respect the conscientious convictions of such people. I would go as far as any one in contending for an "every day religion," and protesting against a mere Sabbath Christianity; but I am satisfied that the theory is unsound and unscriptural. I am convinced that, taking human nature as it is, the attempt to regard every day as a Lord's Day would result in having no Lord's Day at all. None but a thorough fanatic, I presume, would say that it is wrong to have stated seasons for private prayer, on the ground that we ought to "pray always;" and few, I am persuaded, who look at the world with the eyes of common sense, will fail to see, that to bring religion to bear on men with full effect, there must be one day in the week set apart for its business.

Now I believe I have advanced nothing that can be fairly gainsaid. I believe that if every church and chapel were pulled down, and every minister of religion banished from this kingdom, it would still be an unmixed benefit for the nation to preserve untouched the institution of the Sabbath, and an act of suicidal folly to part with it. Whether Englishmen know it or not, their Sabbath is one of their richest possessions, and the grand secret of their position in the world. It is good for their bodies, minds, and souls. Of it the famous words may be truly used, that "it is the cheap defence of a nation."

III. I propose, in the third place, to show *the manner in which the Sabbath ought to be kept*.

This is a branch of the subject on which great difference of opinion exists: it is one on which even the friends of the Sabbath are not thoroughly agreed. Many, I believe, would contend as strongly as I do for a Sabbath, but not for the Sabbath for which I contend. In a matter like this I can call no man master. My desire is simply to state what appears to be the mind of God as revealed in Holy Scripture.

Once for all, I must plainly say, that I cannot entirely agree with those who tell us that they do not want a Jewish Sabbath, but a Christian one. I doubt whether such persons clearly know what they mean. If they object to a Pharisaic Sabbath, I agree with them; if they object to a Mosaic Sabbath, I would have them consider well what they say. I can find no clear evidence that the Old Testament Sabbath was intended by Moses to be more strictly kept than the Christian Sunday. The case of the man stoned for gathering sticks on the Sabbath, is clearly not a case in point: it was a special offence, committed under specially heinous aggravations, in the very face of Mount Horeb, and just after the giving of the law. It is no more a precedent than the striking dead of Ananias and Sapphira, in the Acts, for lying; and there is no proof that such a punishment was ever after repeated. My own belief is, that the explanations of the law of the Sabbath given by our Lord are the very explanations which Moses himself would have given. I have a strong suspicion that, allowing for the difference of the two dispensations, David, and Samuel, and Isaiah would not have kept their Sabbath very differently from St. John and St. Paul.

What then appears to be the will of God about the manner of observing the Sabbath Day? There are two general rules laid down for our guidance in the Fourth Commandment, and by them all questions must be decided.

One plain rule about the Sabbath is, that *it must be kept as a day of rest.* All work of every kind ought to cease as far as possible, both of body and mind. "Thou shalt not do any work, thou, nor thy son, nor thy daughter, thy man-servant nor thy maid-servant, nor thy cattle, nor thy stranger that is within thy gates." Works of necessity and mercy may be done. Our Lord Jesus Christ teaches us this, and teaches also that all such works were allowable in the Old Testament times. "Have ye not read," He says, "what David did?"—"Have ye not read that the priests in the temple profane the Sabbath, and are blameless?" (Matt. xii. 5.) Whatever, in short, is necessary to preserve and maintain life, whether of ourselves, or of the creatures, or to do good to the souls of men, may be done on the Sabbath Day without sin.*

The other great rule about the Sabbath is, that *it must be kept holy.* Our rest is not to be the rest of a beast, like that of the ox and the ass, which have neither mind nor soul. It is not to be a carnal, sensual rest, like that of the worshippers of the golden calf, who "sat down to eat and drink and rose up to play." (Exod. xxxii. 6.) It is to be emphatically a holy rest. It is to be a rest in which, as far as possible, the affairs of the soul may be

---

* "Works needful for the comfortable passing of the Sabbath, as dressing of moderate food and the like, may be done on the Sabbath Day. For, seeing Christ allows us to lead an ox to water, and requireth not to fetch in water for him over night, He alloweth us to dress meats, and requireth not to dress it over night. For the order in the law of not kindling a fire pertained alone to the business of the tabernacle, and that order of dressing what they would dress on the sixth day pertained alone to the matter of manna."—*Leigh's Body of Divinity,* 1654.

"Not only those works which are of absolute necessity, but those which are of great conveniency, may lawfully be done on the Lord's Day: such are kindling of fire, preparing of meat, and many other particulars too numerous to be mentioned.—Only let us take this caution, that we neglect not the doing of those things till the Lord's Day, which might be well done before, and then plead necessity or convenience for it."—*Bishop Hopkins on the Fourth Commandment.* 1690.

attended to, the business of another world minded, and communion with God and Christ kept up. In short, it ought never to be forgotten that it is "the Sabbath of the Lord our God." (Exod. xx. 10.)

I ask attention to these two general rules. I believe that by them all Sabbath questions may be safely tested. I believe that within the bounds of these rules every lawful and reasonable want of human nature is fully met, and that whatsoever transgresses these bounds is sin.

I am no Pharisee. Let no hard-working man, who has been confined to a close room for six weary days, suppose that I object to his taking any lawful relaxation for his body on the Sunday. I see no harm in a quiet walk on a Sunday, provided always that it does not take the place of going to public worship, and is really quiet, and like that of Isaac.* (Gen. xxiv. 63.) I read of our Lord and His disciples walking through the corn-fields on the Sabbath Day. All I say is, beware that you do not turn liberty into licence,—beware that you do not injure the souls of others in seeking relaxation for yourself,—and beware that you never forget you have a soul as well as a body.†

I am no enthusiast. I want no tired labourer to misunderstand my meaning, when I bid him to keep the Sabbath holy. I do not tell any one that he ought to pray all day, or read his Bible all day, or go to church all day, or meditate all day, without let or cessation, on a Sunday. All I say is, that the Sunday rest should be *a holy rest*. God ought to be kept in view; God's Word ought to be studied; God's House ought to be attended; the soul's business ought to be specially considered; and I say that everything which prevents the day being kept holy in this way, ought as far as possible to be avoided.

I am no admirer of a gloomy religion. Let no one suppose that I want Sunday to be a day of sadness and unhappiness. I want every Christian to be a happy man: I wish him to have "joy and peace in believing," and to "rejoice in hope of the glory of God." I want every one to regard Sunday as the brightest, cheerfulest day of all the seven; and I tell every one who finds such a Sunday as I advocate, a wearisome day, that there is something sadly wrong in the state of his heart. I tell him plainly that

---

* "If you walk abroad this day, choose to do it alone as much as possible, for people going in troops to the fields occasion idleness, vain talking, sporting and misspending precious Sabbath time."—*Wilson on the Lord's Day*. (An admirable book.)

† "I cannot see that the employment of horses to take us to church on the Sabbath is wrong, where it is a case of plain necessity and without the use of them the Gospel cannot be heard. But in such cases people should use their own horses if they have them.—The following quotation deserves notice. 'When the Shunammite came to her husband for the ass, he saith to her, Why should you go to him to-day? it is neither Sabbath Day, nor new moon.' The meaning is that the Shunammite was wont to go out to hear the Prophet, and because she had got means would ride. Therefore when the means of sanctification are wanting, a man may take a Sabbath Day's journey. He may go where they are used to be gotten."—*Bishop Andrews on the Moral Law*. 1642.

if he cannot *enjoy* a "holy" Sunday, the fault is not in the day, but in his own soul.

I can well believe that many will think that I am setting the standard of Sabbath observance far too high. The thoughtless and worldly, the lovers of money and lovers of pleasure, will all exclaim that I am requiring what is impossible. It is easy to make such assertions. The only question for a Christian ought to be, "What does the Bible teach?" God's measure of what is right must surely not be brought down to the measure of man: man's measure should rather be brought up to the measure of God.

I want no other standard of Sabbath observance than that which is laid down in the Fourth Commandment. I want neither more nor less. It is a rule which has been sanctioned by the Prayer-book of the Church of England, the writings of all the leading Puritans, and the Scotch Confession of Faith. No English Churchman, no Scotch Presbyterian, no Nonconformist who walks in the steps of his forefathers, has any just right to find fault with it.

I maintain no other standard of Sabbath observance than that which all the best and holiest Christians, of every Church and nation, have maintained almost without exception. It is extraordinary to mark the harmony there is among them on this point. They have differed widely on other subjects in religion:—they have even disagreed as to the grounds on which they defend Sabbath sanctification:—but as soon as you come to the practical question, "how the Lord's Day ought to be observed," the unity among them is truly surprising.

Last, but not least, I want no other standard of Sabbath observance than that to which a calm, rational reflection on things yet to come, will lead every sober-minded person. Are we really going to die one day and leave this world? Are we about to appear before God in another state of existence? Have we any hope that we are about to spend an endless eternity in God's immediate presence? Are these things so, or are they not? Surely, if they are, it is not too much to ask men to give one day in seven to God; it is not too much to require them to test their own meetness for another world, by spending the Sabbath in special preparation for it. Common sense, reason, conscience, will combine, I think, to say, that if we cannot spare God one day in a week, we cannot be living as those ought to live who are going to die.

IV.   The last thing I propose to do, is to expose some of *the ways in which the Sabbath is profaned.*

There are two kinds of Sabbath desecration which require to be noticed. One is that more *private* kind of which thousands are continually guilty, and which can only be checked by awakening men's consciences. The other is that more *public* kind, which can only be remedied by the pressure of public opinion, and the strong arm of the law.

When I speak of *private Sabbath desecration*, I mean that reckless, thoughtless, secular way of spending Sunday, which every one who looks round him must know is common. How many make the Lord's Day a day for visiting their friends and giving dinner parties,—a day for looking over their accounts and making up their books,—a day for going journeys and quietly transacting worldly business,—a day for reading newspapers or new novels,—a day for writing letters, or talking politics and idle gossip,—a day, in short, for anything rather than the things of God.

Now all this sort of thing is wrong, decidedly wrong. Thousands, I firmly believe, never give the subject a thought: they sin from ignorance and inconsideration. They only do as others; they only spend Sunday as their fathers and grandfathers did before them: but this does not alter the case. It is utterly impossible to say, that to spend Sunday as I have described is to "*keep the day holy:*" it is a plain breach of the Fourth Commandment, both in the letter and in the spirit. It is impossible to plead necessity or mercy in one instance of a thousand. And small and trifling as these breaches of the Sabbath may seem to be, they are exactly the sort of things that prevent men communing with God and getting good from His Day.

When I speak of *public desecration of the Sabbath*, I mean those many open, unblushing practices, which meet the eye on Sundays in the neighbourhood of large towns. I refer to the practice of keeping shops open, and buying and selling on Sundays. I refer especially to Sunday travel on railways, Sunday pleasure cruises and excursions to tea gardens and places of public amusement.

These ways of spending the Sabbath are all wrong, decidedly wrong. So long as the Bible is the Bible, and the Fourth Commandment the Fourth Commandment, I dare not come to any other conclusion. They are all wrong.

These ways of spending Sunday *are none of them works of necessity or works of mercy*. There is not the slightest likeness between them and any of the things which the Lord Jesus explains to be lawful on the Sabbath Day. To heal a sick person, or pull an ox or an ass out of a pit, is one thing: to travel in an excursion train is quite another. The difference is as great as between light and darkness.

These ways of spending Sunday are *none of them of a holy tendency, or calculated to do any good to souls*. What soul was ever converted by tearing down to Brighton, or dashing down to Gravesend? What worldly man was ever turned to God by listening to polkas, waltzes, or opera music? No indeed! all experience teaches that it needs something more than the beauties of art and nature to teach man the way to heaven.

These ways of spending Sunday *have never yet conferred moral or spiritual good in any place where they have been tried*. They have been tried for hundreds of years in Italy, in Germany, and in France. The people of Paris have had their Sunday visits to the fountains and statues at Versailles. The Italians and Germans have had their splendid works of art thrown open to the public on Sundays. But what benefit have they derived that we should wish to imitate them? What advantages have we to gain by making a London Sunday like a Sunday at Paris, or Vienna, or Rome? I say decidedly we have nothing to gain. It would be a change for the worse, and not for the better.

Last, but not least, these ways of spending Sunday *inflict a cruel injury on the souls of multitudes of people.* Railway trains and steamboats cannot be run on Sundays without employing hundreds of persons. Clerks, porters, ticket-takers, policemen, guards, engine-drivers, omnibus-drivers, must all work on the Sabbath Day, if people will make Sunday a day for travelling and excursions. Museums, exhibitions, and galleries of pictures, cannot be opened on Sundays without attendants to take care of them and wait on those who visit them. And have not all these unfortunate persons immortal souls? Beyond doubt they have. Do they not all need a day of rest as much as any one else? Beyond doubt they do. But Sunday is no Sunday to them, so long as these public desecrations of the Sabbath are permitted. Their life becomes a long unbroken chain of work, work, unceasing work: in short, what is play to others becomes death to them. Away with the idea that a pleasure-seeking, exhibition-visiting, Continental Sabbath is mercy to any one! It is nothing less than an enormous fallacy to call it so. *Such a Sabbath is real mercy to nobody, and is positive sacrifice to some.*

I write these things with sorrow. I know well to how many myriads of my fellow-countrymen they apply. I have spent many a Sunday in large towns. I have seen with my own eyes how the Day of the Lord is made by multitudes a day of worldliness, a day of ungodliness, a day of carnal mirth, and too often a day of sin. But the extent of the disease must not prevent us exposing it: the truth must be told.

There is one general conclusion to be drawn from the conduct of those who publicly desecrate the Sabbath in the way I have described. They show plainly that they are at present "without God" in the world. They are like those of old who said, "When will the Sabbath be gone?"—"What a weariness is it!" (Amos viii. 5; Mal. i. 13.) It is an awful conclusion, but it is impossible to avoid it. Scripture, history, and experience all combine to teach us, that delight in the Lord's Word, the Lord's service, the Lord's people, and the Lord's Day, will always go together. Sunday railway excursionists and Sunday pleasure-seekers are their own witnesses. They are every week practically declaring, "*We do not like God—we do not want Him to reign over us.*"

It is not the slightest argument, in reply to what I have said, that many great and learned men see no harm in travelling on Sundays and visiting exhibitions. It matters nothing in religious questions, "who does a thing:" the only point to be ascertained is, "whether it be right." Let God be true and every man a liar. We must never follow a multitude to do evil.

The public ways of profaning the Sabbath I have referred to are likely to be often thrust on our notice, if we live many years in England. Let us remember that they are an open breach of God's commandment. Let us have nothing to do with them ourselves, and let us use every lawful means in our power, both publicly and privately, to prevent others having anything to do with them. Let us not mind the epithets of Puritans, Pharisees, bigoted and narrow-minded, or be moved by the specious arguments of newspaper writers. If they only studied their Bibles as much as current affairs, they would not write as they do. Let us fall back on that old Book which has stood the test of many centuries, and of which every word is true. Let us take our stand on the Bible, and hold fast its teaching. Whatever others may think lawful, let our sentence ever be that one day in seven, and one whole day, ought to be kept holy to God.

And now, in concluding this paper, I wish to address a parting word to several classes of persons into whose hands it may fall. I write as a friend to men's souls. I have no interest at heart but that of true religion. I ask for a fair and patient hearing.

(1) I appeal first to *all readers of this paper who are in the habit of breaking the Sabbath.* Whether you break it in public or private, whether you break it in company or alone, I have somewhat to say to you. Do not refuse to read it. Give me a hearing.

I ask you to consider seriously, how you will answer for your present conduct in the day of judgment. I put it solemnly to your conscience. I ask you to think quietly and calmly, how utterly unfit you are to appear before God. You cannot live always: you must one day lie down and die. You cannot escape the great assize in the world to come: you must stand before the great white throne, and give account of all your works. You have before you but two alternatives,—an eternal heaven, or an eternal hell. These are great realities, and you know they are true. I repeat it deliberately: unless you are prepared to take up some silly fable of man's invention, and to be that poor credulous creature, a sceptic, you know these things are true.

Now where is your fitness for the solemn change which is yet before you? Where is your preparedness for meeting the God of the Bible, and reckoning with Him? Where is your readiness for an eternity in His company, and the society of saints and angels? Where is your meetness for a heaven, which is nothing but an eternal Sabbath, an everlasting Sunday, a Lord's Day without end? Yes! *I may well ask, Where?* You cannot give an answer. You cannot give God one single day in seven! It wearies you to spend one-seventh part of your time in attempting to know anything about Him, before whose bar you are going one day to stand! His Bible wearies you! His ministers weary you! His house wearies you! His praises weary you! The excursion train is better! The newspaper is better! The merry dinner-party is better! Anything, in short, anything is better than God! Alas, what an awful state this is to be in! But, alas, how common!

Oh, Sabbath-breaker, unhappy Sabbath-breaker, consider your ways, and be wise! What harm has Sunday done the world, that you should hate it so much? What harm has God done you, that you should so obstinately turn your back on His laws? What injury has religion done to mankind, that you should be so afraid of having too much? Look at that body of yours, and think how soon it will be dust and ashes. Look at that earth on which you walk, and think how soon you will be six feet beneath its surface. Look on the heavens above you, and think of the mighty Being, who is the eternal God. Look into your own heart, and think how much better it would be to be God's friend than God's enemy. As ever you would lie down on your dying-bed with comfort,—as ever you would leave this world with a good hope,—break off from your Sabbath desecration, and sin no more. Let the time past suffice you to have robbed God of His Day. For the time to come give God His own.

The very next Sunday after you read this paper, go to the house of God, and hear the Gospel preached. Confess your past sin at the throne of grace, and ask pardon through that blood which "cleanses from all sin." Arrange your time on Sunday so that you may have leisure for quiet, sober meditation on eternal things. Avoid the company that would lead you to talk only of this world. Take down your long-neglected Bible, and study its pages. Murder no man's soul by obliging him to work on Sunday in order that you may play. *Do it, do it, do it, without a week's delay!* It may be hard at first, but it is worth a struggle. Do it, and it will be well for you both in time and eternity.

(2) I appeal, in the next place, *to all readers of this paper who profess to reverence the Sabbath*, and have no wish to see its character changed. I have only one thing to say to you, but it deserves serious attention.

I ask you, then, to consider whether you may not be more strict in keeping the Sabbath Day holy than you have been hitherto. I am sadly afraid there is much laxity in many quarters on this point. I fear that many who have no thought of infringing the Fourth Commandment, are culpably inconsiderate and careless as to the way in which they obey its precepts. I fear that the world gets into the Sundays of many a respectable church-going family far more than it ought to do. I fear that many keep the Sabbath themselves, but never give their servants a chance of keeping it holy. I fear that many who keep the Lord's Day with much outward propriety when they are at home, are often grievous Sabbath-breakers when they go abroad. I fear that hundreds of English travellers do things

I*

on Sundays on the Continent, which they would never do in their own land.

This is a sore evil. It weakens the hands of all who defend the cause of the Sabbath, to an enormous extent: it supplies the enemies of the Lord's Day with an argument which they know too well how to use. Let us all remember this. If we really love the Lord's Day, let us prove our love by our manner of using it. Wherever we are, whether at home or abroad,—whether in Protestant or Roman Catholic countries,—let our conduct on Sunday be such as becomes the day. Let us never forget that the eyes of the Lord are in every place, and that the Fourth Commandment is just as binding on us in Italy, Switzerland, Germany, or France, as it is in our own country. Last, but not least, let us remember that the Fourth Commandment speaks of our "man-servant and maid-servant," as well as ourselves.

(3) I appeal, in the last place, *to all who love the Lord Jesus Christ in sincerity, and are zealous in His cause.* I have one thing to say to you in connection with the Sabbath question, which I commend to your most serious attention.

I ask you, then, to consider whether it does not become the solemn duty of all true Christians to take far more effectual measures than we have done hitherto, to preserve the holiness of the Lord's Day? For my own part I am satisfied that it is our duty, and that we must go to work in a very different way from that hitherto adopted.

We all complain of Sabbath desecration in large towns: we sorrow over the crowds who every Sunday spend their time in places of sensual amusement, or fill the steamboats and railway trains. They are all evidently in a deplorable state of spiritual ignorance; they are a growing evil, which threatens mischief: but are we taking the right means to remedy the evil? I say unhesitatingly that we are not.

We besiege the House of Commons with petitions when the advocates of these Sabbath-breaking crowds demand an extension of their present licence to sin. But is that enough? No: it is not!

We form societies to defend the Lord's Day, and propose measure after measure in Parliament to stop Sunday trading. But is that enough? No: it is not!

The truth must be spoken:—we must begin lower down. We cannot make people religious by Acts of Parliament alone. We must teach right as well as forbid wrong: we must try to prevent evil as well as repress it. We must strike at the root of the evils we deplore. We must endeavour to evangelize the masses of men and women who now break their Sabbaths every week. We must show them a better way. We must divert this fountain of Sabbath-breaking into different channels, and not content ourselves with damming up its waters when they overflow.

Are there not many parishes in our large towns where you may now find 12,000 or 15,000 people under one clergyman, and with one church to go to? Have we any right to wonder if a large proportion of this population regularly break the Sabbath every week? The bulk of the people in such a parish know nothing hardly about the way to "keep the Sunday holy." They have no place of worship to go to, if they have a mind to keep it. To expect such a population to keep the Sabbath holy, is preposterous and absurd: they are quite as much to be pitied as to be blamed. We have surely little right to find fault with them for not honouring the Lord's Day, while we leave them in utter ignorance of its meaning.

What then ought we to do? We ought to break up these large overgrown parishes into districts of a manageable size, containing not more than 3,000 people at the very most. We ought at once to put a minister of the Gospel and two lay agents in every one of these districts, and give them the spiritual oversight of the people. We must not wait to build a fine church. We must send a man who is able to preach anywhere,—in a garret, a coach-house, an alley, or even in the street,—and give him abundant liberty to work, unfettered by precedent and routine. This is the best antidote for the evils over which we mourn. The preached Gospel applied to the conscience, and not pains and penalties,—the preached Gospel, and not fines and imprisonment,—the preached Gospel carried home to every house in a parish,—this is the grand remedy for Sabbath-breaking.

I know well that all this sounds impracticable and Utopian to many ears. Ecclesiastical laws, rectorial rights, the want of funds, the want of men,—all these, and twenty other like objections, will at once be started.

Be it so. All I say is that until something of this kind is done, we shall never stop the Sabbath-breaking of great towns. It will be a festering sore on the face of our country, which will every now and then break out and lead to enormous mischief.

For my own part I see nothing in the proposal I have made which might not easily be attained, if the subject was fairly grappled with. *Laws* are repealed easily enough when public opinion demands it, and if they are bad the sooner they are repealed the better.—*Rectorial rights* must never stand in competition with the wants of immortal souls.—*Men*, I believe, of the right sort are to be found, if the Bishops will only encourage them to come forward.—*Money*, I am convinced, will never be wanting for a good cause, if a case is really made out. And after all we had better sacrifice fifty Canonries than leave our great town parishes in their present condition.

I commend these things to the attention of all who love the Lord Jesus Christ in sincerity. Let London, Manchester, Liverpool, Glasgow, and other large towns be thoroughly evangelized, and you will strike a deadly blow at the root of all Sabbath-breaking. Leave them alone, or go on at the rate we go at present, and my firm conviction is that we shall never be free from a Sabbath question agitation. It will return periodically, like an ague fit, until the sources which now supply it are dried up.

The plain truth is, that the Sabbath-breaking of the present day is one among many proofs of the low state of vital religion, and the awful want of union among British Christians. We have wasted our time on petty internal quarrels, and neglected the mighty work of converting souls. We have wrangled and squabbled about matter of mint, anise, and cummin, and forgotten our Master's business. We have allowed vast town populations to grow up in semi-heathen ignorance, and are now reaping the fruit of our gross neglect in their Sabbath-breaking propensities. In short, while the doctors have been disputing, the disease has been spreading and the patient dying.

I pray God that we may all learn wisdom, and amend our ways before it be too late. We want less party spirit and sectarianism, and more work for Christ. We want a return to the old paths of the Apostles in every branch of the Church; we want a generation of ministers whose first ambition is to go into every room in their parish, and tell the story of the cross of Christ.

I am not sanguine in my expectations. Routine and precedent seem to bind men now-a-days with iron chains. But I deliberately repeat once more, that unless our large towns are more thoroughly evangelized, we shall never be long without a struggle TO KEEP THE SABBATH HOLY.

NOTE

I take the liberty of recommending to the attention of my brethren in the ministry, the following extract from the Charge of the Venerable Bishop of Calcutta, in the year 1838:—

"Honour especially in your public and private instructions the primæval law of the Sabbath; the chief vestige of our Paradisaical state; the one command inscribed on the order of creation; the grand external symbol of revealed religion; a prominent branch of the first table of the moral law, and standing on the same footing as the love of God and our neighbour; the theme of the Prophets' exhortations in their descriptions of the Evangelical age: vindicated indeed from the uncommanded austerities of the Pharisees, but honoured by the constant practice of our blessed Saviour; transferred by the Lord and His Apostles, after the resurrection, to that great day of the Church's triumph, but remaining the same in its apportionment of time, its spiritual character, and its Divine obligation on the whole human race, and handed down and commended by the constant and unvaried usage of the Church from the very birth of Christianity to the present hour."

The following extracts from a speech of the late Lord Macaulay speak for themselves:—

"I have not the smallest doubt that, if we and our ancestors had, during the last three centuries, worked just as hard on the Sundays as on the week days, we should have been at this moment a poorer people and a less civilized people than we are; that there would have been less production than there has been, that the wages of the labourer would have been lower than they are, and that some other nation would have been now making cotton stuffs and woollen stuffs and cutlery for the whole world. Of course I do not mean to say that a man will not produce more in a week by working seven days than by working six days. But I very much doubt whether, at the end of a year, he will generally have produced more by working seven days a week than by working six days a week; and I firmly believe that, at the end of twenty years, he will have produced much less by working seven days a week than by working six days a week.

"We are not poorer in England, but richer, because we have, through many ages, rested from our labour one day in seven. That day is not lost. While industry is suspended, while the plough lies in the furrow, while the Exchange is silent, while no smoke ascends from the factory, a process is going on quite as important to the wealth of nations as any process which is performed on more busy days. Man, the machine of machinery, the machine compared with which all the contrivances of the Watts and Arkwrights are worthless, is repairing and winding up, so that he returns to his labour on the Monday with clearer intellect, with livelier spirits, with renewed corporal vigour."—*Macaulay's Speech on the Ten Hours Bill. Speeches*, pp. 450, 453, 454.

The famous Blackstone says, "The keeping one day in seven holy, as a time of relaxation and refreshment, as well as for public worship, is of admirable service to a State, considered merely as a civil institution."—*Blackstone's Commentaries*, vol. iv., p. 63.

XV

PHARISEES AND SADDUCEES

"Then Jesus said unto them, Take heed and beware of the leaven of the Pharisees and of the Sadducees."—MATT. xvi. 6.

EVERY word spoken by the Lord Jesus is full of deep instruction for Christians. It is the voice of the Chief Shepherd. It is the Great Head of the Church speaking to all its members,—the King of kings speaking to His subjects,—the Master of the house speaking to His servants,—the Captain of our salvation speaking to His soldiers. Above all, it is the voice of Him who said, "I have not spoken of Myself: the Father which sent Me, He gave Me a commandment what I should say and what I should speak." (John xii. 49.) The heart of every believer in the Lord Jesus ought to burn within him when he hears his Master's words: he ought to say, "This is the voice of my beloved." (Cant. ii. 8.)

And every kind of word spoken by the Lord Jesus is of the greatest value. Precious as gold are all His words of doctrine and precept; precious are all His parables and prophecies; precious are all His words of comfort and of consolation; precious, not least, are all His words of caution and of warning. We are not merely to hear Him when He says, "Come unto Me, all ye that labour, and are heavy laden;" we are to hear Him also when He says, "Take heed and beware."

I am going to direct attention to one of the most solemn and emphatic warnings which the Lord Jesus ever delivered: "Take heed and beware of the leaven of the Pharisees and of the Sadducees." Upon this text I wish to erect a beacon for all who desire to be saved, and to preserve some souls, if possible, from making shipwreck. The times call loudly for such beacons: the spiritual shipwrecks of the last twenty-five years have been deplorably numerous. The watchmen of the Church ought to speak out plainly now, or for ever hold their peace.

I. First of all, I ask my readers to observe *who they were to whom the warning of the text was addressed.*

Our Lord Jesus Christ was not speaking to men who were worldly, ungodly, and unsanctified, but to His own disciples, companions, and friends. He addressed men who, with the exception of the apostate Judas

256

Iscariot, were right-hearted in the sight of God. He spoke to the twelve
Apostles, the first founders of the Church of Christ, and the first ministers
of the Word of salvation. And yet even to them He addresses the solemn
caution of our text: "Take heed and beware."

There is something very remarkable in this fact. We might have thought
that these Apostles needed little warning of this kind. Had they not given
up all for Christ's sake? They had.—Had they not endured hardship for
Christ's sake? They had.—Had they not believed Jesus, followed Jesus,
loved Jesus, when almost all the world was unbelieving? All these things
are true; and yet to them the caution was addressed: "Take heed and
beware." We might have imagined that at any rate the disciples had but
little to fear from the "leaven of the Pharisees and of the Sadducees."
They were poor and unlearned men, most of them fishermen or publicans;
they had no leanings in favour of the Pharisees and the Sadducees; they
were more likely to be prejudiced against them than to feel any drawing
towards them. All this is perfectly true; yet even to them there comes the
solemn warning: "Take heed and beware."

There is useful counsel here for all who profess to love the Lord Jesus
Christ in sincerity. It tells us loudly that the most eminent servants of
Christ are not beyond the need of warnings, and ought to be always on
their guard. It shows us plainly that the holiest of believers ought to walk
humbly with his God, and to watch and pray, lest he fall into temptation,
and be overtaken in a fault. None is so holy, but that he may fall,—not
finally, not hopelessly, but to his own discomfort, to the scandal of the
Church, and to the triumph of the world: none is so strong but that he
may for a time be overcome. Chosen as believers are by God the Father,
justified as they are by the blood and righteousness of Jesus Christ, sanctified as they are by the Holy Ghost,—believers are still only men: they are
yet in the body, and yet in the world. They are ever near temptation: they
are ever liable to err, both in doctrine and in practice. Their hearts, though
renewed, are very feeble; their understanding, though enlightened, is still
very dim. They ought to live like those who dwell in an enemy's land, and
every day to put on the armour of God. The devil is very busy: he never
slumbers or sleeps. Let us remember the falls of Noah, and Abraham, and
Lot, and Moses, and David, and Peter; and remembering them, be humble,
and take heed lest we fall.

I may be allowed to say that none need warnings so much as the ministers of Christ's Gospel. Our office and our ordination are no security
against errors and mistakes. It is, alas, too true, that the greatest heresies
have crept into the Church of Christ by means of ordained men. Neither
Episcopal ordination, nor Presbyterian ordination, nor any other ordination, confers any immunity from error and false doctrine. Our very
familiarity with the Gospel often begets in us a hardened state of mind.
We are apt to read the Scriptures, and preach the Word, and conduct

public worship, and carry on the service of God, in a dry, hard, formal, callous spirit. Our very familiarity with sacred things, except we watch our hearts, is likely to lead us astray. "Nowhere," says an old writer, "is a man's soul in more danger than in a priest's office." The history of the Church of Christ contains many melancholy proofs that the most distinguished ministers may for a time fall away. Who has not heard of Archbishop Cranmer recanting and going back from those opinions he had defended so stoutly, though, by God's mercy, raised again to witness a glorious confession at last? Who has not heard of Bishop Jewel signing documents that he most thoroughly disapproved, and of which signature he afterwards bitterly repented? Who does not know that many others might be named, who, at one time or another, have been overtaken by faults, have fallen into errors, and been led astray? And who does not know the mournful fact that many of them never came back to the truth, but died in hardness of heart, and held their errors to the last?

These things ought to make us humble and cautious. They tell us to distrust our own hearts, and to pray to be kept from falling. In these days, when we are specially called upon to cleave firmly to the doctrines of the Protestant Reformation, let us take heed that our zeal for Protestantism does not puff us up, and make us proud. Let us never say in our self-conceit, "I shall never fall into Popery or Modernism: those views will never suit me." Let us remember that many have begun well and run well for a season, and yet afterwards turned aside out of the right way. Let us take heed that we are spiritual men as well as Protestants, and real friends of Christ as well as enemies of Antichrist. Let us pray that we may be kept from error, and never forget that the twelve Apostles themselves were the men to whom the Great Head of the Church addressed these words: "Take heed and beware."

II. I propose, in the second place, to explain *what were those dangers against which our Lord warned the Apostles.* "Take heed," He says, "and beware of the leaven of the Pharisees and of the Sadducees."

The danger against which He warns them is false doctrine. He says nothing about the sword of persecution, or the open breach of the Ten Commandments, or the love of money, or the love of pleasure. All these things no doubt were perils and snares to which the souls of the Apostles were exposed; but against these things our Lord raises no warning voice here. His warning is confined to one single point: "The leaven of the Pharisees and of the Sadducees."—We are not left to conjecture what our Lord meant by the word "leaven." The Holy Ghost, a few verses after the very text on which I am now dwelling, tells us plainly that by leaven was meant the "doctrine" of the Pharisees and of the Sadducees.

Let us try to understand what we mean when we speak of the "doctrine of the Pharisees and of the Sadducees."

(*a*) The doctrine of the Pharisees may be summed up in three words,—they were formalists, tradition-worshippers, and self-righteous. They attached such weight to the traditions of men, that they practically regarded them as of more importance than the inspired writings of the Old Testament. They valued themselves upon excessive strictness in their attention to all the ceremonial requirements of the Mosaic law. They thought much of being descended from Abraham, and said in their hearts, "We have Abraham to our father." They fancied because they had Abraham for their father that they were not in peril of hell like other men, and that their descent from him was a kind of title to heaven. They attached great value to washings and ceremonial purifyings of the body, and believed that the very touching of the dead body of a fly or gnat would defile them. They made a great ado about the outward parts of religion, and such things as could be seen of men. They made broad their phylacteries, and enlarged the fringes of their garments. They prided themselves on paying great honour to dead saints, and garnishing the sepulchres of the righteous. They were very zealous to make proselytes. They thought much of having power, rank, and pre-eminence, and of being called by men, "Rabbi, Rabbi." These things, and many suchlike things, the Pharisees did. Every well-informed Christian can find these things in the Gospels of St. Matthew and St. Mark. (See Matthew, chaps. xv. and xxiii.; Mark, chap. vii.)

All this time, be it remembered, they did not formally deny any part of the Old Testament Scripture. But they brought in, over and above it, so much of human invention, that they virtually put Scripture aside, and buried it under their own traditions. This is the sort of religion of which our Lord says to the Apostles, "Take heed and beware."

(*b*) The doctrine of the Sadducees, on the other hand, may be summed up in three words,—free-thinking, scepticism, and rationalism. Their creed was one far less popular than that of the Pharisees, and, therefore, we find them less often mentioned in the New Testament Scriptures. So far as we can judge from the New Testament, they appear to have held the doctrine of degrees of inspiration; at all events they attached exceeding value to the Pentateuch above the other parts of the Old Testament, if indeed they did not altogether ignore the latter. They believed that there was no resurrection, no angel, and no spirit, and tried to laugh men out of their belief in these things, by supposing hard cases, and bringing forward difficult questions. We have an instance of their mode of argument in the case which they propounded to our Lord of the woman who had had seven husbands, when they asked, "In the resurrection, whose wife shall she be of the seven?" And in this way they probably hoped, by rendering religion absurd, and its chief doctrines ridiculous, to make men altogether give up the faith they had received from the Scriptures.

All this time, be it remembered, we may not say that the Sadducees

were downright infidels: this they were not. We may not say they denied
revelation altogether: this they did not do. They observed the law of
Moses. Many of them were found among the priests in the times described
in the Acts of the Apostles. Caiaphas who condemned our Lord was a
Sadducee. But the practical effect of their teaching was to shake men's
faith in any revelation, and to throw a cloud of doubt over men's minds,
which was only one degree better than infidelity. And of all such kind of
doctrine,—free-thinking, scepticism, rationalism,—our Lord says, "Take
heed and beware."

Now the question arises, Why did our Lord Jesus Christ deliver this
warning? He knew, no doubt, that within forty years the schools of the
Pharisees and the Sadducees would be completely overthrown. He that
knew all things from the beginning, knew perfectly well that in forty years
Jerusalem, with its magnificent temple, would be destroyed, and the Jews
scattered over the face of the earth. Why then do we find Him giving this
warning about "the leaven of the Pharisees and of the Sadducees?"

I believe that our Lord delivered this solemn warning for the perpetual
benefit of that Church which He came on earth to found. He spoke with
a prophetic knowledge. He knew well the diseases to which human nature
is always liable. He foresaw that the two great plagues of His Church upon
earth would always be the doctrine of the Pharisees and the doctrine of
the Sadducees. He knew that these would be the upper and nether mill-
stones, between which His truth would be perpetually crushed and
bruised until He came the second time. He knew that there always would
be Pharisees in spirit, and Sadducees in spirit, among professing Christians.
He knew that their succession would never fail, and their generation never
become extinct,—and that though the names of Pharisees and Sadducees
were no more, yet their principles would always exist. He knew that during
the time that the Church existed, until His return, there would always be
some that would add to the Word, and some that would subtract from it,
—some that would stifle it, by adding to it other things, and some that
would bleed it to death, by subtracting from its principal truths. And this
is the reason why we find Him delivering this solemn warning: "Take
heed and beware of the leaven of the Pharisees and of the Sadducees."

And now comes the question, Had not our Lord Jesus Christ good
reason to give this warning? I appeal to all who know anything of Church
history, was there not indeed a cause? I appeal to all who remember what
took place soon after the Apostles were dead. Do we not read that in the
primitive Church of Christ there rose up two distinct parties,—one ever
inclined to err, like the Arians, in holding less than the truth, the other ever
inclined to err, like the relic-worshippers and saint-worshippers, in holding
more than the truth, as it is in Jesus?—Do we not see the same thing
coming out in after times, in the form of Romanism on the one side and
Socinianism on the other?—Do we not read in the history of our own

Church of two great parties, the Non-jurors on the one side, and the Latitudinarians on the other?—These are ancient things.—In a short paper like this it is impossible for me to enter more fully into them. They are things well known to all who are familiar with records of past days. There always have been these two great parties,—the party representing the principles of the Pharisee, and the party representing the principles of the Sadducee.—And therefore our Lord had good cause to say of these two great principles, "Take heed and beware."

But I desire to bring the subject even nearer at the present moment. I ask my readers to consider whether warnings like this are not especially needed in our own times. We have, undoubtedly, much to be thankful for in England. We have made great advances in arts and sciences in the last three centuries, and have much of the form and show of morality and religion. But I ask anybody who can see beyond his own door, or his own fireside, whether we do not live in the midst of dangers from false doctrine?

We have amongst us, on the one side, a school of men who, wittingly or unwittingly, are paving the way into the Church of Rome,—a school that professes to draw its principles from primitive tradition, the writings of the Fathers, and the voice of the Church,—a school that talks and writes so much about the Church, the ministry, and the sacraments, that it makes them like Aaron's rod, swallow up everything else in Christianity,—a school that attaches vast importance to the outward form and ceremonial of religion,—to gestures, postures, bowings, crosses, piscinas, sedilia, credence-tables, rood-screens, albs, tunicles, copes, chasubles, altar-cloths, incense, images, banners, processions, floral decorations, and many other like things, about which not a word is to be found in the Holy Scriptures as having any place in Christian worship. I refer, of course, to the school of Churchmen called Ritualists. When we examine the proceedings of that school, there can be but one conclusion concerning them. I believe whatever be the meaning and intention of its teachers, however devoted, zealous, and self-denying many of them are, that upon them has fallen the mantle of the Pharisees.

We have, on the other hand, a school of men, who wittingly or un-wittingly, appear to pave the way to Socinianism,—a school which holds strange views about the plenary inspiration of Holy Scripture,—strange views about the doctrine of sacrifice, and the Atonement of our Lord and Saviour Jesus Christ,—strange views about the eternity of punishment, and God's love to man,—a school strong in negatives, but very weak in positives,—skilful in raising doubts, but impotent in laying them,—clever in unsettling and unscrewing men's faith, but powerless to offer any firm rest for the sole of our foot. And, whether the leaders of this school mean it or not, I believe that on them has fallen the mantle of the Sadducees.

These things sound harsh. It saves a vast deal of trouble to shut our eyes, and say, "I see no danger," and because it is not seen, therefore not to believe it. It is easy to stop our ears and say, "I hear nothing," and because we hear nothing, therefore to feel no alarm. But we know well who they are that rejoice over the state of things we have to deplore in some quarters of our own Church. We know what the Roman Catholic thinks; we know what the Socinian thinks. The Roman Catholic rejoices over the rise of the Tractarian party; the Socinian rejoices over the rise of men who teach such views as those set forth in modern days about the atonement and inspiration. They would not rejoice as they do if they did not see their work being done, and their cause being helped forward. The danger, I believe, is far greater than we are apt to suppose. The books that are read in many quarters are most mischievous, and the tone of thought on religious subjects is deeply unsatisfactory. The plague is abroad. If we love life, we ought to search our own hearts, and try our own faith, and make sure that we stand on the right foundation. Above all, we ought to take heed that we ourselves do not imbibe the poison of false doctrine, and go back from our first love.

I feel deeply the painfulness of speaking out on these subjects. I know well that plain speaking about false doctrine is very unpopular, and that the speaker must be content to find himself thought very uncharitable, very troublesome, and very narrow-minded. Thousands of people can never distinguish differences in religion. To the bulk of men a clergyman is a clergyman, and a sermon is a sermon; and as to any difference between one minister and another, or one doctrine and another, they are utterly unable to understand it. I cannot expect such people to approve of any warning against false doctrine. I must make up my mind to meet with their disapprobation, and must bear it as I best can.

But I will ask any honest-minded, unprejudiced Bible reader to turn to the New Testament and see what he will find there. He will find many plain warnings against false doctrine: "Beware of false prophets,"—"Beware lest any man spoil you through philosophy and vain deceit,"—"Be not carried about with divers and strange doctrines,"—"Believe not every spirit, but try the spirits whether they be of God." (Matt. vii. 15; Col. ii. 8; Heb. xiii. 9; 1 John iv. 1.) He will find a large part of several inspired Epistles taken up with elaborate explanations of true doctrine and warnings against false teaching. I ask whether it is possible for a minister who takes the Bible for his rule of faith to avoid giving warnings against doctrinal error?

Finally, I ask any one to mark what is going on in England at this very day? I ask whether it is not true that hundreds have left the Established Church and joined the Church of Rome within the last thirty years? I ask whether it is not true that hundreds remain within our pale, who in heart are little better than Romanists, and who ought, if they were consistent, to walk in the steps of Newman and Manning, and go to their own place? —I ask again whether it is not true that scores of young men, both at Oxford and Cambridge, are spoiled and ruined by the withering influence of scepticism, and have lost all positive principles in religion? Sneers at religious newspapers, loud declarations of dislike to "parties," high-sounding, vague phrases about "deep thinking," broad views, new light, free handling of Scripture, and the effete weakness of certain schools of theology, make up the whole Christianity of many of the rising generation. —And yet, in the face of these notorious facts, men cry out, "Hold your peace about false doctrine. Let false doctrine alone!" I cannot hold my peace. Faith in the Word of God, love to the souls of men, the vows I took when I was ordained, alike constrain me to bear witness against the errors of the day. And I believe that the saying of our Lord is eminently a truth for the times: "Beware of the leaven of the Pharisees and of the Sadducees."

III. The third thing to which I wish to call attention is *the peculiar name by which our Lord Jesus Christ speaks of the doctrines of the Pharisees and of the Sadducees.*

The words which our Lord used were always the wisest and the best that could be used. He might have said, "Take heed and beware of the doctrine, or of the teaching, or of the opinions, of the Pharisees and of the Sadducees." But He does not say so: He uses a word of a peculiar nature. —He says, "Take heed and beware of the *leaven* of the Pharisees and of the Sadducees."

Now we all know what is the true meaning of the word "leaven." It is what we commonly call yeast,—the yeast which is added to the lump of dough in making a loaf of bread. This yeast, or leaven, bears but a small proportion to the lump into which it is thrown; just so, our Lord would have us know, the first beginning of false doctrine is but small compared to the body of Christianity.—It works quietly and noiselessly; just so, our Lord would have us know, false doctrine works secretly in the heart in which it is once planted.—It insensibly changes the character of the whole mass with which it is mingled; just so, our Lord would have us know, the doctrines of the Pharisees and Sadducees turn everything upside down, when once admitted into a Church or into a man's heart.—Let us mark these points: they throw light on many things that we see in the present day. It is of vast importance to receive the lessons of wisdom that this word "leaven" contains in itself.

False doctrine does not meet men face to face, and proclaim that it is false. It does not blow a trumpet before it, and endeavour openly to turn us away from the truth as it is in Jesus. It does not come before men in broad day, and summon them to surrender. It approaches us secretly, quietly, insidiously, plausibly, and in such a way as to disarm man's suspicion, and throw him off his guard. It is the wolf in sheep's clothing, and Satan in the garb of an angel of light, who have always proved the most dangerous foes of the Church of Christ.

I believe the most powerful champion of the Pharisees is not the man who bids you openly and honestly come out and join the Church of Rome: it is the man who says that he agrees on all points with you in *doctrine*. He would not take anything away from those Evangelical views that you hold;—he would not have you make any change at all;—all he asks you to do is to *add* a little more to your belief, in order to make your Christianity perfect. "Believe me," he says, "we do not want you to give up anything. We only want you to hold a few more clear views about the Church and the sacraments. We want you to add to your present opinions a little more about the office of the ministry, and a little more about Episcopal authority, and a little more about the Prayer-book, and a little more about the necessity of order and of discipline.—We only want you to add *a little more* of these things to your system of religion, and you will be quite right." But when men speak to you in this way, then is the time to remember what our Lord said, and "to take heed and beware." This is the leaven of the Pharisees, against which we are to stand upon our guard.

Why do I say this? I say it because there is no security against the doctrine of the Pharisees, unless we resist its principles in their beginnings. Beginning with a "little more about the Church," you may one day place the Church in the room of Christ.—Beginning with a "little more about the ministry," you may one day regard the minister as "the mediator between God and man."—Beginning with a "little more about the sacraments," you may one day altogether give up the doctrine of justification by faith without the deeds of the law.—Beginning with a "little more reverence for the Prayer-book," you may one day place it above the holy Word of God Himself.—Beginning with a "little more honour to bishops," you may at last refuse salvation to every one who does not belong to an Episcopal Church.—I only tell an old story: I only mark out roads that have been trodden by hundreds of members of the Church of England in the last few years. They began by carping at the Reformers, and have ended by swallowing the decrees of the Council of Trent. They began by crying up Laud and the Non-jurors, and have ended by going far beyond them, and formally joining the Church of Rome. I believe that when we hear men asking us to "add a little more" to our good old plain Evangelical views, we should stand upon our guard. We should remember our Lord's caution: "Of the leaven of the Pharisees, take heed and beware."

I consider the most dangerous champion of the Sadducee school is not the man who tells you openly that he wants you to lay aside any part of the truth, and to become a free-thinker and a sceptic. It is the man who begins with quietly insinuating doubts as to the position that we ought to take up about religion,—doubts whether we ought to be so positive in saying "This is truth, and that falsehood,"—doubts whether we ought to think men wrong who differ from us on religious opinions, since they *may* after all be as much right as we are.—It is the man who tells us we ought

not to condemn anybody's views, lest we err on the side of want of charity.
—It is the man who always begins talking in a vague way about God being
a God of love, and hints that we ought to believe perhaps that all men,
whatever doctrine they profess, will be saved.—It is the man who is ever
reminding us that we ought to take care how we think lightly of men of
powerful minds, and great intellects (*though they are Deists and sceptics*),
who do not think as we do, and that, after all, "great minds are all more
or less taught of God!"—It is the man who is ever harping on the difficulties of inspiration, and raising questions whether all men may not be
found saved in the end, and whether all may not be right in the sight of
God.—It is the man who crowns this kind of talk by a few calm sneers
against what he is pleased to call "old-fashioned views," and "narrow-
minded theology," and "bigotry," and the "want of liberality and charity."
in the present day. But when men begin to speak to us in this kind of way,
then is the time to stand upon our guard. Then is the time to remember
the words of our Lord Jesus Christ, and "to take heed and beware of
leaven."

Once more, why do I say this? I say it because there is no security
against Sadduceeism, any more than against Phariseeism, unless we resist
its principles in the bud. Beginning with a little vague talk about "charity,"
you may end in the doctrine of universal salvation, fill heaven with a mixed
multitude of wicked as well as good, and deny the existence of hell.—
Beginning with a few high-sounding phrases about intellect and the
inner light in man, you may end with denying the work of the Holy
Ghost, and maintaining that Homer and Shakespeare were as truly inspired
as St. Paul, and thus practically casting aside the Bible.—Beginning with
some dreamy, misty idea about "all religions containing more or less
truth," you may end with utterly denying the necessity of missions, and
maintaining that the best plan is to leave everybody alone.—Beginning
with dislike to "Evangelical religion," as old-fashioned, narrow, and exclusive, you may end by rejecting every leading doctrine of Christianity,—
the atonement, the need of grace, and the divinity of Christ. Again I repeat
that I only tell an old story: I only give a sketch of a path which scores
have trodden in the last few years. They were once satisfied with such
divinity as that of Newton, Scott, Cecil, and Romaine; they are now
fancying they have found a more excellent way in the principles which
have been propounded by theologians of the Broad school! I believe there
is no safety for a man's soul unless he remembers the lesson involved in
those solemn words, "Beware of the leaven of the Sadducees."

Let us beware of the *insidiousness* of false doctrine. Like the fruit of
which Eve and Adam ate, it looks at first sight pleasant and good, and a
thing to be desired. Poison is not written upon it, and so people are not
afraid. Like counterfeit coin, it is not stamped "bad:" it passes current
from the very likeness it bears to the truth.

Let us beware of the *very small beginnings* of false doctrine. Every heresy began at one time with some little departure from the truth. There is only a little seed of error needed to create a great tree. It is the little stones that make up the mighty building. It was the little timbers that made the great ark that carried Noah and his family over a deluged world. It is the little leaven that leavens the whole lump. It is the little flaw in one link of the chain cable that wrecks the gallant ship, and drowns the crew. It is the omission or addition of one little item in the doctor's prescription that spoils the whole medicine, and turns it into poison. We do not tolerate quietly a little dishonesty, or a little cheating, or a little lying: just so, let us never allow a little false doctrine to ruin us, by thinking it is but a "little one," and can do no harm. The Galatians seemed to be doing nothing very dangerous when they "observed days and months, and times and years;" yet St. Paul says, "I am afraid of you." (Gal. iv. 10, 11.)

Finally, let us beware of supposing that *we at any rate are not in danger.* "Our views are sound: our feet stand firm: others may fall away, but we are safe!" Hundreds have thought the same, and have come to a bad end. In their self-confidence they tampered with little temptations and little forms of false doctrine; in their self-conceit they went near the brink of danger; and now they seem lost for ever. They appear given over to a strong delusion, so as to believe a lie. Some of them have exchanged the Prayer-book for the Breviary, and are praying to the Virgin Mary, and bowing down to images. Others of them are casting overboard one doctrine after another, and bid fair to strip themselves of every sort of religion but a few scraps of Deism. Very striking is the vision in *Pilgrim's Progress,* which describes the hill Error as "very steep on the farthest side;" and "when Christian and Hopeful looked down they saw at the bottom several men dashed all to pieces by a fall they had from the top."—Never, never let us forget the caution to beware of "leaven;" and if we think we stand, let us "take heed lest we fall."

IV. I propose, in the fourth and last place, to suggest *some safe-guards and antidotes against the dangers of the present day,—the leaven of the Pharisees and the leaven of the Sadducees.*

I feel that we all need more and more the presence of the Holy Ghost in our hearts, to guide, to teach, and to keep us sound in the faith. We all need to watch more, and to pray to be held up, and preserved from falling away. But still, there are certain great truths, which, in a day like this, we are specially bound to keep in mind. There are times when some common epidemic invades a land, when medicines, at all times valuable, become of peculiar value. There are places where a peculiar malaria prevails, in which remedies, in every place valuable, are more than ever valuable in consequence of it. So I believe there are times and seasons in

the Church of Christ when we are bound to tighten our hold upon certain
great leading truths, to grasp them with more than ordinary firmness in
our hands, to press them to our hearts, and not to let them go. Such
doctrines I desire to set forth in order, as the great antidotes to the leaven
of the Pharisees and of the Sadducees. When Saul and Jonathan were slain
by the archers, David ordered the children of Israel to be taught the use
of the bow.

(a) For one thing, if we would be kept sound in the faith, we must take
heed to our doctrine about the *total corruption of human nature*. The
corruption of human nature is no slight thing. It is no partial, skin-deep
disease, but a radical and universal corruption of man's will, intellect,
affections, and conscience. We are not merely poor and pitiable sinners in
God's sight: we are guilty sinners; we are blameworthy sinners; we deserve
justly God's wrath and God's condemnation. I believe there are very few
errors and false doctrines of which the beginning may not be traced up
to unsound views about the corruption of human nature. Wrong views of
a disease will always bring with them wrong views of the remedy. Wrong
views of the corruption of human nature will always carry with them
wrong views of the grand antidote and cure of that corruption.

(b) For another thing, we must take heed to our doctrine about *the
inspiration and authority of the Holy Scriptures*. Let us boldly maintain,
in the face of all gainsayers, that the whole of the Bible is given by inspiration of the Holy Ghost,—that all is inspired completely, not one
part more than another,—and that there is an entire gulf between the
Word of God and any other book in the world.—We need not be afraid
of difficulties in the way of the doctrine of plenary inspiration. There may
be many things about it far too high for us to comprehend: it is a miracle,
and all miracles are necessarily mysterious. But if we are not to believe
until we can entirely explain it, there are very few things indeed that we
shall believe.—We need not be afraid of all the assaults that criticism brings
to bear upon the Bible. From the days of the Apostles the Word of the
Lord has been incessantly "tried," and has never failed to come forth as
gold, uninjured, and unsullied.—We need not be afraid of the discoveries
of science. Astronomers may sweep the heavens with telescopes, and
geologists may dig down into the heart of the earth, and never shake the
authority of the Bible: "The voice of God and the work of God's hands
never will be found to contradict one another."—We need not be afraid
of the researches of travellers. They will never discover anything that
contradicts God's Bible. I believe that if a Layard were to go over all the
earth and dig up a hundred buried Ninevehs, there would not be found
a single inscription which would contradict a single fact in the Word of
God.

Furthermore, we must boldly maintain that this Word of God is the
only rule of faith and of practice,—that whatsoever is not written in it

cannot be required of any man as needful to salvation,—and that however plausibly new doctrines may be defended, if they be not in the Word of God they cannot be worth our attention. It matters nothing who says a thing, whether he be bishop, archdeacon, dean, or presbyter. It matters nothing that the thing is well said, eloquently, attractively, forcibly, and in such a way as to turn the laugh against you. We are not to believe it except it be proved to us by Holy Scripture.

Last, but not least, we must use the Bible as if we believed it was given by inspiration. We must use it with reverence, and read it with all the tenderness with which we would read the words of an absent father. We must not expect to find, in a book inspired by the Spirit of God, no mysteries. We must rather remember that in nature there are many things we cannot understand; and that as it is in the book of nature, so it will always be in the book of Revelation. We should draw near to the Word of God in that spirit of piety recommended by Lord Bacon many years ago. "Remember," he says, speaking of the book of nature, "that man is not the master of that book, but the interpreter of that book." And as we deal with the book of nature, so we must deal with the book of God. We must draw near to it, not to teach, but to learn,—not like the master of it, but like a humble scholar, seeking to understand it.

(c) For another thing, we must take heed to our doctrine respecting *the atonement and priestly office of our Lord and Saviour Jesus Christ.* We must boldly maintain that the death of our Lord upon the cross was no common death. It was not the death of one who only died like Cranmer, Ridley, and Latimer, as a martyr. It was not the death of one who only died to give us a mighty example of self-sacrifice and self-denial. The death of Christ was an offering up unto God of Christ's own body and blood, to make satisfaction for man's sin and transgression. It was a sacrifice and propitiation; a sacrifice typified in every offering of the Mosaic law, a sacrifice of the mightiest influence upon all mankind. Without the shedding of that blood there could not be—there never was to be—any remission of sin.

Furthermore, we must boldly maintain that this crucified Saviour ever sitteth at the right hand of God, to make intercession for all that come to God by Him; that He there represents and pleads for them that put their trust in Him; and that He has deputed His office of Priest and Mediator to no man or set of men on the face of the earth. We need none besides. We need no Virgin Mary, no angels, no saint, no priest, no person ordained or unordained, to stand between us and God, but the one Mediator, Christ Jesus.

Furthermore, we must boldly maintain that peace of conscience is not to be bought by confession to a priest, and by receiving a man's absolution from sin. It is to be had only by going to the great High Priest, Christ Jesus; by confession before Him, not before man; and by absolution from Him only, who alone can say, "Thy sins be forgiven thee: go in peace."

Last, but not least, we must boldly maintain that peace with God, once obtained by faith in Christ, is to be kept up, not by mere outward cere-monial acts of worship,—not by receiving the sacrament of the Lord's Supper every day,—but by the daily habit of looking to the Lord Jesus Christ by faith,—eating by faith His body, and drinking by faith His blood; that eating and drinking of which our Lord says that he who eats and drinks shall find His "body meat indeed, and His blood drink indeed." Holy John Owen declared, long ago, that if there was any one point more than another that Satan wished to overthrow, it was the Priestly office of our Lord and Saviour Jesus Christ. Satan knew well, he said, that it was the "principal foundation of faith and consolation of the Church." Right views upon that office are of essential importance in the present day, if men would not fall into error.

(d) One more remedy I must mention. We must take heed to our doctrine about *the work of God the Holy Ghost*. Let us settle it in our minds that His work is no uncertain invisible operation upon the heart: and that where He is, He is not hidden, not unfelt, not unobserved. We do not believe that the dew, when it falls, cannot be felt, or that where there is life in a man it cannot be seen and observed by his breath. So is it with the influence of the Holy Ghost. No man has any right to lay claim to it, except its fruits—its experimental effects—can be seen in his life. Where He is, there will ever be a new creation, and a new man. Where He is, there will ever be new knowledge, new faith, new holiness, new fruits in the life, in the family, in the world, in the Church. And where these new things are not to be seen we may well say, with confidence, there is no work of the Holy Ghost. These are times in which we all need to be upon our guard about the doctrine of the work of the Spirit. Madame Guyon said, long ago, that the time would perhaps come when men might have to be martyrs for the work of the Holy Ghost. That time seems not far distant. At any rate, if there is one truth in religion that seems to have more contempt showered upon it than another, it is the work of the Spirit.

I desire to impress the immense importance of these four points upon all who read this paper: (a) clear views of the sinfulness of human nature; (b) clear views of the inspiration of Scripture; (c) clear views of the Atonement and Priestly office of our Lord and Saviour Jesus Christ; (d) and clear views of the work of the Holy Ghost. I believe that strange doctrines about the Church, the ministry, and the sacraments,—about the love of God, the death of Christ, and the eternity of punishment,—will find no foothold in the heart which is sound on these four points. I believe that they are four great safe-guards against the leaven of the Pharisees and of the Sadducees.

I will now conclude this paper with a few remarks by way of practical application. My desire is to make the whole subject useful to those into whose hands these pages may fall, and to supply an answer to the questions which may possibly arise in some hearts,—What are we to do? What advice have you got to offer for the times?

(1) In the first place, I will ask every reader of this paper to find out whether he has *saving personal religion for his own soul*. This is the principal thing after all. It will profit no man to belong to a sound visible Church, if he does not himself belong to Christ. It will avail a man nothing to be intellectually sound in the faith, and to approve sound doctrine, if he is not himself sound at heart. Is this the case with you? Can you say that your heart is right in the sight of God? Is it renewed by the Holy Ghost? Does Christ dwell in it by faith? O, rest not, rest not, till you can give a satisfactory answer to these questions! The man who dies unconverted, however sound his views, is as truly lost for ever as the worst Pharisee or Sadducee that ever lived.

(2) In the next place, let me beseech every reader of this paper who desires to be sound in the faith, *to study diligently the Bible*. That blessed Book is given to be a light to our feet, and a lantern to our path. No man who reads it reverently, prayerfully, humbly, and regularly, shall ever be allowed to miss the way to heaven. By it every sermon, and every religious book, and every ministry, ought to be weighed and proved. Would you know what is truth? Do you feel confused and puzzled by the war of words which you hear on every side about religion? Do you want to know what you ought to believe, and what you ought to be and do, in order to be saved? Take down your Bible, and cease from man. Read your Bible with earnest prayer for the teaching of the Holy Ghost; read it with honest determination to abide by its lessons. Do so steadily and perseveringly, and you shall see light: you shall be kept from the leaven of the Pharisees and Sadducees, and be guided to eternal life. The way to do a thing is to do it. Act upon this advice without delay.

(3) In the next place, let me advise every reader of this paper who has reason to hope that he is sound in faith and heart, *to take heed to the proportion of truths*. I mean by that to impress the importance of giving each several truth of Christianity the same place and position in our hearts which is given to it in God's Word. The first things must not be put second, and the second things must not be put first in our religion. The Church must not be put above Christ; the sacraments must not be put above faith and the work of the Holy Ghost. Ministers must not be exalted above the place assigned to them by Christ; means of grace must not be regarded as an end instead of a means. Attention to this point is of great moment: the mistakes which arise from neglecting it are neither few nor small. Here lies the immense importance of studying the whole Word of God, omitting nothing, and avoiding partiality in reading one part more than another. Here again lies the value of having a clear system of Christianity in our minds. Well would it be for the Church of England if all its members read the Thirty-nine Articles, and marked the beautiful order

in which those Articles state the main truths which men ought to believe.

(4) In the next place, let me entreat every true-hearted servant of Christ *not to be deceived by the specious guise* under which false doctrines often approach our souls in the present day. Beware of supposing that a teacher of religion is to be trusted, because, although he holds some unsound views, he yet "teaches a great deal of truth." Such a teacher is precisely the man to do you harm: poison is always most dangerous when it is given in small doses and mixed with wholesome food. Beware of being taken in by the apparent earnestness of many of the teachers and upholders of false doctrine. Remember that zeal and sincerity and fervour are no proof whatever that a man is working for Christ, and ought to be believed. Peter no doubt was in earnest when he bade our Lord spare Himself, and not go to the cross; yet our Lord said to him, "Get thee behind Me, Satan." Saul no doubt was in earnest when he went to and fro persecuting Christians; yet he did it ignorantly, and his zeal was not according to knowledge. The founders of the Spanish Inquisition no doubt were in earnest, and in burning God's saints alive thought they were doing God service; yet they were actually persecuting Christ's members and walking in the steps of Cain.—It is an awful fact that "Satan himself is transformed into an angel of light." (2 Cor. xi. 14.) Of all the delusions prevalent in these latter days, there is none greater than the common notion that "if a man is in earnest about his religion he must be a good man!" Beware of being carried away by this delusion: beware of being led astray by "earnest-minded men!" Earnestness is in itself an excellent thing; but it must be earnestness in behalf of Christ and His whole truth, or else it is worth nothing at all. The things that are highly esteemed among men are often abominable in the sight of God.

(5) In the next place, let me counsel every true servant of Christ *to examine his own heart* frequently and carefully as to his state before God. This is a practice which is useful at all times: it is specially desirable at the present day. When the great plague of London was at its height, people remarked the least symptoms that appeared on their bodies in a way that they never remarked them before. A spot here, or a spot there, which in time of health men thought nothing of, received close attention when the plague was decimating families, and striking down one after another! So ought it to be with ourselves, in the times in which we live. We ought to watch our hearts with double watchfulness. We ought to give more time to meditation, self-examination, and reflection. It is a hurrying, bustling age: if we would be kept from falling, we must make time for being frequently alone with God.

(6) Last of all, let me urge all true believers *to contend earnestly for the faith once delivered to the saints.* We have no cause to be ashamed of that faith. I am firmly persuaded that there is no system so life-giving, so

K

calculated to awaken the sleeping, lead on the inquiring, and build up the saints, as that system which is called the *Evangelical* system of Christianity. Wherever it is faithfully preached, and efficiently carried out, and consistently adorned by the lives of its professors, it is the power of God. It may be spoken against and mocked by some; but so it was in the days of the Apostles. It may be weakly set forth and defended by many of its advocates; but, after all, its fruits and its results are its highest praise. No other system of religion can point to such fruits. Nowhere are so many souls converted to God as in those congregations where the Gospel of Jesus Christ is preached in all its fulness, without any admixture of the Pharisee or Sadducee doctrine. We are not called upon, beyond all doubt, to be nothing but controversialists; but we never ought to be ashamed to testify to the truth as it is in Jesus, and to stand up boldly for Evangelical religion. We have the truth, and we need not be afraid to say so. The judgement-day will prove who is right, and to that day we may boldly appeal.

XVI

DIVERS AND STRANGE DOCTRINES

"Be not carried about with divers and strange doctrines. For it is a good thing that the heart be established with grace; not with meats, which have not profited them that have been occupied therein."—HEB. xiii. 9.

THE text which heads this paper is an Apostolic caution against false doctrine. It forms part of a warning which St. Paul addressed to Hebrew Christians. It is a caution just as much needed now as it was eighteen hundred years ago. Never, I think, was it so important for Christian ministers to cry aloud continually, "Be not carried about."

That old enemy of mankind, the devil, has no more subtle device for ruining souls than that of spreading false doctrine. "A murderer and a liar from the beginning," he never ceases going to and fro in the earth, "seeking whom he may devour."—Outside the Church he is ever persuading men to maintain barbarous customs and destructive superstitions. Human sacrifice to idols,—gross, revolting, cruel, disgusting worship of abominable false deities,—persecution, slavery, cannibalism, child-murder, devastating religious wars,—all these are a part of Satan's handiwork, and the fruit of his suggestions. Like a pirate, his object is to "sink, burn, and destroy."—Inside the Church he is ever labouring to sow heresies, to propagate errors, to foster departures from the faith. If he cannot prevent the waters flowing from the Fountain of Life, he tries hard to poison them. If he cannot destroy the medicine of the Gospel, he strives to adulterate and corrupt it. No wonder that he is called "Apollyon, the destroyer."

The Divine Comforter of the Church, the Holy Ghost, has always employed one great agent to oppose Satan's devices. That agent is the Word of God. The Word expounded and unfolded, the Word explained and opened up, the Word made clear to the head and applied to the heart, —the Word is the chosen weapon by which the devil must be confronted and confounded. The Word was the sword which the Lord Jesus wielded in the temptation. To every assault of the Tempter, He replied, "It is written." The Word is the sword which His ministers must use in the present day, if they would successfully resist the devil. The Bible, faithfully and freely expounded, is the safe-guard of Christ's Church.

I desire to remember this lesson, and to invite attention to the text which stands at the head of this paper. We live in an age when men profess to dislike dogmas and creeds, and are filled with a morbid dislike to controversial theology. He who dares to say of one doctrine that "it is true," and of another that "it is false," must expect to be called narrow-minded and uncharitable, and to lose the praise of men. Nevertheless, the Scripture was not written in vain. Let us examine the mighty lessons contained in St. Paul's words to the Hebrews. They are lessons for us as well as for them.

I.   First, we have here a *broad warning:* "Be not carried about with divers and strange doctrines."

II. Secondly, we have here a *valuable prescription:* "It is good that the heart be established with grace, not with meats."

III. Lastly, we have here an *instructive fact:* Meats "have not profited them which have been occupied therein."

On each of these points I have somewhat to say. If we patiently plough up this field of truth, we shall find that there is precious treasure hidden in it.

I.   First comes the *broad warning:* "Be not carried about with divers and strange doctrines."

The meaning of these words is not a hard thing which we cannot understand. "Be not tossed to and fro," the Apostle seems to say, "by every blast of false teaching, like ships without compass or rudder. False doctrines will arise as long as the world lasts, in number many, in minor details varying, in one point alone always the same,—strange, new, foreign, and departing from the Gospel of Christ. They do exist now. They will always be found within the visible Church. Remember this, and be not carried away." Such is St. Paul's warning.

The Apostle's warning does not stand alone. Even in the midst of the Sermon on the Mount there fell from the loving lips of our Saviour a solemn caution: "Beware of false prophets, which come unto you in sheep's clothing, but inwardly they are ravening wolves." (Matt. vii. 15.) Even in St. Paul's last address to the Ephesian elders, though he finds no time to speak about the sacraments, he does find time to warn his friends against false doctrine: "Of your own selves shall men arise, speaking perverse things to draw away disciples after them." (Acts xx. 30.) What says the Second Epistle to the Corinthians? "I fear, lest by any means, as the serpent beguiled Eve through his subtlety, so your minds should be corrupted from the simplicity that is in Christ." (2 Cor. xi. 3.) What says the Epistle to the Galatians? "I marvel that ye are so soon removed from him that called you into the grace of Christ unto another Gospel."— "Who hath bewitched you that ye should not obey the truth?"—"Having begun in the Spirit, are ye now made perfect by the flesh."—"How turn ye again to weak and beggarly elements?"—"Ye observe days, and months,

and times, and years. I am afraid of you."—"Stand fast in the liberty
where with Christ hath made us free, and be not entangled again in the
yoke of bondage." (Gal. i. 6; iii. 1, 3; iv. 9, 10, 11; v. 1.) What says the
Epistle to the Ephesians? "Be no more children, tossed to and fro, and
carried about with every wind of doctrine." (Eph. iv. 14.) What says the
Epistle to the Colossians? "Beware lest any man spoil you through philosophy and vain deceit, after the tradition of men." (Col. ii. 8.) What says
the First Epistle to Timothy? "The Spirit speaketh expressly, that in the
latter times some shall depart from the faith." (1 Tim. iv. 1.) What says
the Second Epistle of Peter? "There shall be false teachers among you,
who privily shall bring in damnable heresies." (2 Peter ii. 1.) What says
the First Epistle of John? "Believe not every spirit. Many false prophets
are gone out into the world." (1 John iv. 1.) What says the Epistle of Jude?
"Contend earnestly for the faith once delivered to the saints. For there
are certain men crept in unawares." (Jude 3, 4.) Let us mark well these
texts. These things were written for our learning.

What shall we say to these texts? How they may strike others I cannot
say. I only know how they strike me. To tell us, as some do, in the face
of these texts, that the early Churches were a model of perfection and
purity, is absurd. Even in Apostolic days, it appears, there were abundant
errors both in doctrine and practice.—To tell us, as others do, that clergymen ought never to handle controversial subjects, and never to warn their
people against erroneous views, is senseless and unreasonable. At this rate
we might neglect not a little of the New Testament. Surely the dumb dog
and the sleeping shepherd are the best allies of the wolf, the thief, and the
robber. It is not for nothing that St. Paul says, "If thou put the brethren
in remembrance of these things, thou shalt be a good minister of Jesus
Christ." (1 Tim. iv. 5.)

A plain warning against false doctrine is specially needed in England
in the present day. The school of the Pharisees, and the school of the
Sadducees, those ancient mothers of all mischief, were never more active
than they are now. Between men adding to the truth on one side, and men
taking away from it on the other,—between those who bury truth under
additions, and those who mutilate it by subtractions,—between superstition and infidelity,—between Romanism and Modernism,—between
Ritualism and Rationalism,—between these upper and nether mill-stones
the Gospel is well nigh crushed to death!

Strange views are continually propounded by clergymen about subjects
of the deepest importance. About the atonement, the divinity of Christ,
the inspiration of the Bible, the reality of miracles, the eternity of future
punishment,—about the Church, the ministerial office, the sacraments,
the confessional, the honour due to the Virgin, prayers for the dead,—
about all these things there is nothing too monstrous to be taught by
some English ministers in these latter days. By the pen and by the tongue,

by the press and by the pulpit, the country is incessantly deluged with a flood of erroneous opinions. To ignore the fact is mere affectation. Others see it, if we pretend to be ignorant of it. The danger is real, great, and unmistakable. Never was it so needful to say, "Be not carried about."

Many things combine to make the present inroad of false doctrine peculiarly dangerous. There is an undeniable zeal in some of the teachers of error: their "earnestness" (to use an unhappy cant phrase) makes many think they must be right. There is a great appearance of learning and theological knowledge: many fancy that such clever and intellectual men must surely be safe guides. There is a general tendency to free-thought and free inquiry in these latter days: many like to prove their independence of judgment, by believing novelties. There is a wide-spread desire to appear charitable and liberal-minded: many seem half ashamed of saying that anybody can be in the wrong. There is a quantity of half-truth taught by the modern false teachers: they are incessantly using Scriptural terms and phrases in an unscriptural sense. There is a morbid craving in the public mind for a more sensuous, ceremonial, sensational, showy worship: men are impatient of inward, invisible heart-work. There is a silly readiness in every direction to believe everybody who talks cleverly, lovingly, and earnestly, and a determination to forget that Satan is often "transformed into an angel of light." (2 Cor. ii. 14.) There is a wide-spread "gullibility" among professing Christians: every heretic who tells his story plausibly is sure to be believed, and everybody who doubts him is called a persecutor and a narrow-minded man. All these things are peculiar symptoms of our times. I defy any observing man to deny them. They tend to make the assaults of false doctrine in our day peculiarly dangerous. They make it more than ever needful to cry aloud, "Be not carried about."

Does any one ask me, What is the best safe-guard against false doctrine? —I answer in one word, "The Bible: the Bible regularly read, regularly prayed over, regularly studied." We must go back to the old prescription of our Master: "Search the Scriptures." (John v. 39.) If we want a weapon to wield against the devices of Satan, there is nothing like "the sword of the Spirit, the Word of God." But to wield it successfully, we must read it habitually, diligently, intelligently, and prayerfully. This is a point on which, I fear, many fail. In an age of hurry and bustle, few read their Bibles as much as they should. More books perhaps are read than ever, but less of the one Book which makes man wise unto salvation. Rome and Neology could never have made such havoc in the Church in the last fifty years, if there had not been a most superficial knowledge of the Scriptures throughout the land. A Bible-reading laity is the strength of a Church.

"Search the Scriptures." Mark how the Lord Jesus Christ and His Apostles continually refer to the Old Testament, as a document just as authoritative as the New. Mark how they quote texts from the Old Testament, as the voice of God, as if every word was given by inspiration. Mark how the greatest miracles in the Old Testament are all referred to in the New, as unquestioned and unquestionable facts. Mark how all the leading events in the Pentateuch are incessantly named as historical events, whose reality admits of no dispute. Mark how the atonement, and substitution, and sacrifice, run through the whole Bible from first to last, as essential doctrines of revelation. Mark how the resurrection of Christ, the greatest of all miracles, is proved by such an overwhelming mass of evidence, that he who disbelieves it may as well say he will believe no evidence at all. Mark all these things, and you will find it very hard to be a Rationalist! Great are the difficulties of infidelity: it requires more credulity to be an infidel than a Christian. But greater still are the difficulties of Rationalism. Free handling of Scripture,—results of modern criticism,—broad and liberal theology,—all these are fine, swelling, high-sounding phrases, which please some minds, and look very grand at a distance. But the man who looks below the surface of things will soon find that there is no sure standing-ground between ultra-Rationalism and Atheism.

"Search the Scriptures." Mark what a conspicuous absence there is in the New Testament of what may be called the sacramental system, and the whole circle of Ritualistic theology. Mark how extremely little there is said about the effects of baptism. Mark how very seldom the Lord's Supper is mentioned in the Epistles. Find, if you can, a single text in which New Testament ministers are called sacrificing priests,—or the Lord's Supper is called a sacrifice,—or private confession to ministers is recommended and practised.—Turn, if you can, to one single verse in which sacrificial vestments are named as desirable,—or in which lighted candles and pots of flowers on the Lord's Table, or—processions, and incense, and flags, and banners, and turning to the east, and bowing down to the bread and wine,—or prayer to the Virgin Mary and the angels,—are sanctioned. Mark these things well, and you will find it very hard to be a Ritualist! You may find your authority for Ritualism in garbled quotations from the Fathers,—in long extracts from monkish, mystical, or Popish writers; but you certainly will not find it in the Bible. Between the plain Bible, honestly and fairly interpreted, and extreme Ritualism, there is a gulf which cannot be passed.

If we would not be carried about by "divers and strange doctrines," we must remember the words of our Lord Jesus Christ: "Search the Scriptures." Ignorance of the Bible is the root of all error. Knowledge of the Bible is the best antidote against modern heresies.

II. I now proceed to examine St. Paul's *valuable prescription:* "It is good that the heart be established with grace; not with meats."

There are two words in this prescription which require a little explanation. A right understanding of them is absolutely essential to a proper use of the Apostle's advice. One of these words is "meats," and the other is "grace."

To see the full force of the word "meats", we must remember the immense importance attached by many Jewish Christians to the distinctions of the ceremonial law about food. The flesh of some animals and birds, according to Leviticus, might be eaten, and that of others might not be eaten. Some meats were, consequently, called "clean," and others were called "unclean." To eat certain kinds of flesh made a Jew ceremonially unholy before God, and no strict Jew would touch and eat such food on any account.—Now were these distinctions still to be kept up after Christ ascended into heaven, or were they done away by the Gospel? Were heathen converts under any obligation to attend to the ceremonial of the Levitical law about food? Were Jewish Christians obliged to be as strict about the meats they ate as they were before Christ died, and the veil of the temple was rent in twain? Was the ceremonial law about meats entirely done away, or was it not? Was the conscience of a believer in the Lord Jesus to be troubled with fear lest his food should defile him?

Questions like these appear to have formed one of the great subjects of controversy in the Apostolic times. As is often the case, they assumed a place entirely out of proportion to their real importance. The Apostle Paul found it needful to handle the subject in no less than three of his Epistles to the Churches.—"Meat," he says, "commends us not to God." —"The kingdom of God is not meat and drink."—"Let no man judge you in meat and drink." (1 Cor. viii. 8; Rom. xiv. 17; Col. ii. 16.) Nothing shows the fallen nature of man so clearly as the readiness of morbid and scrupulous consciences to turn trifles into serious things. At last the controversy seems to have spread so far and obtained such dimensions, that "meats" became an expression to denote anything ceremonial added to the Gospel as a thing of primary importance, any Ritual trifle thrust out of its lawful place and magnified into an essential of religion. In this sense, I believe, the word must be taken in the text now before us. By "meats" St. Paul means ceremonial observances, either wholly invented by man, or else built on Mosaic precepts which have been abrogated and superseded by the Gospel. It is an expression which was well understood in the Apostolic days.

The word "grace," on the other hand, seems to be employed as a comprehensive description of the whole Gospel of Jesus Christ. Of that glorious Gospel, grace is the main feature,—grace in the original scheme—grace in the execution—grace in the application to man's soul. Grace is the fountain of life from which our salvation flows. Grace is the agency through which our spiritual life is kept up. Are we justified? it is by grace. —Are we called? it is by grace.—Have we forgiveness? it is through the riches of grace.—Have we good hope? it is through grace.—Do we believe? it is through grace.—Are we elect? it is by the election of grace.—

Are we saved? it is by grace.—Why should I say more? The time would fail me to exhibit fully the part that grace does in the whole work of redemption. No wonder that St. Paul says to the Romans, "We are not under the law, but under grace;" and tells Titus, "The grace of God, which bringeth salvation, hath appeared unto all men." (Rom. iii. 24; Gal. i. 15; Ephes. i. 7; 2 Thess. ii. 16; Acts xviii. 27; Rom. i. 5; Ephes. ii. 5; Rom. vi. 15; Titus ii. 11.)

Such are the two great principles which St. Paul puts in strong contrast in the prescription we are now considering. He places opposite to one another "meats" and "grace,"—Ceremonialism and the Gospel—Ritualism and the free love of God in Christ Jesus. And then he lays down the great principle that it is by "grace," and "not meats," that the heart must be established.

Now "establishment of heart" is one of the great wants of many professing Christians. Specially is it longed after by those whose knowledge is imperfect, and whose conscience is half enlightened. Such persons often feel in themselves much indwelling sin, and at the same time see very indistinctly God's remedy and Christ's fulness. Their faith is feeble, their hope dim, and their consolations small. They want to realize more sensible comfort. They fancy they ought to feel more and see more. They are not at ease. They cannot attain to joy and peace in believing. Whither shall they turn? What shall set their consciences at rest? Then comes the enemy of souls, and suggests some short-cut road to establishment. He hints at the value of some addition to the simple plan of the Gospel, some man-made device, some exaggeration of a truth, some flesh-satisfying invention, some improvement on the old path, and whispers, "Only use this, and you shall be established." Plausible offers flow in at the same time from every quarter, like quack medicines. Each has its own patrons and advocates. On every side the poor unstable soul hears invitations to move in some particular direction, and then shall come perfect establishment.

"Come to us," says the Roman Catholic. "Join the Catholic Church, the Church on the Rock, the one, true, holy Church; the Church that cannot err. Come to her bosom, and repose your soul on her protection. Come to us, and you will find establishment."

"Come to us," says the extreme Ritualist. "You need higher and fuller views of the priesthood and the sacraments, of the Real Presence in the Lord's Supper, of the soothing influence of daily service, daily masses, auricular confession, and priestly absolution. Come and take up sound Church views, and you will find establishment."

"Come to us," says the violent Liberationist. "Cast off the trammels and fetters of established Churches. Come out from all alliance with the State. Enjoy religious liberty. Throw away forms and Prayer-books. Use our shibboleth. Join our party. Cast in your lot with us, and you will soon be established."

"Come to us," say the Plymouth Brethren. "Shake off all the bondage of creeds and Churches and systems. We will soon show you higher, deeper, more exalting, more enlightened views of truth. Join the Brethren, and you will soon be established."

"Come to us," says the Rationalist. "Lay aside the old worn-out clothes of effete schemes of Christianity. Give your reason free scope and play. Begin a freer mode of handling Scripture. Be no more a slave to an ancient old-world book. Break your chains, and you shall be established."

Every experienced Christian knows well that such appeals are constantly made to unsettled minds in the present day. Who has not seen that, when boldly and confidently made, they produce a painful effect on some people? Who has not observed that they often beguile unstable souls, and lead them into misery for years?

"What saith the Scripture?" This is the only sure guide. Hear what St. Paul says. Heart establishment is not to be obtained by joining this party or that. It comes "by grace, and not by meats." Other things have a "show of wisdom," perhaps, and give a temporary satisfaction "to the flesh." (Col. ii. 23.) But they have no healing power about them in reality, and leave the unhappy man who trusts them nothing bettered, but rather worse.

A clearer knowledge of the Divine scheme of grace, its eternal purposes, its application to man by Christ's redeeming work,—a firmer grasp of the doctrine of grace, of God's free love in Christ, of Christ's full and complete satisfaction for sin, of justification by simple faith,—a more intimate acquaintance with Christ the Giver and Fountain of grace, His offices, His sympathy, His power,—a more thorough experience of the inward work of grace in the heart,—this, this, this is the grand secret of heart-establishment. This is the old path of peace. This is the true panacea for restless consciences. It may seem at first too simple, too easy, too cheap, too commonplace, too plain. But all the wisdom of man will never show the heavy-laden a better road to heart-rest. Secret pride and self-righteousness, I fear, are too often the reason why this good old road is not used.

I believe there never was a time when it was more needful to uphold the old Apostolic prescription than it is in the present day. Never were there so many unestablished and unsettled Christians wandering about, and tossed to and fro, from want of knowledge. Never was it so important for faithful ministers to set the trumpet to their mouths and proclaim everywhere, "Grace, grace, grace, not meats, establishes the heart."

From the days of the Apostles there have never been wanting quack spiritual doctors, who have professed to heal the wounds of conscience with man-made remedies. In our own beloved Church there have always been some who have in heart turned back to Egypt, and, not content with the simplicity of our worship, have hankered after the ceremonial fleshpots of the Church of Rome. Laud, of unhappy memory, did a little in this way, but his doings were nothing compared to those of some clergymen in the present day. To hear the sacraments incessantly exalted, and preaching cried down,—to see the Lord's Supper turned into an idol under the specious pretext of making it more honourable,—to find plain Prayer-book worship overlaid with so many new-fangled ornaments and cere-monies that its essentials are quite buried,—how common is all this! These things were once a pestilence that walked in darkness. They are now a destruction that wastes in noonday. They are the joy of our enemies, the sorrow of the Church's best children, the damage of English Christ-ianity, the plague of our times. And to what may they all be traced? To neglect or forgetfulness of St. Paul's simple prescription: "Grace, and not meats, establishes the heart."

Let us take heed that in our own personal religion, grace is all. Let us have clear systematic views of the Gospel of the grace of God. Nothing else will do good in the hour of sickness, in the day of trial, on the bed of death, and in the swellings of Jordan. Christ dwelling in our hearts by faith, Christ's free grace the only foundation under the soles of our feet,—this alone will give peace. Once let in self, and forms, and man's inventions, as a necessary part of our religion, and we are on a quicksand. We may be amused, excited, or kept quiet for a time, like children with toys, by a religion of "meats." Such a religion has "a show of wisdom." But unless our religion be one in which "grace" is all, we shall never feel established.

III. In the last place, I proceed to examine *the instructive fact* which St. Paul records. He says, "Meats have not profited them that have been occupied therein."

We have no means of knowing whether the Apostle, in using this language, referred to any particular Churches or individuals. Of course it is possible that he had in view the Judaizing Christians of Antioch and Galatia,—or the Ephesians of whom he speaks to Timothy in his pastoral Epistle,—or the Colossians who caused him so much inward conflict,—or the Hebrew believers in every Church, without exception. It seems to me far more probable, however, that he had no particular Church or Churches in view. I rather think that he makes a broad, general, sweeping statement about all who in any place had exalted ceremonial at the expense of the doctrines of "grace." And he makes a wide declaration about them all. They have got no good from their favourite notions. They have not been more inwardly happy, more outwardly holy, or more generally use-ful. Their religion has been most unprofitable to them. Man-made altera-tions of God's precious medicine for sinners,—man-made additions to Christ's glorious Gospel,—however speciously defended and plausibly supported, do no real good to those that adopt them. They confer no increased inward comfort; they bring no growth of real holiness; they give no enlarged usefulness to the Church and the world. Calmly, quietly, and mildly, but firmly, decidedly, and unflinchingly, the assertion is made, "Meats have *not profited* them that have been occupied therein."

The whole stream of Church history abundantly confirms the truth of the Apostle's position. Who has not heard of the hermits and ascetics of the early centuries? Who has not heard of the monks and nuns and re- cluses of the Romish Church in the middle ages? Who has not heard of the burning zeal, the devoted self-denial, of Romanists like Xavier and Ignatius Loyola? The earnestness, the fervour, the self-sacrifice of all these classes, are matters beyond dispute. But none who read carefully and intelligently the records of their lives, yea, some of the best of them, can fail to see that they had no solid peace or inward rest of soul. Their very feverish restlessness is enough to show that their consciences were not at ease. None can fail to see that, with all their furious zeal and self- denial, they never did much good to the world. They gathered round themselves admiring partisans. They left a high reputation for self-denial and sincerity. They made men wonder at them while they lived, and some- times canonize them when they died. But they did nothing to *convert souls.* And what is the reason of this? They attached an overweening importance to man-made ritual and ceremonial, and made less than they ought to have done of the Gospel of the grace of God. Their principle was to make much of "meats," and little of "grace." Hence they verified the words of St. Paul, "Meats do not profit them that are occupied therein."

The very history of our own times bears a striking testimony to the truth of St. Paul's assertion. In the last twenty-five years some scores of clergymen have seceded from the Church of England, and joined the Church of Rome. They wanted more of what they called Catholic doctrine and Catholic ceremonial. They honestly acted up to their principles, and went over to Rome. They were not all weak, and illiterate, and second-rate, and inferior men; several of them were men of commanding talents, whose gifts would have won for them a high position in any profession. Yet what have they gained by the step they have taken? What profit have they found in leaving "grace" for "meats," in exchanging Protestantism for Catholi- cism? Have they attained a higher standard of holiness? Have they procured for themselves a greater degree of usefulness? The religious system which exalts ceremonial and man-made ritual does no real good to its adherents, compared to the simple old Gospel of the grace of God.

Let us turn now, for a few moments, to the other side of the picture, and see what "grace" has done. Let us hear how profitable the doctrines of the Gospel have proved to those who have clung firmly to them, and have not tried to mend and improve and patch them up by adding, as essentials, the "meats" of man-made ceremonial.

It was "grace, and not meats," that made Martin Luther do the work that he did in the world. The key to all his success was his constant declaration of justification by faith, without the deeds of the law. This was the truth which enabled him to break the chains of Rome, and let light into Europe.

It was "grace, and not meats," that made our English martyrs, Latimer and Hooper, exercise so mighty an influence in life, and shine so brightly in death. They saw clearly, and taught plainly, the true priesthood of Christ, and salvation only by grace. They honoured God's grace, and God put honour on them.

It was "grace, and not meats," that made Romaine and Venn, and their companions, turn the world upside down in England, one hundred years ago. In themselves they were not men of extraordinary learning or intellectual power. But they revived and brought out again the real pure doctrines of grace.

It was "grace, and not meats," that made Simeon and Bishop Daniel Wilson and Bickersteth such striking instruments of usefulness in the first half of the present century. God's free grace was the great truth on which they relied, and continually brought forward. For so doing God put honour on them. They made much of God's grace, and the God of grace made much of them.

The list of ministerial biographies tells a striking tale. Who are those who have shaken the world, and left their mark on their generation, and aroused consciences, and converted sinners, and edified saints? Not those who have made asceticism, and ceremonials, and sacraments, and services, and ordinances the main thing; but those who have made most of God's free grace! In a day of strife, and controversy, and doubt, and perplexity, men forget this. Facts are stubborn things. Let us look calmly at them, and be not moved by those who tell us that daily services, frequent communions, processions, incense, bowings, crossings, confessions, absolutions, and the like, are the secret of a prosperous Christianity. Let us look at plain facts. Facts in old history, and facts in modern days, facts in every part of England, support the assertion of St. Paul. The religion of "meats" does "not profit those that are occupied therein." It is the religion of grace that brings inward peace, outward holiness, and general usefulness.

Let me wind up this paper with a few words of practical application. We are living in an age of peculiar religious danger. I am quite sure that the advice I am going to offer deserves serious attention.

(1) In the first place, *let us not be surprised* at the rise and progress of false doctrine. It is a thing as old as the old Apostles. It began before they died. They predicted that there would be plenty of it before the end of the world. It is wisely ordered of God for the testing of our grace, and to prove who has real faith. If there were no such thing as false doctrine or heresy upon earth, I should begin to think the Bible was not true.

(2) In the next place, let us make up our minds *to resist false doctrine*, and not to be carried away by fashion and bad example. Let us not flinch because all around us, high and low, rich and poor, are swept away, like

geese in a flood, before a torrent of semi-Popery. Let us be firm and stand our ground.

Let us resist false doctrine, and contend earnestly for the faith once delivered to the saints. Let us not be ashamed of showing our colours and standing out for New Testament truth. Let us not be stopped by the cuckoo cry of "controversy." The thief likes dogs that do not bark, and watchmen that give no alarm. The devil is a thief and a robber. If we hold our peace, and do not resist false doctrine, we please him and displease God.

(3) In the next place, let us try *to preserve* the Old Protestant principles of the Church of England, and to hand them down uninjured to our children's children. Let us not listen to those faint-hearted Churchmen who would have us forsake the ship, and desert the Church of England in her time of need.

The Church of England is worth fighting for. She has done good service in days gone by, and she may yet do more, if we can keep her free from Popery and infidelity. Once re-admit and sanction the Popish mass and auricular confession, and the Church of England will be ruined. Then let us fight hard for the Church of England being kept a Protestant Church. Let us read our Thirty-nine Articles every year with attention, and learn from these Articles what are real Church principles. Let us arm our memories with these Articles, and be able to quote them. Before the edge and point of these Articles, fairly interpreted, ultra-Ritualists and ultra-Rationalists can never stand.

(4) In the last place, *let us make sure work of our own personal salvation.* Let us seek to know and feel that we ourselves are "saved."

The day of controversy is always a day of spiritual peril. Men are apt to confound orthodoxy with conversion, and to fancy that they must go to heaven if they know how to answer Papists. Yet mere earnestness without knowledge, and mere head-knowledge of Protestantism, alike save none. Let us never forget this.

Let us not rest till we feel the blood of Christ sprinkled on our consciences, and have the witness of the Spirit within us that we are born again. This is reality. This is true religion. This will last. This will never fail us. It is the possession of grace in the heart, and not the intellectual knowledge of it, that profits and saves the soul.

XVII

THE FALLIBILITY OF MINISTERS

"But when Peter was come to Antioch, I withstood him to the face, because he was to be blamed.

"For before that certain came from James, he did eat with the Gentiles: but when they were come, he withdrew and separated himself, fearing them which were of the circumcision.

"And the other Jews dissembled likewise with him; insomuch that Barnabas also was carried away with their dissimulation.

"But when I saw that they walked not uprightly according to the truth of the Gospel, I said unto Peter before them all, If thou, being a Jew, livest after the manner of Gentiles, and not as do the Jews, why compellest thou the Gentiles to live as do the Jews?

"We who are Jews by nature, and not sinners of the Gentiles,

"Knowing that a man is not justified by the works of the law, but by the faith of Jesus Christ, even we have believed in Jesus Christ, that we might be justified by the faith of Christ, and not by the works of the law for by the works of the law shall no flesh be justified."—GALATIANS ii. 11-16.

HAVE we ever considered what the Apostle Peter once did at Antioch? It is a question that deserves serious consideration.

What the Apostle Peter did *at Rome* we are often told, although we have hardly a jot of authentic information about it. Roman Catholic writers furnish us with many stories about this. Legends, traditions, and fables abound on the subject. But unhappily for these writers, Scripture is utterly silent upon the point. There is nothing in Scripture to show that the Apostle Peter ever was at Rome at all!

But what did the Apostle Peter do *at Antioch?* This is the point to which I want to direct attention. This is the subject of the passage from the Epistle to the Galatians, which heads this paper. On this point, at any rate, the Scripture speaks clearly and unmistakably.

The six verses of the passage before us are striking on many accounts. They are striking, if we consider the *event* which they describe: here is one Apostle rebuking another!—They are striking, when we consider who the two *men* are: Paul, the younger, rebukes Peter, the elder!—They are striking, when we remark the *occasion:* this was no glaring fault, no flagrant sin, at first sight, that Peter had committed! Yet the Apostle Paul says, "I withstood him to the face, because he was to be blamed." He does more than this:—he reproves Peter publicly for his error before all the Church at Antioch. He goes even further:—he writes an account of the matter, which is now read in two hundred languages all over the world.

It is my firm conviction that the Holy Ghost means us to take particular notice of this passage of Scripture. If Christianity had been an invention of man, these things would never have been recorded. An impostor, like Mahomet, would have hushed up the difference between two Apostles. The Spirit of truth has caused these verses to be written for our learning, and we shall do well to take heed to their contents.

There are three great lessons from Antioch, which I think we ought to learn from this passage.

I. The *first* lesson is, that *great ministers may make great mistakes.*

II. The *second* is, that *to keep the truth of Christ in His Church is even more important than to keep peace.*

III. The *third* is, that *there is no doctrine about which we ought to be so jealous as justification by faith without the deeds of the law.*

I.   The first great lesson we learn from Antioch is, that *great ministers may make great mistakes.*

What clearer proof can we have than that which is set before us in this place; Peter, without doubt, was one of the greatest in the company of the Apostles. He was an old disciple. He was a disciple who had had peculiar advantages and privileges. He had been a constant companion of the Lord Jesus. He had heard the Lord preach, seen the Lord work miracles, enjoyed the benefit of the Lord's private teaching, been numbered among the Lord's intimate friends, and gone out and come in with Him all the time He ministered upon earth. He was the Apostle to whom the keys of the kingdom of heaven were given, and by whose hand those keys were first used. He was the first who opened the door of faith to the Jews, by preaching to them on the day of Pentecost. He was the first who opened the door of faith to the Gentiles, by going to the house of Cornelius, and receiving him into the Church. He was the first to rise up in the Council of the fifteenth of Acts, and say, "Why tempt ye God, to put a yoke upon the neck of the disciples, which neither our fathers nor we were able to bear?" And yet here this very Peter, this same Apostle, plainly falls into a great mistake. The Apostle Paul tells us, "I withstood him to the face." He tells us "that he was to be blamed." He says "he feared them of the circumcision." He says of him and his companions, that "they walked not uprightly according to the truth of the Gospel." He speaks of their "dissimulation." He tells us that by this dissimulation even Barnabas, his old companion in missionary labours, "was carried away."

What a striking fact this is. This is Simon Peter! This is the third great error of his, which the Holy Ghost has thought fit to record! Once we find him trying to keep back our Lord, as far as he could, from the great work of the cross, and severely rebuked. Then we find him denying the Lord three times, and with an oath. Here again we find him endangering the leading truth of Christ's Gospel. Surely we may say, "Lord, what is man?" The Church of Rome boasts that the Apostle Peter is her founder and first Bishop. Be it so: grant it for a moment. Let us only remember, that of all the Apostles there is not one, excepting, of course, Judas Iscariot, of whom we have so many proofs that he was a *fallible* man. Upon her own showing, the Church of Rome was founded by the most fallible of the Apostles.*

But it is all meant to teach us that even the Apostles themselves, when not writing under the inspiration of the Holy Ghost, were at times liable to err. It is meant to teach us that the best men are weak and fallible so long as they are in the body. Unless the grace of God holds them up, any one of them may go astray at any time. It is very humbling, but it is very true. True Christians are converted, justified, and sanctified. They are living members of Christ, beloved children of God, and heirs of eternal life. They are elect, chosen, called, and kept unto salvation. They have the Spirit. But they are *not infallible*.

Will not rank and dignity confer infallibility? No: they will not! It matters nothing what a man is called. He may be a Czar, an Emperor, a King, a Prince. He may be a Pope or a Cardinal, an Archbishop or a Bishop, a Dean or an Archdeacon, a Priest or a Deacon. He is still a *fallible man*. Neither the crown, nor the diadem, nor the anointing oil, nor the mitre, nor the imposition of hands, can prevent a man making mistakes.

Will not numbers confer infallibility? No: they will not! You may gather together princes by the score, and bishops by the hundred; but, when gathered together, they are still liable to err. You may call them a council, or a synod, or an assembly, or a conference, or what you please. It matters nothing. Their conclusions are still the conclusions of *fallible men*. Their collective wisdom is still capable of making enormous mistakes. Well says the Twenty-first Article of the Church of England, "General

* It is curious to observe the shifts to which some writers have been reduced in order to explain away the plain meaning of the verses which head this paper. Some have maintained that Paul did not really rebuke Peter, but only feignedly, for show and appearance sake! Others have maintained that it was not Peter the Apostle who was rebuked, but another Peter, one of the seventy! Such interpretations need no remark. They are simply absurd. The truth is that the plain honest meaning of the verses strikes a heavy blow at the favourite Roman Catholic doctrine of the primacy and superiority of Peter over the rest of the Apostles.

councils may err, and sometimes have erred, even in things pertaining unto God."

The example of the Apostle Peter at Antioch is one that does not stand alone. It is only a parallel of many a case that we find written for our learning in Holy Scripture. Do we not remember Abraham, the father of the faithful, following the advice of Sarah, and taking Hagar for a wife? Do we not remember Aaron, the first high priest, listening to the children of Israel, and making a golden calf? Do we not remember Nathan the prophet telling David to build a temple? Do we not remember Solomon, the wisest of men, allowing his wives to build their high places? Do we not remember Asa, the good king of Judah, seeking not to the Lord, but to the physicians? Do we not remember Jehoshaphat, the good king, going down to help wicked Ahab? Do we not remember Hezekiah, the good king, receiving the ambassadors of Babylon? Do we not remember Josiah, the last of Judah's good kings, going forth to fight with Pharaoh? Do we not remember James and John wanting fire to come down from heaven? These things deserve to be remembered. They were not written without cause. They cry aloud, *No infallibility*!

And who does not see, when he reads the history of the Church of Christ, repeated proofs that the best of men can err? The early fathers were zealous according to their knowledge, and ready to die for Christ. But many of them countenanced monkery, and nearly all sowed the seeds of many superstitions.—The Reformers were honoured instruments in the hand of God for reviving the cause of truth on earth. Yet hardly one of them can be named who did not make some great mistake. Martin Luther held pertinaciously the doctrine of consubstantiation. Melanchthon was often timid and undecided. Calvin permitted Servetus to be burned. Cranmer recanted and fell away for a time from his first faith. Jewel subscribed to Popish doctrines for fear of death. Hooper disturbed the Church of England by over-scrupulosity about vestments. The Puritans, in after times, denounced toleration as Abaddon and Apollyon. Wesley and Toplady, last century, abused each other in most shameful language. Irving, in our own day, gave way to the delusion of speaking in unknown tongues. All these things speak with a loud voice. They all lift up a beacon to the Church of Christ. They all say, "Cease ye from man;"—"Call no man master;"—"Call no man father upon earth;"—"Let no man glory in man;"—"He that glorieth, let him glory in the Lord." They all cry, *No infallibility*!

The lesson is one that we all need. We are all naturally inclined to lean upon man whom we can see, rather than upon God whom we cannot see. We naturally love to lean upon the ministers of the visible Church, rather than upon the Lord Jesus Christ, the great Shepherd, and Bishop, and High Priest, who is invisible. We need to be continually warned and set upon our guard.

I see this tendency to lean on man everywhere. I know no branch of the Protestant Church of Christ which does not require to be cautioned upon the point. It is a snare, for example, to the English Episcopalian to make idols of Bishop Pearson and the "Judicious Hooker." It is a snare to the Scotch Presbyterian to pin his faith on John Knox, the Covenanters, and Dr. Chalmers. It is a snare to the Methodists in our day to worship the memory of John Wesley. It is a snare to the Independent to see no fault in any opinion of Owen and Doddridge. It is a snare to the Baptist to exaggerate the wisdom of Gill, and Fuller, and Robert Hall. All these are snares, and into these snares how many fall!

We all naturally love to have a Pope of our own. We are far too ready to think, that because some great minister or some learned man says a thing,—or because our own minister, whom we love, says a thing,—it must be right, without examining whether it is in Scripture or not. Most men dislike the trouble of thinking for themselves. They like following a leader. They are like sheep,—when one goes over the gap all the rest follow. Here at Antioch even Barnabas was carried away. We can well fancy that good man saying, "An old Apostle, like Peter, surely cannot be wrong. Following him, I cannot err."

And now let us see what practical lessons we may learn from this part of our subject.

(a) For one thing, let us learn not to put implicit confidence in any man's opinion, merely *because he lived many hundred years ago*. Peter was a man who lived in the time of Christ Himself, and yet he could err.

There are many who talk much in the present day about "the voice of the primitive Church." They would have us believe that those who lived nearest the time of the Apostles, must of course know more about truth than we can. There is no foundation for any such opinion. It is a fact that the most ancient writers in the Church of Christ are often at variance with one another. It is a fact that they often changed their own minds, and retracted their own former opinions. It is a fact that they often wrote foolish and weak things, and often showed great ignorance in their explanations of Scripture. It is vain to expect to find them free from mistakes. *Infallibility is not to be found in the early fathers, but in the Bible.*

(b) For another thing, let us learn not to put implicit confidence in any man's opinion, *merely because of his office as a minister*. Peter was one of the very chiefest Apostles, and yet he could err.

This is a point on which men have continually gone astray. It is the rock on which the early Church struck. Men soon took up the saying, "Do nothing contrary to the mind of the Bishop!" But what are bishops, priests, and deacons? What are the best of ministers but men,—dust, ashes, and clay,—men of like passions with ourselves, men exposed to temptations, men liable to weaknesses and infirmities? What saith the Scripture, "Who is Paul and who is Apollos, but ministers by whom ye believed,

even as the Lord gave to every man?" (1 Cor. iii. 5.) Bishops have often
driven the truth into the wilderness, and decreed that to be true which
was false. The greatest errors have been begun by ministers. Hophni and
Phinehas, the sons of the High Priest, made religion to be abhorred by
the children of Israel. Annas and Caiaphas, though in the direct line of
descent from Aaron, crucified the Lord. Arius, that great heresiarch, was
a minister. It is absurd to suppose that ordained men cannot go wrong.
We should follow them so far as they teach according to the Bible, but no
further. We should believe them so long as they can say, "Thus it is
written,"—"Thus saith the Lord;" but further than this we are not to go.
Infallibility is not to be found in ordained men, but in the Bible.

(c) For another thing, let us learn not to place implicit confidence in
any man's opinion, *merely because of his learning.* Peter was a man who
had miraculous gifts, and could speak with tongues, and yet he could err.

This is a point, again, on which many go wrong. This is the rock on
which men struck in the middle ages. Men looked on Thomas Aquinas,
and Duns Scotus, and Peter Lombard, and many of their companions,
as almost inspired. They gave epithets to some of them in token of their
admiration. They talked of "the irrefragable" doctor, "the seraphic"
doctor, "the incomparable" doctor,—and seemed to think that whatever
these doctors said must be true! But what is the most learned of men, if
he be not taught by the Holy Ghost? What is the most learned of all
divines but a mere fallible child of Adam at his very best? Vast knowledge
of books and great ignorance of God's truth may go side by side. They
have done so, they may do so, and they will do so, in all times. I will
engage to say that the two volumes of Robert M'Cheyne's Memoirs and
Sermons have done more positive good to the souls of men, than any
one folio that Origen or Cyprian ever wrote. I doubt not that the one
volume of *Pilgrim's Progress*, written by a man who knew hardly any
book but his Bible, and was ignorant of Greek and Latin,—will prove in
the last day to have done more for the benefit of the world than all the
works of the schoolmen put together. Learning is a gift that ought not
to be despised. It is an evil day when books are not valued in the Church.
But it is amazing to observe how vast a man's intellectual attainments
may be, and yet how little he may know of the grace of God. I have no
doubt the authorities of Oxford in the last century knew more of Hebrew,
Greek, and Latin, than Wesley, Whitefield, Berridge, or Venn. But they
knew little of the Gospel of Christ. *Infallibility is not to be found among
learned men, but in the Bible.*

(d) For another thing, let us take care that we do not place implicit
confidence *on our own minister's opinion,* however godly he may be. Peter
was a man of mighty grace, and yet he could err.

Your minister may be a man of God indeed, and worthy of all honour
for his preaching and practice; but do not make a Pope of him. Do not

place his word side by side with the Word of God. Do not spoil him by flattery. Do not let him suppose he can make no mistakes. Do not lean your whole weight on his opinion, or you may find to your cost that he can err.

It is written of Joash, King of Judah, that he "did that which was right in the sight of the Lord all the days of Jehoiada the priest." (2 Chron. xxiv. 2.) Jehoiada died, and then died the religion of Joash. Just so your minister may die, and then your religion may die too;—may change, and your religion may change;—may go away, and your religion may go. Oh, be not satisfied with a religion built upon man! Be not content with saying, "I have hope, because my own minister has told me such and such things." Seek to be able to say, "I have hope, because I find it thus and thus written in the Word of God." If your peace is to be solid, you must go yourself to the Fountain of all Truth. If your comforts are to be lasting, you must visit the well of life yourself, and draw fresh water for your own soul. Ministers may depart from the faith. The visible Church may be broken up. But he who has the Word of God written in his heart has a foundation beneath his feet which will never fail him. Honour your minister as a faithful ambassador of Christ. Esteem him very highly in love for his work's sake. But never forget that *infallibility is not to be found in godly ministers, but in the Bible.*

The things I have mentioned are worth remembering. Let us bear them in mind, and we shall have learned one lesson from Antioch.

II. I now pass on to the second lesson that we learn from Antioch. That lesson is, *that to keep Gospel truth in the Church is of even greater importance than to keep peace.*

I suppose no man knew better the value of peace and unity than the Apostle Paul. He was the Apostle who wrote to the Corinthians about charity. He was the Apostle who said, "Be of the same mind one toward another;"—"Be at peace among yourselves;"—"Mind the same things;" —"The servant of God must not strive;"—"There is one body and there is one Spirit, even as ye are called in one hope of your calling, one Lord, one faith, one baptism." He was the Apostle who said, "I become all things to all men, that by all means I may save some." (Rom. xii. 16; 1 Thess. v. 13; Phil. iii. 16; Eph. iv. 5; 1 Cor. ix. 22.) Yet see how he acts here! He withstands Peter to the face. He publicly rebukes him. He runs the risk of all the consequences that might follow. He takes the chance of everything that might be said by the enemies of the Church at Antioch. Above all, he writes it down for a perpetual memorial, that it never might be forgotten,—that, wherever the Gospel is preached throughout the world, this public rebuke of an erring Apostle might be known and read of all men.

Now, why did he do this? Because he dreaded false doctrine—because he knew that a little leaven leaveneth the whole lump,—because he would teach us that we ought to contend for the truth jealously, and to fear the loss of truth more than the loss of peace.

St. Paul's example is one we shall do well to remember in the present day. Many people will put up with anything in religion, if they may only have a quiet life. They have a morbid dread of what they call "controversy." They are filled with a morbid fear of what they style, in a vague way, "party spirit," though they never define clearly what party spirit is. They are possessed with a morbid desire to keep the peace, and make all things smooth and pleasant, even though it be at the expense of truth. So long as they have outward calm, smoothness, stillness, and order, they seem content to give up everything else. I believe they would have thought with Ahab that Elijah was a troubler of Israel, and would have helped the princes of Judah when they put Jeremiah in prison, to stop his mouth. I have no doubt that many of these men of whom I speak, would have thought that Paul at Antioch was a very imprudent man, and that he went too far!

I believe this is all wrong. We have no right to expect anything but the pure Gospel of Christ, unmixed and unadulterated,—the same Gospel that was taught by the Apostles,—to do good to the souls of men. I believe that to maintain this pure truth in the Church men should be ready to make any sacrifice, to hazard peace, to risk dissension, and run the chance of division. *They should no more tolerate false doctrine than they would tolerate sin.* They should withstand any adding to or taking away from the simple message of the Gospel of Christ.

For the truth's sake, our Lord Jesus Christ denounced the Pharisees, though they sat in Moses' seat, and were the appointed and authorized teachers of men. "Woe unto you, Scribes and Pharisees, hypocrites," He says, eight times over, in the twenty-third chapter of Matthew. And who shall dare to breathe a suspicion that our Lord was wrong?

For the truth's sake, Paul withstood and blamed Peter, though a brother. Where was the use of unity when pure doctrine was gone? And who shall dare to say he was wrong?

For the truth's sake, Athanasius stood out against the world to maintain the pure doctrine about the divinity of Christ, and waged a controversy with the great majority of the professing Church. And who shall dare to say he was wrong?

For the truth's sake, Luther broke the unity of the Church in which he was born, denounced the Pope and all his ways, and laid the foundation of a new teaching. And who shall dare to say that Luther was wrong?

For the truth's sake, Cranmer, Ridley, and Latimer, the English Reformers, counselled Henry VIII. and Edward VI. to separate from Rome, and to risk the consequences of division. And who shall dare to say that they were wrong?

For the truth's sake, Whitefield and Wesley denounced the mere barren moral preaching of the clergy of their day, and went out into the highways and byways to save souls, knowing well that they would be cast out from the Church's communion. And who shall dare to say that they were wrong?

Yes! peace without truth is a false peace; it is the very peace of the devil. Unity without the Gospel is a worthless unity; it is the very unity of hell. Let us never be ensnared by those who speak kindly of it. Let us remember the words of our Lord Jesus Christ: "Think not that I came to send peace upon earth. I came not to send peace, but a sword." (Matt. x. 34.) Let us remember the praise He gives to one of the Churches in the Revelation: "Thou canst not bear them which are evil. Thou hast tried them which say they are Apostles, and are not, and hast found them liars." (Rev. ii. 2.) Let us remember the blame He casts upon another: "Thou sufferest that woman Jezebel to teach." (Rev. ii. 20.) Never let us be guilty of sacrificing any portion of truth upon the altar of peace. Let us rather be like the Jews, who, if they found any manuscript copy of the Old Testament Scriptures incorrect in a single letter, burned the whole copy, rather than run the risk of losing one jot or title of the Word of God. Let us be content with nothing short of the whole Gospel of Christ.

In what way are we to make practical use of the general principles which I have just laid down? I will give my readers one simple piece of advice. I believe it is advice which deserves serious consideration.

I warn, then, every one who loves his soul, *to be very jealous as to the preaching he regularly hears, and the place of worship he regularly attends.* He who deliberately settles down under any ministry which is positively unsound, is a very unwise man. I will never hesitate to speak my mind on this point. I know well that many think it a shocking thing for a man to forsake his parish church. I cannot see with the eyes of such people. I draw a wide distinction between teaching which is *defective* and teaching which is thoroughly *false*,—between teaching which errs on the negative side and teaching which is positively unscriptural. But I do believe, if false doctrine is unmistakably preached in a parish church, a parishioner who loves his soul is quite right in not going to that parish church. To hear unscriptural teaching fifty-two Sundays in every year is a serious thing. It is a continual dropping of slow poison into the mind. I think it almost impossible for a man wilfully to submit himself to it, and not take harm. I see in the New Testament we are plainly told to "prove all things," and "hold fast that which is good." (1 Thess. v. 21.) I see in the Book of Proverbs that we are commanded to "cease to hear the instruction which causeth to err from the paths of knowledge." (Prov. xix. 27.) If these words do not justify a man in ceasing to worship at a church, if positively false doctrine is preached in it, I know not what words can.

Does any one mean to tell us that to attend the parish church is absolutely needful to an Englishman's salvation? If there is such an one, let him speak out, and give us his name.—Does any one mean to tell us that going to the parish church will save any man's soul, if he dies unconverted and ignorant of Christ? If there is such an one, let him speak out, and give us his name.—Does any one man mean to tell us that going to the parish church will teach a man anything about Christ, or conversion, or faith, or repentance, if these subjects are hardly ever named in the parish church, and never properly explained? If there is such an one, let him speak out, and give us his name.—Does any one mean to say that a man who repents, believes in Christ, is converted and holy, will lose his soul, because he has forsaken his parish church and learned his religion elsewhere? If there is such an one, let him speak out, and give us his name. —For my part I abhor such monstrous and extravagant ideas. I see not a jot of foundation for them in the Word of God. I trust that the number of those who deliberately hold them is exceedingly small.

There are not a few parishes in England where the religious teaching is little better than Popery. Ought the laity of such parishes to sit still, be content, and take it quietly? They ought not. And why? Because, like St. Paul, they ought to prefer truth to peace.

There are not a few parishes in England where the religious teaching is little better than morality. The distinctive doctrines of Christianity are never clearly proclaimed. Plato, or Seneca, or Confucius, or Socinus, could have taught almost as much. Ought the laity in such parishes to sit still, be content, and take it quietly? They ought not. And why? Because, like St. Paul, they ought to prefer truth to peace.

I am using strong language in dealing with this part of my subject: I know it.—I am trenching on delicate ground: I know it. I am handling matters which are generally let alone, and passed over in silence: I know it.—I say what I say from a sense of duty to the Church of which I am a minister. I believe the state of the times, and the position of the laity in some parts of England, require plain speaking. Souls are perishing, in many parishes, in ignorance. Honest members of the Church of England, in many districts, are disgusted and perplexed. This is no time for smooth words. I am not ignorant of those magic expressions, "the parochial system, order, division, schism, unity, controversy," and the like. I know the cramping, silencing influence which they seem to exercise on some minds. I too have considered those expressions calmly and deliberately, and on each of them I am prepared to speak my mind.

(*a*) The *parochial system* of England is an admirable thing in theory. Let it only be well administered, and worked by truly spiritual ministers, and it is calculated to confer the greatest blessings on the nation. But it is useless to expect attachment to the parish church, when the minister of the parish is ignorant of the Gospel or a lover of the world. In such a case we must never be surprised if men forsake their parish church, and seek truth wherever truth is to be found. If the parochial minister does not preach the Gospel and live the Gospel, the conditions on which he claims the attention of his parishioners are *virtually violated*, and his claim to be heard is at an end. It is absurd to expect the head of a family to endanger the souls of his children, as well as his own, for the sake of "parochial order." There is no mention of parishes in the Bible, and we have no right to require men to live and die in ignorance, in order that they may be able to say at last, "I always attended my parish church."

(*b*) *Divisions and separations* are most objectionable in religion. They weaken the cause of true Christianity. They give occasion to the enemies of all godliness to blaspheme. But before we blame people for them, we must be careful that we lay the blame *where it is deserved*. False doctrine and heresy are even worse than schism. If people separate themselves from teaching which is positively false and unscriptural, they ought to be praised rather than reproved. In such cases separation is a virtue and not a sin. It is easy to make sneering remarks about "itching ears," and "love of excitement;" but it is not so easy to convince a plain reader of the Bible that it is his duty to hear false doctrine every Sunday, when by a little exertion he can hear truth. The old saying must never be forgotten, "He is the schismatic who causes the schism."

(*c*) *Unity, quiet, and order* among professing Christians are mighty blessings. They give strength, beauty, and efficiency to the cause of Christ. But even gold may be bought too dear. Unity which is obtained by the sacrifice of truth is worth nothing. It is not the unity which pleases God. The Church of Rome boasts loudly of a unity which does not deserve the name. It is unity which is obtained by taking away the Bible from the people, by gagging private judgment, by encouraging ignorance, by forbidding men to think for themselves. Like the exterminating warriors of old, the Church of Rome "makes a solitude and calls it peace." There is quiet and stillness enough in the grave, but it is not the quiet of health, but of death. It was the false prophets who cried "Peace," when there was no peace.

(*d*) *Controversy* in religion is a hateful thing. It is hard enough to fight the devil, the world, and the flesh, without private differences in our own camp. But there is one thing which is even worse than controversy, and that is false doctrine tolerated, allowed, and permitted without protest or molestation. It was controversy that won the battle of Protestant Reformation. If the views that some men hold were correct, it is plain we never ought to have had any Reformation at all! For the sake of peace, we ought to have gone on worshipping the Virgin, and bowing down to images and relics to this very day! Away with such trifling! There are times when controversy is not only a duty but a benefit. Give me the mighty thunder-storm rather than the pestilential malaria. The one walks in darkness and poisons us in silence, and we are never safe. The other frightens and alarms for a little season. But it is soon over, and it clears the air. It is a plain Scriptural duty to "contend earnestly for the faith once delivered to the saints." (Jude 3.)

I am quite aware that the things I have said are exceedingly distasteful to many minds. I believe many are content with teaching which is not the whole truth, and fancy it will be "all the same" in the end. I am sorry for them. I am convinced that nothing but *the whole truth* is likely, as a general rule, to do good to souls. I am satisfied that those who wilfully put up with anything short of the whole truth, will find at last that their souls have received much damage. Three things there are which men never ought to trifle with,—a little poison, a little false doctrine, and a little sin.

I am quite aware that when a man expresses such opinions as those I have just brought forward, there are many ready to say, "He is no Churchman." I hear such accusations unmoved. The day of judgment will show who were the true friends of the Church of England and who were not. I have learned in the last thirty-two years that if a clergyman leads a quiet life, lets alone the unconverted part of the world, and preaches so as to offend none and edify none, he will be called by many "a good Churchman." And I have also learned that if a man studies the Articles and Homilies, labours continually for the conversion of souls, adheres closely to the great principles of the Reformation, bears a faithful testimony against Popery, and preaches as Jewel and Latimer used to preach, he will probably be thought a firebrand and "troubler of Israel," and called no Churchman at all! But I can see plainly that they are not the best Churchmen who talk most loudly about Churchmanship. I remember that none cried "Treason" so loudly as Athaliah (2 Kings xi. 14.) Yet she was a traitor herself. I have observed that many who once talked most about Churchmanship have ended by forsaking the Church of England, and going over to Rome. Let men say what they will. *They are the truest friends of the Church of England who labour most for the preservation of truth.*

I lay these things before the readers of this paper, and invite their serious attention to them. I charge them never to forget that truth is of more importance to a Church than peace. I ask them to be ready to carry out the principles I have laid down, and to contend zealously, if needs be, for the truth. If we do this, we shall have learned something from Antioch.

III.   But I pass on to the third lesson from Antioch. That lesson is, that *there is no doctrine about which we ought to be so jealous as justification by faith without the deeds of the law.*

The proof of this lesson stands out most prominently in the passage of Scripture which heads this paper. What one article of the faith had the Apostle Peter denied at Antioch? None.—What doctrine had he publicly preached which was false? None.—What, then, had he done? He had done this. After once keeping company with the believing Gentiles as "fellow-heirs and partakers of the promise of Christ in the Gospel" (Ephes. iii. 6), he suddenly became shy of them and withdrew himself. He seemed to think they were less holy and acceptable to God than the circumcised Jews. He seemed to imply that the believing Gentiles were in a lower state than they who had kept the ceremonies of the law of Moses. He seemed, in a word, to add something to simple *faith* as needful to give man an interest in Jesus Christ. He seemed to reply to the question, "What shall I do to be saved?" not merely "Believe on the Lord Jesus Christ," but "Believe on the Lord Jesus Christ, *and be circumcised*, and keep the ceremonies of the law."

Such conduct as this the Apostle Paul would not endure for a moment. Nothing so moved him as the idea of adding anything to the Gospel of Christ. "I withstood him," he says, "to the face." He not only rebuked him, but he recorded the whole transaction fully, when by inspiration of the Spirit he wrote the Epistle to the Galatians.

I invite special attention to this point. I ask men to observe the remarkable jealousy which the Apostle Paul shows about this doctrine, and to consider the point about which such a stir was made. Let us mark in this passage of Scripture the immense importance of justification by faith without the deeds of the law. Let us learn here what mighty reasons the Reformers of the Church of England had for calling it, in our Eleventh Article, "a most wholesome doctrine and very full of comfort."

(*a*) This is the doctrine which is *essentially necessary to our own personal comfort.* No man on earth is a real child of God, and a saved soul, till he sees and receives salvation by faith in Christ Jesus. No man will ever have solid peace and true assurance, until he embraces with all his heart the doctrine that "we are accounted righteous before God for the merit of our Lord Jesus Christ, by faith, and not for our own works and deservings." One reason, I believe, why so many professors in this day are tossed to and fro, enjoy little comfort, and feel little peace, is their ignorance on this point. They do not see clearly justification by faith without the deeds of the law.

(*b*) This is the doctrine which *the great enemy of souls hates, and labours to overthrow.* He knows that it turned the world upside down at the first beginning of the Gospel, in the days of the Apostles. He knows that it turned the world upside down again at the time of the Reformation. He is therefore always tempting men to reject it. He is always trying to seduce Churches and ministers to deny or obscure its truth. No wonder that the Council of Trent directed its chief attack against this doctrine, and pronounced it accursed and heretical. No wonder that many who think themselves learned in these days denounce the doctrine as theological jargon, and say that all "earnest-minded people" are justified by Christ, whether they have faith or not! The plain truth is that the doctrine is all gall and wormwood to unconverted hearts. It just meets the wants of the awakened soul. But the proud unhumbled man who knows not his own sin, and sees not his own weakness, cannot receive its truth.

(c) This is the doctrine, the *absence of which accounts for half the errors of the Roman Catholic Church*. The beginning of half the unscriptural doctrines of Popery may be traced up to rejection of justification by faith. No Romish teacher, if he is faithful to his Church, can say to an anxious sinner, "Believe on the Lord Jesus Christ and thou shalt be saved." He cannot do it without additions and explanations, which completely destroy the good news. He dare not give the Gospel medicine, without adding something which destroys its efficacy, and neutralizes its power. Purgatory, penance, priestly absolution, the intercession of saints, the worship of the Virgin, and many other man-made services of Popery, all spring from this source. They are all rotten props to support weary consciences. But they are rendered necessary by the denial of justification by faith.

(d) This is the doctrine which is *absolutely essential to a minister's success among his people*. Obscurity on this point spoils all. Absence of clear statements about justification will prevent the utmost zeal doing good. There may be much that is pleasing and nice in a minister's sermons, much about Christ and sacramental union with Him,—much about self-denial,—much about humility,—much about charity. But all this will profit little, if his trumpet gives an uncertain sound about justification by faith without the deeds of the law.

(e) This is the doctrine which is *absolutely essential to the prosperity of a Church*. No Church is really in a healthy state, in which this doctrine is not prominently brought forward. A Church may have good forms and regularly ordained ministers, and the sacraments properly administered, but a Church will not see conversion of souls going on under its pulpits, when this doctrine is not plainly preached. Its schools may be found in every parish. Its ecclesiastical buildings may strike the eye all over the land. But there will be no blessing from God on that Church, unless justification by faith is proclaimed from its pulpits. Sooner or later its candle-stick will be taken away.

Why have the Churches of Africa and the East fallen to their present state?—Had they not bishops? They had.—Had they not forms and liturgies? They had.—Had they not synods and councils? They had.—But they cast away the doctrine of justification by faith. They lost sight of that mighty truth, and so they fell.

Why did our own Church do so little in the last century, and why did the Independents, and Methodists, and Baptists do so much more?— Was it that their system was better than ours? No.—Was it that our Church was not so well adapted to meet the wants of lost souls? No.— But their ministers preached justification by faith, and our ministers, in too many cases, did not preach the doctrine at all.

Why do so many English people go to Dissenting chapels in the present day? Why do we so often see a splendid Gothic parish Church as empty of worshippers as a barn in July, and a little plain brick building, called a meeting-house, filled to suffocation? Is it that people in general have an abstract dislike to Episcopacy, the Prayer-Book, the surplice, and the establishment? Not at all! The simple reason is, in the vast majority of cases, that people do not like preaching in which justification by faith is not fully proclaimed. When they cannot hear it in the parish church they will seek it elsewhere. No doubt there are exceptions. No doubt there are places where a long course of neglect has thoroughly disgusted people with the Church of England, so that they will not even hear truth from its ministers. But I believe, as a general rule, when the parish church is empty and the meeting-house full, it will be found on inquiry that *there is a cause*.

If these things be so, the Apostle Paul might well be jealous for the truth, and withstand Peter to the face. He might well maintain that anything ought to be sacrificed, rather than endanger the doctrine of justification in the Church of Christ. He saw with a prophetical eye coming things. He left us all an example that we should do well to follow. Whatever we tolerate, let us never allow any injury to be done to that blessed doctrine,—that we are justified by faith without the deeds of the law.

Let us always beware of any teaching which either directly or indirectly obscures justification by faith. All religious systems which put anything between the heavy-laden sinner and Jesus Christ the Saviour, except simple faith, are dangerous and unscriptural. All systems which make out faith to be anything complicated, anything but a simple, childlike dependence,—the hand which receives the soul's medicine from the physician,—are unsafe and poisonous systems. All systems which cast discredit on the simple Protestant doctrine which broke the power of Rome, carry about with them a plague-spot, and are dangerous to souls.

Baptism is a sacrament ordained by Christ Himself, and to be used with reverence and respect by all professing Christians. When it is used rightly, worthily, and with faith, it is capable of being the instrument of mighty blessings to the soul. But when people are taught that *all* who are baptized are as a matter of course born again, and that *all* baptized persons should be addressed as "children of God," I believe their souls are in great danger. Such teaching about baptism appears to me to overthrow the doctrine of justification by faith. They only are children of God who have faith in Christ Jesus. And all men have not faith.

The Lord's Supper is a sacrament ordained by Christ Himself, and intended for the edification and refreshment of true believers. But when people are taught that all persons ought to come to the Lord's Table, whether they have faith or not; and that all alike receive Christ's body and blood who receive the bread and wine, I believe their souls are in great danger. Such teaching appears to me to darken the doctrine of justification by faith. No man eats Christ's body and drinks Christ's blood except the justified man. And none are justified until they believe.

Membership of the Church of England is a great privilege. No visible Church on earth, in my opinion, offers so many advantages to its members, when rightly administered. But when people are taught that because they are members of the Church, they are as a matter of course members of Christ, I believe their souls are in great danger. Such teaching appears to me to overthrow the doctrine of justification by faith. They only are joined to Christ who believe. And all men do not believe.

Whenever we hear teaching which obscures or contradicts justification by faith, we may be sure there is a screw loose somewhere. We should watch against such teaching, and be upon our guard. Once let a man get wrong about justification, and he will bid a long farewell to comfort, to peace, to lively hope, to anything like assurance in his Christianity. An error here is a worm at the root.

(1) In conclusion, let me first of all ask every one who reads this paper, to arm himself with a thorough *knowledge of the written Word of God.* Unless we do this we are at the mercy of any false teacher. We shall not see through the mistakes of an erring Peter. We shall not be able to imitate the faithfulness of a courageous Paul. An ignorant laity will always be the bane of a Church. A Bible-reading laity may save a Church from ruin. Let us read the Bible regularly, daily, and with fervent prayer, and become familiar with its contents. Let us receive nothing, believe nothing, follow nothing, which is not in the Bible, nor can be proved by the Bible. Let our rule of faith, our touch-stone of all teaching, be the written Word of God.

(2) In the next place, let me recommend every member of the Church of England to make himself acquainted with *the Thirty-nine Articles of his own Church.* They are to be found at the end of most Prayer-books. They will abundantly repay an attentive reading. They are the true standard by which Churchmanship is to be tried, next to the Bible. They are the test by which Churchmen should prove the teaching of their ministers, if the want to know whether it is "Church teaching" or not. I deeply lament the ignorance of systematic Christianity which prevails among many who attend the services of the Church of England. It would be well if such books as Archbishop Usher's *Body of Divinity* were more known and studied than they are. If Dean Nowell's Catechism had ever been formally accredited as a formulary of the Church of England, many of the heresies of the last twenty years could never have lived for a day.* But unhappily many persons really know no more about the true doctrines of their own communion, than the heathen or Mahometans. It is useless

---

* Dean Nowell was Prolocuter of the Convocation which drew up the Thirty-nine Articles in the form in which we now have them, in the year 1562. His Catechism was approved and allowed by the Convocation.

to expect the laity of the Church of England to be zealous for the maintenance of true doctrine, unless they know what their own Church has defined true doctrine to be.

(3) In the next place, let me entreat all who read this paper to be always *ready to contend for the faith of Christ*, if needful. I recommend no one to foster a controversial spirit. I want no man to be like Goliath, going up and down, saying, "Give me a man to fight with." Always feeding upon controversy is poor work indeed. It is like feeding upon bones. But I do say that no love of false peace should prevent us striving jealously against false doctrine, and seeking to promote true doctrine wherever we possibly can. True Gospel in the pulpit, true Gospel in every religious society we support, true Gospel in the books we read, true Gospel in the friends we keep company with,—let this be our aim, and never let us be ashamed to let men see that it is so.

(4) In the next place, let me entreat all who read this paper *to keep a jealous watch over their own hearts* in these controversial times. There is much need of this caution. In the heat of the battle we are apt to forget our own inner man. Victory in argument is not always victory over the world or victory over the devil. Let the meekness of St. Peter in taking a reproof, be as much our example as the boldness of St. Paul in reproving. Happy is the Christian who can call the person who rebukes him faithfully, a "beloved brother." (2 Peter iii. 15.) Let us strive to be holy in all manner of conversation, and not least in our tempers. Let us labour to maintain an uninterrupted communion with the Father and with the Son, and to keep up constant habits of private prayer and Bible reading. Thus we shall be armed for the battle of life, and have the sword of the Spirit well fitted to our hand when the day of temptation comes.

(5) In the last place, let me entreat all members of the Church of England who know what real praying is, *to pray daily for the Church to which they belong*. Let us pray that the Holy Spirit may be poured out upon it, and that its candle-stick may not be taken away. Let us pray for those parishes in which the Gospel is now not preached, that the darkness may pass away, and the true light shine in them. Let us pray for those ministers who now neither know nor preach the truth, that God may take away the veil from their hearts, and show them a more excellent way. Nothing is impossible. The Apostle Paul was once a persecuting Pharisee; Luther was once an unenlightened monk; Bishop Latimer was once a bigoted Papist; Thomas Scott was once thoroughly opposed to evangelical truth. Nothing I repeat, is impossible. The Spirit can make clergymen preach that Gospel which they now labour to destroy. Let us therefore be instant in prayer.

I commend the matters contained in this paper to serious attention. Let us ponder them well in our hearts. Let us carry them out in our daily practice. Let us do this, and we shall have learned something from the story of St. Peter at Antioch.

XVIII

APOSTOLIC FEARS

"I fear, lest by any means, as the serpent beguiled Eve by his subtilty, so your minds should be corrupted from the simplicity that is in Christ."—
2 COR. xi. 3.

THE text which heads this page, contains one part of the experience of a very famous Christian. No servant of Christ perhaps has left such a mark for good on the world as the Apostle St. Paul. When he was born, the whole Roman Empire, excepting one little corner, was sunk in the darkest heathenism; when he died, the mighty fabric of heathenism was shaken to its very centre, and ready to fall. And none of the agents whom God used to produce this marvellous change did more than Saul of Tarsus, after his conversion. Yet even in the midst of his successes and usefulness we find him crying out, "I fear."

There is a melancholy ring about these words which demands our attention. They show a man of many cares and anxieties. He who supposes that St. Paul lived a life of ease, because he was a chosen Apostle, wrought miracles, founded Churches, and wrote inspired Epistles, has yet much to learn. Nothing can be more unlike the truth! The eleventh chapter of the second Epistle to the Corinthians tells a very different tale. It is a chapter which deserves attentive study. Partly from the opposition of the heathen philosophers and priests, whose craft was in danger,—partly from the bitter enmity of his own unbelieving countrymen,—partly from false or weak brethren,—partly from his own thorn in the flesh,—the great Apostle of the Gentiles was like his Master,—"a man of sorrows and acquainted with grief." (Isa. liii. 3.)

But of all the burdens which St. Paul had to carry, none seems to have weighed him down so much as that to which he refers, when he writes to the Corinthians,—"the care of all the Churches." (2 Cor. xi. 28.) The scanty knowledge of many primitive Christians, their weak faith,—their shallow experience,—their dim hope,—their low standard of holiness,—all these things made them peculiarly liable to be led astray by false teachers, and to depart from the faith. Like little children, hardly able to walk, they required to be treated with immense patience. Like exotics in a hothouse, they had to be watched with incessant care. Can we doubt that they kept their Apostolic founder in a state of constant tender anxiety? Can we wonder that he says to the Colossians, "What great conflict I have for you"?—and to the Galatians, "I marvel that ye are so soon removed from Him who called you into the grace of Christ unto another Gospel;"—"O foolish Galatians, who hath bewitched you?" (Col. ii. 1; Gal. i. 6; iii. 1.) No attentive reader ean study the Epistles without seeing this subject repeatedly cropping up. And the text I have placed at the head of this paper is a sample of what I mean:—"I fear, lest by any means, as the serpent beguiled Eve by his subtilty, so your minds should be corrupted from the simplicity that is in Christ." That text contains three important lessons, which I wish to press on the attention of all my readers. I believe in my conscience they are lessons for the times.

I. First, the text shows us *a spiritual disease to which we are all liable, and which we ought to fear.* That disease is corruption of our minds:—"I fear, lest your minds be corrupted."

II. Secondly, the text shows us *an example which we ought to remember, as a beacon:*—"The serpent beguiled Eve by his subtilty."

III. Thirdly, the text shows us *a point about which we ought specially to be on our guard.* That point is corruption "from the simplicity that is in Christ."

The text is a deep mine, and is not without difficulty. But let us go down into it boldly, and we shall find it contains much precious metal.

I. First, then, there is *a spiritual disease, which we ought to fear:* "Corruption of mind."

I take "corruption of mind" to mean injury of our minds by the reception of false and unscriptural doctrines in religion. And I believe the sense of the Apostle to be, "I fear lest your minds should imbibe erroneous and unsound views of Christianity. I fear lest you should take up, as truths, principles which are not the truth. I fear lest you should depart from the faith once delivered to the saints, and embrace views which are practically destructive to the Gospel of Christ.

The fear expressed by the Apostle is painfully instructive, and at first sight may create surprise. Who would have thought that under the very eyes of Christ's own chosen disciples,—while the blood of Calvary was hardly yet dry, while the age of miracles had not yet passed away,—who would have thought that in a day like this there was any danger of Christians departing from the faith? Yet nothing is more certain than that "the mystery of iniquity" began already to work before the Apostles were dead. (2 Thess. ii. 7.) "Even now," says St. John, "There are many Antichrists." (1 John ii. 18.) And no fact in Church history is more clearly proved than this,—that false doctrine has never ceased to be the plague of Christendom for the last eighteen centuries. Looking forward with the eye of a prophet,

St. Paul might well say, "I fear:"—"I fear not merely the corruption of your morals, but of your minds."

The plain truth is that *false doctrine* has been the chosen engine which Satan has employed in every age to stop the progress of the Gospel of Christ. Finding himself unable to prevent the Fountain of Life being opened, he has laboured incessantly to poison the streams which flow from it. If he could not destroy it, he has too often neutralized its usefulness by addition, subtraction, or substitution. In a word, he has "corrupted men's minds."

(*a*) False doctrine soon overspread the Primitive Church after the death of the Apostles, whatever some may please to say of primitive purity. Partly by strange teaching about the Trinity and the Person of Christ, partly by an absurd multiplication of new-fangled ceremonies, partly by the introduction of monasticism and a man-made asceticism, the light of the Church was soon dimmed and its usefulness destroyed. Even in Augustine's time, as the preface to the English Prayer-book tells us, "Ceremonies were grown to such a number that the estate of Christian people was in worse case concerning this matter than were the Jews." Here was the corruption of men's minds.

(*b*) False doctrine in the middle ages so completely over-spread the Church, that the truth as it is in Jesus was well nigh buried or drowned. During the last three centuries before the Reformation, it is probable that very few Christians in Europe could have answered the question, "What must I do to be saved?" Popes and Cardinals, Abbots and Priors, Archbishops and Bishops, Priests and Deacons, Monks and Nuns, were, with a few rare exceptions, steeped in ignorance and superstition. They were sunk into a deep sleep, from which they were only partially roused by the earthquake of the Reformation. Here, again, was the "corruption of men's minds."

(*c*) False doctrine, since the days of the Reformation, has continually been rising up again, and marring the work which the Reformers began. Modernism in some districts of Europe, Socinianism in others, formalism and indifferentism in others, have withered blossoms which once promised to bear good fruit, and made Protestantism a mere barren form. Here, again, has been the "corruption of the mind."

(*d*) False doctrine, even in our own day and under our own eyes, is eating out the heart of the Church of England and perilling her existence. One school of Churchmen does not hesitate to avow its dislike to the principles of the Reformation, and compasses sea and land to Romanize the Establishment.—Another school, with equal boldness, speaks lightly of inspiration, sneers at the very idea of a supernatural religion, and tries hard to cast overboard miracles as so much lumber.—Another school proclaims liberty to every shade and form of religious opinion, and tells us that all teachers are equally deserving our confidence, however heterogeneous and contradictory their opinions, if they are only clever, earnest, and sincere. To each and all the same remark applies. They illustrate the "corruption of men's minds."

In the face of such facts as these, we may well lay to heart the words of the Apostle in the text which heads the paper. Like him we have abundant cause to feel afraid. Never, I think, was there such need for English Christians to stand on their guard. Never was there such need for faithful ministers to cry aloud and spare not. "If the trumpet give an uncertain sound, who shall prepare himself for the battle?" (1 Cor. xiv. 8.)

I charge every loyal member of the Church of England to open his eyes to the peril in which his own Church stands, and to beware lest it takes damage through apathy and a morbid love of peace. Controversy is an odious thing; but there are days when it is a positive duty. Peace is an excellent thing; but, like gold, it may be bought too dear. Unity is a mighty blessing; but it is worthless if it is purchased at the cost of truth. Once more I say, Open your eyes and be on your guard.

The nation that rests satisfied with its commercial prosperity, and neglects its national defences, because they are troublesome or expensive, is likely to become a prey to the first Alaric, or Attila, or Tamerlane, or Napoleon, who chooses to attack it. The Church which is "rich, and increased with goods," may think it has "need of nothing," because of its antiquity, orders, and endowments. It may cry "Peace, peace," and flatter itself it shall see no evil. But if it is not careful about the maintenance of sound doctrine among its ministers and members, it must never be surprised if its candlestick is taken away.

I deprecate, from the bottom of my heart, despondency or cowardice at this crisis. All I say is, let us exercise a godly fear. I do not see the slightest necessity for forsaking the old ship, and giving it up for lost. Bad as things look inside our ark, they are not a whit better outside. But I do protest against that careless spirit of slumber which seems to seal the eyes of many Churchmen, and to blind them to the enormous peril in which we are placed by the rise and progress of false doctrine in these days. I protest against the common notion so often proclaimed by men in high places, that *unity* is of more importance than sound doctrine, and *peace* more valuable than truth. And I call on every reader who really loves the Church of England to recognize the dangers of the times, and to do his duty, manfully and energetically, in resisting them by united action and by prayer. It was not for nothing that our Lord said, "He that hath no sword, let him sell his garment and buy one." (Luke xxii. 36.) Let us not forget St. Paul's words, "Watch ye: stand fast in the faith. Quit you like men: be strong." (1 Cor. xvi. 13.) Our noble Reformers bought the truth at the price of their own blood, and handed it down to us. Let us take heed that we do not basely sell it for a mess of pottage, under the specious names of unity and peace.

II.   Secondly, the text shows us *an example we shall do well to remember,
as a beacon:* "The serpent beguiled Eve by his subtilty."

I need hardly remind my readers that St. Paul in this place refers to
the story of the fall in the third chapter of Genesis, as a simple historical
fact. He does not afford the least countenance to the modern notion
that the book of Genesis is nothing more than a pleasing collection of
myths and fables. He does not hint that there is no such being as the devil,
and that there was not any literal eating of the forbidden fruit, and that it
was not really in this way that sin entered into the world. On the contrary,
he narrates the story of the third of Genesis as a veracious history of a
thing that really took place.

You should remember, moreover, that this reference does not stand
alone. It is a noteworthy fact that several of the most remarkable histories
and miracles of the Pentateuch are expressly mentioned in the New Testament, and always as historical facts. Cain and Abel, Noah's ark, the destruction of Sodom, Esau's selling his birthright, the destruction of the
first-born in Egypt, the passage of the Red Sea, the brazen serpent, the
manna, the water flowing from the rock, Balaam's ass speaking,—all
these things are named by the writers of the New Testament, and named as
matters of fact and not as fables. Let that never be forgotten. Those who
are fond of pouring contempt on Old Testament miracles, and making
light of the authority of the Pentateuch, would do well to consider whether
they know better than our Lord Jesus Christ and the Apostles. To my
mind, to talk of Gensis as a collection of myths and fables, in the face of
such a text of Scripture as we have before us in this paper, sounds alike
unreasonable and profane. Was St. Paul mistaken or not, when he narrated
the story of the temptation and the fall? If he was, he was a weak-minded,
credulous person, and may have been mistaken on fifty other subjects.
At this rate there is an end of all his authority as a writer! From such a
monstrous conclusion we may well turn away with scorn. But it is well to
remember that much infidelity begins with irreverent contempt of the Old
Testament.

The point, after all, which the Apostle would have us mark in the
history of Eve's fall, is the "subtilty" with which the devil led her into
sin. He did not tell her flatly that he wished to deceive her and do her harm.
On the contrary, he told her that the thing forbidden was a thing that
was "good for food, and pleasant to the eyes, and to be desired to make
one wise." (Gen. iii. 6.) He did not scruple to assert that she might eat
the forbidden fruit and yet "not die." He blinded her eyes to the sinfulness
and danger of transgression. He persuaded her to believe that to depart
from God's plain command was for her benefit and not for her ruin. In
short, "he beguiled her by his subtilty."

Now this "subtilty," St. Paul tells us, is precisely what we have to
fear in false doctrine. We are not to expect it to approach our minds in

the garment of error, but in the form of truth. Bad coin would never obtain currency if it had not some likeness to good. The wolf would seldom get into the fold if he did not enter it in sheep's clothing. Popery and infidelity would do little harm if they went about the world under their true names. Satan is far too wise a general to manage a campaign in such a fashion as this. He employs fine words and high-sounding phrases, such as "Catholicity, Apostolicity, Unity, Church order, sound Church views, free thought, broad sense, kindly judgment, liberal interpretation of Scripture," and the like, and thus effects a lodgment in unwary minds. And this is precisely the "subtilty" which St. Paul refers to in the text. We need not doubt that he had read his Master's solemn words in the Sermon on the Mount: "Beware of false prophets, which come to you in sheep's clothing, but inwardly they are ravening wolves." (Matt. vii. 15.)

I ask your special attention to this point. Such is the simplicity and innocence of many Churchmen in this day, that they actually expect false doctrine to look false, and will not understand that the very essence of its mischievousness, as a rule, is its resemblance to God's truth. A young Churchman, for instance, brought up from his cradle to hear nothing but Evangelical teaching, is suddenly invited some day to hear a sermon preached by some eminent teacher of semi-Romish, or semi-sceptical opinions. He goes into the church, expecting in his simplicity to hear nothing but *heresy* from the beginning to the end. To his amazement he hears a clever, eloquent sermon, containing a vast amount of truth, and only a few homœopathic drops of error. Too often a violent reaction takes place in his simple, innocent, unsuspicious mind. He begins to think his former teachers were illiberal, narrow, and uncharitable, and his confidence in them is shaken, perhaps for ever. Too often, alas! it ends with his entire perversion, and at last he is enrolled in the ranks of the Ritualists or the Broad Churchmen! And what is the history of the whole case? Why, a foolish forgetfulness of the lesson St. Paul puts forward in this text. "As the serpent beguiled Eve by his subtilty," so Satan beguiles unwary souls in the nineteenth century by approaching them under the garb of truth.

I beseech every reader of this paper to remember this part of my subject, and to stand upon his guard. What more common than to hear it said of some false teacher in this day,—"He is so good, so devoted, so kind, so zealous, so laborious, so humble, so self-denying, so charitable, so earnest, so fervent, so clever, so evidently sincere, there can be no danger and no harm in hearing him. Besides, he preaches so much real Gospel: no one can preach a better sermon than he does sometimes! I never can and never will believe he is unsound."—Who does not hear continually such talk as this? What discerning eye can fail to see that many Churchmen expect unsound teachers to be open vendors of poison, and cannot realize that they often appear as "angels of light," and are far too wise to be always

saying all they think, and showing their whole hand and mind. But so
it is. Never was it so needful to remember the words, "The serpent beguiled Eve by his subtilty."

I leave this part of my subject with the sorrowful remark that we have
fallen upon times when *suspicion* on the subject of sound doctrine is not
only a duty but a virtue. It is not the avowed Pharisee and Sadducee that
we have to fear, but the *leaven* of the Pharisees and Sadducees. It is the
"show of wisdom" with which Ritualism is invested that makes it so
dangerous to many minds. (Col. ii. 23.) It seems so good, and fair, and
zealous, and holy, and reverential, and devout, and kind, that it carries
away many well-meaning people like a flood. He that would be safe must
cultivate the spirit of a sentinel at a critical post. He must not mind being
laughed at and ridiculed, as one who "has a keen nose for heresy." In
days like these he must not be ashamed to *suspect* danger. And if any
one scoffs at him for so doing, he may well be content to reply, "The
serpent beguiled Eve by his subtilty."

III.   The third and last lesson of the text remains yet to be considered.
It shows us *a point about which we ought to be especially on our guard.*
That point is called "The simplicity that is in Christ."

Now the expression before us is somewhat remarkable, and stands
alone in the New Testament. One thing at any rate is abundantly clear:
the word *simplicity* means that which is single and unmixed, in contradistinction to that which is mixed and double. Following out that idea,
some have held that the expression means "singleness of affection towards
Christ;"—we are to fear lest we should divide our affections between
Christ and any other. This is no doubt very good theology; but I question
whether it is the true sense of the text.—I prefer the opinion that the expression means the simple, unmixed, unadulterated, unaltered doctrine
of Christ,—the simple "truth as it is in Jesus," on all points,—without
addition, subtraction, or substitution. Departure from the simple genuine
prescription of the Gospel, either by leaving out any part or adding any
part, was the thing St. Paul would have the Corinthians specially dread.
The expression is full of meaning, and seems specially written for our
learning in these last days. We are to be ever jealously on our guard, lest
we depart from and corrupt the *simple* Gospel which Christ once delivered
to the saints.

The expression before us is exceedingly instructive. The principle it
contains is of unspeakable importance. If we love our souls and would
keep them in a healthy state, we must endeavour to adhere closely to the
simple doctrine of Christ, in every jot, tittle, and particular. Once add to
it or take away anything from it, and you risk spoiling the Divine medicine,
and may even turn it into poison. Let your ruling principle be,—"No other
doctrine but that of Christ; nothing less, and nothing more!" Lay firm

hold on that principle, and never let it go. Write it on the table of your heart, and never forget it.

(1) Let us settle it, for example, firmly in our minds, that there is *no way of peace* but the simple way marked out by Christ. True rest of conscience and inward peace of soul will never come from anything but direct faith in Christ Himself and His finished work. Peace by auricular confession, or bodily asceticism, or incessant attendance at Church services, or frequent reception of the Lord's Supper, is a delusion and a snare. It is only by coming straight to Jesus Himself, labouring and heavy laden, and by believing, trusting communion with Him, that souls find rest. In this matter let us stand fast in "the simplicity that is in Christ."

(2) Let us settle it next in our minds that there is *no other priest* who can be in any way a Mediator between yourself and God but Jesus Christ. He Himself has said, and His word shall not pass away, "No man cometh unto the Father but by Me." (John xiv. 6.) No sinful child of Adam, whatever be his orders, and however high his ecclesiastical title, can ever occupy Christ's place, or do what Christ alone is appointed to do. The priesthood is Christ's peculiar office, and it is one which He has never deputed to another. In this matter also let us stand fast in "the simplicity that is in Christ."

(3) Let us settle it next in our minds that there is *no sacrifice for sin* except the one sacrifice of Christ upon the cross. Listen not for a moment to those who tell you that there is any sacrifice in the Lord's Supper, any repetition of Christ's offering on the cross, or any oblation of His body and blood, under the form of consecrated bread and wine. The one sacrifice for sins which Christ offered was a perfect and complete sacrifice, and it is nothing short of blasphemy to attempt to repeat it. "By one offering He has perfected for ever them that are sanctified." (Heb. x. 14.) In this matter also let us stand fast in the "simplicity that is in Christ."

(4) Let us settle it next in our minds that there is *no other rule of faith*, and judge of controversies, but that simple one to which Christ always referred,—the written Word of God. Let no man disturb our souls by such vague expressions as "the voice of the Church, primitive antiquity, the judgment of the early Fathers," and the like tall talk. Let our only standard of truth be the Bible, God's Word written. "What saith the Scripture?"—"What is written?"—"How readest thou?"—"To the law and the testimony!"—"Search the Scriptures." (Rom. iv. 3; Luke x. 26; Isa. viii. 20; John v. 39.) In this matter also let us stand fast in the "simplicity that is in Christ."

(5) Let us settle it next in our minds that there are *no other means of grace* in the Church which have any binding authority, excepting those well-known and simple ones which Christ and the Apostles have sanctioned. Let us regard with a jealous suspicion all ceremonies and forms of man's invention, when they are invested with such exaggerated importance as to

thrust into the background God's own appointments. It is the invariable tendency of man's inventions to supersede God's ordinances. Let us beware of making the Word of God of none effect by human devices. In this matter also let us stand fast in the "simplicity that is in Christ."

(6) Let us settle it next in our minds that *no teaching about the sacraments* is sound which gives them a power of which Christ says nothing. Let us beware of admitting that either baptism or the Lord's Supper can confer grace "*ex opere operato*,"—that is, by their mere outward administration, independently of the state of heart of those who receive them. Let us remember that the only proof that baptized people and communicants have grace, is the exhibition of grace in their lives. The fruits of the Spirit are the only evidences that we are born of the Spirit and one with Christ, and not the mere reception of the sacraments. In this matter also let us stand fast in the "simplicity that is in Christ."

(7) Let us settle it next in our minds that *no teaching about the Holy Ghost* is safe which cannot be reconciled with the simple teaching of Christ. They are not to be heard who assert that the Holy Ghost actually dwells in all baptized people, without exception, by virtue of their baptism, and that this grace within such people only needs to be "stirred up." The simple teaching of our Lord is, that He dwells only in those who are His believing disciples, and that the world neither knows, nor sees, nor can receive the Holy Spirit. (John xiv. 17.) His indwelling is the special privilege of Christ's people, and where He is He will be seen. On this point also let us stand fast in the "simplicity that is in Christ."

(8) Finally, let us settle it in our minds that no teaching can be thoroughly sound, in which truth is not set forth in *the proportion of Christ and the Apostles*. Let us beware of any teaching in which the main thing is an incessant exaltation of the Church, the ministry, or the sacraments, while such grand verities as repentance, faith, conversion, holiness, are comparatively left in a subordinate and inferior place. Place such teaching side by side with the teaching of the Gospels, Acts, and Epistles. Count up texts. Make a calculation. Mark how little *comparatively* is said in the New Testament about baptism, the Lord's Supper, the Church, and the ministry; and then judge for yourself what is the proportion of truth. In this matter also, I say once more, let us stand fast in the "simplicity that is in Christ."

The simple doctrine and rule of Christ, then—nothing added, nothing taken away, nothing substituted—this is the mark at which we ought to aim. This is the point from which departure ought to be dreaded. Can we improve on His teaching? Are we wiser than He? Can we suppose that He left anything of real vital importance unwritten, or liable to the vague reports of human traditions? Shall we take on ourselves to say that we can mend or change for the better any ordinance of His appointment? Can we doubt that in matters about which He is silent we have need to act very cautiously, very gently, very moderately, and must beware of pressing them on those who do not see with our eyes? Above all, must we not beware of asserting anything to be needful to salvation of which Christ has said nothing at all? I only see one answer to such questions as these. We must beware of anything which has even the appearance of departure from the "simplicity that is in Christ."

The plain truth is that we cannot sufficiently exalt the Lord Jesus Christ as the great Head of the Church, and Lord of all ordinances, no less than as the Saviour of sinners. I take it we all fail here. We do not realize how high and great and glorious a King the Son of God is, and what undivided loyalty we owe to One who has not deputed any of His offices, or given His glory to another. The solemn words which John Owen addressed to the House of Commons, in a sermon on the "Greatness of Christ," deserve to be remembered. I fear the House of Commons hears few such sermons in the present day.

"Christ is the *way:* men without Him are Cains, wanderers, vagabonds. He is the *truth:* men without Him are liars, like the devil of old. He is the *life:* men without Him are dead in trespasses and sins. He is the *light:* men without Him are in darkness, and go they know not whither. He is the *vine:* men that are not in Him are withered branches prepared for the fire. He is the *rock:* men not built on Him are carried away with a flood. He is the *Alpha and Omega*, the first and the last, the author and ender, the founder and finisher of our salvation. He that hath not Him hath neither beginning of good nor shall have end of misery. Oh, blessed Jesus, how much better were it not to be than to be without Thee! never to be born than not to die in Thee! A thousand hells come short of this, eternally to want Jesus Christ." This witness is true. If we can say Amen to the spirit of this passage it will be well with our souls.

And now let me conclude this paper by offering a few parting words of counsel to any one into whose hands it may fall. I offer them not as one who has any authority, but one who is affectionately desirous to do good to his brethren. I offer them especially to all who are members of the Church of England, though I believe they will be found useful by all English Christians. And I offer them as counsels which I find helpful to my own soul, and as such I venture to think they will be helpful to others.

(1) In the first place, if we would be kept from falling away into false doctrine, *let us arm our minds with a thorough knowledge of God's Word.* Let us read our Bibles from beginning to end with daily diligence, and constant prayer for the teaching of the Holy Spirit, and so strive to become thoroughly familiar with their contents. Ignorance of the Bible is the root of all error, and a superficial acquaintance with it accounts for many of the sad perversions and defections of the present day. In a hurrying age of railways and telegraphs, I am firmly persuaded that many

Christians do not give time enough to private reading of the Scriptures. I doubt seriously whether English people did not know their Bibles better two hundred years ago than they do now. The consequence is, that they are "tossed to and fro by, and carried about with, every wind of doctrine, and fall an easy prey to the first clever teacher of error who tries to influence their minds. I entreat my readers to remember this counsel, and take heed to their ways. It is as true now as ever, that the good *textuary* is the only good theologian, and that a familiarity with great leading texts is, as our Lord proved in the temptation, one of the best safe-guards against error. Arm yourself then with the sword of the Spirit, and let your hand become used to it. I am well aware that there is no royal road to Bible knowledge. Without diligence and pains no one ever becomes "mighty in the Scriptures." "Justification," said Charles Simeon, with his characteristic quaintness, "is by faith, but knowledge of the Bible comes by works." But of one thing I am certain: there is no labour which will be so richly repaid as laborious regular daily study of God's Word.

(2) In the second place, if we would keep a straight path, as Churchmen, in this evil day, *let us be thoroughly acquainted with the Thirty-nine Articles of the Church of England.* Those Articles, I am bold to say, are the authorized Confession of the Church of England, and the true test by which the teaching of every clergyman ought to be tried. The "teaching of the Prayer-book" is a common phrase in many mouths, and the Prayer-book is often held up as a better standard of Churchmanship than the Articles. But I venture to assert that the Articles, and not the Prayer-book, are the Church's standard of Church doctrine. Let no one suppose that I think lightly of the Prayer-book, because I say this. In loyal love to the Liturgy, and deep admiration of its contents, I give place to no man. Taken for all in all, it is an incomparable book of devotion for the use of a Christian congregation. But the Church's Prayer-book was never meant to be the Church's fixed standard of Bible doctrine, in the same way that the Articles are. This was not meant to be its office: this was not the purpose for which it was compiled. It is a manual of devotion; it is not a Confession of faith. Let us value it highly; but let us not exalt it to the place which the Articles alone can fill, and which common sense, statute law, and the express opinion of eminent divines agree in assigning to them.

I entreat every reader of this paper to search the Articles, and to keep up familiar acquaintance with them by reading them carefully at least once a year. Settle it in your mind that no man has a right to call himself a sound Churchman who preaches, teaches, or maintains anything contrary to the Church's Confession of faith. I believe the Articles in this day are unduly neglected. I think it would be well if in all middle-class schools connected with the Church of England, they formed a part of the regular system of religious instruction. Like the famous Westminster

Confession in Scotland, they would be found a mighty barrier against the tendency to return to Rome.

(3) The third and last counsel which I venture to offer is this: *Let us make ourselves thoroughly acquainted with the history of the English Reformation.* My reason for offering this counsel is my firm conviction that this highly important part of English history has of late years been undeservedly neglected. Thousands of Churchmen now-a-days have a most inadequate notion of the amount of our debt to our martyred Reformers. They have no distinct conception of the state of darkness and superstition in which our fathers lived, and of the light and liberty which the Reformation brought in. And the consequence is that they see no great harm in the Romanizing movement of the present day, and have very indistinct ideas of the real nature and work of Popery. It is high time that a better state of things should begin. Of one thing I am thoroughly convinced: a vast amount of the prevailing apathy about the Romanizing movement of the day may be traced up to gross ignorance, both of the true nature of Popery and of the Protestant Reformation.

Ignorance, after all, is one of the best friends of false doctrine. More light is one of the great wants of the day, even in the nineteenth century. Thousands are led astray by Popery or infidelity from sheer want of reading and information. Once more I repeat, if men would only study with attention the Bible, the Articles, and the History of the Reformation, I should have little fear of their "minds being corrupted from the simplicity that is in Christ." They might not, perhaps be "converted" to God, but at any rate they would not be "perverted" from the Church of England.

XIX

IDOLATRY

"Flee from idolatry."—1 Cor. x. 14.

THE text which heads this page may seem at first sight to be hardly needed in England. In an age of education and intelligence like this, we might almost fancy it is waste of time to tell an Englishman to "flee from idolatry."

I am bold to say that this is a great mistake. I believe that we have come to a time when the subject of idolatry demands a thorough and searching investigation. I believe that idolatry is near us, and about us, and in the midst of us, to a very fearful extent. The Second Commandment, in one word, is in peril. "The plague is begun."

Without further preface, I propose in this paper to consider the four following points:—

I. *The definition of idolatry.* WHAT IS IT?

II. *The cause of idolatry.* WHENCE COMES IT?

III. *The form idolatry assumes in the visible Church of Christ.* WHERE IS IT?

IV. *The ultimate abolition of idolatry.* WHAT WILL END IT?

I feel that the subject is encompassed with many difficulties. Our lot is cast in an age when truth is constantly in danger of being sacrificed to toleration, charity, and peace falsely so called. Nevertheless, I cannot forget, as a clergyman, that the Church of England is a Church which has "given no uncertain sound" on the subject of idolatry; and, unless I am greatly mistaken, truth about idolatry is, in the highest sense, truth for the times.

I. Let me, then, first of all, supply *a definition of idolatry.* Let me show WHAT IT IS.

It is of the utmost importance that we should understand this. Unless I make this clear, I can do nothing with the subject. Vagueness and indistinctness prevail upon this point, as upon almost every other in religion. The Christian who would not be continually running aground in his spiritual voyage, must have his channel well buoyed, and his mind well stored with clear definitions.

314

I say, then, that "*idolatry is a worship in which the honour due to God in Trinity, and to Him only, is given to some of His creatures, or to some invention of His creatures.*" It may vary exceedingly. It may assume exceedingly different forms, according to the ignorance or the knowledge, the civilization or the barbarism, of those who offer it. It may be grossly absurd and ludicrous, or it may closely border on truth, and admit of being most speciously defended. But whether in the adoration of the idol of Juggernaut, or in the adoration of the Host in St. Peter's at Rome, the principle of idolatry is in reality the same. In either case the honour due to God is turned aside from Him, and bestowed on that which is not God. And whenever this is done, whether in heathen temples or in professedly Christian churches, there is an act *of idolatry*.

It is not necessary for a man formally to deny God and Christ, in order to be an idolator. Far from it. Professed reverence for the God of the Bible, and actual idolatry, are perfectly compatible. They have often gone side by side, and they still do so. The children of Israel never thought of renouncing God when they persuaded Aaron to make the golden calf. "These be thy gods," they said (thy Elohim), "which brought thee up out of the land of Egypt." And the feast in honour of the calf was kept as "a feast unto the Lord" (Jehovah). (Exodus xxxii. 4, 5.) Jeroboam, again, never pretended to ask the ten tribes to cast off their allegiance to the God of David and Solomon. When he set up the calves of gold in Dan and Bethel, he only said, "It is too much for you to go up to Jerusalem: behold thy gods, O Israel (thy Elohim), which brought thee up out of the land of Egypt." (1 Kings xii. 28.) In both instances, we should observe, the idol was not set up as a rival to God, but under the pretence of being a help—a stepping-stone to His service. But, in both instances, a great sin was committed. The honour due to God was given to a visible representation of Him. The majesty of Jehovah was offended. The second commandment was broken. There was, in the eyes of God, a flagrant act of *idolatry*.

Let us mark this well. It is high time to dismiss from our minds those loose ideas about idolatry, which are common in this day. We must not think, as many do, that there are only two sorts of idolatry,—the spiritual idolatry of the man who loves his wife, or child, or money more than God; and the open, gross idolatry of the man who bows down to an image of wood, or metal, or stone, because he knows no better. We may rest assured that idolatry is a sin which occupies a far wider field than this. It is not merely a thing in Hindostan, that we may hear of and pity at missionary meetings; nor yet is it a thing confined to our own hearts, that we may confess before the Mercy-seat upon our knees. It is a pestilence that walks in the Church of Christ to a much greater extent than many suppose. It is an evil that, like the man of sin, "sits in the very temple of God." (2 Thess. ii. 4.) It is a sin that we all need to watch and pray against continually. It creeps into our religious worship insensibly, and is upon us before we are aware. Those are tremendous words which Isaiah spoke to the formal Jew,—not to the worshipper of Baal, remember, but to the man who actually came to the temple (Isa. lxvi. 3): "He that killeth an ox is as if he slew a man; he that sacrificeth a lamb, as if he cut off a dog's neck; he that offereth an oblation, as if he offered swine's blood; he that burneth incense, as if he blessed an idol."

This is that sin which God has especially denounced in His Word. One commandment out of ten is devoted to the prohibition of it. Not one of all the ten contains such a solemn declaration of God's character, and of His judgments against the disobedient:—"I the Lord thy God am a jealous God, visiting the iniquity of the fathers upon the children unto the third and fourth generation of them that hate Me," (Exod. xx. 5.) Not one, perhaps, of all the ten is so emphatically repeated and amplified, and especially in the fourth chapter of the book of Deuteronomy.

This is the sin, of all others, to which the Jews seem to have been most inclined before the destruction of Solomon's temple. What is the history of Israel under their judges and kings but a melancholy record of repeated falling away into idolatry? Again and again we read of "high places" and false gods. Again and again we read of captivities and chastisements on account of idolatry. Again and again we read of a return to the old sin. It seems as if the love of idols among the Jews was naturally bone of their bone and flesh of their flesh. The besetting sin of the Old Testament Church, in one word, was idolatry. In the face of the most elaborate ceremonial ordinances that God ever gave to His people, Israel was incessantly turning aside after idols, and worshipping the work of men's hands.

This is the sin, of all others, which has brought down the heaviest judgments on the visible Church. It brought on Israel the armies of Egypt, Assyria, and Babylon. It scattered the ten tribes, burned up Jerusalem, and carried Judah and Benjamin into captivity. It brought on the Eastern Churches, in later days, the overwhelming flood of the Saracenic invasion, and turned many a spiritual garden into a wilderness. The desolation which reigns where Cyprian and Augustine once preached, the living death in which the Churches of Asia Minor and Syria are buried, are all attributable to this sin. All testify to the same great truth which the Lord proclaims in Isaiah: "My glory will I not give to another." (Isa. xlii. 8.)

Let us gather up these things in our minds, and ponder them well. Idolatry is a subject which, in every Church of Christ that would keep herself pure, should be thoroughly examined, understood, and known. It is not for nothing that St. Paul lays down the stern command, "Flee from idolatry."

II. Let me show, in the second place, *the cause to which idolatry may be traced.* WHENCE COMES IT?

To the man who takes an extravagant and exalted view of human intellect and reason, idolatry may seem absurd. He fancies it too irrational for any but weak minds to be endangered by it.

To a mere superficial thinker about Christianity, the peril of idolatry may seem very small. Whatever commandments are broken, such a man will tell us, professing Christians are not very likely to transgress the second.

Now, both these persons betray a woeful ignorance of human nature. They do not see that there are secret roots of idolatry within us all. The prevalence of idolatry in all ages among the heathen must necessarily puzzle the one,—the warnings of Protestant ministers against idolatry in the Church must necessarily appear uncalled for to the other. Both are alike blind to its cause.

The cause of all idolatry is the natural corruption of man's heart. That great family disease, with which all the children of Adam are infected from their birth, shows itself in this, as it does in a thousand other ways. Out of the same fountain from which "proceed evil thoughts, adulteries, fornications, murders, thefts, covetousness, wickedness, deceit," and the like (Mark vii. 21, 22),—out of that same fountain arise false views of God, and false views of the worship due to Him; and therefore, when the Apostle Paul tells the Galatians (Gal. v. 20) what are the "works of the flesh," he places prominently among them "idolatry."

A religion of some kind man will have. God has not left Himself without a witness in us all, fallen as we are. Like old inscriptions hidden under mounds of rubbish,—like the almost obliterated under-writing of Palimpsest manuscripts,*—even so there is a dim *something* engraven at the bottom of man's heart, however faint and half-erased,—a *something* which makes him feel he must have a religion and a worship of some kind. The proof of this is to be found in the history of voyages and travels in every part of the globe. The exceptions to the rule are so few, if indeed there are any, that they only confirm its truth. Man's worship in some dark corner of the earth may rise no higher than a vague fear of an evil spirit, and a desire to propitiate him; but a worship of some kind man will have.

But then comes in the effect of the fall. Ignorance of God, carnal and low conceptions of His nature and attributes, earthly and sensual notions of the service which is acceptable to Him, all characterize the religion of the natural man. There is a craving in his mind after something he can see,

---

* "Palimpsest" is the name given to ancient parchment manuscripts which have been twice written over, that is, the work of a comparatively modern writer has been written over or across the work of an older writer. Before the invention of cheap paper, the practice of so writing over an old manuscript was not uncommon. The object of the practice, of course, was to save expense. The misfortune was that the second writing was often far less valuable than the first.

and feel, and touch in his Divinity. He would fain bring his God down to his own crawling level. He would make his religion a thing of sense and sight. He has no idea of the religion of heart, and faith, and spirit. In short, just as he is willing to live on God's earth, but, until renewed by grace, a fallen and degraded life, so he has no objection to worship after a fashion, but, until renewed by the Holy Ghost, it is always with a fallen worship. In one word, idolatry is a natural product of man's heart. It is a weed which, like the earth uncultivated, the heart is always ready to bring forth.

And now does it surprise us, when we read of the constantly recurring idolatries of the Old Testament Church,—of Peor, and Baal, and Moloch, and Chemosh, and Ashtaroth,—of high places and hill altars, and groves and images,—and this in the full light of the Mosaic ceremonial? Let us cease to be surprised. It can be accounted for. There is a cause.

Does it surprise us when we read in history how idolatry crept in by degrees into the Church of Christ,—how little by little it thrust out Gospel truth, until, in Canterbury, men offered more at the shrine of Thomas à Becket than they did at that of the Virgin Mary, and more at that of the Virgin Mary than at that of Christ? Let us cease to be surprised. It is all intelligible. There is a cause.

Does it surprise us when we hear of men going over from Protestant Churches to the Church of Rome, in the present day? Do we think it unaccountable, and feel as if we ourselves could never forsake a pure form of worship for one like that of the Pope? Let us cease to be surprised. There is a solution for the problem. There is a cause.

That cause is nothing else but the deep corruption of man's heart. There is a natural proneness and tendency in us all to give God a sensual, carnal worship, and not that which is commanded in His Word. We are ever ready, by reason of our sloth and unbelief, to devise visible helps and stepping stones in our approaches to Him, and ultimately to give these inventions of our own the honour due to Him. In fact, idolatry is all natural, down-hill, easy, like the broad way. Spiritual worship is all grace, all uphill, and all against the grain. Any worship whatsoever is more pleasing to the natural heart, than worshipping God in the way which our Lord Christ describes, "in spirit and in truth." (John iv. 23.)

I, for one, am not surprised at the quantity of idolatry existing, both in the world and in the visible Church. I believe it perfectly possible that we may yet live to see far more of it than some have ever dreamed of. It would never surprise me if some mighty personal Antichrist were to arise before the end,—mighty in intellect, mighty in talents for government, aye, and mighty, *perhaps*, in miraculous gifts too. It would never surprise me to see such an one as him setting up himself in opposition to Christ, and forming an infidel conspiracy and combination against the Gospel. I believe that many would rejoice to do him honour, who now glory in saying, "We will not have this Christ to reign over us." I believe that many would make a god of him, and reverence him as an incarnation of truth, and concentrate their idea of hero-worship on his person. I advance it as a *possibility*, and no more. But of this at least I am certain,—that no man is less safe from danger of idolatry than the man who now sneers at every form of religion; and that from infidelity to credulity, from atheism to the grossest idolatry, there is but a single step. Let us not think, at all events, that idolatry is an old-fashioned sin, into which we are never likely to fall. "Let him that thinketh he standeth, take heed lest he fall." We shall do well to look into our own hearts: the seeds of idolatry are all there. We should remember the words of St. Paul: "Flee from idolatry."

III. Let me show, in the third place, *the forms which idolatry has assumed, and does assume, in the visible Church.* WHERE IS IT?

I believe there never was a more baseless fabric than the theory which obtains favour with many,—that the promises of perpetuity and preservation from apostacy, belong to the visible Church of Christ. It is a theory supported neither by Scripture nor by facts. The Church against which "the gates of hell shall never prevail," is not the visible Church, but the whole body of the elect, the company of true believers out of every nation and people. The greater part of the visible Church has frequently maintained gross heresies. The particular branches of it are never secure against deadly error, both of faith and practice. A departure from the faith,—a falling away,—a leaving of first love in any branch of the visible Church,— need never surprise a careful reader of the New Testament.

That idolatry would arise, seems to have been the expectation of the Apostles, even before the canon of the New Testament was closed. It is remarkable to observe how St. Paul dwells on this subject in his Epistle to the Corinthians. If any Corinthian called a brother was an idolator, with such an one the members of the Church "were not to eat." (1 Cor. v. 11.) "Neither be ye idolators, as were some of our fathers." (1 Cor. x. 7.) He says again, in the text which heads this paper, "My dearly beloved, flee from idolatry." (1 Cor. x. 14.) When he writes to the Colossians, he warns them against "worshipping of angels." (Col. ii. 18.) And St. John closes his first Epistle with the solemn injunction, "Little children, keep yourselves from idols." (1 John v. 21.) It is impossible not to feel that all these passages imply an expectation that idolatry would arise, and that soon, among professing Christians.

The famous prophecy in the fourth chapter of the first Epistle to Timothy contains a passage which is even more directly to the point: "The Spirit speaketh expressly, that in the latter times some shall depart from the faith, giving heed to seducing spirits, and doctrines of devils." (1 Tim. iv. 1.) I will not detain my readers with any lengthy discussion of that remarkable expression, "doctrines of devils." It may be sufficient to say that our excellent translators of the Bible are considered for once to have missed the full meaning of the Apostle, in their rendering of the word translated as "devils" in our version, and that the true meaning of the expression is, "doctrines about departed spirits." And in this view, which, I may as well say, is maintained by all those who have the best right to be heard on such a question, the passage becomes a direct prediction of the rise of that most specious form of idolatry, the *worship of dead saints*. (See Mede's Works.)

The last passage I will call attention to, is the conclusion of the ninth chapter of Revelation. We there read, at the twentieth verse: "The rest of the men which were not killed by these plagues, yet repented not of the works of their hands, that they should not worship devils" (this is the same word, we should observe, as that in the Epistle to Timothy just quoted), "and idols of gold, and silver, and brass, and stone, and wood: which neither can see, nor hear, nor walk." Now, I am not going to offer any comment on the chapter in which this verse occurs. I know well there is a difference of opinion as to the true interpretation of the plagues predicted in it. I only venture to assert that it is the highest probability these plagues are to fall upon the visible Church of Christ; and the highest improbability that St. John was here prophesying about the heathen, who never heard the Gospel. And this once conceded, the fact that idolatry is *a predicted sin of the visible Church*, does seem most conclusively and for ever established.

And now, if we turn from the Bible to facts, what do we see? I reply unhesitatingly, that there is unmistakable proof that Scripture warnings and predictions were not spoken without cause, and that idolatry has actually arisen in the visible Church of Christ, and does still exist.

The rise and progress of the evil in former days, we shall find well summed up in the Homily of the Church of England on "Peril of Idolatry." To that Homily I beg to refer all Churchmen, reminding them once for all, that in the judgment of the Thirty-nine Articles, the Book of Homilies "contains a godly and wholesome doctrine, and necessary for these times." —There we read, how, even in the FOURTH CENTURY, Jerome complains "that the errors of images have come in, and passed to the Christians from the Gentiles;" and Eusebius says, "We do see that images of Peter and Paul, and of our Saviour Himself, be made, and tables be painted, which I think to have been derived and kept indifferently by an heathenish custom."—There we may read how "Pontius Paulinus, Bishop of Nola, in the *fifth century*, caused the walls of the temples to be painted with stories taken out of the Old Testament; that the people beholding and considering these pictures, might the better abstain from too much surfeiting and riot. But from learning by painted stories, it came by little and little to idolatry."—There we may read how Gregory the First, Bishop of Rome, in the beginning of the *seventh century*, did allow the free having of images in churches.—There we may read how Irene, mother of Constantine the Sixth, in the *eighth century*, assembled a Council at Nicæa, and procured a decree that "images should be put up in all the churches of Greece, and that honour and worship should be given to the said images." And there we may read the conclusion with which the Homily winds up its historical summary,—"that laity and clergy, learned and unlearned, all ages, sorts, and degrees of men, women, and children of whole Christendom, have been at once drowned in abominable idolatry, of all other vices most detested of God, and most damnable to man, and that by the space of 800 years and more."

This is a mournful account, but it is only too true. There can be little doubt the evil began even before the time just mentioned by the Homily writers. No man, I think, need wonder at the rise of idolatry in the Primitive Church, who considers calmly the excessive reverence which it paid, from the very first, to the visible parts of religion. I believe that no impartial man can read the language used by nearly all the Fathers about the Church, the bishops, the ministry, baptism, the Lord's Supper, the martyrs, the dead saints generally,—no man can read it without being struck with the wide difference between their language and the language of Scripture on such subjects. You seem at once to be in a new atmosphere. You feel that you are no longer treading on holy ground. You find that things which in the Bible are evidently of second-rate importance, are here made of first-rate importance. You find the things of sense and sight exalted to a position in which Paul, and Peter, and James, and John, speaking by the Holy Ghost, never for a moment placed them. It is not merely the weakness of uninspired writings that you have to complain of; it is something worse: it is a new system. And what is the explanation of all this? It is, in one word, that you have got into a region where the malaria of idolatry has begun to arise. You perceive the first workings of the mystery of iniquity. You detect the buds of that huge system of idolatry which, as the Homily describes, was afterwards formally acknowledged, and ultimately blossomed so luxuriantly in every part of Christendom.

But let us now turn from the past to the present. Let us examine the question which most concerns ourselves. Let us consider in what form idolatry presents itself to us as a sin of the visible Church of Christ in our own time.

I find no difficulty in answering this question. I feel no hesitation in affirming that idolatry never yet assumed a more glaring form than it does *in the Church of Rome at this present day*.

And here I come to a subject on which it is hard to speak, because of the times we live in. But the whole truth ought to be spoken by ministers of Christ, without respect of times and prejudices. And I should not lie down in peace, after writing on idolatry, if I did not declare my solemn conviction that idolatry is one of the crying sins of which the Church of

322 KNOTS UNTIED

Rome is guilty. I say this in all sadness. I say it, acknowledging fully that we have our faults in the Protestant Church; and practically, perhaps, in some quarters, not a little idolatry. But from formal, recognized, systematic idolatry, I believe we are almost entirely free. While, as for the Church of Rome, if there is not in her worship an enormous quantity of systematic, organized idolatry, I frankly confess I do not know what idolatry is.

(a) To my mind, it is idolatry to have images and pictures of saints in churches, and to give them a reverence for which there is no warrant or precedent in Scripture. And if this be so, I say there is *idolatry in the Church of Rome.*

(b) To my mind, it is idolatry to invoke the Virgin Mary and the saints in glory, and to address them in language never addressed in Scripture except to the Holy Trinity. And if this be so, I say, there is *idolatry in the Church of Rome.*

(c) To my mind, it is idolatry to bow down to mere material things, and attribute to them a power and sanctity far exceeding that attached to the ark or altar of the Old Testament dispensation; and a power and sanctity, too, for which there is not a tittle of foundation in the Word of God. And if this be so with the holy coat of Treves, and the wonderfully multiplied wood of the true cross, and a thousand other so-called relics in my mind's eye, I say there is *idolatry in the Church of Rome.*

(d) To my mind, it is idolatry to worship that which man's hands have made,—to call it God, and adore it when lifted up before our eyes. And if this be so, with the notorious doctrine of transubstantiation, and the elevation of the Host in my recollection, I say there is *idolatry in the Church of Rome.*

(e) To my mind, it is idolatry to make ordained men mediators between ourselves and God, robbing, as it were, our Lord Christ of His office, and giving them an honour which even Apostles and angels in Scripture flatly repudiate. And if this be so, with the honour paid to Popes and Priests before my eyes, I say there is *idolatry in the Church of Rome.*

I know well that language like this jars the minds of many. Men love to shut their eyes against evils which it is disagreeable to allow. They will not see things which involve unpleasant consequences. That the Church of Rome is an *erring* Church, they will acknowledge. That she is *idolatrous*, they will deny.

They tell us that the reverence which the Romanish Church gives to saints and images does not amount to idolatry. They inform us that there are distinctions between the worship of "latria" and "dulia," between a mediation of redemption, and a mediation of intercession, which clear her of the charge. My answer is, that the Bible knows nothing of such distinctions; and that, in the actual practice of the great bulk of Roman Catholics, they have no existence at all.*

They tell us, that it is a mistake to suppose that Roman Catholics really worship the images and pictures before which they perform acts of adoration; that they only use them as helps to devotion, and in reality look far beyond them. My answer is, that many a heathen could say just as much for his idolatry;—that it is notorious, in former days, that they did say so. But the apology does not avail. The terms of the second commandment are too stringent. It prohibits *bowing down*, as well as worshipping. And the very anxiety which the Church of Rome has often displayed to exclude that second commandment from her catechisms, is of itself a great fact which speaks volumes to a candid observer.

They tell us that we have no evidence for the assertions we make on this subject; that we found our charges on the abuses which prevail among the ignorant members of the Romish communion; and that it is absurd to say that a Church containing so many wise and learned men, is guilty of idolatry. My answer is, that the devotional books in common use among Roman Catholics supply us with unmistakable evidence. Let any one examine that notorious book, *The Garden of the Soul*, if he doubts my assertion, and read the language there addressed to the Virgin Mary. Let him remember that this language is addressed to a woman who, though highly favoured, and the mother of our Lord, was yet one of our fellow-sinners,—to a woman who actually confesses her need of a Savour for herself. She says, "My spirit hath rejoiced in God my Saviour." (Luke i. 47.) Let him examine this language in the light of the New Testament, and then let him tell us fairly whether the charge of idolatry is not fully made out.—But I answer, beside this, that we want no better evidence than that which is supplied in the city of Rome itself. What do men and women do under the light of the Pope's own countenance? What is the religion that prevails around St. Peter's and under the walls of the Vatican? What is Romanism at Rome, unfettered, unshackled, and free to develop itself in full perfection? Let a man honestly answer these questions, and I ask no more. Let him read such a book as Seymour's *Pilgrimage to Rome*, or *Alfred's Letter's*, and ask any visitor to Rome if the picture is too highly coloured. Let him do this, I say, and I believe he cannot avoid the conclusion that Romanism in perfection is a gigantic system of Church-worship, sacrament-worship, Mary-worship, saint-worship, image-worship, relic-worship, and priest-worship,—that it is, in one word, a *huge organized idolatry*.

I know how painful these things sound to many ears. To me it is no

* "Latria" and "dulia" are two Greek words, both meaning "worship" or "service," but the former being a much stronger word than the latter. The Roman Catholic admits that the worship of "latria" may not be given to saints, but maintains that "dulia" may be given.

pleasure to dwell on the shortcomings of any who profess and call themselves Christians. I can say truly that I have said what I have said with pain and sorrow.

I draw a wide distinction between the accredited dogmas of the Church of Rome and the private opinions of many of her members. I believe and hope that many a Roman Catholic is in heart inconsistent with his profession, and is better than the Church to which he belongs. I cannot forget the Jansenists, and Quesnel, and Martin Boos. I believe that many a poor Italian at this day is worshipping with an idolatrous worship, simply because he knows no better. He has no Bible to instruct him. He has no faithful minister to teach him. He has the fear of the priest before his eyes, if he dares to think for himself. He has no money to enable him to get away from the bondage he lives under, even if he feels a desire. I remember all this; and I say that the Italian eminently deserves our sympathy and compassion. But all this must not prevent my saying that the Church of Rome is an *idolatrous Church*.

I should not be faithful if I said less. The Church of which I am a minister has spoken out most strongly on the subject. The Homily on "Peril of Idolatry," and the solemn protest following the Rubrics at the end of our Prayer-book Communion Service, which denounces the adoration of the sacramental bread and wine as "idolatry to be abhorred of all faithful Christians," are plain evidence that I have said no more than the mind of my own Church. And in a day like this,—when some are disposed to secede to the Church of Rome, and many are shutting their eyes to her real character, and wanting us to be reunited to her,—in a day like this, my own conscience would rebuke me if I did not warn men plainly that the Church of Rome is an idolatrous Church, and that if they will join her they are "*joining themselves to idols.*"

But I may not dwell longer on this part of my subject. The main point I wish to impress on men's minds is this,—that idolatry has decidedly manifested itself in the visible Church of Christ, and nowhere so decidedly as in the Church of Rome.

IV. And now let me show, in the last place, *the ultimate abolition of all idolatry.* WHAT WILL END IT?

I consider that man's soul must be in an unhealthy state who does not long for the time when idolatry shall be no more. That heart can hardly be right with God which can think of the millions who are sunk in heathenism, or honour the false prophet Mahomet, or daily offer up prayers to the Virgin Mary, and not cry, "O my God, what shall be the end of these things? How long, O Lord, how long?"

Here, as in other subjects, the sure word of prophecy comes in to our aid. The end of all idolatry shall one day come. Its doom is fixed. Its overthrow is certain. Whether in heathen temples, or in so-called Christian churches, idolatry shall be destroyed at the second coming of our Lord Jesus Christ.

Then shall be fulfilled the prophecy of Isaiah, "The idols He shall utterly abolish." (Isa. ii. 18.)—Then shall be fulfilled the words of Micah (v. 13): "Their graven images also will I cut off, and their standing images out of the midst of thee, and thou shalt no more worship the work of thine hands."—Then shall be fulfilled the prophecy of Zephaniah (ii. 11): "The Lord will be terrible unto them: for He will famish all the gods of the earth; and men shall worship Him, every one from his place, even all the isles of the heathen."—Then shall be fulfilled the prophecy of Zechariah (xiii. 2). "It shall come to pass at that day, saith the Lord of hosts, that I will cut off the names of the idols out of the land, and they shall no more be remembered."—In a word, the ninety-seventh Psalm shall then receive its full accomplishment: "The Lord reigneth: let the earth rejoice; let the multitude of isles be glad thereof. Clouds and darkness are round about Him: righteousness and judgment are the habitation of His throne. A fire goeth before Him, and burneth up His enemies round about. His lightnings enlightened the world: the earth saw, and trembled. The hills melted like wax at the presence of the Lord, at the presence of the Lord of the whole earth. The heavens declare His righteousness, and all the people see His glory. Confounded be all they that serve graven images, that boast themselves of idols: worship Him, all ye gods."

The second coming of our Lord Jesus Christ is that blessed hope which should ever comfort the children of God under the present dispensation. It is the pole-star by which we must journey. It is the one point on which all our expectations should be concentrated. "Yet a little while, and He that shall come will come, and will not tarry." (Heb. x. 37.) Our David shall no longer dwell in Adullam, followed by a despised few, and rejected by the many. He shall take to Himself His great power, and reign, and cause every knee to bow before Him.

Till then our redemption is not perfectly enjoyed; as Paul tells the Ephesians, "We are sealed unto the day of redemption." (Eph. iv. 30.) Till then our salvation is not completed; as Peter says, "We are kept by the power of God through faith unto salvation ready to be revealed in the last time." (1 Peter i. 5.) Till then our knowledge is still defective; as Paul tells the Corinthians: "Now we see through a glass darkly; but then face to face: now I know in part; then shall I know even also as I am known." (1 Cor. xiii. 12.) In short, our best things are yet to come.

But in the day of our Lord's return every desire shall receive its full accomplishment. We shall no more be pressed down and worn out with the sense of constant failure, feebleness, and disappointment. In His presence we shall find there is a *fulness* of joy, if nowhere else; and when we awake up after His likeness we shall be *satisfied*, if we never were before. (Psalm xvi. 11; xvii. 15.)

There are many abominations now in the visible Church, over which we can only sigh and cry, like the faithful in Ezekiel's day. (Ezek. ix. 4.) We cannot remove them. The wheat and the tares will grow together until the harvest. But a day comes when the Lord Jesus shall once more purify His temple, and cast forth everything that defiles. He shall do that work of which the doings of Hezekiah and Josiah were a faint type long ago. He shall cast forth the images, and purge out idolatry in every shape.

Who is there now that longs for the conversion of the heathen world? You will not see it in its fulness until the Lord's appearing. Then, and not till then, will that often-misapplied text be fulfilled: "A man shall cast his idols of silver, and his idols of gold, which they made each one for himself to worship, to the moles and to the bats." (Isa. ii. 20.)

Who is there now that longs for the redemption of Israel? You will never see it in its perfection till the Redeemer comes to Zion. Idolatry in the professing Church of Christ has been one of the mightiest stumbling-blocks in the Jew's way. When it begins to fall, the veil over the heart of Israel shall begin to be taken away. (Psalm cii. 16.)

Who is there now that longs for the fall of Antichrist, and the purification of the Church of Rome? I believe that will never be until the winding up of this dispensation. That vast system of idolatry may be consumed and *wasted* by the Spirit of the Lord's mouth, but it shall never be *destroyed* excepting by the brightness of His coming. (2 Thess. ii. 8.)

Who is there now that longs for a perfect Church—a Church in which there shall not be the slightest taint of idolatry? You must wait for the Lord's return. Then, and not till then, shall we see a perfect Church,—a Church having neither spot nor wrinkle, nor any such thing (Eph. v. 27),—a Church of which all the members shall be regenerate, and every one a child of God.

If these things be so, men need not wonder that we urge on them the study of prophecy, and that we charge them above all to grasp firmly the glorious doctrine of Christ's second appearing and kingdom. This is the "light shining in a dark place," to which we shall do well to take heed. Let others indulge their fancy if they will, with the vision of an imaginary "Church of the future." Let the children of this world dream of some "coming man," who is to understand everything, and set everything right. They are only sowing to themselves bitter disappointment. They will awake to find their visions baseless and empty as a dream. It is to such as these that the Prophet's words may be well applied: "Behold, all ye that kindle a fire, that compass yourselves about with sparks: walk in the light of your fire, and in the sparks that ye have kindled. This shall ye have of Mine hand; ye shall lie down in sorrow." (Isa. 1. 11.)

But let our eyes look right onward to the day of Christ's second advent. That is the only day when every abuse shall be rectified, and every corruption and source of sorrow completely purged away. Waiting for that day let us each work on and serve our generation; not idle, as if nothing could be done to check evil, but not disheartened because we see not yet all things put under our Lord. After all, the night is far spent, and the day is at hand. Let us wait, I say, on the Lord.

If these things be so, men need not wonder that we warn them to beware of all leanings towards the Church of Rome. Surely, when the mind of God about idolatry is so plainly revealed to us in His Word, it seems the height of infatuation in any one to join a Church so steeped in idolatries as the Church of Rome. To enter into communion with her, when God is saying, "Come out of her, that ye be not partakers of her sins, and receive not of her plagues" (Rev. xviii. 4),—to seek her when the Lord is warning us to leave her,—to become her subjects when the Lord's voice is crying, "Escape for thy life, flee from the wrath to come;"—all this is mental blindness indeed,—a blindness like that of him who, though fore-warned, embarks in a sinking ship,—a blindness which would be almost incredible, if our own eyes did not see examples of it continually.

We must all be on our guard. We must take nothing for granted. We must not hastily suppose that we are too wise to be ensnared, and say, like Hazael, "Is Thy servant a dog, that he should do this thing?" Those who preach must cry aloud and spare not, and allow no false tenderness to make them hold their peace about the heresies of the day. Those who hear must have their loins girt about with truth, and their minds stored with clear prophetical views of the end to which all idol-worshippers must come. Let us all try to realize that the latter ends of the world are upon us, and that the abolition of all idolatry is hastening on. Is this a time for a man to draw nearer to Rome? Is it not rather a time to draw further back and stand clear, lest we be involved in her downfall? Is this a time to extenuate and palliate Rome's manifold corruptions, and refuse to see the reality of her sins? Surely we ought rather to be doubly jealous of everything of a Romish tendency in religion,—doubly careful that we do not connive at any treason against our Lord Christ,—and doubly ready to protest against unscriptural worship of every description. Once more, then, I say, let us remember that the destruction of all idolatry is certain, and remembering that, *beware of the Church of Rome.*

The subject I now touch upon is of deep and pressing importance, and demands the serious attention of all Protestant Churchmen. It is vain to deny that a large party of English clergy and laity in the present day are moving heaven and earth to reunite the Church of England with the idolatrous Church of Rome. The publication of that monstrous book, Dr. Pusey's *Eirenicon,* and the formation of a "Society for Promoting the Union of Christendom," are plain evidence of what I mean. He that runs may read.

The existence of such a movement as this will not surprise any one who has carefully watched the history of the Church of England during the

last forty years. The tendency of Tractarianism and Ritualism has been
steadily towards Rome. Hundreds of men and women have fairly honestly
left our ranks, and become downright Papists. But many hundreds more
have stayed behind, and are yet nominal Churchmen within our pale.
The pompous semi-Romish ceremonial which has been introduced into
many churches, has prepared men's minds for changes. An extravagantly
theatrical and idolatrous mode of celebrating the Lord's Supper has
paved the way for transubstantiation. A regular process of *unprotestantizing*
has been long and successfully at work. The poor old Church of England
stands on an inclined plane. Her very existence, as a Protestant Church,
is in peril.

I hold, for one, that this Romish movement ought to be steadily and
firmly resisted. Notwithstanding the rank, the learning, and the devoted-
ness of some of its advocates, I regard it as a most mischievous, soul-
ruining, and unscriptural movement. To say that re-union with Rome
would be an insult to our martyred Reformers, is a very light thing; it
is far more than this: it would be a sin and an offence against God!
Rather than be re-united with the idolatrous Church of Rome, I would
willingly see my own beloved Church perish and go to pieces. Rather
than become Popish once more, she had better die!

Unity in the abstract is no doubt an excellent thing: but unity without
truth is useless. Peace and uniformity are beautiful and valuable: but
peace without the Gospel,—peace based on a common Episcopacy, and
not on a common faith,—is a worthless peace, not deserving of the name.
When Rome has repealed the decrees of Trent, and her additions to the
Creed,—when Rome has recanted her false and unscriptural doctrines,—
when Rome has formally renounced image-worship, Mary-worship, and
transubstantiation,—then, and not till then, it will be time to talk of re-
union with her. Till then there is a gulf between us which cannot be honestly bridged. Till then I call on all Churchmen to resist to the death this
idea of reunion with Rome. Till then let our watchwords be, "No peace
with Rome! No communion with idolators!" Well says the admirable
Bishop Jewel, in his *Apology*, "We do not decline concord and peace with
men; but we will not continue in a state of war with God that we might
have peace with men!—If the Pope does indeed desire we should be reconciled to him, he ought first to reconcile himself to God." This witness
is true! Well would it be for the Church of England, if all her bishops had
been like Jewel!

I write these things with sorrow. But the circumstances of the times
make it absolutely necessary to speak out. To whatever quarter of the
horizon I turn, I see grave reason for alarm. For the true Church of Christ
I have no fears at all. But for the Established Church of England, and for
all the Protestant Churches of Great Britain, I have very grave fears indeed. The tide of events seems running strongly against Protestantism and

in favour of Rome. It looks as if God had a controversy with us, as a nation, and was about to punish us for our sins.

I am no prophet. I know not where we are drifting. But at the rate we are going, I think it quite within the verge of possibility that in a few years the Church of England may be re-united to the Church of Rome. The Crown of England may be once more on the head of a Papist. Protestantism may be formally repudiated. A Romish Archbishop may once more preside at Lambeth Palace. Mass may be once more said at Westminister Abbey and St. Paul's. And one result will be, that all Bible-reading Christians must either leave the Church of England, or else sanction idol-worship and become idolaters! God grant we may never come to this state of things! But at the rate we are going, it seems to me quite possible.

And now it only remains for me to conclude what I have been saying, by mentioning some safe-guards for the souls of all who read this paper. We live in a time when the Church of Rome is walking amongst us with renewed strength, and loudly boasting that she will soon win back the ground that she has lost. False doctrines of every kind are continually set before us in the most subtle and specious forms. It cannot be thought unseasonable if I offer some practical safe-guards against idolatry. What it is, whence it comes, where it is, what will end it,—all this we have seen. Let me point out how we may be safe from it, and I will say no more.

(1) Let us arm ourselves, then, for one thing, with *a thorough knowledge of the Word of God*. Let us read our Bibles more diligently than ever, and become familiar with every part of them. Let the Word dwell in us richly. Let us beware of anything which would make us give less time, and less heart, to the perusal of its sacred pages. The Bible is the sword of the Spirit;—let it never be laid aside. The Bible is the true lantern for a dark and cloudy time;—let us beware of travelling without its light. I strongly suspect,—if we did but know the secret history of the numerous secessions from our Church to that of Rome, which we deplore,—I strongly suspect that in almost every case one of the most important steps in the down-ward road would be found to have been a neglected Bible,—more attention to forms, sacraments, daily services, primitive Christianity, and so forth, and diminished attention to the written Word of God. The Bible is the King's highway. If we once leave that for any by-path, however beautiful, and old, and frequented it may seem, we must never be surprised if we end with worshipping images and relics, and going regularly to a con-fessional.

(2) Let us arm ourselves, in the second place, with a *godly jealousy about the least portion of the Gospel*. Let us beware of sanctioning the slightest attempt to keep back any jot or title of it, or to throw any part of it into the shade by exalting subordinate matters in religion. When Peter withdrew himself from eating with the Gentiles, it seemed but a

little thing; yet Paul tells the Galatians, "I withstood him to the face, because he was to be blamed." (Gal. ii. 11.) Let us count nothing little that concerns our souls. Let us be very particular whom we hear, where we go, and what we do, in all the matters of our own particular worship; and let us care nothing for the imputation of squeamishness and excessive scrupulosity. We live in days when great principles are involved in little acts, and things in religion, which fifty years ago were utterly indifferent, are now by circumstances rendered indifferent no longer. Let us beware of tampering with anything of a Romanizing tendency. It is foolishness to play with fire. I believe that many of our perverts and seceders began with thinking there could be no mighty harm in attaching a *little* more importance to certain outward things than they once did. But once launched on the downward course, they went on from one thing to another. They provoked God, and He left them to themselves! They were given over to strong delusion, and allowed to believe a lie. (2 Thess. ii. 11.) They tempted the devil, and he came to them! They started with trifles, as many foolishly call them. They have ended with downright idolatry.

(3) Let us arm ourselves, last of all, with *clear sound views of our Lord Jesus Christ*, and of the salvation that is in Him. He is the "image of the invisible God,"—the express "image of His person,"—and the true preservative against all idolatry, when truly known. Let us build ourselves deep down on the strong foundation of His finished work upon the cross. Let us settle it firmly in our minds, that Christ Jesus has done everything needful in order to present us without spot before the throne of God, and that simple, childlike faith on our part is the only thing required to give us an entire interest in the work of Christ. Let us not doubt that, having this faith, we are completely justified in the sight of God,—will never be more justified if we live to the age of Methuselah and do the works of the Apostle Paul,—and CAN add nothing to that complete justification by any acts, deeds, words, performances, fastings, prayers, almsdeeds, attendance on ordinances, or anything else of our own.

Above all, let us keep up continual communion with the person of the Lord Jesus! Let us abide in Him daily, feed on Him daily, look to Him daily, lean on Him daily, live upon Him daily, draw from His fulness daily. Let us realize this, and the idea of other mediators, other comforters, other intercessors, will seem utterly absurd. "What need is there?" we shall reply: "I have Christ, and in Him I have all. What have I to do with idols? I have Jesus in my heart, Jesus in the Bible, and Jesus in heaven, and I want nothing more!"

Once let the Lord Christ have His rightful place in our hearts, and all other things in our religion will soon fall into their right places.—Church, ministers, sacraments, ordinances, all will go down, and take the second place.

Except Christ sits as Priest and King upon the throne of our hearts, that little kingdom within will be in perpetual confusion. But only let Him be "all in all" there, and all will be well. Before Him every idol, every Dagon shall fall down. CHRIST RIGHTLY KNOWN, CHRIST TRULY BELIEVED, AND CHRIST HEARTILY LOVED, IS THE TRUE PRESERVATIVE AGAINST RITUALISM, ROMANISM AND EVERY FORM OF IDOLATRY.

NOTE

I ask every reader of this paper to read, mark, learn, and inwardly digest the language of the following declaration. It is the declaration which, under the "Act of Settlement" and by the law of England, every Sovereign of this country, at his or her coronation, must "make, subscribe, and audibly repeat."

"I, . . ., do solemnly and sincerely, in the presence of God, profess, testify, and declare that I do believe that in the sacrament of the Lord's Supper there is not any transubstantiation of the elements of bread and wine into the body and blood of Christ, at or after the consecration thereof, by any person whatsoever; and that the invocation or adoration of the Virgin Mary or any other Saint, and the sacrifice of the mass, as they are now used in the Church of Rome, are superstitious, and *idolatrous*. And I do solemnly, in the presence of God, profess, testify, and declare, that I do make this declaration, and every part thereof, in the plain and ordinary sense of the words read unto me, as they are commonly understood by English Protestants, without any evasion, equivocation, or mental reservation, and without any dispensation already granted me for this purpose by the Pope or any other authority or person whatsoever, or without any hope of any such dispensation from any person or authority whatsoever, or without thinking that I am or can be acquitted before God or man, or absolved of this declaration or any part thereof, although the Pope, or any other person or persons or power whatsoever, shall dispense with or annul the same, or declare that it was null and void from the beginning."

May the day never come when British Sovereigns shall cease to make the above declaration!

Also from Benediction Books ...
Wandering Between Two Worlds: Essays on Faith and Art
Anita Mathias
Benediction Books, 2007
152 pages
ISBN: 0955373700

In these wide-ranging lyrical essays, Anita Mathias writes, in lush, lovely prose, of her naughty Catholic childhood in Jamshedpur, India; her large, eccentric family in Mangalore, a sea-coast town converted by the Portuguese in the sixteenth century; her rebellion and atheism as a teenager in her Himalayan boarding school, run by German missionary nuns, St. Mary's Convent, Nainital; and her abrupt religious conversion after which she entered Mother Teresa's convent in Calcutta as a novice. Later rich, elegant essays explore the dualities of her life as a writer, mother, and Christian in the United States-- Domesticity and Art, Writing and Prayer, and the experience of being "an alien and stranger" as an immigrant in America, sensing the need for roots.

About the Author

Anita Mathias is the author of *Wandering Between Two Worlds: Essays on Faith and Art.* She has a B.A. and M.A. in English from Somerville College, Oxford University, and an M.A. in Creative Writing from the Ohio State University, USA. Anita won a National Endowment of the Arts fellowship in Creative Nonfiction in 1997. She lives in Oxford, England with her husband, Roy, and her daughters, Zoe and Irene.

Visit Anita at http://www.anitamathias.com.

The Church That Had Too Much
Anita Mathias
Benediction Books, 2010
ISBN: 9781849026567

The Church That Had Too Much was very well-intentioned. She wanted to love God, she wanted to love people, but she was both hampered by her muchness and the abundance of her possessions, and beset by ambition, power struggles and snobbery. Read about the surprising way The Church That Had Too Much began to resolve her problems in this deceptively simple and enchanting fable.

The Meek Shall Inherit the Earth
Anita Mathias
Benediction Books, 2013
ISBN: 9781781393956

"Blessed are the meek, for they shall inherit the earth," Jesus says in his most puzzling Beatitude. Puzzling, because, if we are honest, it does not feel true to our experience. So do the meek inherit the earth? Is this true? Or isn't it? In The Meek Shall Inherit the Earth, an extended meditation on the power of gentleness, Anita Mathias grapples with this mystifying Beatitude.

Francesco, Artist of Florence: The Man Who Gave Too Much
Anita Mathias
Benediction Books, 2014
52 pages (full colour)
ISBN: 978-1781394175

In this lavishly illustrated book by Anita Mathias, Francesco, artist of Florence, creates magic in pietre dure, inlaying precious stones in marble in life-like "paintings." While he works, placing lapis lazuli birds on clocks, and jade dragonflies on vases, he is purely happy. However, he must sell his art to support his family. Francesco, who is incorrigibly soft-hearted, cannot stand up to his haggling customers. He ends up almost giving away an exquisite jewellery box to Signora Farnese's bambina, who stands, captivated, gazing at a jade parrot nibbling a cherry. Signora Stallardi uses her daughter's wedding to cajole him into discounting his rainbowed marriage chest. His old friend Girolamo bullies him into letting him have the opulent table he hoped to sell to the Medici almost at cost. Carrara is raising the price of marble; the price of gems keeps rising. His wife is in despair. Francesco fears ruin.

* * *

Sitting in the church of Santa Maria Novella at Mass, very worried, Francesco hears the words of Christ. The lilies of the field and the birds of the air do not worry, yet their Heavenly Father looks after them. As He will look after us. He resolves not to worry. And as he repeats the prayer the Saviour taught us, Francesco resolves to forgive the friends and neighbours who repeatedly put their own interests above his. But can he forgive himself for his own weakness, as he waits for the eternal city of gold whose walls are made of jasper, whose gates are made of pearls, and whose foundations are sapphire, emerald, ruby and amethyst? There time and money shall be no more, the lion shall live with the lamb, and we shall dwell trustfully together. Francesco leaves Santa Maria Novella, resolving to trust the One who told him to live like the lilies and the birds, deciding to forgive those who haggled him into bad bargains--while making a little resolution for the future.

www.ingramcontent.com/pod-product-compliance
Lightning Source LLC
Chambersburg PA
CBHW030728150426
42813CB00051B/337